DISCARD

DATE

6/13
2
1/11

9

~~14 DAY LOAN~~

BEFORE
ROE v. WADE

BEFORE
ROE v. WADE

VOICES THAT SHAPED THE ABORTION DEBATE BEFORE THE SUPREME COURT'S RULING

EDITED BY

LINDA GREENHOUSE
AND REVA SIEGEL

KAPLAN

PUBLISHING

New York

This publication is designed to provide accurate and authoritative information in regard to the subject matter covered. It is sold with the understanding that the publisher is not engaged in rendering legal, accounting, or other professional service. If legal advice or other expert assistance is required, the services of a competent professional should be sought.

© 2010 by Linda Greenhouse and Reva B. Siegel

Published by Kaplan Publishing, a division of Kaplan, Inc.
1 Liberty Plaza, 24th Floor
New York, NY 10006

Library of Congress Cataloging-in-Publication Data has been applied for.

Printed in the United States of America

10 9 8 7 6 5 4 3 2 1

ISBN: 978-1-60714-671-6

Kaplan Publishing books are available at special quantity discounts to use for sales promotions, employee premiums, or educational purposes. For more information or to purchase books, please call the Simon & Schuster special sales department at 866-506-1949.

TABLE OF CONTENTS

FOREWORD

This book's purpose is to recapture a time that is rapidly fading from memory. During the years before January 22, 1973, the day on which the Supreme Court decided *Roe v. Wade* and proclaimed that the Constitution protected a woman's right to decide whether to bring a pregnancy to term, Americans conducted a vigorous debate about abortion's morality and meaning. It is obvious today that the Supreme Court's decision did not end this debate. Neither, of course, did the Court start it—although public discussion of *Roe v. Wade* implies not infrequently that it did. By the spring of 1971, when the justices agreed to decide *Roe*—a case challenging the constitutionality of a nineteenth-century Texas law that prohibited all abortions except those necessary to save a woman's life—the legal pipeline was rapidly filling up with challenges to abortion laws from around the country.

By declaring unconstitutional laws that criminalized abortion in states across the country, the decision in *Roe v. Wade* also swept away much of the collective memory of what had gone before. Records of court cases that had taken years to build were now rendered irrelevant, and transcripts of testimony once painstakingly compiled were carelessly misfiled or discarded. And beyond the loss of paper records, the Supreme Court decision itself proved a distorting lens through which to look back on what had preceded it.

For example, the fact that neither women nor fetuses figured very prominently in *Roe v. Wade* makes it plausible to assume that feminist voices and right-to-life voices were simply missing, both from the arguments presented to the Supreme Court and from the public conversation. In fact, feminist and right-to-life positions were passionately expressed in public debate and in friend-of-the-court briefs filed in *Roe*. Yet, the Supreme Court issued a decision that appeared mainly responsive to the arguments of the medical community. In page after page, *Roe* reasoned from medical science, and in its main holding affirmed the autonomy of doctors to act in what they believed to be the best interest of their patients. The organized medical profession, which had spurred the criminalization of abortion a century earlier, had come only lately to view the hundreds of thousands of illegal abortions performed every year as a public health problem of urgent dimensions. The Court responded to these medical voices—which the justices heard through legal briefs and, more informally, through their reading and in their daily lives.

As this book demonstrates, doctors and public health advocates played an important role in setting the nation on the road to *Roe,* but so too did movements for human freedom. In the pages that follow, we trace how arguments for liberalizing abortion law in the name of public health gave way over time to claims of the women's movement seeking for women liberty, equality, and dignity: women's right to control their own bodies and lives; to have their voices and decisions treated with respect; and to participate as equals in private and public life. As the women's movement connected the abortion right to these larger claims of principle, the abortion conflict was constitutionalized. And these claims for repeal of laws criminalizing abortion in turn moved other Americans to appeal to widely held principles to defend the "right to life" of the unborn.

In this early period, the Catholic Church played a key role in helping mobilize its members to vote in defense of laws criminalizing abortion and, as importantly, to translate faith-based convictions about abortion into claims on secular forms of authority. Newly organized right-to-life chapters invoked secular sources of law, including the Declaration of Independence and international human rights treaties, to assert the claim that life in the womb was fully human life, as fully deserving of the state's protection before birth as after. And right-to-life advocates appealed to the authority of science, incorporating newly available and widely published photographs of developing fetuses into their arguments for preserving the nineteenth-century statutes that criminalized abortion. The women's movement and the right-to-life movement shaped arguments made to the Court in *Roe.* But the Court responded to these arguments only indirectly. Perhaps these movement voices were sufficiently alien to the nine middle-aged-to-elderly men—eight Protestants and one liberal Catholic—who decided *Roe v. Wade* that the Court simply *could not* hear them. Or, more likely, the justices, hearing support for abortion's decriminalization from doctors, the bar, many religious leaders, and the rising tide of public opinion, chose to emphasize these mainstream sources of authority in *Roe* as offering a firmer basis for its decision than the nascent arguments of the feminist and right-to-life movement, which the justices may have heard as voices from the margins. Excerpts from the briefs filed to the Court are included in this book so that readers can sample for themselves the range of arguments that were being made for and against a right to abortion at the time the Court decided *Roe.*

This book does not offer a conventional history of a Supreme Court decision. It does not trace the various legal doctrines on which the Court drew in deciding *Roe*, nor does it follow litigation in the case from the filing of the complaint to its ultimate disposition in the Supreme Court. Numerous other sources tell the story of *Roe v. Wade* in narrative form, including David Garrow's monumental *Liberty and Sexuality: The Right to Privacy and the Making of* Roe v. Wade (2nd edition, 1998) and Roe v. Wade: *The Abortion Rights Controversy in American History* by E. H. Hull and Peter Charles Hoffer (2001). Through the documents collected here, our effort is rather to re-create the public conversations from which the case emerged. In the years before the Court decided *Roe,* what had Americans been doing and saying about abortion laws? With what other issues was abortion associated? How did these conversations change the meaning and social significance of abortion and alter views about the proper role for the government in regulating it?

Although both of us believe that women should be free to decide for themselves whether and when to bear children, this is not a work of advocacy. Our purpose in presenting original texts reflecting many points of view is to permit readers to come to their own informed conclusions about a consequential, but widely misunderstood, chapter in American social, political, and legal history. Indeed, while each of us has studied and written about the abortion issue for many years, every path we traveled in our search for relevant and representative documents enriched our own understanding of the period even as it raised new questions. We found ourselves on a journey of discovery that took us to public and private archives and that placed in our hands crumbling and long-forgotten legal documents retrieved from participants' attics and basements. We heard the voices of women and men—well-known, little-known, and completely unknown—calling from across the years. It is a privilege to enable them to speak again in their own words in these pages. We benefitted from the generosity of those for whom the right to abortion has been a lifelong cause—especially those who challenged Connecticut's nineteenth-century abortion statute in the years before *Roe*—as well as of two of the country's most influential opponents of abortion reform, Phyllis Schlafly and Dr. Jack Willke. We are grateful to all those who permitted us to republish portions of their work. The result is a book that contains passionate appeals from contending movements, weaving together arguments that were once forged responsively.

While our story does not offer a traditional legal history of *Roe v. Wade*, it does situate the case in a decade-long national conversation over the question of abortion's decriminalization. The documents gathered in this book reconstruct a debate about reform that begins within shared premises and then breaks their bounds. Advocates progressively link questions concerning abortion law to wider issues of social life and fundamental principles of justice. As advocates appeal to principle and to different pictures of a just political order, they divide and grow progressively more estranged from one another. They begin to make claims on the Constitution to make their positions audible to public officials and to other citizens whom they might persuade to join their cause. Conflict is constitutionalized, and we are on the road to *Roe*.

The book is organized in four parts. Part I collects documents that show both the early stirrings of the abortion-reform movement and the eventual shift in goals from reform to the outright repeal of the laws that made abortion a crime. This part also demonstrates the reaction these developments produced among people whose religious faith made abortion problematic or deeply immoral. It shows the efforts of the opponents to develop secular arguments in order to mobilize a broader constituency to join their cause. At the same time, the documents demonstrate that there was no single religious view, just as there was no single view of abortion among women or among members of either political party.

The documents in Part I tell a story about the roots of abortion reform in the mid-twentieth century that surprised us in its complexity and fluidity. The motivation for challenging long-unexamined assumptions about restrictions on abortion arose separately from distinct communities of interest. Medical science proved better able to identify high-risk pregnancies, but doctors faced prosecution for helping women who feared that they should not bring a pregnancy to term. Public health advocates increasingly raised concern about women killed and injured by illegal abortions. Environmentalists began to warn of the consequences of an unbridled "population explosion" and increasingly came to support sex education, access to contraception, and the decriminalization of abortion.

The women's movement came to the abortion cause from still another route. Feminists sought to free women to participate fully and equally in the workplace, calling for contraception and abortion rights that would give women control over the timing of motherhood, at the same time that the movement sought public support for child care. Only gradually, against the backdrop of the 1960s' understanding that sexual expression was a good independent of its procreative aims, did abortion migrate to the top of the women's rights agenda. At a time when abortion remained a crime in all states, feminists began to associate giving women control over reproductive decisions, not simply with economic independence, but also with respect for women's decision-making authority. With this shift in background understandings, securing reproductive rights now concerned fundamental questions of dignity, promising women both practical and symbolic forms of autonomy, and the capacity to lead equal and self-governing lives.

This set of reasons for changing abortion laws was very different from concerns driving the public-health agenda. Feminist calls for repeal of nineteenth-century abortion laws threatened to legitimize a practice about which many were ambivalent and some believed to be deeply immoral, a violation of life and human dignity. And the women's movement did not only call for the decriminalization of abortion to protect women from dangerous illegal procedures; feminists asserted that women had the right to control their own bodies and lives, and claimed the right to child care as well as to abortion so that women, no less than men, would be able to participate fully in education, work, and politics. As abortion arguments came to challenge fundamental features of the social order, the prospect of finding common ground in the debate diminished.

The different arguments for reforming abortion law advanced during the 1960s proved influential. As Part I shows, organized religions responded with a range of views about the acceptability of abortion—a range of response that may appear surprising in the contemporary political climate, when religious faith is routinely assumed to equate to opposition to abortion. Some denominations supported liberalization, and there were individual clergy who organized, as a religious mission, to assist women in finding safe, even if illegal, abortions. A number of denominations that today oppose abortion were in this period beginning, however tentatively, to open the door to reform.

But the Catholic Church opposed reform and opposed it ever more energetically the more audible cries for reform became. In the years before *Roe*, it was the Church that planted and nurtured the seeds of the modern right-to-life movement. Part I closes by surveying early expressions of opposition to abortion's liberalization, considering both individual statements of conviction and the arguments constructed by early leaders of an organized political movement as they worked to translate religious convictions about the wrongs of abortion into claims rooted in secular forms of authority that might speak to a wider audience.

As Part II shows, the appeal to principle escalated conflict and gave it constitutional form. In the American experience, once people start talking about rights and the principles that should define a just community, they are necessarily—even if unconsciously—making claims on the Constitution itself. They make claims on the Constitution in the streets and in state legislatures. And when they are unable to prevail in those domains, they turn to the courts.

Part II examines documents from the conflict over liberalization of abortion laws in the years just before *Roe*, featuring case studies from New York and Connecticut. In both states, litigation was entwined with developments in the state legislatures. A case filed in New York became moot when the legislature repealed New York's abortion law in 1970, but not before the lawyers challenging the old law framed a new and vigorous argument for the right to abortion based not only on liberty, but also on the Constitution's guarantee of equal protection. The women's movement successfully employed both liberty and equality arguments to challenge Connecticut's nineteenth-century abortion in federal court. These early victories in the New York legislature and Connecticut federal court prompted counter-mobilization of right-to-life organizations that sought to reinstate the abortion bans. The Connecticut legislature actually re-enacted the state's abortion ban, which the federal court again invalidated in a case that was on appeal to the Supreme Court when the Court issued *Roe v. Wade*.

The case studies from New York and Connecticut offer a window on the constitutionalization of the abortion conflict, illustrating how the political arguments of each side assumed legal form. The record of legislation and litigation in these states is resurrected here from the category of cases that were largely lost to memory in the aftermath of *Roe*. Cases from Illinois, Louisiana, Missouri, North Carolina, and Utah, as well as Connecticut, had all reached the Supreme Court and were awaiting action when the Court issued its decision in *Roe*. Sometimes depicted today as an historical aberration, the case that became *Roe v. Wade* was in fact one ripple in a nationwide tide.

The documents in Part II show how the meaning of the abortion issue evolved in the crucible of this increasingly profound debate, and close with a glimpse of claims about abortion in the national arena in 1972. An individual's position on abortion now conveyed membership in a community with common views on social and political priorities, on the respective roles of men and women, on the appropriate trajectory for women's lives, on the structure of society itself. Well before the justices took their seats on the bench to announce the decision in *Roe v. Wade*, a backlash engendered by the success that the reform movement had already achieved was already building, attracting the attention of alert strategists for the national political parties in the 1972 presidential campaign.

Part III presents excerpts from the briefs that lawyers for "Jane Roe" and for

Dallas County District Attorney Henry Wade filed in the Supreme Court. We have not included the decision itself, largely for reasons of space. While we might have included excerpts from the 51-page majority opinion, as well as from the three concurring and two dissenting opinions, excerpts are necessarily selective, and, given the ease of finding the decision on the Internet, we encourage readers to tackle it themselves. In its place, we have included the text of the announcement that the decision's author, Justice Harry A. Blackmun, made from the bench on the morning of January 22, 1973, in which he outlined the decision and explained what he thought the Court had accomplished. (Excerpts from briefs filed by *amici curiae* ("friends of the Court") for both sides are presented in the fourth section of the book, a separate appendix.)

An afterword discusses *Roe* and its aftermath and explores the deepest paradox the decision presents: why the Supreme Court's ratification of a reform that had wide public acceptance has been followed by decades of strife. Was *Roe* the moving cause of that conflict or, instead, a symbol that emerged from it? The documents this book collects precede the Court's decision and thus reveal the grammar of the conflict that produced *Roe*. In surprising ways, they also shed light on the conflict that was to come.

Linda Greenhouse and Reva B. Siegel, 2010

PART I

Reform, Repeal, Religion and Reaction

INTRODUCTION

In the early 1960s, the practice of abortion was prohibited by criminal law throughout the United States, but the forces that would prompt change had begun to appear.

Abortion had been outlawed for at least a century, except as necessary to save a pregnant woman's life or, in a few jurisdictions, to preserve her health. The organized medical profession, which led the effort to criminalize abortion in the mid-19th century, still opposed liberalizing abortion laws. But specialists in public health were beginning to raise alarms about the health consequences of illegal abortion, obtained by an estimated one million American women every year. Increasingly, Americans recoiled from the harms that laws criminalizing abortion inflicted on women and their families.

Several streams of concern fed the growing public sense that criminalization of abortion was wrong—at least in certain cases. A German measles epidemic in 1965 that resulted in the birth of thousands of babies with serious disabilities, along with one pregnant woman's highly publicized encounter with Thalidomide, a drug that caused devastating harm to a developing fetus, made abortion a topic of media attention and public conversation as never before.

There was new attention paid by public health authorities, the media, and local prosecutors to the injuries that illegal abortionists inflicted on women, particularly on poor women who lacked the connections necessary to obtain an authorized abortion and the money needed to travel to Japan, England, Sweden, or other countries that had legalized abortion. The invention of oral contraception, "the Pill," in 1960 helped make control over the timing and spacing of parenthood feasible, acceptable, and, for some, even ethically required, in turn altering sexual mores and leading to public concern about "unwanted babies." By the end of the decade, a growing movement for women's liberation advanced the claim for "repeal" of abortion laws, as part of a more broad-based challenge to traditional sexual mores and family roles.

While no single narrative explains the shift in public consciousness, it is clear that increasingly, Americans came to believe that, at least in some cases, abortion ought to be permitted. The elite reaches of the legal profession began to advocate reform of abortion laws. The American Law Institute proposed a model statute that authorized committees of doctors to evaluate a woman's reasons for seeking an abortion and to grant permission if the woman's situation met specified criteria. By the end of the decade, 12 state legislatures would relax their criminal prohibitions and enact all or part of the institute's reform model. Four other states—three by legislation and one by public referendum—would act by the end of 1970 to eliminate all or nearly all restrictions on access to abortion.

Organized religion responded to these signs of change in different ways. Some denominations supported the cause of change, and liberal members of the clergy formed a network to help women find safe, even if illegal, abortions. Other Protestant denominations sat on the sidelines. The Catholic Church, however, alarmed by the spread of new mores and riven by internal dispute over whether and how to enforce its longstanding prohibition on the use of contraception, began to focus on abortion. By the decade's end, as forces mobilized in support of liberalizing abortion laws, the Church began to make increasingly visible and organized efforts to block reform—first speaking in religious registers and then shifting to secular and nondenominational grounds for opposing abortion. Catholic legal scholars began calling on secular sources of law from which to argue for a legally protected right to life for the unborn.

Even as the Church was beginning to organize the right-to-life movement, support for liberalizing abortion was emerging from sources that would fatefully change abortion's social meaning and expression. In the mid-1960s, an increasingly invigorated women's movement was training its attention on discrimination in the workplace and had not yet assigned a high priority to giving women the right to control their reproductive lives. But by the decade's end, feminists had begun to frame a right to abortion as essential both to women's autonomy and to their full participation in economic and political life.

In short, debate about abortion in the mid-1960s had many moving and intersecting parts, offering a snapshot of a society on the cusp of change, as the documents collected in Part I reflect. In what follows, we present voices from that debate as it unfolded over the course of the decade, as the winds of reform became a demand for repeal of the old laws, in turn generating an increasingly strategic and politicized reaction from those opposed to change.

Our documents are organized thematically rather than strictly chronologically. We endeavor to reconstruct a national conversation that endowed abortion with weighty and increasingly contradictory social and political meanings that over the course of the decade began to crowd out the space available for consensus and compromise.

REFORM

Letter to the Society for Humane Abortion

The first two documents are from the files of the Society for Humane Abortion, founded in California in 1961. The group was small, but it made an impact through such activities as publicly advertising sessions in private homes at which women could learn techniques of self-abortion. (A Chicago-based group known as Jane was created later in the decade. At first, it referred women for safe, although illegal abortions; women were instructed to call a telephone number and ask for "Jane." Later, members of the group began performing abortions themselves in private apartments.)

Women who had nowhere else to turn sought help from these organizations. This letter appeared in the August 1965 newsletter (vol. 1, no. 2) of the Society for Humane Abortion, which published it with the writer's name withheld. At the age of 41, the letter-writer was passionate in her conviction that she faced social and economic ruin if forced to carry her unwanted pregnancy to term. For many today, the stigma of unwed motherhood and illegitimacy may be a distant memory, but this letter is a reminder of the personal crisis that the situation once created, driving desperate women to the danger of the back alley.

I have the money (up to a certain amount) but not the influence I need. I have gone from doctor to doctor and told my sad little tale, spent endless sums on shots, pills, gasoline, more shots, pills and more gasoline and nothing has happened: my sad tale is that I am 41 (old enough to know better, so I am told), not married, no chance for marriage, will lose my job, house, car, if I am forced by law to go thru with this pregnancy—a simple operation would solve my problem, and I know how simple it is, as I have worked for doctors and seen it done legally under our laws.

I attempted suicide once and have attempted to abort myself but knowing anatomy and what I could do to myself have, unfortunately, been overcautious and nothing has resulted....

I hesitate to write because if this is against the law then how could you help me unless you know a doctor who would really help me....

Since I don't intend to go thru this I figure an illegal abortion is my only out of suicide. So what to do—I want to live just like anyone else but I won't live thru this...feeling like my back is to the wall and no place to go but down....

Please help me.

Printed by permission of the Schlesinger Library, Radcliffe Institute for Advanced Study, Harvard University, Society for Humane Abortion Collection, MC 289, box 1, folder 4.

"Rush" Procedure for Going to Japan

The Society for Humane Abortion kept lists of doctors who were willing to help, and referred thousands of women for abortions. Japan, where abortion became legal in the late 1940s, was a destination of choice for women from the West Coast who could afford the trip. This list of instructions for getting an abortion in Japan, poorly typed on two pages, carries no identifying information, so the source of the advice is unknown. But the specificity of the instructions for organizing the trip from San Francisco to Tokyo suggests that this is a journey that many women undertook. The Society for Humane Abortion claimed to have sent 12,000 women out of the country for abortions. Mexico and Japan were destinations for women on the West Coast. East Coast women with money and the right connections could go to Puerto Rico, England, or Scandinavia. Numbers are difficult to come by, but abortions obtained overseas were undoubtedly a small fraction of the illegal abortions that women obtained by the hundreds of thousands every year. (See the article by Mary Steichen Calderone, M.D. in this section, page 22.)

START AT 8 A.M. MONDAY.

1. Obtain three passport photos: 1 is required for passport, 2 extra are to carry with extra copy of birth certificate as identification. Cost is $3.50 plus tax. There are 3 or 4. photo shops around the Federal Building and it takes about 1 hour to get the photos.

2. Take copy of birth certificate, photos and $12 in cash or check to passport service office in Federal Building on Golden Gate near Van Ness. Fill out request form and give them the photo and birth certificate and money. Have some form of identification such as a driver's license, or someone to vouch for you

that you are who the birth certificate says you are. If they want to know why you want to get the passport in a hurry, tell them you are meeting a tour group in Japan and you didn't know you could go till just now. Passport should be ready at 8:30 A.M. Wednesday.

3. Get smallpox shot and have the health card signed and stamped by doctor; you also need the vaccine batch number on the card. Take the card to the S.F. Health Dept. (Rm. 305, building at Hayes and Larkin), and for $1 they will stamp it for you. All this can be done on Monday after taking care of the passport. You may be able to get the shot free at the Public Health Dept.

4. Go to Japan Air Lines ticket office at Powell and O'Farrell and book economy fare round trip ticket to Tokyo ($680 to $722 depending on season). Book for Thursday or Friday. (There are 2 flights daily, one at about 4:30 P.M. and the other 10:30 A.M.: the latter is better as it arrives in Tokyo at 4:30 P.M. Tokyo time, while the other arrives around 11 P.M. Tokyo time. Book open return in San Francisco.

The ticket must be paid for by about 3 P.M. the day before the flight. Bank of Tokyo on Sutter Street in S.F. may finance the fare (90%): you pay 10% down on a 12-to-18 month pay back plan. If you are local, a credit check will take about 72 hours and you have to hand-carry the application blank to the bank, stay on top of them every day to see it goes through, and then make arrangements with the bank and JAL to hand-carry the travel loan check from the bank to the airline to get it all completed from Monday A.M. to Wednesday afternoon. If the bank mails the check to the JAL office it will take at least one extra day to get the money for your ticket.

5. When you are fairly certain of your arrival time, phone the doctor direct and discuss your case with him and get a price quoted. He will talk first and then switch you to his cashier. Try to get the price reduced. Tell them you are a student or a poor working girl and don't have much money. Phone again or cable before your departure, giving name, JAL or PanAm flight number, date and Tokyo time of arrival, as they will be expecting you at the clinic in a couple of hours after your arrival.

Call blank [Here, the notation "Dr. #20" was hand-written on the instructions] about 5 or 6 P.M. S.F. time. Your call will reach him in the morning at a reasonable time. Dr. will ask your blood type; this is necessary, because Japan doesn't have large quantities of negative blood.

6. Tuesday at 4 P.M. (they close at 4:30) call the passport office to see if you can pick up your passport at 8:30 A.M. on Wednesday. If it is ready pick it up Wednesday A.M. Sign it on page two and take it to the Japan Consulate Office in the 1600 block on Post street (at Laguna) at the Japan Trade Center. They will stamp in their visa free of charge. You have to fill out a one-page questionnaire as to who you are and why you want to go to Japan. If you are under age you may have to make up a fake name and address (use the Palace Hotel in Tokyo) as someone who will be responsible for you while in Japan. If questioned, you are going on vacation and this is the name of a relative or tour leader you are going to be with. Visa should take about 1 hour; no charge. Be at airport 1 hour before flight time. Have passport, shot record, birth certificate, and extra photos.

7. When you arrive in Tokyo airport, go immediately to JAL ticket office and book flight for the 5th day or so (you must give the airline 72 hours reconfirming notice, so have the doctor notify you of your progress so you can give notice to the airline). JAL phone number is on the ticket; dial direct. Dial tone sounds like our busy signal.

8. Bank of Tokyo at the Tokyo airport is open 24 hours a day, so you can change U.S. money there. Dr. Blank will take U.S. travelers' checks.

9. Change your money in Tokyo going and coming as you get a better rate.

10. There is an American-speaking information booth right outside of customs at Tokyo airport. Ask them to direct you to the taxi stand. If the taxi driver doesn't speak English make signs that he is to phone the number listed for the clinic and get directions. If he doesn't get the directions the first time, stay with it until he does, then he will deliver you to the door. Be sure you have about $10 U.S., in yen to pay for the taxi both ways. If you don't understand the money, just hold out some bills and coins and he will take just what is needed. They are very honest and there is no tipping in Japan for this type of service. A U.S. dollar = 360 (yen). The taxis in Tokyo are metered so you know what to pay. By all means stay off the street car, buses, or subway as you are bound to get lost. Take a taxi only, directly to and from the airport and clinic.

11. Coming back, the 5 P.M. flight is non-stop to S.F. and you go through customs in S.F. The 10 A.M. flight stops in Hawaii and you go through customs there: this means getting off the plane and standing around the airport for about 1½ hours. Customs will ask you the usual questions of where were you, what did

you buy, and how long you were out of the U.S. If they say anything about how short the time is, you can tell them you had a cablegram that there was a death or sickness in the family and you had to cut your vacation short.

Printed by permission of the Schlesinger Library, Radcliffe Institute for Advanced Study, Harvard University, Society for Humane Abortion Collection, MC 289, box 4, folder 73.

The Lesser of Two Evils
by Sherri Chessen Finkbine

In 1962 Sherri Chessen Finkbine, host of a popular children's television program in Phoenix, was pregnant with a much-wanted fifth child when she learned that the sleeping pill she had been taking was linked to an epidemic of babies being born in Europe without arms or legs. The drug contained thalidomide, which her husband had acquired by prescription while on a business trip to England. It was popular in Europe but had not yet received federal approval for sale in the United States.

Her doctor recommended abortion. What followed became an international drama. A cover story in Life *magazine on August 10, 1962, depicted Mrs. Finkbine wrestling with "the wracking moral question of abortion" as she packed a suitcase to leave the country. Mrs. Finkbine's plight, along with shocking photographs of limbless babies, some 5,000 of whom had been born to women who took the drug in early pregnancy, sparked widespread public discussion for the first time about whether it made sense under such a circumstance for abortion to be treated as a crime. The conversation took place in the nation's heartland as well as its more liberal coasts. "Must a woman bring a monster into the world because the law*

Society for Humane Abortion, Inc.
NEWSLETTER
Vol. 4, No. 1   September 1968

"We continue to believe that birth control should not be based upon a lottery system; i.e. if your means of control breaks down you lose, and gain a child. After all, if a couple does not desire a child, that should be that. It is not a game. Children are not meant to be a punishment . . ."

Send us the tired, the poor
The uncounted women pleading to breathe unpregnant,
The abandoned, unwed, daughters from overfilled homes.
Send us these and the abortion committee rejects,
The frightened, deserted female mendicant.
We'll study our map beside the golden door
And send them forth South, East, West and North
To another shore.

Printed by permission of the Schlesinger Library, Radcliffe Institute for Advanced Study, Harvard University, Society for Humane Abortion Collection, MC 289, folder 4.

chooses to be blind?" the Tulsa Tribune *asked in an editorial, which then answered its own question: "Here is need for common sense." Over the course of the decade, this rationale for liberalizing access to abortion would provoke increasing debate.*

On January 9, 1966, Mrs. Finkbine recounted her experience at a conference in San Francisco on "abortion and human dignity," sponsored by the Society for Humane Abortion.

I speak to you today not as a doctor who can give medical insights into the dangers of illegal abortion nor as a lawyer who can speak on the absurdities of our archaic laws. I speak not as a religious person with dogma decrying the murderous aspects of the subject. I speak to you rather as a person who is much more deeply involved than any of those people could ever be. I speak to you as a mother who desperately needed a pregnancy terminated. I can truthfully say to you that an abortion was to me a very sad, ugly experience but definitely the lesser of two evils.

Three and a half years ago I discovered that I had inadvertently while pregnant taken a drug that would force me to give birth to a limbless child, a child, as it turned out, that would be just a head and a torso. Believe me, the thought now, years later, still makes my heart pound and gives me shivers all over. Faced with what at that time was an unfortunate choice on either hand, my husband and I chose what we considered under the circumstances to be the most humane course of action. We could not knowingly bring a grossly deformed baby into the world to suffer. Also, we had at that time four small children all under the age of 7 years to consider. What would giving birth to a grossly deformed baby do to their lives? I think any mother listening to me now knows that the desire to protect your children is a very, very strong trait in a woman. We had no religious convictions that preordained any answers for it. Newsmen would hound me with the question: Did I think the fetus had a soul?

To tell you the honest truth, I had never even thought of it before. It sounds almost too wholesome to be true, but I grew up in a family of five children. I had been an avid Girl Scout, camper, playground director, and camp counselor before I met my husband at the University of Wisconsin. He was a football player majoring in history and I was a cheer leader. It sounds like some True Story but it really is. I was majoring in radio and TV and we got married while we were still in college and spent the summer after graduation teaching swimming to children at a co-educational camp.

After two years in the service Bob settled down to teaching more children and I decided to have six children. Between babies I did manage to get into the field for which I had studied. And our discussion of pregnancy and babies at that time never seemed to extend beyond the fact that we had the normal concern for healthy children and his wondering if I really did crave onion rings and the fact that we were rapidly running out of names. We were what I would call very child-oriented. It was in fact this love of children that brought the world in on us. Bob and two other teachers took 63 high school students on a tour through Europe one summer, and at the trip's inception in England he felt the need for something to help him rest. The doctor in England gave him a prescription for some little pills which he subsequently barely used as the pressures and responsibilities of the trip lessened. He carried them in his camera case all summer and when he came home set them up on a shelf in a kitchen cupboard.

As someone who has lived through 49½ months and 14 days of pregnancy, I can honestly tell you that morning sickness is a very real thing, except that it's not always confined to the morning. I was doing at this time a TV program for and with preschool children. I think you have the program in San Francisco; it was called Romper Room. I had 4 small children to care for and I was, as always, trying every anti-nausea drug or shot my doctor could think of. One day I decided that if a tranquilizer could calm you down why couldn't it calm down the queasiness of a pregnant tummy? I was wrong; I take every blame for it. I know most doctors kill patients like me, but I took someone else's prescribed medicine. But never, never in a million, zillion years did I ever dream that a little white pill could actually destroy potential life.

Not too many weeks after I started doing this I read on page 11 of our local paper a little, tiny wire-press story on England's desire to practice abortion on mothers who had taken what they called in the article a sleeping pill, or even more horrible, practice euthanasia on the grotesque babies that were being born because of the drug. Well, I read it, my heart cried in empathy, and I thought no more about it. The next day a similar story appeared still receiving no real dominance, but this time the drug was called a tranquilizer. Instantly of course, I thought about those little brown bottles and asked my doctor to check them out. He sent a wire to the pharmacy and I sat in his office and he read the wire to me. He said, "Sherri, if you were my own wife, I'd tell you the exact same thing. The odds for a normal baby are so against you that I am recommending termination of pregnancy." At that time it seemed very simple to me. He explained that from 10 to 25 therapeutic abortions were done every year in Phoenix. I had only to write a little note to a three-doctor medical board explaining my reasons for wanting the operation. I asked him what we could do if they didn't approve it, and he said,

"Don't worry, it's already approved. I've already spoken with them." That was Saturday and the operation was set for Thursday. To show you how naïve I was, I even requested a bed in St. Joseph's Hospital! I had had my last baby there and I liked it there. And this is what I knew about it.

At that point I really felt that they would be taking a part of me. I was two months pregnant and the baby seemed very, very unreal to me. But by my own hand, seeking to help others, I turned the whole thing into a really black, unforgettable experience. I know it sounds altruistic and pollyanna-ish now, but the next day I began thinking how a little article was going to help our family avert a real and life-long tragedy. Naturally the thought came to me that if I'd obtained Thalidomide it was conceivable that others had done so. In fact a contingent of Arizona National Guardsmen had been in Germany that whole past year, the Wall had just gone up that last August, and that is where the drug was first manufactured. It was this concern that made me pick up the telephone the next morning—it was Sunday—and call Ed Murray who is the editor of the Arizona paper. Incidentally, his own son was with Bob in England when he got the pills; he was one of the high school students on tour. He wasn't home but I spoke with Mrs. Murray and she agreed that some warning should indeed be published and asked me if their medical reporter, who was preparing an article on Thalidomide, could phone me. I said yes if he wouldn't use my name and she assured me that he would not. So I agreed.

Well, the paper kept their promise, but rather than merely an article warning of the drug, the front-page, black-bordered story screamed in bold print: "Baby-deforming drug may cost woman her child here." Well, that did it. The story went out on the wire and before the day was two hours along it stirred international interest. London was debating the Thalidomide problem, and here were examples of what their drug was doing in what to them, I am sure, was the remotest corner of the United States. Well, bathed in the merciless glare of national publicity, the doctors cancelled the operation. From this point on they put me in a little hospital bed, and when everybody asks me when did you decide to do this and when did you decide to petition the court, I can truthfully say that I didn't do much deciding. All I did was a lot of arguing as to why I couldn't get out of there, but to no avail. The surgery, they felt at that point, could be challenged by any citizen. Anyone could have gone to the prosecuting attorney and the doctor, the hospital and myself could face criminal prosecution no matter how noble or how right we felt our justification was. So the hospital board and the doctors and lawyers and everyone conferred. They felt the existing laws were so vague—what did "life" mean in the term "necessary to save the life of the mother"? They decided that to gain judicial clarity the hospital would petition the Supreme Court of Arizona for a declaratory judgment prior to doing this.

That's when our names became a matter of court—and thus public—record, and we were swept from there into a ridiculous maelstrom of newsprint. The case was dismissed in court without a hearing. The judge related 9 minutes of legal terminology and concluded with the words: "As a human being, I would like to hear the case; as a judge under existing Arizona law, I cannot." There is an interesting postscript that lawyers especially may appreciate, and I have to be careful because a very dear friend of mine who is a lawyer in Phoenix is listening. The young attorneys who were handling the case passed by the first judge who was supposed to sit on the case because he was the only judge before whom my lawyer had ever lost a case; later on he found out that this judge would have been very sympathetic because he had raised a Mongoloid sister.

Now we faced a blank wall in the United States because of the publicity. We had thousands of letters from people giving all sorts of advice and offering an infinite variety of aids, some perhaps new even to doctors here. For instance, a man told me that for 30 cents I could get a dandy abortion—to go out and get a pint of agua ammonia but dilute it, because he said raw ammonia would loosen a rusty bolt in five minutes. (And I can think of a great pun, which I won't give you.) But he didn't say whether to drink the ammonia or sit in it, so I thought I'd better not try. A roller coaster ride was prescribed; smelling turpentine fumes; a hypnotist from Berkeley claimed that he could hypnotize me into an abortion, over the telephone yet; a skydiver offered me the thrill of my life and a miscarriage as well. And these people were sincere, honestly, they really believed it. (I know me, I'd break my leg and keep the baby!)

From New York came the advice of two quarts of gin for three days with hot baths, hard work, no food and no sleep. There was advice of doctors to see in Beaver Dam, Milwaukee, Georgia, Chicago, Los Angeles, Juarez, Puerto Rico, in practically every city and you'd be surprised at some of the places that were recommended. A doctor from New York offered to do the operation for $1500 in an airplane, thereby out of the state's jurisdiction, he said.

The actual horror of the situation was brutally compounded for me by the thousands of pieces of hate mail we received. It is unbelievable really that so much hate could be spewed in the name of religion. The worst letters—and I do admit that I am overly sensitive and always have been, but the worst ones were those that threatened the lives of my husband and my children. How people can be so unfeel-

nothing controversial and nothing too thought-provoking or deep. At least one high-positioned person in the station believed I had done something murderous and hoped that the program would remain unsponsored and thus die a natural death. But rather it caught on, became sponsored, and they had to extend the time.... [W]hen I did become pregnant again, it was a very graceful excuse for the station to ease me off the air without alienating those people who thought I had done the right thing.

I could have remained silent that fateful Sunday back in 1962, but knowing myself, I don't think I ever would have rested knowing that an apathetic attitude on my part had let babies go on being born without arms, legs, and God knows what deformities. If by speaking out against the drug I prevented even one baby from this type of birth and one mother the heartbreak of seeing it born, then my hurt has been small indeed. Then too I hope that our case serves as a catalyst of sorts for abortion reform in our country. I think it pointed up a real human need and forced people to at least talk about it and face the issue. I still get at least three calls a week mostly from mothers with daughters in trouble, and the sadness of some of the situations is shattering. Everyone is powerless to help them and they grasp in their dire desperation for any straw in the wind.

I'm thankful that President Kennedy issued a national plea in '62 to throw away any foreign pills from medicine cabinets; that was my initial aim and it was achieved. He also increased the personnel of the Food and Drug Administration, and many drug laws now have been tightened to prevent such tragedies in the future.

I'm thankful that my own children were really too young to understand what went on that awful summer, or were bright enough not to be overly inquisitive if they did understand. I always had a very, very deep feeling for compensation after the abortion. And to show you how God did feel about the entire matter, just 11 months ago we welcomed the most beautiful, lovely, perfect, normal baby I've ever seen.

Thank you.

Published by permission of Sherri Chessen and of the Schlesinger Library, Radcliffe Institute for Advanced Study, Harvard University, Society for Humane Abortion Collection, MC 281, box 1, folder 21.

Abortion: The Law and the Reality in 1970

by Jane E. Hodgson, M.D.

Dr. Jane E. Hodgson (1915–2006) was an obstetrician and gynecologist in Saint Paul, Minnesota. Driven by her belief that abortion, even if illegal, was nonetheless sometimes consistent with the "highest standards of medical practice," in 1970 she performed an abortion on a 23-year-old patient who had contracted German measles early in pregnancy. Although the disease carried a high likelihood of serious injury to the fetus—an epidemic in the 1960s had resulted in tens of thousands of babies born deaf, blind, or with heart defects or mental retardation—Minnesota law at the time permitted abortion only to save a pregnant woman's life. The operation that Dr. Hodgson performed was therefore illegal.

Dr. Hodgson had gone to federal court in advance of the procedure to get a ruling enabling her to proceed. But the judge declined to act immediately, and with her patient's pregnancy advancing, Dr. Hodgson went ahead with the abortion and then notified the authorities. As she expected, she was arrested and, after a trial in state court, was convicted and sentenced to 30 days in jail and a year's probation. Her sentence was suspended to enable her to appeal, and while her appeal was pending, the Supreme Court decided Roe v. Wade.

The following excerpt is from an article Dr. Hodgson published in the Mayo Clinic's alumni magazine on the eve of her trial. She had trained at the clinic, in Rochester, Minnesota, on a postgraduate fellowship, and retained many ties there. Her case received widespread attention. The Rochester Post-Bulletin *reprinted her article in full in its issue of November 17, 1970. Following her conviction, the* Minneapolis Tribune *published an editorial praising her for bringing a "courageous and dignified test case" that shed light on the country's "anachronistic abortion laws."*

I am probably the only Mayo alumnus with the dubious distinction of having been arraigned and tried for committing a felony. I am constantly asked: What motivating factors led to a situation where I have been arraigned on an abortion charge and am at present awaiting trial? Have I always felt so strongly about abortion reform?

As an otherwise law-abiding citizen with the utmost respect for the law, my reply is that my attitude has gradually evolved during 23 years of practicing obstetrics and gynecology.... My complete reversal of attitude has been gradual—a reeducation, perhaps—and the direct result of years of frustration in attempting to provide a high grade of medical care under an archaic and cruel law.

....

I cannot equate therapeutic abortion prior to 12 weeks with murder. Call it feticide if you will, but its purpose and end result are the same as those of contraception and sterilization, both of which have become acceptable to most opponents of abortion law reform. Feticide is merely intervention in the continuum of life for the sake of quality....

As doctors, we all tend to be rigid and moralistic. Instead, we should strive to be more humanistic, more involved with the needs of society and individual patient, rather than passing superficial judgments. There is no room for a punitive attitude toward the woman with the unwanted pregnancy.

Should the 14-year-old victim of incest be punished?... Should the relatively innocent college girl who underestimates the power of alcohol and becomes pregnant during a casual date be "punished" to the degree of being forced to give up her college education and social standing, bringing untold hardships on her family? Or should her punishment be a trip to a criminal abortionist, with resultant sterility a strong possibility? What about the housewife with several children, living precariously on a marginal income, who has a contraceptive failure in spite of conscientious use?...

ALTHOUGH IT MIGHT APPEAR otherwise, I have the greatest respect for the law and have performed very few so-called "legal" abortions—not over a dozen, perhaps, in 23 years. It is not the ones I have performed that bother me; rather it is the ones I refused to perform that have haunted me.

....

I have persuaded many patients to continue their pregnancies; I would continue to do so regardless of the law when such a course seemed to be in the patient's best interest. A doctor must always be able to choose the proper course for the patient, or to guide the patient to make the choice. A competent physician—not a legislator—is in the best position to decide. If the patient does not agree with the physician, hopefully, she is free to choose another....

A suitable test case might help to illustrate the cruelty of our present system and hasten a declaratory judgment of unconstitutionality or help to prod the legislature in 1971.

So when Mrs. John Doe, already a mother of three, appeared in my office on April 14, 1970, having contracted German measles during her fourth week of pregnancy, I did not send her to England or Mexico or Montreal. She could have afforded it—but what about future patients who could not? She could have been aborted here in a local hospital with proper consultations (nothing would have been said)—but what about the next case? And what about respect for law? We both knew we could not dodge the issue.

Therefore, two days later, the Federal District Court was asked for a declaratory judgment on the constitutionality of our law and for an injunction to prevent my prosecution by the state....

When it became obvious that no judicial help was forthcoming, the abortion was performed on April 29, 1970, in the best interests of my patient, with consultations having been obtained from my colleagues....

I was indicted by the grand jury and the legal battle was begun....

I feel confident that the battle is already won.

As far as my legal problem is concerned, no matter how long it requires, I am certain as to the ultimate outcome. The cause is just. Repeal of the old law is inevitable. Some day, abortion will be a humane medical service, not a felony.

Excerpted from the October 1970 issue of the *Mayo Alumnus,* pp. 1–4. Printed by permission of the Mayo Clinic, 200 First Street SW, Rochester, MN 55905.

Dr. Hodgson's Affidavit

Following is an excerpt from the statement Dr. Hodgson filed in the Minnesota state district court in Saint Paul in support of her motion to dismiss the indictment. In her affidavit, she swore under oath:

That your Affiant [Dr. Hodgson] firmly believed it to be her professional, ethical, and moral duty to her patient to perform the abortion to prevent a fetal deformity....

....That your Affiant was aware of the existing law, having had to decline almost daily requests over the years, many of which were medically or psychiatrically indicated but illegal under the law; that many of the pregnant women turned away later had illegal abortions by unqualified persons; that your Affiant has had to treat many women, including some of those Affiant declined to abort, who were infected, some of whom were in serious Danger of death.

....

That the State law does not at all correlate with medical indications.

....

That the law also directly results in tremendous societal problems...that your Affiant does have respect for the law; that she has endeavored to govern her actions in accordance with the law; but that your Affiant is in great conflict because the law prevents her from practicing medicine in the highest standards of the medical practice; that the law directly results in tragic personal and societal injury of devastating and shocking proportion; that your Affiant, having been thrust into this conflicting position, had to make a choice between following the existing law or fulfilling her obligation to her patient, her profession and her society, and chose to fulfill her obligations by openly performing the abortion to test this law.

Statement of Dr. Hodgson's Patient

Dr. Hodgson's patient Nancy Kay Widmyer gave this statement during the trial to explain why she chose to have an abortion and why she agreed to let Dr. Hodgson use her situation as a test case. After describing her understanding that the fetus faced a likelihood of severe disability, she said:

I felt that it would be very cruel to the baby. I don't think I could do this to a child. I couldn't make a child suffer. And I don't think that I could have lived with myself knowing that I could have done something about this and I didn't.

Both documents are records of the State of Minnesota District Court, Second Judicial District (Ramsey County). Minnesota Historical Society, Jane E. Hodgson Papers, 149.D.11.10F, box 3.

Illegal Abortion as a Public Health Problem
by Mary Steichen Calderone

As medical director of Planned Parenthood from 1953 to 1964, Dr. Mary Steichen Calderone (1904–1998) prodded the public health profession to acknowledge the dimensions and consequences of illegal abortion and to take action to address the problem. She was also one of the country's leading advocates for sex education as cofounder and president of the Sex Information and Education Council of the United States (SIECUS). Calderone presented this paper at the Maternal and Child Health Section of the American Public Health Association on October 19, 1959.

These women are as often married as unmarried, more often white than colored, more often of college level education than of high school education. They are also from all religious groups. Here, as elsewhere, the difficulty lies in determining the incidence, because the groups for which we have available statistical data are very restricted. The best statistical experts we could find would only go so far as to estimate that, on the basis of present studies, the frequency of illegally induced abortion in the United States might be as low as 200,000 and as high as 1,200,000 per year. During the course of the conference, however, it was notable that the figure of 1,000,000 abortions yearly, or one to every four births in the United States, was advanced again and again by the various participants. Fact number five, therefore, is that whether the incidence is as low as 200,000 or as high as 1,200,000, nevertheless, we do have an illegal abortion problem.

Should public health people look upon it as a problem? Can they shrug off even 200,000 invasions of pregnant uteri as of no medico-social importance? But, one can say, only 260 deaths from all types of abortions—that is a low mortality rate. Why should illegal abortion be a public health problem?

The answer is that we have passed the stage where public health concerns itself only with death rates.... As public health people, we are interested in the whole body, that is, in society. We are also interested in the whole body of the individual who is a part of society. Here are some of the symptoms of this disease of society, illegal abortion.

First, medical indecision regarding the interpretation of the law: We do not have that kind of indecision concerning permissible bacteria counts above which milk or drinking water are not considered safe. One can interpret the law in only one way as far as most public health measures are concerned, but the interpretation of the law regarding abortion depends upon who is interpreting it and how far he is willing to go....

A second symptom, inequity of application of a medical procedure: Remember the woman with $300 who knows the right person and is successful in getting herself legally aborted on the private service of a voluntary hospital, in contrast to her poorer, less influential sister on the ward service of the same hospital or in a public hospital in the same city, a woman in exactly the same physical and mental state as the first one—whose application is turned down?

A third symptom, inconsistency of application: Even with $300 a woman applying at one hospital may be turned down and go to another hospital in the same city where, with the right combination of medical opinions, she may obtain a legal abortion. Is this sound medicine, soundly practiced?

Another symptom, and probably the worst of all, the quasi-legal subterfuges and hypocrisies that must be undertaken by an honest and concerned medical man when he wants to provide his patient with a procedure that in his best medical judgment is indicated.

And last but not least, as a symptom of a disease of our whole social body, the frightening hush-hush, the cold shoulders, the closed doors, the social ostracism and punitive attitude toward those who are greatly in need of concrete help and sympathetic understanding, the unwillingly pregnant women of all ages, both married and unmarried....

I ask you not to assume that I am indiscriminately for abortion. Believe me, I am not. Aside from the fact that abortion is the taking of a life, I am also mindful of what was brought out by our psychiatrists—that in almost every case abortion, whether legal or illegal, is a traumatic experience that may have severe consequences later on. So I am not for abortion but, trained in public health, I am for preventing any need for abortion, and I also am for facing the problem of illegal abortion which is with us....

American Law Institute Abortion Policy, 1962

In 1962 the American Law Institute (ALI), a respected organization of judges, lawyers, and law professors who make periodic recommendations for revisions to state laws in light of new developments, proposed a new legal approach to abortion. Appearing as part of a "model penal code" proposed for adoption by individual states, the abortion sections proposed legalizing what are usually referred to as "therapeutic" abortions. These are abortions that, in a doctor's judgment, are warranted because of a condition affecting the physical or mental health of the woman or the development of the fetus, or because the pregnancy itself resulted from a criminal act. As Dr. Calderone's article indicates, these were not the typical reasons for which women sought abortion. But situations like Sherri Chessen Finkbine's had begun to persuade leaders of the basically conservative professions of law and medicine that it was time to relax the old strictures, at least for abortions that could be deemed "therapeutic."

The institute's proposal, excerpted here, proved influential in the early abortion-reform movement. In fairly short order, 12 states relaxed their existing abortion prohibition and adopted all or part of the institute's recommendation. The twelve were Arkansas, California, Colorado, Delaware, Georgia, Kansas, Maryland, Mississippi, New Mexico, North Carolina, South Carolina, and Virginia.

It is worth noting that the American Law Institute's emphasis was on shielding doctors from liability ("A licensed physician is justified in terminating a pregnancy...") rather than on effectuating a woman's choice in how to deal with an unwanted pregnancy. Georgia's ALI-style law would be successfully challenged as unduly restrictive in Doe v. Bolton, *a case the U.S. Supreme Court considered alongside the challenge to the Texas law in* Roe v. Wade.

SECTION 230.3. ABORTION.

(2) Justifiable Abortion. A licensed physician is justified in terminating a pregnancy if he believes there is substantial risk that continuance of the pregnancy would gravely impair the physical or mental health of the mother or that the child would be born with grave physical or mental defect, or that the pregnancy resulted from rape, incest, or other felonious intercourse. All illicit intercourse with a girl below the age of 16 shall be deemed felonious for purposes of this subsection. Justifiable abortions shall be performed only in a licensed hospital except in case of emergency when hospital facilities are unavailable. [Additional exceptions from the requirement of hospitalization may be incorporated here to take account of situations in sparsely settled areas where hospitals are not generally accessible.]

(3) Physicians' Certificates; Presumption from Non-Compliance. No abortion shall be performed unless two physicians, one of whom may be the person performing the abortion, shall have certified in writing the circumstances which they believe to justify the abortion. Such certificate shall be submitted before the abortion to the hospital where it is to be performed and, in the case of abortion following felonious intercourse, to the prosecuting attorney or the police. Failure to comply with any of the requirements of this Subsection gives rise to a presumption that the abortion was unjustified.

American Medical Association Policy Statements, 1967 and 1970

The American Medical Association, which played a central role in the criminalization of abortion in the 19th century, began reconsidering its position in the mid-1960s. Its first steps were tentative, as shown by the policy statement adopted by the organization's House of Delegates at its annual meeting in June 1967. The delegates adopted a proposal for therapeutic abortion that followed the American Law Institute's Model Penal Code. The recommendation and its accompanying report made clear that the delegates envisioned nothing more than a modest step that would apply to "an occasional obstetric patient." The report disavowed any effort to loosen the legal restrictions on abortions that lacked therapeutic indications, noting that "the Committee on Human Reproduction is unequivocally opposed to any relaxation of the criminal abortion statutes...." The report also acknowledged strong opposition from Catholic members to any relaxation of abortion restrictions.

The tone of the AMA's next effort, a new policy adopted at the June 1970 annual meeting, is very different. The organization was now willing to leave the abortion question to the "sound clinical judgment" of its members, without the definitional strictures of the earlier policy. Taken together, the two documents present a portrait of a profession—like the society it served—on the cusp of change. Justice Harry A. Blackmun had both documents, in manuscript form, in his file when he was working on his opinion in Roe v. Wade, *with check marks indicating that he read them closely.*

I. JUNE 1967

F. Therapeutic Abortion

....This report is addressed only to the medical aspects of therapeutic abortion. It is in no way related or intended to cope with the problem of criminal abortion. The Committee believes that the frequency of criminal abortions would not be reduced at all if the recommendations contained in this report were implemented on a national scale. The Committee on Human Reproduction is unequivocally opposed to any relaxation of the criminal abortion statutes....

Conclusions

The Committee on Human Reproduction is of the opinion that the American Medical Association should have a policy statement on therapeutic abortion in keeping with modern scientific knowledge and medical practice. The Committee realizes, however, that no policy by the AMA on this subject will prove to be acceptable to all physicians. There are some practitioners who honestly believe that there are no circumstances which warrant therapeutic abortion. There are also those equally conscientious physicians who believe that all women should be masters of their own reproductive destinies and that the interruption of an unwanted pregnancy, no matter what the circumstances, should be solely an individual matter between the patient and her doctor.

The policy which the Committee advocates is designed to afford ethical physicians the right to exercise their sound medical judgment concerning therapeutic abortion just as they do in reaching any other medical decision.

The Committee on Human Reproduction is aware that one major religious group opposes abortion under any circumstances. The Committee respects the right of this group to express and practice its belief. However, the Committee believes that physicians who hold other views should be legally able to exercise sound medical judgment which they and their colleagues feel to be in the best interest of the patient. In making recommendations on this subject, the Committee does not intend to raise the question of rightness or wrongness of therapeutic abortion. This is a personal and moral consideration which in all cases must be faced according to the dictates of the conscience of the patient and her physician....

Recommendation

The Committee on Human Reproduction is now of the opinion that, rather than recommending changes in state laws, the American Medical Association should adopt its own statement of position which can be used as a guide for component and constituent societies in states contemplating legislative reform. Accordingly, it is recommended that the following statement be adopted as the policy of the AMA:

> The American Medical Association is cognizant of the fact that there is no consensus among physicians regarding the medical indications for therapeutic abortion. However, the majority of physicians believe that, in the light of recent advances in scientific medical knowledge, there may be substantial medical evidence brought forth in the evaluation of an occasional obstetric patient which would warrant the institution of therapeutic abortion either to safeguard the health or life of the patient, or to prevent the birth of a severely crippled, deformed or abnormal infant.

Under these special circumstances, it is consistent with the policy of the American Medical Association for a licensed physician, in a hospital accredited by the Joint Commission on Accreditation of Hospitals, and in consultation with two other physicians chosen because of their recognized professional competence who have examined the patient and have concurred in writing, to be permitted to prescribe and administer treatment for his patient commensurate with sound medical judgment and currently established scientific knowledge. Prior to the institution of a therapeutic abortion, the patient and her family should be fully advised of the medical implications and the possible untoward emotional and physical sequelae of the procedure. In view of the above, and recognizing that there are many physicians who on moral or religious grounds oppose therapeutic abortion under any circumstances, the American Medical Association is opposed to induced abortion except when:

1. There is documented medical evidence that continuance of the pregnancy may threaten the health or life of the mother, or

2. There is documented medical evidence that the infant may be born with incapacitating physical deformity or mental deficiency, or

3. There is documented medical evidence that continuance of a pregnancy, resulting from legally established statutory or forcible rape or incest may constitute a threat to the mental or physical health of the patient,

4. Two other physicians chosen because of their recognized professional competence have examined the patient and have concurred in writing, and

5. The procedure is performed in a hospital accredited by the Joint Commission on Accreditation of Hospitals.

It is to be considered consistent with the principles of ethics of the American Medical Association for physicians to provide medical information to State Legislatures in their consideration of revision and/or the development of new legislation regarding therapeutic abortion.

II. JUNE 1970

Therapeutic Abortion

RESOLUTION NO. 44,
INTRODUCED BY SOUTH CAROLINA DELEGATION

House Action: Adopted

WHEREAS, Abortion, like any other medical procedure, should not be performed when contrary to the best interests of the patient since good medical practice requires due consideration for the patient's welfare and not mere acquiescence to the patient's demand; and

WHEREAS, The standards of sound clinical judgment, which, together with informed patient consent should be determinative according to merits of each individual case; therefore be it

RESOLVED, That abortion is a medical procedure and should be performed only by a duly licensed physician and surgeon in an accredited hospital acting only after consultation with two other physicians chosen because of their professional competency and in conformance with standards of good medical practice and the Medical Practice Act of his State; and be it further

RESOLVED, That no physician or other professional personnel shall be compelled to perform any act which violates his good medical judgment. Neither physician, hospital, nor hospital personnel shall be required to perform any act violative of personally-held moral principles. In these circumstances good medical practice requires only that the physician or other professional personnel withdraw from the case so long as the withdrawal is consistent with good medical practice.

THE JUDICIAL COUNCIL rendered the following opinion relative to the relationship of medical ethics and abortion: The Principles of Medical Ethics of the AMA do not prohibit a physician from performing an abortion that is performed in accordance with good medical practice and under circumstances that do not violate the laws of the community in which he practices.

House of Delegates Proceedings: Annual Convention 1967, "F. Therapeutic Abortion," pp. 40–51, copyright American Medical Association, 1967. All rights reserved/Courtesy AMA Archives. Annual convention 1970, "Resolution No. 44, Therapeutic Abortion," p. 221. Published by permission of the American Medical Association, copyright American Medical Association, 1970. All rights reserved/Courtesy AMA Archives.

Clergy Statement on Abortion Law Reform and Consultation Service on Abortion (1967)

The Clergy Consultation Service on Abortion, founded in 1967 by a group of ministers and rabbis in New York City and later expanded into a nationwide network, was one of the most important sources of information for women seeking safe abortions in states where the procedure was not yet legal. Its longtime leader was the Reverend Howard Moody of the Judson Memorial Church in New York City's Greenwich Village. By 1970, the service was operating in 26 states and counseling as many as 150,000 women a year. Chapters in states where abortion restrictions had been relaxed helped women navigate the sometimes daunting eligibility rules. Chapters in states where abortion was still illegal under nearly all circumstances referred women to doctors willing to perform the procedure safely and at reasonable cost. As an example of the service's reputation, a booklet written in 1971 by a student committee at Yale University and distributed nationally as The Student Guide to Sex on Campus *(excerpted in Part I.B) contained a list of 43 Clergy Consultation contacts in the United States and Canada. It urged readers to use the service as an alternative to seeking out an illegal abortion on their own.*

By invoking allegiance to "higher laws and moral obligations transcending legal codes," the ministers and rabbis who participated in the Clergy Consultation Service were not only engaging in a form of civil disobedience. They were enacting their own view of "the sanctity of human life"—the lives of the women whom their statement here describes as suffering severe anguish and unnecessary death and the lives of children left motherless—that differed profoundly from the theological view requiring all women to carry pregnancies to term.

The present abortion laws require over a million women in the United States each year to seek illegal abortions which often cause severe mental anguish, physical suffering, and unnecessary death of women. These laws also compel the birth of unwanted, unloved, and often deformed children; yet a truly human society is one in which the birth of a child is an occasion for genuine celebration, not the imposition of a penalty or punishment upon the mother. These laws brand as criminals wives and mothers who are often driven as helpless victims to desperate acts. The largest percentage of abortion deaths are found among 35–39-year-old married women who have five or six children. The present abortion law in New York is most oppressive of the poor and minority groups. A 1965 report shows that 94% of abortion deaths in New York City occurred among Negroes and Puerto Ricans.

We are deeply distressed that recent attempts to suggest even a conservative change in the New York State abortion law, affecting only extreme cases of rape, incest, and deformity of the child, have met with such immediate and hostile reaction in some quarters, including the charge that all abortion is "murder." We affirm that there is a period during gestation when, although there may be embryo life in the fetus, there is no living child upon whom the crime of murder can be committed.

Therefore we pledge ourselves as clergymen to a continuing effort to educate and inform the public to the end that a more liberal abortion law in this state and throughout the nation be enacted. In the meantime women are being driven alone and afraid into the underworld of criminality or the dangerous practice of self-induced abortion. Confronted with a difficult decision and the means of implementing it, women today are forced by ignorance, misinformation, and desperation into courses of action that require humane concern on the part of religious leaders. Belief in the sanctity of human life certainly demands helpfulness and sympathy to women in trouble and concern for living children, many of whom today are deprived of their mothers, who die following self-induced abortions or those performed under submedical standards. We are mindful that there are duly licensed and reputable physicians who in their wisdom perform therapeutic abortions which some may regard as illegal. When a doctor performs such an operation motivated by compassion and concern for the patient, and not simply for monetary gain, we do not regard him as a criminal, but as living by the highest standards of religion and of the Hippocratic oath. Therefore believing as clergymen that there are higher laws and moral obligations transcending legal codes, we believe that it is our pastoral responsibility and religious duty to give aid and assistance to all women with problem pregnancies. To that end, we are establishing a Clergymen's Consultation Service on Abortion which will include referral to the best available medical advice and aid to women in need.

From Howard Moody, *A Voice in the Village: A Journey of a Pastor and a People* (Xlibris, 2009). Copyright Howard Moody. Published by permission.

Abortion Law Reform in the United States

by Jimmye Kimmey

The Association for the Study of Abortion, Inc. was organized in 1965 by two obstetricians, Alan F. Guttmacher (1898–1974), president of the Planned Parenthood Federation of America, and Robert E. Hall (1925–1995), a professor at Columbia University's College of Physicians and Surgeons, to support the early reform movement in New York and to serve as a clearinghouse of information for activist groups around the country. The organization maintained ties to the medical establishment and to groups advocating more moderate reform as well as repeal of abortion laws.

The association's executive director, Jimmye Kimmey, spoke at the California Conference on Abortion in San Francisco in May 1969. She surveyed the growing momentum for change and cautioned against "flamboyant tactics" and self-defeating activism. Her remarks demonstrate that by the late 1960s, the abortion reform movement was far from unified, as the momentum within the movement was shifting from supporting reform to advocating outright repeal of the old abortion laws. This is a speech about reform, not repeal; its premise is that doctors make decisions about abortion, hence reform required changing their professional norms.

That the movement for abortion law reform in the United States is gaining momentum is quite apparent: there is increasing support from the public as shown by public opinion polls and by the formation of state and local groups working for legislative change; there is increasing support for such change from national, state, and local religious, civic, and professional groups; and there is increasing activity on the legislative scene.

....

In sum, we know of a total of forty-nine abortion reform measures which were introduced this year. Of these, twenty-nine are based on the ALI model code, twelve provide only that abortions must be done by licensed physicians (some specify that they must be done in licensed hospitals), four would repeal existing abortion statutes, and four are more restrictive than the ALI code.

Increasing legislative interest in abortion reform measures is perhaps a function of increasing public acceptance of the essential justice of such reform....

Thus, we have a picture of a movement which has evoked much interest and support from the general public, from professionals, from politicians. The question is: What is the abortion law reform movement going to do with this growing support? Where is the movement going?

....

By the end of my first year or year and a half with ASA, the meaning of the word *reform* seemed to undergo a change. There were those in the movement who began to talk about reform as though it were some kind of evil against which one must fight in the name of repeal.

....

I would like to share with you some tentative observations on the problem of social change. In any social movement there are those who refuse to compromise, who refuse to meet their opponents (or, sometimes, even their friends) half-way. The no-compromisers enjoy one great advantage—they can argue openly for their position on ideological grounds and therefore appear to themselves and others to be pure of heart. That sensation is, no doubt about it, a great source of energy, but it is apparently such a heady sensation that it sometimes tends to induce blindness.

....

Since the basic objective is to change medical practice, it may be that any disagreements over the content of legislation are not only debilitating to the movement but irrelevant to the goal, because if a change in medical practice is the ultimate objective, then the vital constituency to bear in mind is the medical community. Perhaps some consideration should be given to the question of whether flamboyant tactics such as demonstrating, picketing hospitals and disrupting legislative hearings will gain or lose the respect of the rather conservative medical community. If their respect is lost, changing the law may have only a most limited impact on medical practice.

In fact, it may be that even if their sensibilities are not offended, a change in the law—including repeal of the law—would make less difference in medical practice than one might hope. Voluntary sterilization is not illegal in any state but patients often have a difficult time securing that medical service. Might this be in part because the physician (and, more especially, the hospital administrator) feels no necessity to do something just because it is not illegal? Again, I simply suggest that the possibility be considered.

....

All this is conjectural, but it would seem a wise policy when deciding on tactics to bear in mind that the objective is not just to reform the law but to change medical practice. No matter what the law says, if physicians and hospitals continue to assume that abortions can be done for only a limited number of reasons and, further, that the decision is theirs to make, women will still be forced to turn to the abortionist for this simple medical procedure and the movement's victory will be a hollow one. Those living in the large metropolitan areas would no doubt find competent medical care but, in spite of all the talk of our being an urban society, the large metropolitan area is still the exception and women in small cities and towns might find their situation unchanged.

The abortion law reform movement to be successful must not settle for less than the acceptance of abortion as a normal part of medical practice. Anything the reform movement does which jeopardizes that goal is self-defeating.

Right to Choose Memorandum

by Jimmye Kimmey

In a memorandum to colleagues in December 1972 under the heading "education campaign re: abortion rights," Jimmye Kimmey discussed "the need to find a phrase to counter the Right to Life slogan." Her preferred alternative, the "Right to Choose," indicates that by now, the Association for the Study of Abortion, born in the spirit of reform, had fully embraced the cause of repeal, and that it now saw women, rather than their doctors, as the primary actors.

The alternatives seem to be Freedom of Conscience and Right to Choose. I hope someone can think of a clearly better one but, in the meantime, let me say why I think the latter preferable. There are two reasons—the first superficial, the second, less so:

a. Right to Life is short, catchy, and is composed of monosyllabic words (an important consideration in English). We need something comparable—Right to Choose would seem to do the job.

b. More important, though, is the fact that conscience is an internal matter while choice has to do with action—and it is action we are concerned with.

A woman's conscience may well tell her abortion is wrong, but she may choose (and must have the right to choose) to have one anyway for compelling practical reasons. A woman's conscience may tell her that abortion is right, but she may choose to run the risk of having a defective baby anyway.

What we are concerned with is, to repeat, the woman's right to choose—not with her right (or anyone else's right) to make a judgment about whether that choice is morally licit.

Both documents printed by permission of Jimmye Kimmey and of the Schlesinger Library, Radcliffe Institute for Advance Study, Harvard University, NARAL Collection, MC 313, box 6 ("ASA" file).

REPEAL

The early movement toward reform came from several directions. As we have seen, one motivation was a public health concern to protect women from the consequences of illegal abortion; the members of the Clergy Consultation Service expressed this woman-protective concern as a pastoral obligation. Another motivation was to shield doctors from liability for acting in what they regarded as their patients' best interests. With some notable exceptions, women's voices were heard only infrequently on the subject of abortion during this early period, except as victims of unhappy circumstance.

The movement from reform to repeal also arose from several convergent paths. We begin with the women's movement. Abortion was not initially high on the agenda of the women who organized during the 1960s to press for equal access to higher education, opportunity in the workplace, and social policies, including childcare, that would enable women to combine motherhood and career. It did not take long for women to connect control of their reproductive lives with increased social authority and the opportunity to become full participants in the economy. A right to abortion thus appeared on the women's movement agenda anchored in a broader call for social re-ordering that inspired some women even as it disturbed others. Implicit in the new argument was the notion that, once the goals were achieved, sex and reproduction would no longer be bound together, and a woman's biology would no longer be her destiny.

It was not only feminists who sought sexual freedom. Americans from different walks of life increasingly mistrusted laws that viewed procreation as the only legitimate reason for adult intimacy. Many Americans came to talk about these matters in the language of "population control," a rallying cry of a new environmental movement concerned about conserving the planet's scarce resources. Documents later in this section explore these themes.

National Organization for Women Bill of Rights

The National Organization for Women (NOW) was established in 1966 with the goal of ending discrimination against women in the workplace. Initially its focus was on the Equal Employment Opportunity Commission (EEOC), the federal agency charged with enforcing the antidiscrimination provisions of the Civil Rights Act of 1964. To the dismay of those who had looked to the commission as an agent of change, the EEOC had refused to treat as prohibited sex discrimination the separate help-wanted advertisements for men and women that were then very common and that presented a serious obstacle to women seeking to break down barriers and enter traditionally male-dominated occupations. It required movement pressure to prompt the government to enforce the prohibition on sex discrimination in employment seriously and to consider the possibility that the government itself might wrongfully discriminate against women. It was not until 1971 that the Supreme Court, for the first time, struck down a statute under the equal protection clause of the Constitution for discriminating on the basis of sex.

The women and men who came together to form NOW—electing Betty Friedan (1921–2006) as the first president—adopted a "Bill of Rights" in 1967 that listed workplace and education issues ahead of birth control and abortion. Access to contraception and abortion were not framed as goals in themselves, but as a means to alleviate the burdens that society placed on women, burdens that included mandatory pregnancy leaves with no guarantee that a new mother could reclaim her old job, and a lack of reliable child care preventing many mothers from working at all. NOW's "Bill of Rights" challenged the traditional organization of work and family as perpetrating a wrong against women.

While there was general agreement within NOW on its economic and equality goals, not all the women who were drawn to the organization's workplace-focused antidiscrimination agenda were interested in, or even particularly comfortable with, making abortion reform a priority. One group of such women split off from NOW in 1968 to form the Women's Equity Action League (WEAL), which lobbied and litigated for educational and workplace equality for more than two decades, before closing its doors in 1989.

   I. Equal Rights Constitutional Amendment

  II. Enforce Law Banning Sex Discrimination in Employment

 III. Maternity Leave Rights in Employment and in Social Security Benefits

 IV. Tax Deduction for Home and Child Care Expenses for Working Parents

V. Child Day Care Centers

VI. Equal and Unsegregated Education

VII. Equal Job Training Opportunities and Allowances for Women in Poverty

VIII. The Right of Women to Control their Reproductive Lives

We Demand:

I. That the United States Congress immediately pass the Equal Rights Amendment to the Constitution to provide that "Equality of rights under the law shall not be denied or abridged by the United States or by any State on account of sex" and that such then be immediately ratified by the several States.

II. That equal employment opportunity be guaranteed to all women, as well as men by insisting that the Equal Employment Opportunity Commission enforce the prohibitions against sex discrimination in employment under Title VII of the Civil Rights Act of 1964 with the same vigor as it enforces the prohibitions against racial discrimination.

III. That women be protected by law to insure their rights to return to their jobs within a reasonable time after childbirth without loss of seniority or other accrued benefits and be paid maternity leave as a form of social security and/or employee benefit.

IV. Immediate revision of tax laws to permit the deduction of home and child care expenses for working parents.

V. That child care facilities be established by law on the same basis as parks, libraries and public schools adequate to the needs of children, from the pre-school years through adolescence, as a community resource to be used by all citizens from all income levels.

VI. That the right of women to be educated to their full potential equally with men be secured by Federal and State legislation, eliminating all discrimination and segregation by sex, written and unwritten, at all levels of education including college, graduate and professional schools, loans and fellowships and Federal and State training programs, such as the Job Corps.

VII. The right of women in poverty to secure job training, housing and family allowances on equal terms with men, but without prejudice to a parent's right to remain at home to care for his or her children; revision of welfare legislation and poverty programs which deny women dignity, privacy and self respect.

VIII.   The right of women to control their own reproductive lives by removing from penal codes the laws limiting access to contraceptive information and devices and laws governing abortion.

Published with permission of the National Organization for Women. "This is a historical document and may not reflect the current language or priorities of the organization."

Abortion: A Woman's Civil Right

by Betty Friedan

Implicit in NOW's agenda was a profound critique of existing social arrangements as they affected women and, especially, women with children. The organization's founding president, Betty Friedan, spoke in Chicago in February 1969, at what was billed as the First National Conference on Abortion Laws, sponsored by the Illinois Citizens for the Medical Control of Abortion. This conference gave rise to a new organization: the National Association for Repeal of Abortion Laws (NARAL).

The Chicago conference, and particularly Betty Friedan's speech, marked the public convergence of the women's rights movement and the abortion rights movement. Friedan declared to the assembled abortion rights activists that their movement "is now mine."

The right to abortion emerged front and center for the women's movement, framed in this speech no longer as one element among many necessary to enable women to participate in the economy, but as a right, essential to the "full human dignity and personhood" of women, to control not only one's reproductive life but one's place in society. This new synthesis marked a fundamental reframing of the abortion issue, with radical implications for social change. Friedan's language is passionate, even raw, as she demands that women no longer be treated as mere objects of regulation and that they must have the same ability to be heard in the public sphere, the same claim to self-determination, and the same authority as men to control their own bodies. She asserts that "women's voices are going to be heard and heard strongly"—not only at this conference but as part of a demand for full inclusion in a movement to reshape the social framework.

I am not going to express my gratitude for being here. I think that this is the first conference that's been held on abortion that is a decent conference, because this is the first conference in which women's voices are going to be heard and heard strongly. We are in a new stage here, in the whole unfinished sexual revolution in America—the whole revolution of American women toward full equality, full participation, human dignity and freedom in our society.

We are moving forward again, after many decades of standing still, which has been in effect to move backward, and a very basic part of this, and my only claim to be here, is our belated recognition, if you will, that there is no freedom, no equality, no full human dignity and personhood possible for women until we assert and demand the control over our own bodies, over our own reproductive process.

There is only one voice that needs to be heard on the question of the final decision as to whether a woman will or will not bear a child, and that is the voice of the woman herself. Her own conscience, her own conscious choice.

Then and only then will women move out of their enforced passivity, their enforced integration, their definition as sex objects as *things* to human personhood, to self-determination, to human dignity, and the new stage in your movement, which is now mine, although I am no expert on abortion, but I am the only kind of expert that there needs to be now....

Women are denigrated in this country, because women are not deciding the conditions of their own society and their own lives. Women are not taken seriously as people. Women are not seen seriously as people. So this is the new name of the game on the question of abortion: that women's voices are heard.

....[W]omen are the ones who therefore must decide, and what we are in the process of doing, it seems to me, is realizing that there are certain rights that have never been defined as rights, that are essential to equality for women, and they were not defined in the Constitution of this, or any country, when that Constitution was written only by men. The right of woman to control her reproductive process must be established as a basic and valuable human civil right not to be denied or abridged by the state.

So must we address all questions governing the reproductive process: access to birth control, to contraceptive devices, and laws governing abortion. Reform, don't talk to me about reform—reform is still the same—women, passive object. Reform is something dreamed up by men, abortion reform. Maybe good ordered men, good ordered men, but they can only think from their point of view of men. Women are the passive objects that somehow must be regulated—thalidomide, rape, incest, what have you, you know. What right have they to say? What right has any man to say to any woman: you must bear this child?

....[T]his is woman's right, and not a technical question needing the sanction of the state to be debated in terms of technicalities, they are irrelevant.... This can only really be confronted in terms of the basic personhood and dignity of woman, which is violated forever if she does not have the right to control her own reproductive process, and this question, the guts of it, the heart of it, goes far beyond the question of abortion, as such. It seems to me almost self-evident that this is the only way to handle abortion....

Am I saying that women must be liberated from motherhood? No, I am not. I am saying that motherhood will only be liberated to be a joyous and responsible human act when women are free to make with full conscious choice and full human responsibility the decision to be mothers....

Am I saying that women have to be liberated from men? That men are the enemy? No, I am not. I am saying that men will only be truly liberated. Men will only be truly liberated to love women and to be fully themselves when women are liberated to be full people. To have a full say in the decisions of their life and their society and a full part in that society, a basic part of which is the control of their own reproductive process....

So this is the real sexual revolution. Not what they so cheaply make headlines in the papers, at what age boys and girls go to bed with each other and whether they do it with or without the benefit of marriage. That's the least of it. The real sexual revolution is the emergence of women from passivity, from *thing-ness*...to full self-determination, to full dignity....

NARAL Policy Statement

The organization born at the Chicago conference, the National Association for Repeal of Abortion Laws (NARAL), was founded on a new premise: the goal was not reform, but repeal of existing abortion laws. Its language was also new, emphasizing the rights of women rather than those of doctors. After the Chicago meeting, NARAL adopted these statements of purpose and policy.

PURPOSE

NARAL, recognizing the basic human right of a woman to limit her own reproduction, is dedicated to the elimination of all laws and practices that would compel any woman to bear a child against her will. To that end, it proposes to initiate and co-ordinate political, social, and legal action of individuals and groups concerned with providing safe abortions by qualified physicians for all women seeking them regardless of economic status.

STATEMENT OF POLICY AND PROGRAM

1. Safe abortions performed by physicians should be readily available to all women on a voluntary basis, regardless of economic status and without legal encumbrance.

2. As a medical procedure, abortion should be subject only to the general laws regulating medical licensure and practice.

Printed by permission of NARAL Pro-Choice America.

Call to Women's Strike for Equality, August 26, 1970

by Betty Friedan

Reprinted here from a typed and hand-edited draft in Betty Friedan's papers, this document summons women to mark the 50th anniversary of women's suffrage by abandoning hearth, home, and office for a day of marching, demonstrating, and lobbying for an agenda that included the right to abortion as part of a call for "drastic social change." The demonstrations around the country on August 26, 1970, received considerable publicity, which Friedan avidly sought, and bolstered the prominence of the National Organization for Women.

The strike's message was that the equal right to vote had not yet secured for women equal citizenship. Through the strike, the movement sought ratification of an Equal Rights Amendment to the United States Constitution, which would have provided that "Equality of rights under the law shall not be denied or abridged by the United States or by any State on account of sex." Furthermore, to enable women to exercise guarantees of equal citizenship, the strike advanced three other claims: equality in education and the workplace, abortion rights, and government-financed child care.

Friedan speaks here in terms of "revolution." Her message is that while women have had the vote for a half century, they have not yet achieved equality, and will do so now only through a radical reordering of women's roles in work, family, and sex.

Our movement toward true equality for all women in America in fully equal partnership with men has reached this year a point of critical mass. The chain reaction of events and breakthroughs against sex discrimination and the denigration of women as we begin this new decade is unmistakable evidence that the unfinished revolution of women towards full human freedom, dignity, self determination and full participation in the main stream of society has exploded into the consciousness, into the actions of millions of women across the lines of generation, across the lines of nation, of color, of man-made politics.

It is only three years since employers and even government commissioners empowered to enforce the civil rights acts ban on sex discrimination in employment were treating it as a slightly dirty joke.... It is only two years ago that we dared to first say that the right of a woman to control her own body's reproductive process should be an inalienable human right for the first time—women's voice was heard on the question of abortion, up until then, completely decided by men. I still remember the courage it took for us to dare to confront this question in terms of the basic principle involved and how even the abortion reformers laughed when we changed the terms of the debate from reform to repeal....

All of us this past year have learned in our gut that sisterhood is powerful. The awesome power of women united, the awesome political power of 53% of the population, is visible now and is being taken seriously, as all of us who define ourselves as people now take the actions that need to be taken in every city and state, and together make our voices heard....

And so we face now the awesome responsibility of this beautiful miracle of our own power as women to change society, to change the conditions that oppress us in government, industry, the professions, the churches, the political parties, the unions, in education, in medicine and in our own homes, in the very images that confine us. I think it is urgent that we confront in all seriousness the power we have to make this revolution happen now, not in some abstract future, when the Apocalypse comes, but in our own lives, in the mainstream of our own society. We have the power to restructure the institutions and conditions that oppress all women now, and it is our responsibility to history, to ourselves, to all who will come after us, to use this power NOW. For there is an urgency in this moment....

It is possible, you know, for revolutions to be aborted. No revolution is inevitable. As we visibly become the fastest growing movement for drastic social change in this country, it would be naïve not to recognize that there are and will be many trying to destroy our strength, to divide us and divert us....

We must use our power to end the war between the sexes by confronting politically the conditions, the institutions that keep women in this impotent state. If we confront the real conditions that oppress men now as well as women and translate our rage into action, then and only then will sex really be liberated to be an active joy and a receiving joy for women and for men, when we are both really free to be all we can be. This is not a war to be fought in the bedroom, but in the city, in the political arena....

I therefore propose that we accept the responsibility of mobilizing the chain reaction we have helped release, for instant revolution against sexual oppression in this year, 1970. I propose that on Wednesday, August 26, we call a 24-hour general strike, a resistance both passive and active, of all women in America against the concrete conditions of their oppression. On that day, 50 years after the amendment that gave women the vote became part of the Constitution, I propose we use our power to declare an ultimatum on all who would keep us from using our rights as Americans. I propose that the women who are doing menial chores in the offices cover their typewriters and close their notebooks and the telephone operators unplug their switchboards, the waitresses stop waiting, cleaning women stop cleaning, and everyone who is doing a job for which a man would be paid more— stop; every woman pegged forever as "assistant-to," doing jobs for which men get the credit, stop. In every office, every laboratory, every school, all the women to whom we get word will spend the day discussing, analyzing the conditions which keep us from being all we might be. And if the condition that keeps us down is the lack of a child care center, we will bring our babies to the office that day and sit them on our bosses' laps. We do not know how many will join our day of abstention from so-called women's work, but I expect it will be millions. We will then present concrete demands to those who so far have made all the decisions.

And when it begins to get dark, instead of cooking dinner or making love, we will assemble, and we will carry candles symbolic of that flame of the passionate journey down through history—relit anew in every city—to converge the visible power of women at city hall—at the political arena where the larger options of our life are decided. If men want to join us, fine. If politicians, if political bosses, if mayors and governors wish to discuss our demands, fine, but we will define the terms of the dialogue. And we will send our most skillful scouts to track down senators one by one, until we have his commitment to the equal rights of women. And by the time these 24 hours are ended, our revolution will be a fact.

This flyer summoned women to a meeting to press the demands made during the Women's Strike for Equality six weeks earlier, on August 26, 1970. As the flyer indicates, the slogan "abortion on demand" originated with the women's movement and not, as many have since assumed, with abortion opponents seeking to characterize the abortion-rights agenda as extreme. By the word "demand," the women's movement intended to underscore the limitations of the "therapeutic abortion" model, under which women had to plead with doctors and hospital review boards for the right to terminate a pregnancy. Such a system was not only paternalistic, in the

Printed by permission of the Schlesinger Library, Radcliffe Institute for Advanced Study, Harvard University, Betty Friedan Collection, MC 575, folder 1187.

feminist view, but it stripped women of their dignity; women should be able to obtain abortions as any other medical service and should not be required to justify their choice to committees of doctors. The demand for child care to enable women to combine motherhood and work emphasized that the women's movement was not at war with motherhood itself. However, this part of the platform necessarily underscored that the movement was seeking not only equal rights in a technical, legal sense but a basic change in family structure and relationships that would allow women to exercise these rights. The centrality to this agenda of the right to abortion amounted to a reframing of the abortion issue, from a question of women's health and safety to a key element in the transformation of women's role in society—and of society itself.

Speak-Out-Rage

Socially privileged members of women's movement worked self-consciously, although not always successfully, to reach out to less privileged women. They sought alliances with other movements, as demonstrated by this request for testimony at a "speak-out" on "abortion, contraception, & forced sterilization" scheduled for October 1972 in Boston. The effort at outreach reflected an understanding of the different forms of reproductive control faced by women across race and class lines. Many such documents from the period refer to "forced sterilization." Social service agencies were known to have pushed sterilization on women who had already had several children, even requiring sterilization as the price for continued eligibility for welfare benefits. The burden of such policies fell disproportionately on the non-white poor and engendered suspicion and bitterness. Feminists advocating for abortion rights raised the issue as one of personal autonomy, underscoring their support for motherhood freely undertaken.

At a conference in July 1972, a group of women of color had passed a resolution in support of the campaign for decriminalizing abortion, emphasizing that the right to control their bodies required not only the legalization of abortion but also the end of forced sterilization:

> *"There is a myth that Third World women do not want to control our bodies, that we do not want the right to contraception and abortion. But we know that Third World women have suffered the most because of this denial of our rights and will continue to suffer as long as the anti-abortion laws remain on the books. We know that more Third World women die every year from illegal back-street abortions than the rest of the female population. We know that Third World women are the first victims of forced sterilization. And we know that we intend to fight for our freedom as women."*

A WOMAN'S RIGHT TO CHOOSE
Boston, Oct. 14 [1972]

- The Women's National Abortion Action Coalition is a national organization uniting women in an action and education campaign for the repeal of all abortion laws, for the repeal of all restrictive contraception laws, and for an end to forced sterilization. The Boston Women's Abortion Action Coalition is the Boston local affiliate.

- Speak-Out-Rage Project is women working with the endorsement of concerned organizations to build the best possible public hearings in Boston.

TESTIMONY IS NEEDED FROM ALL WOMEN: Black, Latina, Chicana, Native American and Asian women, gay women, high school and college women, working women, women in the military, Catholic women, from all across the United States and the rest of the world, from Boston especially for the local hearings.

IF: You have experienced illegal abortion

You have met with opposition to voluntary sterilization

You have been victim of forced sterilization

You have been forced to bear an unwanted child

You have been raped and could not obtain an abortion

You have been discriminated against in pre-natal care

You have gone through other experiences resulting from the lack of control over your reproductive life

You are a doctor or lawyer or counselor involved with these issues

THEN: Your testimony and active involvement in the International Tribunal and/or Speak-Out-Rage is needed. Please send in the coupon below if you can help work for these or would like to present testimony of your experiences.

Reprinted by permission of the Schlesinger Library, Radcliffe Institute for Advanced Study, Harvard University, Feminist Ephemera Collection, Pr-11, 63.2.1, box 1.

Feminist as Anti-Abortionist
by Sidney Callahan

Not all women who considered themselves feminists adopted the abortion rights cause, nor did women who opposed abortion consider that their view on the issue placed them outside the boundaries of feminism.

Since the women's movement began to advance abortion rights claims, there have been those in its ranks who opposed the movement's advocacy, as well as abortion itself. In this early period, when the feminist movement's embrace of abortion rights claims was still relatively new—and those mobilized against abortion had not yet raised the banner of family values—there was more conversation among feminists about whether the availability of abortion served the interests of women.

In the article below, Sidney Callahan argues that abortion violates the fundamental principles of the women's movement. Callahan is a widely published Catholic author

and scholar. She is also a licensed psychologist. This article appeared in the National
Catholic Reporter *in 1972.*

Let's get our feminism together. Right now. The feminist cause is being betrayed
by the men and women pushing for public acceptance of the principle of abortion
on demand. Arguments used in urging routine abortion deny fundamental values
guiding the whole women's movement.

On the issue of abortion radical feminists have completely identified with the
male aggressor; they spout a straight machismo ideology, with a touch of Adam
Smith. The worst of traditional male power plays are being embraced and bran-
dished by those who have suffered from them the most. Every slogan in the pro-
abortion arsenal is male-oriented and a sell-out of feminist values. For instance:

1) "The fetus isn't human and has no right to life." But the feminist movement
   insists that men cease their age-old habit of withholding human status from
   women, blacks, Jews, Indians, Asians and any other helpless or different
   instances of human life. Women encourage rights to life, and value potential
   life. To deny the fact that human life is always a growing process through time
   is a failure of imagination and empathy. Out of sight, out of mind, may do for
   a bombardier's conscience but not for a feminist movement dedicated to ending unilateral suppression of life. Embryonic life is also life, life with a built-in
   future.

2) "Any problem pregnancy should be terminated early by a qualified medical
   professional employing the best technological techniques." Yet the feminist
   movement has persistently protested impersonal professional technologies
   which efficiently ignore not only emotions but the real roots of complex
   human problems. Males have always searched, destroyed, cut, burned, and
   aggressively attacked anything in the way without regard to context, consequences and natural interrelationships. Women have been committed to
   creative nonviolent alternatives which seek more lasting solutions. Feminist
   values are highly attuned to conservation and the achievement of social and
   ecological health. What irony that a society confronted with a plastic basin
   filled with fetal remains, or fetal "wastage," could worry more about the problem of recycling the plastic. So where have all the flowers gone?

3) "A woman has the right to control her own body." How valiantly the feminist
   movement has struggled against the male obsession to control. As they find

in every prison, to fully control, you kill.... Men have always tried to detach themselves from the body, viewing female bodies in particular as a form of property. Men are only too happy to separate female "reproductive systems" from the self. More middle-class men favor elective abortion than any other group, not only because it accords with male convenience, male strategies, but also because it suits the male norm of a human body....

4) "Males have no right to speak or legislate on the abortion issue, since abortion is solely a matter between a woman and her physician." This argument is used to browbeat men (how to mau-mau the male power structure), but it is contrary to other feminist demands. Women now insist on their right to speak out on war not only because their husbands and sons die, but because it is a human concern. Feminists justly demand equal male-female cooperation, decision-making and mutual responsibility in all areas of social life. In particular, women will no longer bear the sole responsibility for childrearing. They insist (quite rightly) that men and the society at large accept their responsibility for the next generation by providing public daycare, health programs and other measures which will support and help women. Only with abortion does community concern become disallowed. Men are angrily disqualified, although over half the aborted fetuses are male and all fetuses are fathered. Each fetus not only has a direct link to a male, but genetically and physically it is linked to the human species as a whole. Who owns the human species? Or the gene pool? Who owns life? We don't let people in the name of private property pollute their own water, contaminate their own air or shoot their own eagles; so how can aborting potential human life not be a public socio-legal concern?

I propose that a truly feminist approach to abortion would:

1) Display an advocacy of life no matter how immature, helpless or different it is from white, middle-class, adult males who have heretofore preempted the right to be fully human.

2) Affirm that full feminine humanity includes distinctly feminine functions. Women need not identify with male sexuality, male aggression and womb-less male lifestyles in order to win social equality. Getting into the club is not worth the price of alienation from body-life, emotion, empathy and sensitivity.

3) Assert that abortion is a two-sex, community decision in which the rights and welfare of women, fetuses, children, father, families and the rest of the

community be considered and arbitrated. The whole society has a responsibility for human life and the next generation. Women and men should urge and support nonviolent creative alternatives to abortion. Facing such a painful problem we cannot give in to simpleminded sexist slogans and a property rights ethic. Life is not that easy.

Reprinted from the April 7, 1972, issue of *National Catholic Reporter,* by permission of *National Catholic Reporter,* 115 East Armour Boulevard, Kansas City, Missouri 64111, www. ncronline.org.

Black Women's Manifesto;
Double Jeopardy: To Be Black and Female (1969)
by Frances Beal

The movement to expand access to abortion was an object of considerable distrust in the black community, with some prominent African Americans concerned that it was a plot to shrink the black population. In too many settings, race and class considerations had played a role in birth control policies. The debate over abortion was thus approached with varying degrees of mistrust in communities of color. Some viewed abortion as another path to genocide. "My answer to genocide, quite simply is eight black kids—and another baby on the way," Dick Gregory, a popular black comedian and social activist, wrote in Ebony *magazine in 1971.*

The issue was a challenging one for black political leaders. While 63.7% of respondents to a 1971 poll conducted by the black newspaper the Chicago Daily Defender *feared that government-funded abortion posed a genocidal threat to the black community, only 26.4% opposed abortion itself. The Reverend Jesse Jackson, noting that he himself was born out of wedlock to a teen-aged mother, declared himself opposed to abortion during the 1970s. In 1971, speaking before the U.S. Commission on Population and Growth (see page 201), he equated birth control in the black community with genocide. He explained to the commission: "You have to recognize that the American group that has been subjected to as much harassment as our community has is suspect of any programs that would have the effect of either reducing or leveling off our population growth. Virtually all the security we have is in the number of children we produce." It was not only that Jackson was concerned about the dangers of government-sponsored birth control; he opposed limiting the reproduction of black women in any form: "We don't want birth control; we want blacks so we will have power." Later, during his campaign for the White House in 1988, he supported abortion rights, including federal funding for abortions in government-funded health plans.*

If the black community was uniform in its opposition to racially motivated efforts to restrict its growth, its leaders were divided in how they spoke publicly about birth-control and abortion. Many, often women, took a more nuanced position: while opposing any form of mandated birth control, they also opposed any effort to pressure black women to have children.

Shirley Chisholm, the first black woman elected to Congress, recounted in her 1970 autobiography, Unbought and Unbossed, *her journey from opposing the repeal of New York's abortion law to changing her mind and becoming honorary president of the National Association for the Repeal of Abortion Laws (as NARAL was then known). Noting the harm done to black women by illegal abortion, she wrote: "Which is more like genocide, I have asked my black brothers—this, the way things are, or the conditions I am fighting for in which the full range of family planning services is freely available to women of all classes and colors, starting with effective contraception and extending to safe, legal termination of undesired pregnancies, at a price they can afford?"*

In the excerpt below, Frances Beal decried what she viewed as government efforts to sterilize—and thereby disempower—people of color, while at the same time, she opposed abortion restrictions as equally threatening to the welfare of black women and the black community. Beal was active in the Student Nonviolent Coordinating Committee, a grassroots organization that played a visible role in the civil rights movement, and helped found its Black Women's Liberation Committee. She first published the piece below as a pamphlet in 1969. It was revised the following year for inclusion in the anthology Sisterhood Is Powerful.

BEDROOM POLITICS

[P]erhaps the most outlandish act of oppression in modern times is the current campaign to promote sterilization of non-white women in an attempt to maintain the population and power imbalance between the white haves and the non-white have nots.

These tactics are but another example of the many devious schemes that the ruling elite attempt to perpetrate on the black population in order to keep itself in control. It has recently come to our attention that a massive campaign for so-called "birth control" is presently being promoted not only in the underdeveloped non-white areas of the world, but also in black communities here in the United States. However, what the authorities in charge of these programs refer to as "birth control" is in fact nothing but a method of outright surgical genocide.

The United States has been sponsoring sterilization clinics in non-white countries, especially in India where already some 3 million young men and boys in and around New Delhi have been sterilized in make-shift operating rooms set up by the American Peace Corps workers. Under these circumstances, it is understandable why certain countries view the Peace Corps not as a benevolent project, not as evidence of America's concern for underdeveloped areas, but rather as a threat to their very existence. This program could more aptly be named the "Death Corps."

....

THE [STERILIZATION OF WOMEN] has now become the commonest operation in Puerto Rico, commoner than an appendectomy or a tonsillectomy. It is so widespread that it is referred to simply as "la operación." On the Island, 20% of the women between the ages of 15 and 45 have already been sterilized.

And now, as previously occurred with the pill, this method has been imported into the United States. These sterilization clinics are cropping up around the country in the black and Puerto Rican communities. These so-called "Maternity Clinics" specifically outfitted to purge black women or men of their reproductive possibilities, are appearing more and more in hospitals and clinics across the country.

A number of organizations have been formed to popularize the idea of sterilization such as the Association for Voluntary Sterilization and the Human Betterment (!!?) Association for Voluntary Sterilization which has its headquarters in New York City. Front Royal, Virginia, has one such "Maternity Clinic" in Warren Memorial Hospital. The tactics used in the clinic in Fauquier County, Virginia, where poor and helpless black mothers and young girls are pressured into undergoing sterilization are certainly not confined to that clinic alone.

Threatened with the cut-off of relief funds, some black welfare women have been forced to accept this sterilization procedure in exchange for a continuation of welfare benefits. Mt. Sinai Hospital in New York City performs these operations on many of its ward patients whenever it can convince the women to undergo this surgery. Mississippi and some of the other Southern states are notorious for this act. Black women are often afraid to permit any kind of necessary surgery because they know from bitter experience that they are more likely than not to come out of the hospital without their insides....

We condemn this use of the black woman as a medical testing ground for the white middle class. Reports of the ill effects including deaths from the use of the birth control pill only started to come to light when the white privileged class began to be affected. These outrageous Nazi-like procedures on the part of medical researchers are but another manifestation of the totally amoral and dehumanizing brutality that the capitalist system perpetrates on black women. The sterilization experiments carried on in concentration camps some twenty-five years ago have been denounced the world over, but no one seems to get upset by the repetition of these same racist tactics today in the United States of America—land of the free and home of the brave. This campaign is as nefarious a program as Germany's gas chambers and in a long term sense, as effective and with the same objective.

The rigid laws concerning abortions in this country are another vicious means of subjugation, and, indirectly of outright murder. Rich white women somehow manage to obtain these operations with little or no difficulty. It is the poor black and Puerto Rican woman who is at the mercy of the local butcher. Statistics show us that the non-white death rate at the hands of the unqualified abortionist is substantially higher than for white women. Nearly half of the child-bearing deaths in New York City were attributed to abortion alone and out of these, 79% are among non-whites and Puerto Rican women.

We are not saying that black women should not practice birth control or family planning. Black women have the right and the responsibility to determine when it is in the interest of the struggle to have children or not to have them. It is also her right and responsibility to determine when it is in her own best interests to have children, how many she will have, and how far apart and this right must not be relinquished to anyone.

The lack of the availability of safe birth control methods, the forced sterilization practices and the inability to obtain legal abortions are all symptoms of a decadent society that jeopardizes the health of black women (and thereby the entire black race) in its attempts to control the very life processes of human beings. This repressive control of black women is symptomatic of a society that believes it has the right to bring political factors into the privacy of the bedchamber. The elimination of these horrendous conditions will free black women for full participation in the revolution, and thereafter, in the building of the new society.

Reprinted by permission of Frances Beal.

Black Women and the Motherhood Myth

by Bev Cole

This excerpt is from an essay in The Right to Choose Abortion, *a pamphlet published in 1971 by a Boston-based group, Female Liberation, that supported total repeal of abortion laws. The author, Bev Cole, was a member of the group. Although she, like Beal, decides to support a right to abortion, her essay reflects the struggle within the black community over how to approach a subject with many troubling dimensions that continued to cause deep unease.*

The abortion issue must be faced by each and every woman, especially Black and Third World women. The Black woman throughout history has been a breeder—breeder of slaves and breeder of slave owners' bastards. Then today, Black men tell Black women to continue to breed, so that we shall outnumber the White men and seize control. On July 4th, 1970, the Black Panthers came out with the most absurd statement, "Black women love children and like large families." While the Panthers hopscotch on the subject of the Black woman's innate love for children, and declare that the quantity (not mentioning quality) of forces must be overwhelmed to insure victory, they also say that the Black man and Black woman must stand and fight together against the enemy. How can we have this togetherness on the front if women are busy being balled by night and coping with the results, children everywhere, during each and every day. The gun in the hand of every Black man seems also to mean diaper swinging females following close behind.

That the Black woman's only dream is to reproduce is a false myth, as shown by the fact that 70% of the abortions performed in this country are done on Black and Third World women. The economics of this racist society makes it impossible for many of these women to afford safe abortions, thus illegal, unsafe abortions occur. The poor woman's fate is usually injury or death from having flushed detergents and soaps into herself, or having tried to sever the uterine wall to cut away the multiplying cells. These futile abortive attempts have caused a high death rate among Black and Third World women, so that the Black brother's argument against legal, safe abortion is, in itself, genocidal, killing off Black women in the name of the fetus. A Black brother told one of my girl friends that "if any woman of his got pregnant (note that the fault lies solely with the female) and hurt or killed anything of his inside her, he'd kill her." That's a brother's concern for his sister.

There are women who decide to have and keep their children, and to many of these Black women pregnancy is the admission stub to the nearest welfare office. But many a welfare mother finds herself pregnant for the second third, fourth time and wants to avoid sacrificing the lives of her previous children with one more mouth to feed. Some women seek help, but many times Welfare Agencies step in beforehand, promising an abortion only if one will submit to sterilization.

In my hometown, any welfare recipient expecting either her 10th or 11th child is sterilized by court action. Some women do not even have these legal procedures taken against them; they find themselves awakening in the recovery room where they are told, "You don't have to worry no more." In cases such as these, it seems that the government has taken it into its own hands to punish the welfare recipient for having another pregnancy by forcing sterilization. This method totally takes away the woman's right to choose and control her body. A Black woman, and every woman, is entitled to the right of abortion. At the same time, forced sterilization must come to an end.

I want safe, legal abortive practices provided, especially in Black community hospitals run by the Black community to assist Black women and I want all this NOW!

Reprinted by permission of the Schlesinger Library, Radcliffe Institute for Advanced Study, Harvard University, Feminist Ephemera Collection, Pr-11, 63.2.1, box 1.

We now turn to another of the paths leading from reform to repeal. During the 1960's, a long-running conversation about limiting population growth was taken up by advocates who brought to it concerns about protecting the environment and sexual freedom.

The term "population explosion" dates from a 1954 pamphlet that warned of population growth as a threat to world peace. In the post–World War II period, Western elites, concerned about the resource claims of the world's poorer nations, engaged in geopolitical talk about population growth. In domestic variants of the conversation worry about overpopulation expressed class-based concerns that easily slid into assumptions about race: too many of the poor were having more babies than they could support. With increasing government involvement in public assistance in the 1960s, there were those who continued to talk about "family planning" in openly class-based and, implicitly, race-based terms. While the focus of this conversation was birth control rather than abortion, it left some communities wary of and divided over the new and growing movement for abortion's legalization.

By the 1960s, a growing environmental movement had begun to address overpopulation, and to exhort the middle class itself to practice family planning in the interests of protecting the planet's resources. These early "green" advocates were also part of the 1960s sexual revolution; today we might term them "sex positive."

Population control offered publicly respectable, social-welfare reasons for supporting sex education and birth control practices that separated sex from reproduction.
By the decade's end, growing numbers of population-control advocates supported
the repeal of laws criminalizing abortion. "Population control" offered reasons
for liberalizing access to abortion that were more widely acceptable than reasons
associated with the sexual revolution or the women's liberation movement—causes
with which environmental population-control advocates were often affiliated.

Zero Population Growth

*A growing environmental movement brought new concerns to conversation about pop-
ulation growth. Environmentalists argued that burgeoning population growth would
place escalating demands on natural resources, on the capacity of parks and other places
where people could encounter nature, and on the world's food supply. Famine loomed,
Dr. Paul R. Ehrlich, a biologist, warned in his best-selling 1968 book,* The Population
Bomb. *"[H]undreds of millions of people are going to starve to death," the author predicted in the opening pages. David Brower, executive director of the Sierra Club, wrote
the foreword to* The Population Bomb, *thus firmly linking Ehrlich's call for "population
control" with the agenda of the rapidly growing environmental movement.* The Population Bomb *would ultimately sell over two million copies.*

The Population Bomb *was blunt in its endorsement of abortion as "a highly effective weapon in the armory of population control." The book accused mainstream family-
planning groups of "pussyfooting" about abortion and held up postwar Japan, where
abortion was widely available and where the birthrate had been cut in half, as an
example to be emulated. Ehrlich also advocated sexual freedom and argued that a side
benefit of delinking sex from reproduction would be to liberate the American public from
the "pressures of a sexually repressive and repressed society." Women's liberation, as such,
was not an interest of his, however.*

*The organization Zero Population Growth was founded in 1968 in response to
the environmental concerns then animating an important segment of the population-
control movement. This brochure soliciting new members advocated making legal abortion "freely available" as one means of reaching the population-stabilizing goal of no
more than two children per family. Starting with a few hundred members, Zero Population Growth claimed 300,000 members in 300 chapters by the time it joined one of
the briefs filed in* Roe v. Wade. *In 2002 it changed its name to Population Connection,
which in 2010 had a membership of 30,000.*

PROGRESS?

We Americans have a tendency to equate growth with progress. We think that
every time we build a new dam or highway we have made some progress. It never
seems to occur to us that instead of making progress we are barely keeping even.
The new highway is usually built because the old highway has become inadequate
to carry the ever increasing number of cars. Why don't we think about stopping
the increase in the number of cars, instead of increasing the number of highways?
Or, to put it more directly, why don't we stop the constant increase in the number of people? Less increase in the population means less increase in the number
of cars.

Usually, when we build a dam it is because the greater population requires
more electricity and water. Sometimes it is because we have destroyed the forests of
a region—causing floods. The forests are frequently cut down to build more houses
for the ever growing population. Thus we have a chain reaction type of effect. First
we cut down the forests to build more houses for the expanding population, then
we start to have floods because the natural growth has been removed from the
mountains, then we build a dam to prevent the floods. Each step costs a great deal
of money and scars the countryside. It all starts with population growth.

Growth means that the population expands and more facilities are built to
take care of the greater number of people. Progress means that a distinct improvement has taken place in the quality of our lives. More people living in our neigh-
borhood does not necessarily improve the quality of our lives. Usually, in fact,
more people crowded into the same area results in a decrease in the quality of
life for the inhabitants of the area. If your life is polluted by the presence of too
many people too close to you, then be prepared for the situation to get worse. The
population of the United States continues to grow, and all those extra people have
to fit in somewhere. This country has reached the limit in terms of the number
of people that can be supported comfortably. Of course, we could probably support more people at a survival level—but who wants that? In the 1890s, the last
unused, unsettled land was taken up. Since then, we have been crowding more
and more people into the same land area. Of course, there are still great uninhabited areas within the U.S., but these areas are, without exception, uninhabited for
very good reasons. Either it is too hot, too cold, too mountainous, or there isn't
any water.

As we crowd more and more people into our country, we continually run into
more and more problems of waste disposal. Somehow we have to get rid of all the

trash and sewage created by these additional people. Unfortunately, we cannot afford adequate sewage treatment plants—we have to spend our money for more schools and colleges for the increasing population. So we dump the sewage into our lakes and rivers. The predictable result is that after a period of time the lakes and rivers become "dead." The fish and wildlife die and we have a stinking mess instead of a useful and beautiful natural resource. We also dump vast quantities of waste into the atmosphere—over 500 pounds per year for each person in the country. It settles out as soot on our laundry and settles in our lungs as a possible cancer causing agent. When it gets bad enough we call it smog and it keeps us from seeing the scenery. In Los Angeles, one of the worst smog areas, people talk wistfully of someday having 1940 quality air.

IS THERE ANY HOPE OF STOPPING POPULATION GROWTH?

YES! It is a realistic possibility. Some European countries have reached this goal. All that is required is that the average family size be two children. If there are only two children in a family, then the net long term growth is zero, because one child replaces the father and the other replaces the mother. In the United States it is that third and fourth child in a family that is causing population growth.

WHAT IS ZERO POPULATION GROWTH, INC. DOING?

ZPG is a non-profit, volunteer group which advocates that all measures be taken immediately to stem the tide of population growth.

We advocate:

1. That no responsible family should have more than two children. Any family wanting to care for more than two children should adopt further children. Adopting children does not increase the population.

2. All methods of birth control, including legalized abortion, should be freely available—and at no cost in poverty cases.

3. Irresponsible people who have more than two children should be taxed to the hilt for the privilege of irresponsible breeding....

ZPG has been in existence for only a few months, and already we have over 600 members. Funds collected from membership dues will be, and are being used to stop population growth. Many members are volunteering their time and energies to promoting ZPG's goal.

The two most important lines of attack to be used in reaching our goal are:

1. Active lobbying in our legislatures and in the Congress for population ori-
    ented legislation—tax incentives for the smaller family and government sup-
    port of birth control, including legalized abortion.

2. Advertising to reach the general public, which will popularize the two-child
    family and alert the public to the dangers of population growth.

Our goal is 1,000 members before the end of 1969—this goal is in sight and
we expect to exceed it. By the end of 1970 our goal is 10,000 members. By joining
ZPG you will be taking a concrete step to protect the environment that you, your
children, and your grandchildren will have to live in.

Reprinted by permission of Population Connection.

A Sex Counseling Service for College Students
by Philip M. Sarrel, M.D., and Lorna J. Sarrel, M.S.W.

*The 1960s also saw the celebration of human sexuality in a new climate of openness and
experimentation—enabled, to a degree, by the increased availability of new forms of
birth control. Young people found themselves caught up in a sexual revolution for which
many were unprepared.*

*Yale University confronted this aspect of the 1960s earlier and more directly than
many other campuses, due to the simple fact that its undergraduate college became
coeducational in 1969 and suddenly added 600 women to a formerly all-male environment. Some rapid retooling of the university's health service was clearly in order. Dr.
Philip M. Sarrel, a gynecologist at Yale's medical school, and his wife, Lorna J. Sarrel, a
social worker, took the initiative and established a sex counseling service in which they
operated as a team, advising hundreds of individuals and couples every year. They also
offered a lecture series on human sexuality that was quickly oversubscribed. In 1970,
under their guidance, a student committee produced a 60-page booklet,* Sex and the Yale
Student, *which was distributed without charge to all undergraduates and graduate
students. It went through several editions and became the basis for a book,* The Student
Guide to Sex on Campus, *which was distributed nationally and sold more than 100,000
copies in the early 1970s.*

*The Sarrels described their experience counseling students at Yale at a joint meeting
in October 1970 of the American School Health Association and the School Health Sec-*

tion of the American Public Health Association. Their account, while somewhat clinical in tone, presents in vivid detail a portrait of a population—both students and adults— navigating a world of rapidly changing norms of behavior, a world in which abortion played an accepted if legally ambiguous role.

INTRODUCTION

In the fall of 1969 Yale College became coeducational. All at once, 600 undergraduate females were added to the male enrollment of 4,200. In preparation for coeducation the student health service suddenly became acutely aware of a gap in its services. There was not even one obstetrician and gynecologist on the staff! Female graduate students had always been referred to doctors in town. The thought of 600 young women with ailments ranging from cramps to pregnancy was not a little frightening for a health service geared almost exclusively to male needs.

Knowing of his special interest in the sexual problems of college students, the Department of University Health approached the gynecologist author of this paper with the idea of running a gynecology clinic. After several consultations with health staff administrators a plan was evolved to provide something beyond the usual gynecologic care, something to be labeled "sex-counseling." The Sex Counseling Service would be staffed by the authors—husband and wife, gynecologist and social worker respectively, functioning as a team, with the goal of helping students with any problem relating to sexuality. Another gynecologist would handle routine medical problems. In order to stress the special nature of the service and to facilitate close working relations with staff psychiatrists, it was decided to place the sex counseling service within the Mental Hygiene Division of University Health rather than within the medical division.

STARTING THE SEX COUNSELING SERVICE AT YALE

That students needed help, advice and services relating to sexual problems was unquestionable and there was no reason to think Yale would be any different. But it was obviously important to "advertise" the service and to gain students' confidence and respect....

The "advertising" was obviously successful. From the very first day all appointments were taken. Last year, the sex counseling service functioned one day a week and the wait for an appointment grew longer as the year progressed until last spring when the wait was nearing three months. Of course, emergencies were always fit in somehow....

In our first year we saw a total of 387 cases.... Of the 167 undergraduate females, 65 per cent of them came requesting birth control. Eleven per cent thought they were pregnant, but the majority were not. Fourteen students came for the "morning after" pill. Two girls were afraid they had venereal disease and they did. Twelve girls came just to talk about a sexual problem or dilemma and another ten came for miscellaneous reasons. Since the problems seen at the sex counseling service fall into three major categories, (1) requests for birth control, (2) pregnancy, and (3) sexual dysfunction or concern, our approach to each will be described.

CONTRACEPTION

There are very few "routine" requests for birth control in a college population. The students need and want to talk about so much more than just the relative merits of pill versus IUD, or how to use a diaphragm. There are three general areas that we always discuss with students requesting birth control. The first area is sexual history and begins with the question, "Have you had intercourse?" We want to know if the girl and/or her boyfriend have questions or worries about sex response, or specific sexual experiences. We want to know how they feel about their sexual experiences—happy? sad? perplexed? conflicted? ecstatic?

We see many girls or couples who have not yet had intercourse. They are in a close relationship and know they want to have intercourse, but not before they have the most reliable form of contraception they can get. Another even larger group of patients has begun having intercourse only recently. Almost 75 per cent of the freshmen we saw last year fell into one of these two groups. Only 25 per cent had been non-virgins when they arrived on campus. We give these statistics to emphasize the number of students who are just beginning full sexual relations. This is obviously a critical stage in psychosexual development—a time when education and counseling can spell the difference between development and disaster.

The second major area we discuss is the present male-female relationship or relationships. Are there major problems? If a girl is having intercourse with a number of partners, how is this affecting her? What has been a student's pattern of relating in the past?

The third area we try to cover is, broadly speaking, the student's background and relations to family. There are many current issues such as, whether a girl should tell her parents she is having intercourse. For most college students, first sexual intercourse is intimately tied to feelings about growing up and away from parents, establishing individual and sexual identity, and the shifting of focus from family of orientation to their future family of procreation. Talking about their family's attitudes, and the sex education they did or did not receive, usually raises moral issues. We have been impressed by the students' reaction to this sort of discussion. Far from bristling at any mention of ethics or values, they seem to welcome a chance to discuss their own personal moral dilemmas. Perhaps they welcome it because we are not preaching. What we are trying to do is to help them think through the meaning of their sexuality and sexual behavior for themselves and their partners....

PREGNANCY

Pregnancy poses somewhat different issues for the sex counseling service. To begin with, the fact of pregnancy needs to be established. If a girl is pregnant, we talk to her or, more often, to the couple, about alternatives. Abortion has been the decision in almost every case we have seen. There is a need to focus on the realities of the situation—when and how, finances and the involvement or non-involvement of parents. If a girl is to be aborted legally she (and often her boyfriend) is seen by one of the Department of University Health psychiatrists and he, as well as the sex counseling service gynecologist, submit letters to the hospital committee on abortion. If they approve, then the gynecologist member of our team performs the abortion at the Yale-New Haven Hospital. If the girl is under 21, there must be signed permission from one parent. Although most students are resistant to the idea of involving parents, it has been our experience that parents are amazingly supportive in this crisis. In some instances, it has created a relationship between parent and child that is closer than ever before.

The sex counseling service places great stress on the importance of follow-up after an abortion. The same psychiatrist who saw the girl or couple before will see them at least once afterward. Ideally, he will see them within a few days, again a week or two later, and again six months later. In addition to its therapeutic value for the students, it is hoped this procedure will increase our understanding of the emotional sequelae of abortion among college students.

An important subcategory in our consideration of pregnancy are those girls or couples who have intercourse without birth control at a time when they might become pregnant. In these cases, the morning after pill (50 mgs of diethylstilbestrol) is prescribed, and there have been no failures. However, we find that in many instances these students merit the same concern and professional input as girls who actually do become pregnant. Although almost all are seen on an emergency basis, they are given a follow-up appointment so that we can discuss birth control and the possible reasons for their non-use of contraception. We have found certain factors to be significant: ignorance, promiscuity, fear of infertility, desire for pregnancy, crisis over feminine identity, and many misconceptions about sexual response. In other words, the request for the morning after pill may well be an important signal of psychosexual distress....

CAMPUS RESPONSE

The campus response to the sex counseling service seems to be very favorable. Students obviously make use of the service. This year, we are seeing an increasing proportion of males and couples. It is unusual for a student to cancel or miss an appointment but, when this does happen, the appointment is often "given" to a roommate or friend. In a student booklet, *Sex and the Yale Student,* distributed free to all 9,300 undergraduate and graduate students this fall, the students described the sex counseling service in this way:

"Among modern universities, Yale is almost unique in its creation of a special department at DUH (the Department of University Health) to deal with the sexual problems and questions of its students.... So consider yourself very lucky...."
....

The administration of the college and of the health service have been exceptionally helpful. They were instrumental in starting the sex counseling service and have continued to support it. The Department of University Health will be moving into a new building next year, and provision is being made for the sex counseling service to become a regular part of the health care plan which is to be initiated at that time.

At first, we were concerned about the possible reaction of the alumni and parents, for example, to the prescription of contraception. In fact, there has been little or no opposition and some very positive support. The father of one of the girls we saw is a college president and having learned about the experience of his daughter has since started a sex counseling program on his campus modeled after Yale's.

When a widely distributed national newspaper mentioned that Yale had a new service that prescribed contraception, we thought there might be adverse reaction on the part of the alumni, but the Alumni Office forwarded the protest mail to us; it consisted of one letter. In addition, there were many favorable responses.

Excerpted from Philip M. Sarrel and Lorna J. Sarrel, "A Sex Counseling Service for College Students," *American Journal of Public Health,* vol. 61, no. 7 (July 1971), pp. 1341–7. Printed by permission of the American Public Health Association.

Sex and the Yale Student
by the Student Committee on Human Sexuality

The following excerpts are from the original 1970 edition of the Yale sex booklet itself. Among its notable aspects is its frank discussion of abortion as an available alternative, at a time when Connecticut law permitted abortion only to save a pregnant woman's life. The booklet provides a glimpse of the world between abortion law on the books and abortion law as enforced—at least for university students at a time and place when community support for criminalizing abortion was eroding. Note the student writers' observation that "no one is humiliated or lectured" when seeking help at Yale for pregnancy. Note also the authors' self-awareness that their access to professional advice and safe abortion placed them "among a privileged group" at a time when many women, in Connecticut and elsewhere, lacked those options. We place the excerpts concerning sex counseling at Yale among the "repeal" materials because although the students and their counselors were not engaged in advocacy, they proceeded on the assumption that the decision to terminate a pregnancy belonged to the individuals directly involved; for this community, at least, the old prohibitions had functionally ceased to exist.

MAKING A DECISION

If indeed you are pregnant, you must make two major decisions. First you must decide whether or not to have the child. If you decide to have the child, then you must decide whether or not to keep it. Other decisions which you will have to make include whether or not to involve your boyfriend, your family and others. Perhaps, most important is the issue of understanding why you became pregnant.

If you decide not to have the child, your alternative is abortion. The change in social climate and in medical practice in recent years has made legal and safe abortion readily available. Yale students will find detailed information on this subject in the section of this pamphlet on abortion and in the section on Yale services.

If you decide to carry through your pregnancy, you may avoid many of the doubts that often accompany getting an abortion. But, having the child may still involve different problems of its own. You may wish to get married and keep the baby. However, this is not always possible or desirable. Still, one parent alone may want to keep the baby and may be willing to cope with the difficulties. But, if you don't want an abortion and if you don't feel that either of you can keep your child, you might decide to have the child adopted. In any of these cases it should be noted that school policy at Yale allows you to stay in school while you are pregnant. Repeat. No girl will be asked to leave school because she is pregnant. On the other hand, if you wish to leave school because of pregnancy, the Sex Counseling Service will be glad to tell you about living-in resources here and in other communities which students have used in the past.

If you are thinking about having your child adopted, the first thing you should do is to get in touch with one of the licensed child placing agencies in Connecticut. The Counseling Service will be able to advise you, as there are several agencies in New Haven [list of agencies omitted]

AGAIN, IF YOU HAVE ANY doubts about adoption, keeping your child, or carrying through your pregnancy once you are sure that you are pregnant, go to the Sex Counseling Service. Don't panic; you have several alternatives and the Counseling Service can help you make a rational decision that is right for you.

ABORTION

What happens when birth control is no longer the main concern? What happens when you find yourself the potential mother or father of an unwanted child?

At this point it is no use to castigate yourself or doubt your morality. Once you have determined that you are definitely pregnant, you may decide that you want an abortion.

YOU DO NOT HAVE TO HAVE AN ILLEGAL ABORTION. Repeat. YOU DO NOT HAVE TO LOOK FOR A CRIMINAL ABORTIONIST. Excellent services are available for women who need them. Connecticut statute says an abortion may be legally performed to "save the life of the mother or the fetus." While this does sound a bit cryptic, it does allow physicians to save your life by preventing you from taking matters into your own hands and seeking assistance—and perhaps, death, from a criminal abortionist.

In the chapter on Yale services, the necessary steps are outlined. It is a simple, private, and safe way to terminate a pregnancy. No one is humiliated or lectured. In fact, by all accounts, Yale and its excellent personnel not only help to reduce personal trauma, but also, oddly enough, have seen the whole experience evolve into a positive one. Hard to believe—but true.

This section will attempt to explain what the abortion itself is all about, what the methods are, and which are applicable at what time. In all instances, the working definition for abortion is termination of a pregnancy before a fetus can survive.

NON-HOSPITAL ABORTION

If you are under 21 you will need parental consent to have an abortion at Yale-New Haven or most any hospital. Knowing that this will cause unhappiness, disappointment, or real anger in your parents, you may be tempted to find a private abortionist, not connected with hospital facilities. Don't. We don't like to preach—but truly death or permanent disability is not a worthwhile alternative to facing parents with your problem. Not everyone suffers from a criminal abortion, but it is a terrible risk to take—especially when you don't have to. Those students aborted last year who were under the age of 21 were able to involve at least one of their parents, and this was all that was necessary. In almost all instances, the feeling afterwards of the family as well as that of the couple involved was that involvement of the family turned out to be a very good thing in helping the couple handle the crisis.

Opportunity to receive an abortion in this country discriminates against the poor, the ignorant and the disadvantaged. The situation is getting better, but at this writing, college students are among a privileged group. You are privileged in that you have access to information that some would and many have given their lives for in previous times when abortion was a suppressed and criminal practice. If it is impossible for you to have an abortion done at YNH Medical Center the Counseling Service at Dept. of University Health will help you to find a non-hospital abortion done by a physician under safe conditions. In New Haven, the most reputable referral service can be found by calling the Clergy Counseling Service for Problem Pregnancy

....Concerned clergymen, seeing a desperate need, have been able to help frantic women find skilled physicians in order to avoid the atrocities of criminal abortion....

COSTS

Here is the rub. Even at minimal charges, expenses at any hospital, Yale included, pile up. Costs come to between $400 and $500. (A half hour in an operating room today for any reason costs a patient about $100 just for the room. The other costs are for anesthesia, nursing, hospital bed, laboratory work, and the doctor's fee.) Exceptions and terms may be arranged, but at the present time, any way you look at it an abortion is a great deal more expensive than buying the pill once a month. An illegal abortion may cost you anywhere from $400 to $1,000—of course, that is not counting the money any complications and check-ups may cost and certainly not including the added fear and anxiety. Efforts are being made to bring costs down to a feasible scale, and this has been accomplished somewhat both here in New Haven and in New York. But, at the present time abortion is still a large expense.

THE FUTURE OF ABORTION IN THE UNITED STATES

While the trend in abortion laws seems to be towards liberalization, abortion is still not a simple decision by a woman who wishes to end her pregnancy. Although Yale-New Haven has a more equitable procedure than most, it still entails seeing a psychiatrist, getting permission from a hospital committee, paying out large sums of money, and going through channels. Furthermore, even if abortion should become a totally individual decision (it is almost at that stage now), it would not eradicate all of the tension, ambivalence, and emotional upset of having to terminate a pregnancy. While the abortion can be made into a positive part of one's education, it is not an essential lesson....

It is this committee's opinion, however, that while more enlightened abortion procedures are essential, we would not like to see abortion as a means of birth control. Abortions—even inexpensive, quick abortions—demand decisions, emotions, and professional time that need not be so utilized if an effective birth control program is being used. Hopefully, birth control methods will soon be so widespread and so sophisticated that the need for abortions will decrease. In the meantime, should a birth control failure occur, abortion will be increasingly available.

ABORTION UNIT

A special unit has been created at the Yale-New Haven Hospital. Access to this unit is available to all students through DUH. In accordance with Connecticut law, all women desiring a legal abortion must be seen by a gynecologist and a psychiatrist. Students who need and wish these services will be referred by DUH to the hospital unit responsible for submitting a petition to the hospital committee. If the petition meets the requirements of Connecticut law, it will be granted. The decision is reached in a few days' time. All students for whom permission was requested last year were approved.

Parental consent is required by law for minors for any operation, however slight. Abortions are in no way different, so if you are under 21 and desire a legal abortion, at least one of your parents must give consent. In many cases, it is appropriate for one's boyfriend to be involved in the discussions with the professional staff. The cost for abortion is about $400.00. This cost includes all follow-up visits.

If it is impossible for a student to tell her parents and she is under 21, she will be referred through DUH to the Clergy Counseling Service for Problem Pregnancy where she will be told how and where abortion can be performed safely and legally....

REMEMBER, THERE IS ALWAYS SOMETHING YOU CAN DO. DON'T TAKE A CHANCE WITH AN ILLEGAL ABORTIONIST. IT COULD MEAN YOUR LIFE.

RELIGION

Union for Reform Judaism, 49th General Assembly, Montreal, Quebec (November 1967)

Religious denominations that had paid little, if any, attention to abortion began to feel obligated, beginning in the mid-1960s, to take a stand on an increasingly visible issue with implications for personal morality and religious doctrine. In this section, we offer a sampling of the official policy statements that resulted from what was often prolonged and serious study. Protestant churches arrayed themselves along a spectrum, advocating positions from moderate reform to outright repeal of existing abortion laws. It is worth noting that even the most conservative of the Protestant denominations left the door open to reform along a therapeutic model. While all of the statements presented here pre-date the Supreme Court's ruling in Roe v. Wade, *we indicate denominations that revised their positions in the decade after* Roe.*

The Jewish community included a range of viewpoints. The Orthodox Jewish leadership opposed reform. In 1972, the Rabbinical Council of America, the largest Orthodox rabbinical organization, pronounced itself "concerned with the deterioration of moral values in our society of which permissive abortion is a significant symptom" and called for repeal of state laws that had liberalized the grounds for abortion.

The Reform Jewish leadership, by contrast, had issued this statement in 1967.

ABORTION REFORM

Humane considerations motivate us to speak out in the name of our United States members in favor of needed revisions in the abortion laws of many states. In recent months the moral imperative to modernize abortion legislation has become and important issue in the legislatures of many states.

Each year a great number of American women, many of them married, seek abortions. Most existing state statutes penalize the poor who cannot afford recourse to those services which the more affluent in our society can and do find. But for the poor or affluent alike, illegal abortions yearly take a tragic and needless toll.

We commend those states which have enacted humane legislation in this area and we appeal to other states to do likewise and permit abortions under such circumstances as threatened disease or deformity of the embryo or fetus, threats to the physical and mental health of the mother, rape and incest and the social, economic and psychological factors that might warrant therapeutic termination of pregnancy.

We urge our constituent congregations to join with other forward looking citizens in securing needed revisions and liberalization of abortion laws.

Printed by permission of the Union for Reform Judaism.

United Methodist Church, Statement of Social Principles (1972)

The official statements on abortion issued by Protestant denominations before Roe demonstrate that, although there was a diversity of views about abortion, there was widespread agreement—even among conservative and evangelical denominations—that the law ought to be reformed. The Board of Christian Social Concerns of the United Methodist Church (UMC), in 1969, adopted a Statement of Responsible Parenthood, which called for the decriminalization of abortion. The Methodist Statement "challenge[d] society to responsible parenthood," marked by population control, so that the dignity of persons was not threatened by "crises of insufficient food, diminishing space, and pollution of the environment"; and birth control, so that all children were wanted. In 1972, abortion was incorporated into the Methodist Statement of Social Principles. Note that the Methodist statement invokes the sanctity of life, as Catholic doctrinal statements also did. But the Methodists affirmed not only the value of fetal life but also the life of the pregnant woman.

Our belief in the sanctity of unborn human life makes us reluctant to approve abortion. But we are equally bound to respect the sacredness of the life and well-being of the mother, for whom devastating damage may result from an unacceptable pregnancy. In continuity with past Christian teaching, we recognize tragic conflicts of life with life that may justify abortion. We call all Christians to a searching and prayerful inquiry into the sorts of conditions that may warrant abortion. We support the removal of abortion from the criminal code, placing it instead under laws relating to other procedures of standard medical practice. A decision concerning abortion should be made only after thorough and thoughtful consideration by the parties involved, with medical and pastoral counsel.

Excerpted from *The Social Principles* from the *Book of Discipline of the United Methodist Church* (1972). Reprinted by permission.

Southern Baptist Convention, Resolution on Abortion (June 1971)

In 1968, the American Baptist Convention (now called the American Baptist Churches) adopted a statement calling abortion a matter of "responsible personal decision" and declaring that it should be offered as an "elective medical procedure" at the "request of the individual" before the end of the first trimester of pregnancy.

The more conservative evangelical Southern Baptist Convention's (SBC) first resolution on abortion, adopted in June 1971, essentially endorsed the American Law Institute's model for liberalization. While the Convention resolved that it was the state's responsibility to protect the sanctity of life, its justification for doing so was at least in part secular—the obligation of society "to protect those who cannot protect themselves"—and one that must be balanced with other equally important values, such as the life and health of pregnant women. The resolution called on Southern Baptists to work for legislation to permit abortion "under such conditions as rape, incest, clear evidence of fetal deformity, and carefully ascertained evidence of the likelihood of damage to the emotional, mental, and physical health of the mother."

This language is striking today, in light of the SBC's current position, seeking to recriminalize abortion except in cases where childbirth would endanger a woman's life. In the years after Roe, the leadership of the SBC became increasingly conservative and fundamentalist, culminating in 1979 with either the "Conservative Resurgence," in the parlance of those who had succeeded in gaining power within the denomination, or "Fundamentalist Takeover," as it was described by the moderates who were replaced. With this shift in leadership came a fundamental shift in the Convention's understanding of abortion. The 1971 Resolution understands abortion as a difficult question entailing competing values of the sanctity of human life and the health and life of women and discusses the issue only in these terms, without reference to God or the Bible. In contrast, the 1979 Resolution, passed simultaneously with the Conservative Resurgence, cites the Bible as the source of its views on abortion, and understands abortion as a "moral" as well as "spiritual concern," characterizing non-therapeutic abortion as "selfish" and as a threat to "our society's moral sensitivity." By 1980, the SBC had completely transformed its view of abortion, advocating a constitutional amendment that would prohibit abortion except to save the life of the woman—this is the position the Convention holds today.

WHEREAS, Christians in the American society today are faced with difficult decisions about abortion; and

WHEREAS, Some advocate that there be no abortion legislation, thus making the decision a purely private matter between a woman and her doctor; and

WHEREAS, Others advocate no legal abortion, or would permit abortion only if the life of the mother is threatened;

Therefore, be it RESOLVED, that this Convention express the belief that society has a responsibility to affirm through the laws of the state a high view of the sanctity of human life, including fetal life, in order to protect those who cannot protect themselves; and

Be it further RESOLVED, that we call upon Southern Baptists to work for legislation that will allow the possibility of abortion under such conditions as rape, incest, clear evidence of severe fetal deformity, and carefully ascertained evidence of the likelihood of damage to the emotional, mental, and physical health of the mother.

Reprinted by permission of the Southern Baptist Convention.

National Association of Evangelicals, Statement on Abortion (1971)

The National Association of Evangelicals (NAE) also endorsed a moderate reform position during this period. In 1973, the organization denounced Roe, stating that "we deplore in the strongest possible terms the decision of the U.S. Supreme Court which has made it legal to terminate a pregnancy for no better reason than personal convenience or sociological considerations." But at the same time, this 1973 statement reaffirmed support tor therapeutic abortion: "[W]e recognize the necessity for therapeutic abortion to safeguard the health or the life of the mother...." In a 1979 resolution on "Man and Woman," the NAE continued to "[r]eaffirm its resolution of 1971 attesting to the sacredness of life, opposing abortion on demand and recognizing the possible need for therapeutic abortion to preserve the health or life of the mother."

Abortion has been catapulted into the forefront of the ethical problems confronting evangelicals today. The issue has been nurtured in a general climate of moral relativism, a growing sexual permissiveness, and a threatening population explosion.

The moral issue of abortion is more than a question of the freedom of a woman to control the reproductive functions of her body. It is rather a question of those circumstances under which a human being may be permitted to take the life of another. We believe that all life is a gift of God, so that neither the life of the unborn child nor the mother may be lightly taken. We believe that God, Himself, in Scripture, has conferred divine blessing upon unborn infants and has provided penalties for actions which result in the death of the unborn.

Evangelicals, as much if not more than other citizens, must be involved in the decision making process as virtually every state legislature considers abortion legislation. The National Association of Evangelicals therefore affirms its conviction that abortion on demand for reasons of personal convenience, social adjustment or economic advantage is morally wrong, and expresses its firm opposition to any legislation designed to make abortion possible for these reasons.

At the same time we recognize the necessity for therapeutic abortions to safeguard the health or the life of the mother, as in the case of tubular pregnancies. Other pregnancies, such as those resulting from rape or incest may require deliberate termination, but the decision should be made only after there has been medical, psychological and religious counseling of the most sensitive kind.

Printed by permission of the National Association of Evangelicals.

Humanae Vitae, Encyclical Letter of the Supreme Pontiff Paul VI (July 29, 1968)

Traditionally, Christian doctrine—Catholic and Protestant alike—condemned the use of contraception as interfering with the procreative aims of sex. In the early 20th century, however, views on birth control began to shift. The first official proclamation of this shift was a resolution by the Anglican bishops in 1930, reversing the Anglican Church's earlier prohibition on contraception, and declaring its use permissible for those with a "clearly felt moral obligation to limit or avoid parenthood, and...a morally sound reason for avoiding complete abstinence." The Catholic Church refused to follow suit. Proclaiming itself the guardian of "integrity and purity of morals," the Church, in an encyclical written in 1930 by Pope Pius XI, denounced those who would separate wedlock from sex and sex from reproduction, and declared that "any use whatsoever of matrimony exercised in such a way that the act is deliberately frustrated in its natural power to generate life is an offense against the law of God and of nature, and those who indulge in such are branded with the guilt of a grave sin." The encyclical also condemned abortion, even in cases where a woman's life or health was endangered, as a violation of "the precept of God and the law of nature." The life of the fetus ought not be sacrificed to save that of its mother, for "[t]he life of each is equally sacred." The wrong of abortion was not only that it was murder—though, to be sure, abortion was understood as "direct murder of the innocent"—but also that it reflected a desire for childlessness, which was in itself "wicked."

In the years that followed, Protestant denominations largely followed the Anglicans' lead, permitting the use of birth control. By the 1960s, however, birth control was the site of contestation not only between Catholics and Protestants, but also among Catholics. Priests, theologians, and laypeople alike began to question the Church's stance; of particular concern was the possibility that the Church's rigidity would alienate young Catholics from the Church. In 1964 Pope Paul VI, acknowledging that in the face of recent "scientific, social, and psychological" developments, birth control had become an "extremely complex and delicate problem," announced that a Church study of contraception was already underway.

The following year, the United States Supreme Court, in Griswold v. Connecticut *(1965), ruled that Connecticut's law banning the use of birth control violated the constitutional right to privacy. In what was taken as a sign of the Church's changing stance on contraception, U.S. Catholic bishops did not protest that decision. While maintaining that* Griswold *had no bearing on the morality of birth control, they did not dispute the Court's holding that contraception fell within a realm of marital privacy that ought to be free from state regulation.*

Not long after Griswold, *the Pontifical Study Commission had reached its conclusions. In 1966, after two years of study, a majority of the Commission agreed that "[t]he regulation of conception appears necessary for many couples who wish to achieve a responsible, open and reasonable parenthood in today's circumstances." In its report entitled "Responsible Parenthood," the majority concluded that "the morality of sexual acts between married people....does not...depend upon the direct fecundity of each and every particular act," but rather "from the ordering of their actions in a fruitful married life, that is one which is practiced with responsible, generous and prudent parenthood." Contraception, though pointedly not abortion, was permissible in aid of this responsible parenthood.*

The Minority Report rejected this conclusion. If contraception were deemed licit, the report warned, the very legitimacy of the papacy would be threatened: "If it should be declared that contraception is not evil in itself, then we should have to concede frankly that the Holy Spirit had been on the side of the Protestant churches in 1930." Furthermore, permitting contraception would lead to "more serious evils," such as masturbation, homosexuality, or abortion.

Both papers, intended to be confidential, were leaked to the National Catholic Reporter *in 1967. It was therefore a shock when the Pope, in 1968, issued* Humanae Vitae, *an encyclical adopting the minority position. With procreation the only "meaning and purpose" of the "act of mutual love" between husband and wife, the encyclical reasoned, there could be no "direct interruption of the generative process." That meant, of course, that abortion was prohibited—a conclusion so obvious and logically impelled by the rest of the encyclical as to appear almost as an aside to the document's main argument. Note that this articulation of the wrong of abortion is embedded in an account of the wrong of contraception; indeed, it is understood to be the same wrong. Abortion is listed as one of several "unlawful birth control methods," all of which "contradict[] the moral order," by separating sex from reproduction.*

The encyclical also adopted the slippery-slope argument of the Minority Report: not only was it immoral for humans to use technology to thwart the natural procreative consequences of sex, but to permit such a use could lead to "marital infidelity and a general lowering of moral standards." Interestingly, the encyclical is directed not only at Catholics, but also makes a direct appeal to "public authorities," urging the "rulers of nations" to adopt policies that aid families and facilitate population control without violating the "moral law."

The transmission of human life is a most serious role in which married people collaborate freely and responsibly with God the Creator. It has always been a source of great joy to them, even though it sometimes entails many difficulties and hardships.

The fulfillment of this duty has always posed problems to the conscience of married people, but the recent course of human society and the concomitant changes have provoked new questions. The Church cannot ignore these questions, for they concern matters intimately connected with the life and happiness of human beings.

....

FAITHFULNESS TO GOD'S DESIGN

13. Men rightly observe that a conjugal act imposed on one's partner without regard to his or her condition or personal and reasonable wishes in the matter, is no true act of love, and therefore offends the moral order in its particular application

to the intimate relationship of husband and wife. If they further reflect, they must also recognize that an act of mutual love which impairs the capacity to transmit life which God the Creator, through specific laws, has built into it, frustrates His design which constitutes the norm of marriage, and contradicts the will of the Author of life. Hence to use this divine gift while depriving it, even if only partially, of its meaning and purpose, is equally repugnant to the nature of man and of woman, and is consequently in opposition to the plan of God and His holy will. But to experience the gift of married love while respecting the laws of conception is to acknowledge that one is not the master of the sources of life but rather the minister of the design established by the Creator. Just as man does not have unlimited dominion over his body in general, so also, and with more particular reason, he has no such dominion over his specifically sexual faculties, for these are concerned by their very nature with the generation of life, of which God is the source. "Human life is sacred—all men must recognize that fact," Our predecessor Pope John XXIII recalled. "From its very inception it reveals the creating hand of God."

UNLAWFUL BIRTH CONTROL METHODS

14. Therefore We base Our words on the first principles of a human and Christian doctrine of marriage when We are obliged once more to declare that the direct interruption of the generative process already begun and, above all, all direct abortion, even for therapeutic reasons, are to be absolutely excluded as lawful means of regulating the number of children. Equally to be condemned, as the magisterium of the Church has affirmed on many occasions, is direct sterilization, whether of the man or of the woman, whether permanent or temporary.

Similarly excluded is any action which either before, at the moment of, or after sexual intercourse, is specifically intended to prevent procreation—whether as an end or as a means....

....

APPEAL TO PUBLIC AUTHORITIES

23. And now We wish to speak to rulers of nations. To you most of all is committed the responsibility of safeguarding the common good. You can contribute so much to the preservation of morals. We beg of you, never allow the morals of your peoples to be undermined. The family is the primary unit in the state; do not tolerate any legislation which would introduce into the family those practices which are opposed to the natural law of God. For there are other ways by which a government can and should solve the population problem—that is to say by enact-

ing laws which will assist families and by educating the people wisely so that the moral law and the freedom of the citizens are both safeguarded.

Reprinted by permission of Libreria Editrice Vaticana.

Human Life in Our Day: Pastoral Letter by the National Conference of Catholic Bishops (November 15, 1968)

By the time Humanae Vitae *was promulgated, a majority of Catholics in the United States supported the use of artificial birth control. The encyclical met with swift, fierce, and public opposition, from clergy and laity alike. The day after its release, 87 Roman Catholic theologians issued a statement, published in the* New York Times, *dissenting from the encyclical. Married couples, the theologians stated, "may responsibly decide according to their conscience that artificial contraception in some circumstances is permissible and indeed necessary to preserve and foster the values and sacredness of marriage." Eventually, over 600 theologians joined this statement.*

The Association of Washington Priests issued a similar "Declaration of Conscience," signed by 51 priests of the Washington diocese. When the dissenting priests refused to back down, Cardinal O'Boyle, the Archbishop of Washington disciplined them, removing several from their parishes. This galvanized resistance among lay Catholics, thousands of whom demonstrated at the November meeting of the National Conference of Catholic Bishops. Their keynote speaker was Senator Eugene McCarthy.

On November 15, 1968, the National Conference of Catholic Bishops issued a pastoral letter hoping to calm the controversy. Although the letter strongly supported the Pope's stance, referring to "artificial contraception" as an "objective evil," the Bishops also acknowledged that certain "circumstances may reduce moral guilt," and that the decision to use contraception is a matter of individual conscience. The wide-ranging pastoral letter "in defense of life" not only presented this compromise on birth control, but also expressed an understanding of the sanctity of human life as threatened by more than just nonprocreative sex. These "[f]urther threats to life" included not only abortion, but also nuclear arms, the war in Vietnam, and limitations on the number of children those receiving social support were permitted to have.

INTRODUCTORY STATEMENT

1. We honor God when we reverence human life. When human life is served, man is enriched and God is acknowledged. When human life is threatened, man is diminished and God is less manifest in our midst.

2. A Christian defense of life should seek to clarify in some way the relationship between the love of life and the worship of God. One cannot love life unless he worships God, at least implicitly, nor worship God unless he loves life.

3. The purpose of this Pastoral Letter of the United States bishops is precisely the doctrine and defense of life....

4. We are prompted to speak this year in defense of life for reasons of our pastoral obligation to dialogue within the believing community concerning what faith has to say in response to the threat to life in certain problems of the family and of war and peace.

....

THE ENCYCLICAL AND CONSCIENCE

43. Married couples faced with conflicting duties are often caught in agonizing crises of conscience. For example, at times it proves difficult to harmonize the sexual expression of conjugal love with respect for the life-giving power of sexual union and the demands of responsible parenthood....

45. We feel bound to remind Catholic married couples, when they are subjected to the pressures which prompt the Holy Father's concern, that however circumstances may reduce moral guilt, no one following the teaching of the Church can deny the objective evil of artificial contraception itself. With pastoral solicitude we urge those who have resorted to artificial contraception never to lose heart but to continue to take full advantage of the strength which comes from the Sacrament of Penance and the grace, healing, and peace in the Eucharist....

NEGATIVE REACTIONS TO THE ENCYCLICAL

46. The position taken by the Holy Father in his encyclical troubled many. The reasons for this are numerous. Not a few had been led and had led others to believe that a contrary decision might be anticipated. The mass media which largely shape public opinion have, as the Holy Father himself pointed out, at times amplified the voices which are contrary to the voice of the Church. Then, too, doctrine on this point has its effect not only on the intellects of those who hear it but on their deepest emotions; it is hardly surprising that negative reactions have ranged from sincere anguish to angry hurt or bitter disappointment, even among devout believers. Finally, a decision on a point so long uncontroverted and only recently confronted by new questions was bound to meet with mixed reactions.

....

FURTHER THREATS TO LIFE

83. At this tense moment in our history, when external wars and internal violence make us so conscious of death, an affirmation of the sanctity of human
life by renewed attention to the family is imperative. Let society always be on
the side of life. Let it never dictate, directly or indirectly, recourse to the prevention of life or to its destruction in any of its phases; neither let it require as
a condition of economic assistance that any family yield conscientious determination of the number of its children to the decision of persons or agencies
outside the family.

84. Stepped-up pressures for moral and legal acceptance of directly procured
abortion make necessary pointed reference to this threat to the right to life.
Reverence for life demands freedom from direct interruption of life once it is
conceived. Conception initiates a process whose purpose is the realization of
human personality. A human person, nothing more and nothing less, is always
at issue once conception has taken place. We expressly repudiate any contradictory suggestion as contrary to Judeo-Christian traditions inspired by love
for life, and Anglo-Saxon legal traditions protective of life and the person.

REACTION

In this section, we show how opponents of legalized abortion, led by the Catholic Church, reacted against the forces of change. They sought common cause with allies in other communities by framing their arguments in secular rather than religious terms and increasingly by entering the political arena. In the documents here, we see organizations moving into action and searching for strategies. The documents illustrate a fact that is often overlooked today: a vigorous reaction was underway well before the Supreme Court decision. The Court, of course, was to become a focus of the reaction, but the decision in *Roe v. Wade* neither started nor ended the debate over abortion.

New Jersey Catholic Bishops' Letter

A pamphlet issued in 1970 by the New Jersey Catholic Conference while the state's legislature was considering whether to repeal New Jersey's law criminalizing abortion represents an effort by the Catholic Church to mobilize the broader community —"all of our fellow citizens"— in common opposition to the legislation. The pamphlet not only emphasizes the ecumenical nature of the cause but also draws on secular sources of law—including the Declaration of Independence and the United Nations Declaration on the Rights of the Child—to anchor its argument in common ground that is not exclusively Catholic. The references to secular law, such as the law's recognition that damages can be collected in some circumstances for prenatal injuries, will reappear in briefs filed on behalf of the state in Roe v. Wade. *The pamphlet seeks to demonstrate that opposition to abortion need not depend on acceptance of Catholic religious doctrine.*

This was only one of many such efforts, by the Church itself, by Catholic organizations, and by individuals, to translate opposition to abortion that was based on religious faith into secular language that could persuade others outside their religious tradition. The National Right to Life Committee (NRLC), for example, which had been under the supervision of—and funded by—the National Conference of Catholic Bishops since its founding (under a different name) in 1967, broke off its formal affiliation with the Church in 1973 in order to increase its appeal to non-Catholic audiences. But the NRLC retained its orientation to the Catholic tradition, struggling to reconcile the opposition of many of its members to birth control with the organization's aim to broaden its appeal.

To: The Catholic Community of New Jersey
    and to all of Our Fellow Citizens of the State.

From: New Jersey's Catholic Bishops.

Once again it becomes necessary for us to address ourselves to the problem of the protection of human life.

Recently, the State Study Commission on Abortion concluded its work. Unfortunately, the results of this study are under a shadow. Four of the nine Commission members felt it necessary to issue dissenting opinions from the report written by the Commission chairman, and at least one other member was never present at any of the three public hearings where testimony was gathered. We, too, must conscientiously dissent from the chairman's report, which attempts to solve many of society's problems at the expense of unborn human life.

This controversy is raging not only in New Jersey but throughout the country. In recent months, the pressure has shifted from limited changes in the law to a determined drive for abortion on demand.

We speak today as religious leaders, not to our Catholic community of faith and worship alone but to all of our fellow citizens. The question of abortion is a moral problem transcending a particular theological approach. We have been heartened by the support of many leaders of other religious persuasions. In particular we commend the efforts of those clergymen and laity, of all religious persuasions and of none, who have formed the State Right to Life Committee. We invite the cooperation of all to recognize and eliminate the danger of the erosion of respect for human life that proposed bills may sanction for our State.

We are saddened by those who accuse us of being insensitive to human problems, even some who have been our allies in the fight against poverty and discrimination, and for the improvement of the quality of life in our society.

Certainly, the Catholic people have demonstrated their concern for human needs: among many manifestations of this, we note the hospitals, guidance clinics, homes for the elderly and homes for unwed mothers which have been built by their financial contributions, often at great personal sacrifice.

Now, Catholics must assume their responsibility to involve themselves in the abortion issue, which will have such a profound and long-range effect upon our society and our family life.

It is, indeed, the very matter of life which is at stake. Medical science has informed us that at the moment of conception there comes into being a unique human life in the microscopically tiny egg cell. Contained in this cell is the blueprint for the development of the whole human person, factors which will influence the temperament, physique, eye, hair and skin color, and even intellectual capacity. This cell's tissue composition is distinct from its mother's tissue and would be rejected from her body were it not to be enclosed in the amniotic sac.

The unborn child's civil rights have increasingly been recognized by the law. We recall, in particular, that case in which the mother was forced by the courts against her religious convictions to have a blood transfusion to maintain her baby's life. Likewise, the unborn child's rights of inheritance and medical or economic support, his right to recover damages for injury suffered in the womb are affirmed by the courts. In short, the law has cast itself in the role of safeguarding the rights of the unborn.

How much more important it is that the law continue to protect that most basic right of life itself—the right upon which all others are based!

As religious leaders, we are involved daily with people in situations of distress. We recognize the complex difficulties facing so many women and families. But abortion not only fails to solve the underlying causes: it raises even deeper problems. We are haunted by the wide spectrum of possibilities opened by an acceptance of easy abortion. Once we sanction, for the sake of expedience, the taking of an innocent human life at its beginnings, how can we logically protect human life at any other point, once that life becomes a burden?

Law is an educator. If it allows the destruction of unwanted life, it unavoidably teaches that life is cheap.

We are willing and anxious to cooperate on positive programs to help erase the demand for abortion. There is great need for thorough education of all our citizens to assist them in marriage, family life and responsible sexual behavior. We urge, also, cooperative efforts in such problems as racial discrimination, economic hardship, birth defects, treatment and education of the handicapped, and increased mental health and counseling facilities.

Our prayer and our plea is that all men of good will in this state will join us in seeking these solutions, and will reject that most destructive recourse, the killing of innocent human life in the womb.

[The pamphlet was signed here by five New Jersey bishops.]

HOW DOES THE LAW REGARD THE UNBORN CHILD?

...."The child, by reason of his physical and mental immaturity, needs special safeguards and care, including appropriate legal protection, before as well as after birth."   —U.N. Declaration on Rights of the Child

..."We hold these truths to be self-evident, that all men are created equal, that they are endowed by their Creator with certain inalienable Rights, that among these are life..."   — U.S. Declaration of Independence

ARE CATHOLICS THE ONLY ONES AGAINST ABORTION?

"...as a practicing Protestant, I believe that a fetus is a life."
                    —Leroy G. Augenstein, COME, LET US PLAY GOD. 1969

"Genetics teaches us that we were from the beginning what we essentially still are in every cell and in every...attribute. Thus...genetics seems to have provided an approximation, from the underside, to the religious belief that there is a soul animating and forming man's bodily being from the very beginning."

                              —Dr. Paul Ramsey, Protestant Theologian,
                              Professor of Religion, Princeton University

"Even if the fetus is the product of incest or rape, or an abnormality of any kind is foreseen, the right to life is still his."

                              —New Jersey Orthodox Rabbinic Council
                    Testimony to N.J. Study Commission on Abortion, 1969

"The Christian position is that human life is sacred, and that it may be forcibly terminated only in certain circumstances, such as by soldiers in war or police in duty (Romans 13) or in capital punishment (Genesis 9). Otherwise, willfully to terminate the image of God, as the Bible calls man, is directly contrary to the revealed will of God."

                              —Edwin H. Palmer, Th.D., Chairman,
                    N.J. Right to Life Committee; Pastor, Christian Reformed Church

"To raise the question whether we are here concerned already with a human being or not is merely to confuse the issue. The simple fact is that God certainly intended to create a human being and that this nascent human being has been deliberately deprived of his life. And that is nothing but murder."

—Lutheran Theologian Dietrich Bonhoeffer, Martyred by the Nazis

"Thou shalt not kill." —The Holy Bible, Exodus 20:18

WHAT CAN I DO?

Can One Person Do Anything About Abortion?

1. Abortion is a highly complex issue, involving medical, legal, social and moral questions. Study it in all its aspects so that your efforts and arguments are informed and accurate...

2. In your personal and business life, use your knowledge and conviction to influence others. Most people have only limited and superficial information about this matter. As citizens, they should be better informed. Don't be afraid to tell them what you know.

3. Write letters to your representatives in the State Legislature, to the governor and to other public officials—attorney general, commissioner of health, etc.— stating your opposition to changing or repealing the law....

4. If possible, contact your representatives personally, by telephone or personal appointment. They are there to represent YOU. Ask them their position on abortion. Provide them with information and reading material. State your expectation that they will vote against liberalization.

5. Seek support from your own organizations—school, social, fraternal, professional, both religious and secular—urging them to take a stand against easy abortion laws. Ask them to sponsor a public forum on abortion.

6. Write letters to local newspapers, radio stations, television stations and programs, in rebuttal to or support of articles, letters, editorials and particular programs. As with political letters, this correspondence should be personal, sincere, well thought-out and reasonably brief.

7. Women ought to be in the forefront of the anti-abortion campaign. As nurturers of society as well as new life, their response to this issue will be crucial in determining which way it goes.

It has been said that "all that is needed for evil to conquer is for good men (and women) to do nothing."

Will You Join Us in Trying to Do Something?

Excerpted from pamphlet prepared by New Jersey Catholic Conference and submitted to New Jersey State Assembly, Public Hearing before the Assembly Judiciary Committee on Assembly Bill No. 762 [Abortion Bill]. Held April 9, 1970, Assembly Chamber of the State House. Trenton, New Jersey. Reprinted by permission of the New Jersey Catholic Conference.

Abortion in Perspective
by Robert M. Byrn

Robert M. Byrn, a law professor at Fordham University and a leader of the early right-to-life movement in New York, published this article in 1966. Although he spoke from a Catholic perspective and was later to serve as one of the lawyers on the National Right to Life Committee's Supreme Court brief in Roe v. Wade, *he directed his arguments against abortion reform to the legal profession in general and aimed particular criticism at the American Law Institute's proposal, which at the time was starting to gain momentum as a framework for changing existing abortion laws.*

The abortion controversy is assuming national proportions. The Association for the Study of Abortion, a nationwide organization dedicated to a liberalization of the law, has enlisted a cadre of speakers "to educate the public to reform." The Association seems to be politically as well as pedagogically oriented. One of its spokesmen recently hailed an abortion liberalization bill, introduced at the 1966 session of the New York State Legislature, as a "rallying point for reform forces in the state." The abortion debate is already in vigorous progress in several states, including Pennsylvania and New York, but these states are not unique. Before long, the entire country will be involved.

What are the issues in the abortion debate? To date, much of what we know has come from the mass media. Consequently, some of the issues, which lawyers might conceive to be vital, have been shunted aside in favor of more commercially exploitable material. Even the legal writing on the subject is tinged with sensationalism and...distortions. As a result, if the Bar is to play a meaningful role in the expanding debate, the issues must be reframed within a legal context....

The American Law Institute has proposed the legalization of abortion if a licensed physician "believes there is a substantial risk that continuance of the pregnancy would gravely impair the physical or mental health of the mother or that the child would be born with a grave physical or mental defect or that the pregnancy resulted from rape, incest or other felonious intercourse [statutory rape.]" Most proposals to liberalize state abortion laws have been similarly structured.

The American Law Institute has classified abortion as an offense against the family, thereby belittling the homicidal aspects of the crime. Actually, no evaluation of abortion legislation is meaningful if it ignores the fact that an abortion kills an innocent human being....

Like a person whose skin pigment is other than white, the unborn child is recognizable as a human being simply because he is a human being. His status must be governed by this fact and not by the irrelevancies of size, shape, and color....

None of the reasons given by the American Law Institute are sufficient for classifying unborn children as inferior human beings. Quite the contrary, the fallacies inherent in the Institute's position serve to demonstrate the equality of the unborn child with all other human beings....

As we have seen, there is no qualitative difference, *scientifically speaking*, between human life in the womb and human life after birth. Hence, legislation, which would remove the life of a person in the womb from the full and equal protection of the law, would be as discriminatory, as "irrational," and as inimical to the equal protection clause as the legislative classification of races....

A medically unnecessary liberalization of the law to include the health of the mother would open a Pandora's box of social engineering, having little to do with medical health. We must ask ourselves, therefore, whether we are prepared to abandon human beings to the moral and social predilections of individual doctors, or whether we shall continue to extend to these persons the equal protection of the law regardless of their socio-economic status....

We have a choice in cases of rape-induced pregnancies. We can either kill the child or we can direct all our ingenuity toward smoothing the way for both the mother and the child. The latter is the truly humane choice....

There is another way to attack the problem of illegal abortion. We, as lawyers, may choose to become the advocates of the cause of the unborn child. In this role, we shall argue to the American people, as we have done before, that differences in size, shape, and color are not valid grounds for taking the life of an innocent human being. We know, of course, how arduous and uphill such a civil rights battle can be, and particularly will it be so here because the minority, whose rights are at stake, is both voiceless and voteless...

Respect for the sanctity of innocent human life may very well be one of those rules of conduct upon which the survival of mankind depends. And permissive abortion seems to go a long way toward abrogating the rule. Perhaps, when all is said and done, respect for the innocent person's right to life will turn out to be the crucial issue in the abortion controversy, and perhaps, it will be lawyers who have made it so.

Excerpted from the *Duquesne University Law Review*, vol. 5, no. 2 (1966–1967), pp. 125–41. Printed by permission of the *Duquesne University Law Review*.

Abortion and Social Justice

Americans United for Life (AUL), founded in 1971, describes itself as "the country's oldest national pro-life organization." Its early fund-raising material declared that "abortion is dehumanizing American society" and called on supporters to "help stop the abortion coalition in its tracks."

AUL was initially associated with, and funded by, a conservative Catholic organization, the Society for a Christian Commonwealth. That organization and its magazine, Triumph, *were founded by L. Brent Bozell Jr. (1926–1997), a founding editor of William F. Buckley's* National Review *and a former speech writer for Senator Joseph McCarthy. AUL and Bozell soon split over questions of policy and tactics. Bozell wanted to prohibit abortion under all circumstances, while AUL's leadership believed that abortion should be permitted if necessary to save a pregnant woman's life. Bozell also advocated more radical protest tactics that AUL's leaders feared could slip into violence.*

Although the organization was founded and run initially almost entirely by Catholics (its honorary chair was a prominent Catholic actress, Loretta Young), it was officially nondenominational, and its goal was to attract broad-based support from Americans of all faiths. The first chairman of its board was George Huntson Williams (1914–2000), a Unitarian minister who was a professor at Harvard Divinity School.

As part of its effort to frame an argument against abortion in secular terms, AUL in 1972 sponsored the publication of Abortion and Social Justice, *excerpted here. In his forward to the volume, Rev. Williams explained that "although undoubtedly a religious conviction inform[ed] many of the [book's] writers," their arguments were not "theological or programmatically religious." The goal of the book, a collection of essays, was to promote arguments that would gain support in "a secular society, where state and church are constitutionally separated," and where arguments against abortion must be presented "in terms acceptable to humanists and theists alike." To that end, the essays*

describe the anti-abortion cause as one of "social justice," identifying it with the contem-
porary struggle for civil rights; in this context, the goal of the struggle is to end "prejudice"
against a "newly created 'unwanted class' of human beings," the "unwanted children"
facing abortion. Excerpts from three of the essays follow. The authors are listed at the
end of each excerpt.

THE LEGAL CASE FOR THE UNBORN CHILD

Abortion is not a private matter. The destruction of human life, even "incipient" or developing human life in the womb, can never be considered a private matter under our law. The contention that it is a private matter would be too ludicrous and absurd to even argue were it not so often put forth under such intellectually impeccable auspices. Would those civil libertarians who argue that abortion is a private matter argue that the exercise of civil rights is purely a private matter between the Black man and the man that thwarts them? Certainly not. Just as the civil right to vote must be protected by law, so too the most fundamental and basic of all civil rights—the Right to Life—must be protected by law.

Nor is abortion a merely sectarian religious problem or one for the area of "private" morality. Abortion is nothing less than a question of civil *rights:* Does the unborn child have a civil right to life? If he or she does, is it not then the duty of *all* citizens in a pluralistic society, regardless of religious faith or private moral sensitivities, to protect the unborn child's civil rights?

In various sections of this paper we have developed the legal rights of the unborn child in torts, property and equity cases, as well as under the criminal law. We argue, in still another section, that the purpose of the abortion statutes in the criminal law was for the protection of the unborn child. Proponents of abortion on demand have very cleverly convinced a segment of the courts that the historical purpose of abortion laws was merely to protect the health of the mother against the onslaught of young and foolhardy surgeons. Nothing could be further from the truth. Although hundreds of types of surgery are performed, why has only abortion been prohibited by the criminal law? The answer is simple, yet ignored. Because only in abortion are we talking about the destruction of another human life.

The position that our law takes on abortion indicates the position it will take on euthanasia, genetic engineering, cloning, and all of the difficult human life problems facing our society in the years ahead. Those who argue for the unborn child's right to life are arguing not only for the unborn child, but for the civil right to life of every human being—the mentally ill, the aged, the genetically incompetent, the idle, the useless. If the law vacates the protection of the civil rights of the innocent child in the womb, it will one day vacate its protection of the civil right to life of the mentally incompetent, the senile and the hopelessly ill. It will vacate its protection of your civil rights....

> by Dennis J. Horan, Jerome A. Frazel Jr., Thomas M. Crisham, Dolores B. Horan, John D. Gorby, John T. Noonan Jr., and David W. Louisell.

IS ABORTION NECESSARY TO SOLVE POPULATION PROBLEMS?

....

In the recent advocacy of more permissive abortion policies, there has been a distinct tendency to take the view that the decision whether or not to resort to abortion is a private, moral decision and is not to be legislated. Many of these same advocates have stressed the failure of restrictive abortion laws to deter people from having abortions. Both of these points need to be challenged.

Increasingly through research in psychology, more is being learned about moral development and its stages. One of the most significant findings of this research is that most adults in any culture are at a stage in moral development where existing laws and customs are the most important bases for deciding what is right and wrong. Private morality is influenced as much by permissive abortion policies as it is by restrictive abortion policies. The choice is one of deciding which of two different moral viewpoints we want to encourage.

Although it is true that restrictive abortion laws never succeed in preventing all abortions, as criminal laws generally never succeed in preventing all crime, they have a demonstrable deterrent effect. Wherever highly permissive laws have been instituted, the data available show that the total abortion rates have been increased thereby. Our question, then, is a moral one—namely, what difference does it make to have a permissive abortion policy rather than a restrictive one? The difference revolves around two issues: the protection of individual life, and the protection of the welfare of the community.

The Protection of Individual Human Life. In the Preamble to the Declaration of Independence, the right to life is declared to be an inalienable right. One of the clear advantages of retaining strict abortion laws is that this policy in no way erodes or abrogates that kind of public commitment. For the kind of restrictive abortion policy that we have in mind permits abortion in *instances* where the life of a pregnant woman is endangered by carrying her fetus to term. Here the principle by which life is taken is that of self-defense. We would not, and we do not, deny people the right to defend themselves against genuine threats to their own lives, even when this means taking another life.

But what happens if we shift to permissive abortion policies? Surely abortion advocates do not wish to decrease the right to life and the sanctity that attaches to life. Their hope is that permissive abortion policies will not have that effect. What are the facts?

New York State since July 1, 1970, has a law that permits abortion to be performed at the request of the pregnant woman and with the compliance of a physician unless the fetus is more than twenty-four weeks old. The principle behind this policy is to leave decisions about fetuses, provided that they are no more than twenty-four weeks old, in the private sphere, and to invoke public sanctions against this decision when this fetus is more than twenty-four weeks old. Presumably, therefore, one could preserve the inalienable right to life of every individual by claiming that individuals acquire that right when they are more than twenty-four weeks old. In practice this is not the way it works. Why not?

Women who do not want to bear a child that is developing in their wombs often resort to abortion because their fetus has been diagnosed as abnormal or likely to be abnormal, or because they project a bad life for this child on other grounds. The argument here is that there are some lives that are not worth living.... A life that is considered unworthy to live at twenty-four weeks because it will be a life of blindness, deafness, mental retardation, or whatever, is logically as unworthy at twenty-five weeks as it is at twenty-three, and is as unworthy at birth.
....

If a fetus is unwanted because in prospect its life would be burdensome to those who would rear it, there is no way of assuring that those who are unwanted at any stage will be protected from being considered burdensome, and hence dispensable....

Protection of the Welfare of the Community. Where a permissive abortion policy is adopted on the principle that abortion is an individual decision, certain consequences result for the familial life and for the life of the whole community. These deserve to be examined and assessed.

One of the apparent benefits of permissive abortion policies is that individual freedom, particularly of women, would seem to be increased. However, a great deal depends upon the rationale for one's policy to make abortion accessible on request. If the argument is that voluntary abortion on request is essential for bringing down birth rates, then this policy would become a candidate for compulsion if this voluntary abortion policy proved unsuccessful. Such a policy would not only fail to protect nascent life but would directly assault the freedom and bodily welfare of women.

Let us examine, however, permissive abortion policies whose purpose is solely to enhance freedom and not to achieve certain birth rates, since as we have shown, abortion is not necessary for this latter purpose anyway.... The Commission on Population Growth and the American Future has asked that abortion on request apply also to minors. These moves are made in accord with the principle of complete individual freedom and privacy in reproductive decisions. Is this what we want? The effect of completely individualizing reproductive decisions is to drive a considerable wedge between husband and wife, and, for that matter, between all sexual partners. Family planning on such a principle would be a totally euphemistic expression.

A similar split and strain in communication occurs between parent and child. Where minors decide reproductive matters for themselves, physicians would, by default, be their parents in such privileged communication. Here again family planning would be a euphemism.

Since the family is the only predictable way in which children can be socialized and brought to maturity in an atmosphere of love, one cannot treat lightly any policy that would further undermine its effectiveness and stability.... The implications of adopting the principles behind permissive abortion policies, therefore, portend great harm and no benefits for familial life....

by Arthur J. Dyck

IS ABORTION THE BEST WE HAVE TO OFFER? A CHALLENGE TO THE ABORTIVE SOCIETY

Why does a "civilized" society become so threatened by its own offspring that it seeks the violence of human abortion to relieve its anxiety? Why do innocent children become such a threat that parents are moved to destroy them? Why does a society which attempts to promote peace and justice continue to advocate the mass slaughter of unborn children? These questions are not easy for anyone to answer. And yet, that alone does not detract from the reality of their implication: the reality of a society which is rapidly engulfing itself in fear—a fear which could eventually mean its dissolution.

This fear, deeply rooted and multicentric in origin, is aiming the fullness of its grip toward our women and children. It is amply manifest, day in and day out, by the members of today's so-termed "affluent society" in their unwillingness to give of themselves to others. For some strange reason (one which is shortchanging more and more people as time passes), we have become, in a very striking way, a society in which one's own personal self takes total precedence over the selves of others. We have reached a state of self-orientation while ignoring—and sometimes eliminating—the other.

As in the case of any new mode of behavior, rationalizations are being devised for our actions. Like the Negro slavery of the nineteenth century and the Black discrimination of the twentieth, we are collectively crying "unwanted!"—and again, it finds its base in the "less than human" penultimate rationale.

Must we not accuse ourselves of actively fostering a new prejudice; one involving a future generation, with its focus on the children of the present generation? Isn't this new prejudice quite as deep in its roots as those of the past and potentially just as destructive? We now callously, and often flippantly, refer to our offspring as "unwanted"; almost as if we never really thought about what it means to *be unwanted* nor paused long enough to recognize *who is doing the unwanting!* Isn't there a strong parallel between the unquestioningly accepted notion of "every pregnancy a planned pregnancy" and the degree to which "unwantedness" has spread in the last decade? Certainly, it is now easy to accept automatically any unplanned pregnancy as an unwanted child. This, to the ultimate abuse of the child—abortion.

Perhaps we must again perceive the creeping nature of bias and the role it has played in this latest development, the "unwanted prejudice." Doesn't this euphemistic categorization of a newly created "unwanted class" of human beings really represent a subtle shift in our national and individual discriminations? In a time when so much progress has been made in re-establishing the rights of the minority—rights which have always been theirs, but through subtle persuasion (and sometimes not so subtle) were denied them—we have, for the lack of a prejudicial target, refocused our discrimination toward the child, his mother and his family. We are literally abandoning women and children, as we abandoned the Indians, the Blacks and others, in the past.

....

The faithless abandonment of women and children, which is so overtly promoted in today's society, is rapidly becoming a part of "Americana." People unthinkingly promote and advocate it as much as they were all for Mom and apple pie in times past. Even the women themselves have undertaken this battle for abandonment, and all under the guise of "liberation"! What will eventually come from this growing irresponsibility is the awareness that it only expands and deepens the abortion of peoples. What gradually begins with the violent abortion of the unborn child, before long becomes de facto "social abortion." Women who seek abortion of their "unwanted child" find themselves "socially aborted" themselves, long before they seek the medical abortionist. They are aborted, rejected and unwanted by those close to them—their husbands, parents and friends....

How do we abolish the aborting society—one which turns its back on those who need assistance and incites people to turn their backs on themselves and their own lives? Certainly, *the hearts of men must change!*....

Certainly, our society cannot accept the "unwanted prejudice," nor can it justly allow the mass slaughter of the unborn. What we can, and must, do is change our hearts, open our hands, extend our help and begin to deeply care. This is really the basis of an active love—an involvement in life, its beauties and its difficulties. This *is the very best* we have to offer the woman pregnant and distressed. And this is the only thing that will abolish the aborting society....

by Thomas W. Hilgers, Marjory Mecklenburg, and Gayle Riordan

Abortion and Social Justice, edited by Thomas W. Hilgers, M.D. and Dennis J. Horan, Esq. Reprinted by permission of Sheed & Ward, an imprint of Rowman & Littlefield Publishers, Inc. The excerpts appear on pages 105-6; 168-72; and177-80.

Similarly I Will Not...Cause Abortion
by Robert D. Knapp, Jr., M.D.

Although the leadership of the medical profession was moving, almost uniformly, toward reform, sentiment within the ranks of the profession was far from uniform. Dr. Robert D. Knapp, Jr., was a physician on the staff of the Mayo Clinic and a frequent lunch companion of Harry Blackmun's when Blackmun, during his pre-judicial career, served as the clinic's general counsel. In 1970 and again in 1972, Dr. Knapp sent his old friend articles that he had published in medical journals depicting liberalized abortion laws as a threat to the integrity of the medical profession—articles very different in tone from the other medical articles in Blackmun's files. Blackmun cordially acknowledged receipt of the material while offering no comment on its content. His possession of the articles nonetheless indicates the Court's awareness that the medical profession held more than one view on the abortion question.

The excerpt here is from an article published in the October 1970 issue of the Journal of the Louisiana State Medical Society.

I will use treatment to help the sick according to my ability and judgment, but never with a view to injury and wrong-doing. Neither will I administer a poison to anybody when asked to do so, nor will I suggest such a course. Similarly, I will not give a woman a pessary to cause abortion [text of the Hippocratic oath].

If I promise to kill no one, I do not mean that I will not kill to defend my own life. On the contrary, I would kill even to defend my neighbor's life. Similarly, if I promise not to cause an abortion, I do not mean that I will avoid such an act even when I think the baby is killing its mother. A man must step apart from mankind to remain inactive while someone kills a person whom he could help.

But what if my neighbor says to me, "I will kill myself unless you kill the man loitering on the sidewalk"? My promise holds in such a case, for the loiterer does not threaten to kill, and I cannot bring myself to kill him just because he offends my neighbor. If the neighbor carries out his threat and kills himself, then he has killed—not I or the loiterer. Similarly, what if a woman says to me, "I will kill myself, unless you perform an abortion for me or refer me to someone who will"? My promise holds again. I cannot take part in the killing of her child, for it poses no threat to her; it is she who threatens to kill.

Also, suppose my neighbor's son has received a call to arms and has been ordered to Vietnam or some other battlefield. Since a percentage of young men are disfigured, crazed, or otherwise rendered abnormal in warfare and since many parents cannot face this prospect, my neighbor may ask me to kill his son to spare him such a fate. My promise holds again; I would not do such a thing if the young man himself asked me to do it. More than that, I would not consider killing him even if the worst one could dream of had already happened. Similarly, if a woman asks me for an abortion because she had German measles during the early weeks of pregnancy, because she took thalidomide during that time, or because her last three children were deformed or had mucoviscidosis [cystic fibrosis], not only my promise but my humanity prevents my agreeing to her request. I could not kill a child if it were deformed or seriously ill. How could I bring myself to kill one because he might be deformed or ill?

What of that other thing? What of rape? Where can one find an analogy? If someone ploughs another man's field, he can make no claim to the products; they belong to the owner. And the owner may tear out the seedlings if he does not want them. But he may do that if he changes his mind about seedlings he planted himself. The death of a person is not involved in either case. I think there is no adequate analogy.

Suppose a girl younger than the age of consent has an affair with a man whom she likes. The man is guilty of statutory rape and may be convicted and punished according to law. But what of the child, if the girl becomes pregnant as a result of the affair? Can one justify killing it? One cannot argue that the girl is being subjected to involuntary servitude, only that she has acquired certain responsibilities through indulging in an act in which the state claims she had no right to participate. Thus, one may argue that she deserves punishment of a kind, but I think one would be hard put to demonstrate that the baby deserves to be cast into oblivion just because its mother did something she should not have done....

In settling other legal wrongs, the state often punishes the offender and requires that reparations be paid in money or land or goods. Perhaps such is the appropriate solution in cases of this kind....

If my neighbor asks me to kill his youngest child so that his other children will have enough to eat, my promise not to kill certainly holds, and I shall refuse. Similarly, if a pregnant woman with 14 children asks for an abortion on the grounds that the baby would compete socially and economically with those already born, depriving them to some extent of food and affection, I shall refuse just as quickly....

In the case where I cause an abortion to save the life of my pregnant patient, I will be named *physician*. But, since the number of situations in which pregnancy poses such a threat to a woman has been reduced almost to zero; one now seldom hears that term properly applied to persons performing abortions. They may be physicians, but they are not necessarily acting in that professional capacity when they cause abortions.

Should I yield to my neighbor's plea and kill the loiterer, my name shall be *murderer*.

Oddly, in the analogous situations where the pregnant woman threatens to kill herself—in many foreign countries and in several states in the United States— one may legally dispatch the baby to kingdom come. My deserved term, if I serve as an abortionist in such an instance, probably should be based on the mode of payment. If the pregnant woman, her husband, or another private party pays, I suggest the term *assassin*. If payment is made by the state, *executioner* would seem more appropriate....

WHAT HAS HAPPENED?

Why has no one pointed out that the laws "liberalizing" abortion laws in communist countries, in Sweden, in England, and in some states in this country have given the physician responsibilities in no way concerned with the practice of medicine, on the one hand, and have suggested a frightening change in one aspect of medical practice, on the other? The departures are so extreme; one wonders why all physicians do not protest....

What have physicians to do with the killing of persons who have misfortunes or who no longer enjoy the protection of the law? If the state determines that intrauterine babies of a given age should be killed because their mothers had German measles or took thalidomide or had seven defective children, then the state should hire executioners or license assassins to kill them. I hold that it is malicious to suggest that physicians act in this capacity....

Physicians should rededicate themselves to their profession. Specifically, they should not allow anyone to burden them with nonmedical responsibilities or to persuade them that killing someone so that he will not be sick constitutes preventative medicine or that killing another person sometimes constitutes appropriate medical therapy for mental illness or socioeconomic hardship....

A license to practice medicine and surgery should not in itself be construed as a license to commit abortion, except in the instance of therapeutic abortion which is a medical problem.

Reprinted by permission from the *Journal of the Louisiana State Medical Society*, vol. 122, no. 10 (1970), pp. 297–301.

New Jersey Assembly Testimony

Just as individual women who favored abortion reform spoke of their own experiences, so did women on the opposite side of the argument. On April 9, 1970, the Judiciary Committee of the New Jersey Assembly held a public hearing to consider repealing the state's law criminalizing abortion. This statement by a woman who appeared as an opposition witness is reprinted from the public hearing record.

Sometimes, when we are faced with a momentous decision, our judgment can become confused, cloudy and even biased by pressures. In the makings of any decision, we are usually hit hard with two sides of something; both sides equally demanding and both sides making sense in their own right.

I believe this description personifies the abortion issue. I also believe that I am in a unique position in regards to this issue. I have been on both sides of this fence and I know abortion is not the answer.

I can speak to you as a distraught mother who, three years ago, unashamedly wanted an abortion. I desperately thought, at the time, that abortion was the only solution in my overburdened circumstances.

I can also speak to you as a woman who sought out principle. I do not believe that depression in pregnancy automatically cancels out the ability to rationalize. I have always valued honesty in myself and in others. I believe that if honesty prevails in our quest for truth, the right answers become clearer....

I am the mother of six children. (And I hope it is still safe to admit this fact, here in N.J.) It was my sixth pregnancy that jolted me into the awareness of abortion. Prior to this, I gave it little thought. My husband and I did not plan, nor did we want a sixth child; but it happened. In view of recent major surgery, physical complications, medication for mental stress, my doctors advised a therapeutic abortion. We agreed with their advice; at least we wanted to agree with it. And so in my mind, I planned to abort; I talked about it and I wanted it. But that thing called honesty knocked on the door of my mind; unrelentlessly [sic]. Honesty recalled to me, the day that I was told for the first time that I was pregnant. Happiness abounded; I shouted to all who would listen: "Hey, guess what? I'm going to have a baby!!" I could hardly believe the immensity and miracle of a child within me. Well, my doctor had just given me the identical news and I was trying to convince myself that it wasn't a baby...yet.... That my denial of this bud of life was a forgivable thing under the present circumstances. Somehow my esteemed honesty dwindled into an obvious double standard. I realized that even if no one else considered an abortion wrong, that I did and I have to live with me. No matter what way I sliced it, the termination of this pregnancy would be the termination of a life due to be born eight months hence. At this point I hated my own intelligence, I cursed myself and I blamed everyone and everything for my predicament. Nothing changed except my shape. I carried my unwanted child to term. My honesty allowed me to be the real winner, when a healthy seven-pound son entered our lives. I find myself looking at my son daily, always with the awareness of just exactly what abortion is. It is grossly unfair to predict that an unwanted pregnancy ultimately leads to an unwanted child; it just isn't so.

Many people call our present abortion laws archaic because they refuse to hear the cry of the unborn....

As a concerned citizen, I beg of you to re-direct your time, efforts and monies away from the sham of abortion repeal (ultimately abortion-on-demand) into the channels of a better way of life for all. Let us hit hard at the problems that create the need for abortion. Let's really work at eradicating ignorance, poverty and especially prejudice. Let's pour our resources into the research of a fool-proof contraceptive, into mental-health clinics, into widespread sex education, into health, nutritional, hygienic clinical programs. Let's make voluntary sterilization easily obtainable for all who so desire; NO woman should be compulsorily [sic] pregnant, I am the first to agree with this. On the other hand, no woman should be at liberty to end a life that has already begun. The choice of what to do with one's body should be made before pregnancy occurs, not afterwards. Once there is a valid pregnancy, there is also a valid life....

I would like to end with something my eight-year-old daughter said to me recently. She is in second grade and she reads well. She asked me what I thought about abortion after reading about it in the headlines. Wisdom of an ancient soul shone through her child-like innocence.

"I'm sure glad you wanted me, Mommy," she said.

"Yes, I wanted you very much, Michelle," I replied. "But wanting a baby isn't always the way it is. I didn't really want David before he was born."

"But you LOVED David before he was born," she quickly added, "and when you love something, you can't hurt it, can you, Mommy?"

Somehow her words summed it all up for me. How about you? Do you honestly LOVE LIFE? Or have you become adept in that role that is so prevalent in the society of today: the role of the Great Pretender.

Excerpted from Testimony before Public Hearing before the Assembly Judiciary Committee on Assembly Bill No. 762 [Abortion Bill]. Held April 9, 1970, Assembly Chamber of the State House. Trenton, New Jersey. (Witness's name withheld to preserve anonymity.)

Handbook on Abortion

by Dr. and Mrs. J. C. Willke (first edition, 1971)

For four decades, Dr. J. C. (Jack) Willke, an obstetrician, has been one of the most influential strategists and leaders of the Right to Life movement. Before becoming engaged by the abortion issue, Willke and his wife, Barbara, a registered nurse, lectured frequently to teenaged audiences on sex education, stressing chastity before marriage and declining to advocate contraception. Urged by their college-aged daughters to write a book on abortion, the Willkes produced Handbook on Abortion. *Self-published in 1971, it sold 1.5 million copies within 18 months. The book quickly went through two dozen printings and was translated into many European and Asian languages.*

The pocket-sized book (141 pages in the first edition, excerpted here) was written in question-and-answer format and illustrated with photographs of fetuses and fetal parts. The images were powerful and established a model for others to use in visual protest against abortion. The book provided a common reference point and recruiting tool for the movement, aimed as it was not only to the committed but also to those skeptical of the anti-abortion cause. It is difficult to overstate this little book's importance in framing the issue for those seeking to preserve—and later, to restore—criminal prohibitions against abortion. In addition to its straightforward and accessible language, its success was no doubt also due to its secular tone. Explicitly addressed to "our pluralistic society" with arguments presented as grounded in logic and in medical literature rather than in dogma and faith, it was able to reach across religious lines and appeal to growing numbers of non-Catholic activists.

FOREWORD

In the past several years, a tremendous push for more permissive abortion laws has occurred in the United States. With a few exceptions, the major newspapers and magazines of our country have participated in this movement by publicizing every new development and every argument, valid or not, in favor of liberalizing abortion laws. Those whose deep-felt convictions are pro-life have been labeled "anti" (abortion) and have been dismissed as traditional religionists and often, by inference, either Roman Catholic or influenced by that church's teaching.

Population explosion, illegal abortions and their fancied toll of maternal lives, the pitiable rape or incest victim, the deformed baby, the mother's physical or mental health—these all in turn have been given top billing as reasons for change.

The movement has been sweeping away all who disagree. The pro-abortionists, who only two years ago were setting as their highest goal the incorporation in state laws of the controversial provisions of the American Law Institute's suggested changes, have now discarded that step-on-the-way and have been openly espousing nothing less than abortion-on-demand.

With little being said or written in the public press to counter this wave of propaganda, only a few private and religious publications, it seems, have attempted to present the other side.

The average citizen, when asked his opinion about abortion, will demonstrate an almost total lack of factual knowledge about the subject. He will tend to completely oppose "wide open" permissiveness, but will have a reason or two, stemming from the often false and misleading pro-abortion propaganda which has filled the public media, for which he feels abortion should probably be permitted.

When pushed to define when human life begins, he usually will be even more indefinite. While only a very small minority of vocal people are aggressive proponents of abortion-on-demand, the great bulk of swing voters seem relatively apathetic.

To date, those committed to a pro-life philosophy have produced several excellent (and expensive) books and a rapidly increasing flow of pamphlets. The strength (and weakness) of most of the more modest efforts is that they are limited to only one aspect of the problem, are religiously sectarian, or try to cover too much too briefly. In an attempt to bridge this gap, we have written HAND-BOOK ON ABORTION. Hopefully, it is small, concise, and inexpensive enough to be useful, without sacrificing too much detail.

Our emphasis, we are convinced, must be on the scientific, medical and social aspects of this issue if we hope to present the facts in a way that can influence our pluralistic society. Theological considerations are critical to each person individually but cannot be imposed upon other non-believers in the culture. This is not to minimize religious conviction. The value, dignity, and right to life of each individual which has been a hallmark of and lies at the core of western culture is, at least in part, directly related to our Judeo-Christian heritage.

Knowing full well that the anti-life side has been presented in its fullest by our public media, this book is an honest effort to present the pro-life side of the abortion issue. With this in his pocket or her purse may the legislator, doctor, clergyman, concerned layman, woman's activist, and all who value human life make their voices heard.

The hour is late.

....

IS THIS HUMAN LIFE?

Is this human life? This is the question that must first be considered, pondered, discussed, and finally answered. It cannot be brushed aside or ignored. It must be faced and honestly met. Upon its answer hinges the entire abortion question, as all other considerations pale to insignificance when compared with it. In a sense nothing else really matters. If what is growing within the mother is not human life, is just a piece of meat, a glob of protoplasm, then it deserves no respect or consideration at all, and the only valid concern is the mother's physical and mental health, her social well-being, and at times even her convenience.

But if this growing being is a *human* being, then we are in an entirely different situation. If human, he (or she) must be granted the same dignity and protection of his life, health, and well being that our western civilization has always granted to every other human person.

For two millennia in our western culture, written into our Constitution and Bill of Rights, specifically protected by our laws, and deeply imprinted into the hearts of all men has existed the absolute value of honoring and protecting the right of each person to live. This has been an inalienable and unequivocal right. The only exceptions have been that of balancing a life for a life in certain situations or by due process of law.

Never in modern times, except by Hitler, has a nation put a price tag of economic or social usefulness on an individual human life as the price of its continued existence.

Never in modern times, except by Hitler, has a nation demanded a certain physical perfection as a condition necessary for the continuation of that life.

Never since the ancient law of paterfamilias in Rome, has a major nation granted to a father or mother total dominion over the life or death of their child.

Never has our nation legally allowed innocent humans to be deprived of life without due process of law.

Yet our newly enacted permissive abortion laws do all of the above. They represent a complete about-face, a total rejection of one of the core values of western man, and an acceptance of a new ethic in which life has only a relative value. No longer will every human have an absolute right to live simply because he exists. Man will now be allowed to exist only if he measures up to certain standards of independence, physical perfection, or utilitarian usefulness to others. This is a momentous change that strikes at the root of western civilization.

It makes no difference to vaguely assume that human life is more human post-born than pre-born. What is critical is to judge it to be, or not to be, human life. By a measure of "more" or "less" human, one can easily and logically justify infanticide and euthanasia. By the measure of economic and/or social usefulness, the ghastly atrocities of Hitlerian mass murders came to be. One cannot help but be reminded of the anguished comment of a condemned Nazi judge who said to an American judge after the Nuremberg trials: "I never knew it would come to this." The American judge answered simply: *"It came to this the first time you condemned an innocent life."*

Back to our basic question. Is this unborn being, growing within the mother, a human person? Make this judgment with the utmost care, scientific precision, and honesty. Upon it may hinge much of the basic freedom of man in the years to come.

Judge it to be a mass of cells, a piece of meat? Then vote for abortion-on-demand.

Judge it to be a human person? Then join us in fighting for his right to live, with all the energy and resources at your command.

WHEN DOES HUMAN LIFE BEGIN?

....

But what if a person would sincerely doubt that this is human life in the womb?

Even if a person did doubt the presence of actual human life in the uterus at a particular time, what would be the fully human way to go? Perhaps a guide then would be how we have always treated other human life when there has been a doubt that it exists. Would we not resolve a doubt in favor of life? We do not bury those who are doubtfully dead. We would work frantically to help rescue entombed miners, a child lost in the mountains, or a person under a collapsed building. We would suggest that the truly human thing would be to give life the benefit of the doubt.

DEVELOPMENT IN THE UTERUS

....

What does legal "viability" mean as far as legal rights of the unborn child are concerned?

Some states use "viability" as a measure of judgment as to whether or not the unborn child has the basic human right to protection of his life by the state. The frightening aspect of using this as a dimension of right to life is quickly apparent when we consider that, by this standard, a defective newborn child or a defective child of any age is also not "viable." By the above criteria, the senile old person rendered incompetent by a stroke, the completely psychotic individual, or even the quadriplegic veteran from Vietnam are all not "viable," as they are not capable of independent existence. Some of the above also do not have mental "viability." To make a judgment of an unborn child's right to live or not in our society by his mental or physical competence, rather than merely by the fact that he is human and alive, brings only too close the state's determination of a person's right to continued life as measured by their mental or physical competence or whatever the current price tag is.

....

RAPE, INCEST

Picture the poor helpless girl, possibly your daughter, assaulted by an unknown assailant, by inference possibly of another racial extraction, frightened, tearful, and emotionally upset. Then a few weeks later, confirmation of her worst fears—she's pregnant.

Who would be so heartless and so cruel as to refuse her an abortion? Why must this innocent girl be forced through the ordeal of pregnancy and childbirth? Talk is easy, as long as this is theoretical, but what if this was your daughter?

The above situation, charged as it is with emotionalism, pathos, and sympathy, has been sufficient to convince some state legislators to enact laws that permit abortion for rape or for incest. Is there anything more that can be said?

Is pregnancy from rape very common?

No. It is extremely rare.

Why is this so?

If a girl is raped or subjected to incestuous intercourse and reports the fact promptly, she is usually taken immediately for medical attention. This consists of a douche, commonly a scraping of the uterus, and at times doses of medication, one or all of which, while done partially to prevent venereal disease, will almost invariably prevent her from getting pregnant. If the rape victim would report her assault properly, there would be, for all practical purposes, no pregnancies from rape.

Do most young women know this?

If they don't, they certainly should.

Are there any statistics to support the fact that pregnancy is rare?

There have been a few good statistical studies in this country. In Czechoslovakia, however, out of 86,000 consecutive induced abortions, only twenty-two were done for rape. This figures out to one in 4,000. At a recent obstetric meeting at a major Midwest hospital, a poll taken of those physicians present (who had delivered over 19,000 babies) revealed that not one had delivered a bona fide rape pregnancy.

What has been the English experience?

English law does not even list rape as a reason for abortion, because of "the difficulty of proving rape."

What is meant by "difficulty of proving rape"?

This is the crux of the problem and it goes something like this: Let's assume a young woman is raped, but that through fright or ignorance she does not report it and quietly nurses her fears. She misses her period and hopes against hope that it isn't what she thinks it is. Another week, yet another week, and finally in tears she reports to her mother, her physician, or some other counselor or confidante. Let's assume that the law permits abortion for rape and that her parents bring her to the District Attorney and request that this be performed. The representative of the law may be quite sympathetic and more than willing to help her, but he has one request that must be met: "Since this is a law, and I must have reasonable proof that you were raped, you must furnish me with one reliable witness to corroborate your story." This she cannot do. Therefore, he cannot authorize the abortion for this reason.

But think of the poor girl.

True, if in fact she was actually raped against her will. As everyone knows, there are many degrees of resistance or consent on the part of a woman to the act of intercourse. It is easy for a woman rejected by a lover to then accuse him of raping her. For any kind of justice, some type of proof must be asked.

What of incest?

Incest is intercourse by a father with his daughter, uncle with niece, etc. The same dynamics mentioned above apply. Will Uncle John admit to having relations with his niece? Never! It would be her word against his. The court might even believe her, but could not act on it legally. Incestuous intercourse is seldom reported and when pregnancy does occur, it is not usually reported as being from incest.

What of a law for rape or incest then?

We would call them non-laws, as they would be almost totally inoperative. We believe that rape and incest as reasons for liberalizing abortion laws are little but an emotional smoke screen behind which to open the door for permissive abortion for many other reasons.

But, even if rare, some girls are forcefully raped and some do get pregnant. Should they be forced to carry an unwanted child?

Legal authorities say that to change the entire law for a very few cases would possibly open a Pandora's box.

But think of the poor girl—the trauma to her!

Unquestionably, many would want her to destroy the growing baby within her. But before making this decision, remember that most of the trauma has already occurred. She has been raped. That trauma will live with her all of her life. Furthermore, this girl did not report for help but kept this to herself. For several weeks she thought of little else as the panic builds up. Now she has finally asked for help, has shared her upset, and should be in a supportive situation.

The utilitarian question from the mother's standpoint is whether or not it would now be better to kill the developing baby within her. But will abortion now be best for her, or will it bring her more harm yet? What has happened and its damage has already occurred. She's old enough to know and have an opinion as to whether she carries a "baby" or a "blob of protoplasm."

Will she be able to live comfortably with the memory that she killed her developing baby? Or would she ultimately be more mature and more at peace with herself if she could remember that, even though she was unwillingly pregnant, she nevertheless gave her child life and a good home (perhaps through adoption).

Even from only the mother's standpoint, the choice is one which deserves the most serious deliberation, and no answer is easy or automatically right.

And finally:

Isn't it a twisted logic
that would kill an innocent
unborn baby for the crime
of his father!

MENTAL HEALTH

"Maternal mental health was the commonest indication for hospital abortion in 1969, accounting for 93.7% of all cases."

> — Abortion Surveillance Report Annual Summary
> U.S. Dept. of Health, Education & Welfare

How new is mental health as an indication for abortion?

It is quite new and has been spoken of only in the last few years. Since the decline and virtual disappearance of therapeutic abortion of the type that once was necessary to save the life of the mother, many major university hospitals have gone a decade or more without doing a single therapeutic abortion. For instance, the University Hospital of the College of Medicine at the University of Cincinnati did not do a single therapeutic abortion for fifteen years prior to 1968. This experience is not unusual. (W. Stone, Dept. of Psychiatry, U. of C., Feb. 1971.)

Already in 1951, Dr. R. J. Heffernan, of Tufts University, speaking to the Congress of the American College of Surgeons, said: "Anyone who performs a therapeutic abortion [for physical disease] is either ignorant of modern methods of treating the complications of pregnancy, or is unwilling to take time to use them."

So abortion is rarely necessary today to save a mother's life?

Yes, abortion is almost never necessary anymore.

But isn't it sometimes necessary to preserve her mental health?

The word "mental health" is so broad and vague as to be almost meaningless. In fact, in the last few years, it has become a catch-all reason for which all sorts of abortions have been justified, only rarely in fact being done for serious psychiatric reasons.

What would be a serious psychiatric reason?

Frank Ayd, M.D., medical editor and nationally known psychiatrist said: "True psychiatric reasons for abortion have become practically non-existent. Modern psychiatric therapy has made it possible to carry a mentally ill woman to term."

It can be flatly stated that no mental disease known to man can be cured by abortion. The most that can be said is that possible mental breakdowns or complications might be prevented by abortion. To predict this accurately, however, is quite frankly beyond the competence of ordinary men, and we include psychiatrists in this group. There are so many variables, people are so different, and react in so many different ways, that no one, no matter what his training, can accurately predict what effect a pregnancy or an abortion will have on a woman.

....

Competent medical opinion is deeply divided as to whether psychiatric reasons ever justify an abortion. The phrase "mental health," written into some of our state laws, has opened a Pandora's box of abortion-on-demand. It bears serious reconsideration by those states that have incorporated this phrase into their laws, and almost certainly it should be stricken from them.

UNWANTED CHILD—RIGHT TO HER OWN BODY

"Editor:

I would like to write to you to let you know that I am in full accord with the abortions

that are being performed in New York City. For every early physiologic process inter-
rupted, we are preventing a candidate for our relief rolls, our prison population, and
our growing list of unwanted and frequently battered children."

The above, taken from a letter to the editor of the *A.M.A. News*, reflects the
thinking of some people today. If the above were true, the proponents of abortion at the mother's request would certainly have added weight to their side of the
balance arm of the scale weighing the value of the life of the unborn child. If the
above is not true, then pro-abortionists have deluded themselves with more wish-
ful thinking.

I believe every child should be a wanted child, don't you?

We agree that every child should be wanted. A world without unwanted children
would be an idyllic place in which to live. No one would quarrel with that as an ide-
alistic goal. Wouldn't it also be a wonderful world if there were no unwanted wives
by husbands, no unwanted aging parents by their children, no unwanted Jews,
Black People, Catholics, Chicanos, or ever again a person who at one time or place
finds himself unwanted or persecuted. Let's all try to achieve this, but also remember that people have clay feet and, sadly, the unwanted will always be with us.

The measure of our humanity is not that there aren't unwanted ones, but what
we do with them. Shall we care for them or kill them?

But why should a mother carry to term an unwanted pregnancy?

Physicians who deliver babies will all agree that a significant percentage of all pregnancies are not planned, and, at the time these women are first seen in the doctor's
office, they definitely have "unwanted pregnancies." Overwhelmingly, however, a
mother adjusts to the initial surprise and shock, accepts the baby growing within
her, and comes to anticipate the birth of her child. After more than twenty years
of medical practice, your author personally can say without hesitancy that he has
seen many unwanted pregnancies, but has yet to see the first unwanted newborn
child. If we permit abortion for an unwanted pregnancy, we will be destroying
vast numbers of children, who, by the time of their birth and through their child-
hood would have been very dearly wanted and deeply loved children indeed. If the
judgment of being wanted at an early stage of pregnancy were a final judgment,
and abortions were permitted freely, a high percentage of everyone reading this
book would never have been born.

....

What of the right of a woman to the privacy of her own body?

At least one pro-abortion court decision has referred to this. We think it is an entirely fallacious bit of reasoning. If you, as a citizen, stand outside of a door and listen to a mother battering her child, even to the point of killing it, what would you do? Would you respect the privacy of her home? You would not! You would open or break down the door and rescue the child. By virtue of her assault upon and abuse of another human person, she has surrendered her constitutional right to privacy in this case. The same analogy applies to abortion. The right of the child to live is greater than and supersedes any right that a woman may have to the privacy of her own body.

But a woman does have a right to her own body. Isn't the child, at least in the early stages of pregnancy, part of her body?

A woman's appendix, obviously a part of her body, can be removed for sufficient reason. The cells of the appendix, however, carry the identical genetic code that is present in every other cell in the mother's body. They are, for this reason, undeniably part of her body. The single-celled fertilized ovum or the multi-celled zygote or later developing embryonic human being within her uterus cannot, by any stretch of the imagination, be considered part of her body. This new living being has a genetic code that is totally different from the cells of the mother's body. It is, in truth, a complete separate growing organism and can never be considered part of the mother's body. Does she have a right to her own body? Yes. But this is not part of her own body. It is another person's body.

....

THE POOR SUFFER

A constantly repeated reason to justify abortion-on-demand is that present restrictive laws discriminate against the poor. It is stated that those with money can, in one way or another, obtain abortions if they really want them and that the poor simply cannot.

Isn't it true that restrictive abortion laws are unfair to the poor?

It is probably true that it is safer for a rich person to break almost any law, than for a poor person to do so. Perhaps the poor cannot afford all the heroin they want. Rich people probably can. Does that mean we should make heroin available to everyone? Not everything that money can buy is necessarily good. The solution is not to repeal laws, but to enforce them fairly. Laws restricting abortion can be, and frequently have been, adequately enforced.

But it's still basically unfair, isn't it?

What is unfair is that poor people have not been given an adequate education and an adequate opportunity to better themselves. We will not eliminate poverty by killing poor people. The problem of the poor and the under-educated is their destitution and their lack of opportunity to achieve a better life, not the fact that they have children. Some who live in ivory towers seem unaware of this, but poor people themselves are very much aware of it, as evidenced by the fact that they as a group have cut their birth rate much less than middle and upper class socio-economic groups.

But don't too many children add to the burden of their poverty?

Poverty is more than just a shortage of this world's goods. Poverty is also the lack of spiritual and cultural resources, and often accompanying it is despair, apathy, and helplessness. Those who lack material things, and often find their chances for improvement of their lot in life rather bleak, sometimes find that much of their personal fulfillment is the joy they find in their children.

Do poor people tend not to accept abortion?

The majority certainly have not up until this time. Neither have poor or under-developed or under-educated areas of the world in any significant numbers accepted methods of birth control. It is the middle and upper classes who have accepted and used these methods.

What is the answer then for the poor?

The humane solution is to attempt to raise their standard of living and to help them achieve a more dignified existence. By raising a family's expectations in life, and the degree of education which they hope their children will achieve, people have universally been motivated to limit the number of children they have, in order to take adequate care of those children they have already borne. This seems to be the only way that will consistently motivate people to voluntarily limit their family size.

Are these white people, black people, Indians? Of whom do you speak?

We speak of them all, particularly however non-white people throughout the world who suspect that the imposition of birth control and abortion on their cultures is the white man's method of genocide.

Genocide? Who said this?

In April 1971, Mr. Wm. Darity, head of the Dept. of Public Health, Univ. of Mass. speaking at a Planned Parenthood Conference in Kansas City about his Study of a New England Community said that:

> "The study found parallel increasing evidence of strong opposition to family planning among blacks, including such moderate black civil rights organizations as the Southern Christian Leadership Conference. Considerably more black males under 30 agreed that family planning programs were designed to eliminate blacks." Also, they were "overwhelmingly opposed to sterilization and abortion, 'even if you had all the children you wanted.'"

....

THE WORDS WE USE

"Reform" of abortion laws? Would the denial of the right of the unborn to live truly be a "reform"? To use the word "reform" is to agree with the pro-abortionists that present laws protecting the unborn child should be changed. It is important in this debate to consistently use words that accurately and incisively describe the truths of which we speak. Let's make words work for us, not against us. Let's remove the camouflage and show "repeal" or "updating" of abortion laws for what it is and speak of "permissive laws," "abolishment of all controls," "denial of the unborn child's right to life" or whatever is applicable.

"Product of conception," "fetal tissue," "glob of protoplasm," "prospectus" and other high sounding phrases are all direct denials of the humanity of the growing child. Make up your mind. If you are convinced that this is a human life, call it such. Then consistently speak of "he" or "she," not "it," and speak of the "unborn," "pre-born," or "developing child" or "baby."

"Termination of pregnancy," "interruption of pregnancy," "retroactive conception" are all verbal gymnastics behind which to hide. "Induced abortion" is more accurate. "Killing the life within the mother," "killing the fetus" or most to the point, "killing the unborn baby" directly face the issue, and therefore are the most honorable and preferable terms to use.

"Medical murder" implies a judgment of the abortionist's knowledge of the humanity of the unborn child, and willful killing. This may not be true. We would suggest that the simple phrase of "killing" of the pre-born child cannot be challenged, is not judgmental and directly states what is being done.

"Pre-natal euthanasia" is entirely accurate when describing killing of an unborn child because he is defective. Euthanasia (mercy killing) is killing an adult because he is or has become incompetent or defective. This can also apply to children in which case it is commonly called infanticide.

Do not accept the negative label of being "anti-abortion." Rather, always speak of this movement and philosophy as being "pro-life."

When referring to those who want abortion-on-demand, speak of "abortionists," of the "abortionist mentality," or of the "anti-life movement." Never accuse another person of not being sincere but do insist on accurate terms.

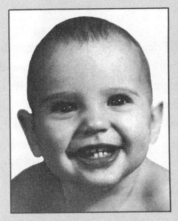

This newspaper advertisement urges readers to spend the postage necessary to urge their "governmental representative" to vote against liberalized abortion laws. Its sponsorship is unknown. First-class postage cost 8 cents from 1971 to 1974.

Abortion Makes Strange Bedfellows: GOP and GOD

by Lawrence T. King

Catholic voters had long been loyal to the Democratic Party. To the extent that abortion reform had a political valence as the issue heated up during the 1960s, it was more Republican than Democratic. Leading advocates for the repeal of New York's law criminalizing abortion, for example, included Republican political figures such as Governor Nelson Rockefeller and Assemblywoman Constance Cook. A Gallup poll in mid-1972 showed that more Republicans than Democrats supported leaving the abortion decision to a woman and her doctor, although a sizeable majority of both groups supported that view. (See p. 207.) The following article illustrates the beginnings of a significant shift, a moment when Republican Party strategists recognized that abortion could provide an opening for Republicans to reach out to Catholics. The incident recounted here occurred in a Catholic church in Southern California. The article appeared in the progressive Catholic magazine Commonweal *in 1970. The author's disapproval of the prospect of a partisan partnership between the Republican Party and the Catholic Church is evident. The reference in the final sentence of the article is to a 1969 book by Kevin Phillips, an aide to Richard Nixon during the 1968 presidential campaign. His book,* The Emerging Republican Majority, *was highly influential in shaping the strategy of President Richard Nixon's 1972 reelection campaign.*

When parishioners showed up for Mass at St. Barbara's Church in Santa Ana, Calif., on the last Sunday in August, their curiosity was aroused by the presence of a battery of voting registrars seated at tables in front of the church. Their curiosity was soon satisfied. During the homily, it was explained that the registrars had been sent there at the request of the pastor who was asking all Democratic members of the congregation to join him after Mass in changing their registration to Republican to protest the adoption of an "abortion on demand" plank at the California Democratic convention. By the time the last Mass was over and the registrars had folded up their tables to call it a day, 530 members of the parish had changed their political affiliation.

To the pastor, the Rev. Michael Collins, the move was the most effective means he could think of to let the state's politicians know how deeply Catholics felt about "legalizing murder." To Edmund G. Brown Jr., the former governor's son who is the Democratic candidate for California secretary of state, it was a "cheap political trick" on the part of the Republican State Central Committee to win over Catholic Democratic voters on the abortion issue.

According to Brown, the incident at St. Barbara's disturbed him to such an extent that he investigated the matter and found out that registrars had been requested at 14 of Orange County's 29 Catholic churches for the following Sunday. Further investigation revealed, he said, that the St. Barbara's incident was not a spontaneous movement, as it had been represented, but the start of a political experiment engineered by the Republican State Central Committee to see if the abortion issue could be used to cause a mass defection of Catholics from the Democratic Party. The Democratic candidates said the experiment was being watched closely by national Republican leaders and if it proved successful it would be used as part of a nationwide campaign to attract Catholic voters.

The day before the re-registration drive was scheduled at the Orange County churches, Brown called a news conference to present the result of his investigations to the news media. When challenged by reporters to substantiate his charges, Brown said, "A personal friend of mine, a member of the State Republican Committee, told me of their plan. He is a Catholic and very upset about this plan to use Catholics as political guinea pigs." He then named the Republican chairman for Orange County, who received the requests for dispatch of registrars, and a woman employee of the county committee office whose job it was, he said, to contact priests throughout the county on the abortion issue and tell them how to set up re-registration drives.

When contacted by newsmen, Father Collins, the county chairman and his staff worker all denied the charges. The county chairman was quoted as saying: "The re-registration drive has not been our initiative. We've had many requests for registrars from various churches and it's our responsibility to get registrars to them when they ask. We have not *overtly* campaigned for voters to switch to the Republican Party on the basis of this issue." (Italics added.)

In California, registrars are quite obliging. They will set up their tables and bring their registration books to any place where people are wont to gather, but when they show up in force at 14 churches on a given Sunday and when their primary objective is not the enrollment of new voters but changing the party affiliation of old voters, then there certainly is legitimate grounds for doubting that the whole thing is a "spontaneous reaction."

....

Since abortion has become a heated political issue in American life, no one can rightfully object to efforts by individuals and groups—this includes the Catholic church—to oppose candidates who favor the removal of all legal restraints on abortion. Candidates must be willing to face the electorate on this issue as well as any other issue. It is quite another thing, however, to take a scattergun approach and make a party issue out of something that is essentially bipartisan.

If the pastors of those Orange County churches had done their homework properly, they would have known that the abortion law that was passed in 1967 was a bipartisan measure. It was introduced by a Democratic state senator and a Republican assemblyman. In the state Senate, 21 votes were needed for passage of the legislation and that is exactly how many votes it received. (Seventeen votes were cast against it.) Twelve Democrats and nine Republicans voted for the measure and seven Democrats and ten Republicans voted against it. How bipartisan can you get? Furthermore, the legislation was signed into law by Republican Gov. Ronald Reagan, despite his knowledge that the Senate could not muster the two-thirds majority needed to override a veto.

Facts such as these might be pondered by pastors in their consideration of political implications of the abortion issue. It will help them in the future in dealing with partisan political workers whose interest in morality is secondary to their interest in winning over Catholic voters as a key tactic in the creation of what they like to call the "emerging Republican majority" (after the book of the same name).

PART II

Conflict Constitutionalized: The Years Before Roe

INTRODUCTION

Over the course of the 1960s, the abortion debate rapidly evolved from a conversation about the legitimate grounds for abortion to an argument about the legitimacy of government control over abortion.

The conversation began, if not exactly on common ground, at least within a shared framework of understanding. Americans who opposed efforts to legalize abortion in cases of rape or maternal health could nonetheless appreciate the concerns motivating those who advocated American Law Institute-style reform.

But with the transition from ALI-style reform to campaigns for abortion repeal, conflict escalated. Advocates for repeal sought more far-reaching changes in the law. And they offered reasons for change that were disquieting to many. While growing numbers of Americans embraced population control, many others opposed it as immoral—as a eugenics project that valued the lives of some more than others or as a pernicious invitation to separate sex from its procreative ends. Many opposed the "new morality" and viewed women's liberation—especially women's demand for abortion rights—as a threat to traditional family values. Calls for unrestricted access to abortion elicited an increasingly vigorous defense of the criminal law's life-protecting purposes.

In fact, public support for the decriminalization of abortion was steadily growing. But swift change in the law stimulated conflict, providing reason for both proponents and opponents of change to mobilize. As movements struggled for authority to shape abortion law and its social meaning, their arguments evolved. With escalation of political conflict, growing numbers of Americans began to appeal to fundamental values and to argue in a constitutional register. Increasingly, they addressed their claims to courts as well as legislatures.

In Part II, we examine this struggle over law in the years just before *Roe*. Between 1969 and 1972, the debate over abortion took hold in legislatures and courtrooms throughout the country. After briefly surveying state law as it stood in 1970, we examine the conflict in New York and Connecticut during in this period, as case studies of the political conflict over abortion taking place in states nationwide. As the documents comprising these case studies make clear, state actors understood themselves as participants in a national drama, much as participants in the same-sex marriage debates do today. Then as now, the abortion conflict traveled across state lines, and from legislature to the courts to the streets and back again. We conclude the Part by sampling new claims about abortion advanced in federal arenas in 1972.

In these debates, one can see public policy arguments evolving into constitutional claims. We have already seen the beginnings of this process in Part I, where social welfare arguments for repeal begin to converge with social justice arguments. There we saw advocates for decriminalization appeal to public health and population control; but they also called for decriminalization on the grounds that the law for poor women should be the same as for wealthy women, and insisted that government respect women as having the right and competence to make the decision whether to bear a child. Some of these "justice" claims were expressly constitutional. Consider, for example, feminist equal-citizenship claims about abortion in the 1970 Strike for Equality that commemorated the half-century anniversary of the Nineteenth Amendment giving women the right to vote. Or the way that opponents of repeal invoked the Declaration of Independence in support of a "right to life."

In the legal conflicts that Part II surveys, we see the rapid constitutionalization of arguments about abortion. As feminists challenge New York's and Connecticut's 19th-century abortion laws in informal speak-outs, in the legislature, and in the courts, the movement increasingly appeals to women's freedom and equality as citizens, prompting its opponents to defend abortion's criminalization in constitutional registers as well. In the brief period from 1970–1972, now-familiar constitutional claims emerge from the crucible of political conflict. Feminists argue that women have a constitutional right to make decisions about bearing children, and their opponents counter with the claim that the unborn, also, have a constitutional right to life. In justifying their respective constitutional claims, adversaries raise the stakes of the conflict, associating abortion with questions of fundamental value. What had been—only recently—intensely private matters of personal experience, religious belief, and moral conviction now find expression as claims about the shape of a just community and as the basis of political identity.

By 1972, abortion law was beginning to emerge as a locus of single-issue voting for some, and symbolic politics for many.

And so, even as public support for decriminalization of abortion continued to grow, the meaning of these changes in the law governing abortion continued rapidly to evolve. The documents concluding Part II show that even while *Roe v. Wade* was pending at the Supreme Court, the very meaning of abortion as an issue was being reshaped outside the Court's quiet precincts, in clashing social movements, in courts and legislatures, in Congress, and on the presidential campaign trail.

Abortion Law Reform and Repeal: Legislative and Judicial Developments (March, 1971)
by Ruth Roemer

We set the stage for the documents of Part II with a 1970 report that observes that the debates of the 1960s had prompted a third of the states to change their abortion laws— most by adopting an ALI-style reform statute and a few by repealing restrictions on abortion during the first months of pregnancy. Other portions of the article consider liberalization of abortion law in a wider transnational context. This report on abortion law reform and repeal was in Justice Blackmun's files.

In the three years from 1967 to 1970, a revolution has occurred in the abortion laws and practices in the United States. That revolution is still in process. Our once highly restrictive anti-abortion laws have been reformed in 13 states and virtually repealed in four states. No other country has a statute which explicitly makes abortion a matter for decision by the woman and her physician. Although other countries permit abortion on request of the woman under certain circumstances, the four American states have pioneered in treating abortion, as a matter of law, like any other medical procedure. As a result of recent developments, the United States has become a laboratory in which three different types of legal regulation of abortion can be compared and evaluated....

LEGISLATIVE DEVELOPMENTS IN THE UNITED STATES

Three kinds of modernized abortion laws have been enacted in the United States since 1967: (1) Twelve states have enacted all or part of the Model Penal Code first proposed in 1957 by the American Law Institute (ALI), under which abortion is not a crime when performed by a licensed physician because of substantial risk that continuance of the pregnancy would gravely impair the physical or mental health of the woman or that the child would be born with grave physical or mental defect, or in cases of pregnancy resulting from rape or incest. (2) One state, Oregon, has expanded the American Law Institute grounds to include a sociomedical ground proposed originally by the American College of Obstetricians and Gynecologists and patterned after a provision of the British Abortion Act of 1967, i.e., that in determining whether or not there is substantial risk to the woman's physical or mental health, account may be taken of her total environment, actual or reasonably foreseeable. (3) Four States—Alaska, Hawaii, New York and the State of Washington (by referendum in November 1970)—have repealed all criminal penalties for abortion, provided only that the abortion is done early in pregnancy and by a licensed physician (Alaska, Hawaii, and Washington also stipulate that the operation must take place in a licensed hospital or other approved facility). Thirty-three states, however, still have laws making abortion a crime except when performed to save the life (or, in a few instances, the health) of the woman. None of these states even requires that the abortion be performed by a licensed physician.

....

Actual practice, of course, may differ from the provisions of the statutes. In some places, doctors will not perform abortions as late as the statute allows. Nonresidents may not be welcomed even though the state has no residency requirement. Consents, consultations, and committee approvals may be required that are not specified in the statutes. It is also possible that residency requirements may not be strictly enforced and procedures may be more simple than those provided in the statute. On the federal level, a bill introduced in Congress by Senator Packwood to legalize abortion throughout the nation made no progress. A recent policy enunciated for U.S. military hospitals, however, permits abortions and sterilizations for military personnel, active or retired, and their families, regardless of state or local laws. [As discussed in Part I, this policy was later reversed.] In October, 1970, a White House task force on the mentally handicapped recommended that, in the interest of both maternal and child mental health, no woman should be forced to bear an unwanted child.

JUDICIAL DEVELOPMENTS IN THE UNITED STATES

Legislative developments have been accompanied by an emerging body of court decisions on the constitutionality of anti-abortion laws. The picture changes almost from day to day. As of autumn, 1970, five cases were on the U.S. Supreme Court docket; more than 20 cases were before three-judge federal courts; and, excluding the 20 states with federal cases, many of which also had state cases, another 11 states had cases pending in local courts. The following important cases may be noted.

1. In September, 1969, the Supreme Court of California, in the first decision on the constitutionality of any anti-abortion statute, invalidated the pre-1967 anti-abortion law of California. In a four-to-three decision in *People v. Belous* (Cal. 1969), the court held the statute unconstitutional on two principal grounds: (1) that the phrase, "necessary to preserve life" was so vague as to be violative of the due process requirements for a criminal law, and (2) that the law was in violation of a woman's fundamental rights to life and to choose whether to bear children. The latter follows from the U.S. Supreme Court's acknowledgment of a right of privacy or liberty in matters related to marriage, family, and sex. The critical issue defined by the California Supreme Court was whether the state had any legitimate interest in the regulation of abortion which would justify so deep an infringement of the fundamental rights of women. The Court held that the state had no such compelling interest....

2. Following the landmark decision of the California Supreme Court, the first decision of a federal court invalidating an anti-abortion statute was handed down. In *United States v. Vuitch* (1971), the U.S. District Court for the District of Columbia held unconstitutional the District of Columbia statute which made abortion a felony unless performed by a licensed physician for the preservation of the mother's life or health. The court held this phrase so uncertain and ambiguous as to invalidate the statute for want of due process, and it recommended appeal to the U.S. Supreme Court....

3. In addition to these two decisions which broke new legal ground, a number of other courts have invalidated pre-ALI style anti-abortion laws. These cases have arisen in both federal and state courts.

   ....

4. Attempts are currently being made to obtain an adjudication of the constitutionality of reformed ALI-style laws. Thus far, only one reformed ALI-style law has been invalidated by a federal court—Georgia's 1968 abortion law. The U.S. District Court in Atlanta held unconstitutional those parts of the 1968 Georgia law that limited the woman's right to abortion to the three ALI

grounds. The basis of the court's decision was violation of the woman's right of privacy. Retained as a proper exercise of state power, however, were the requirements for medical consultation, hospital committee approval, hospital accreditation and exemption provisions, and the residency requirement.

On the state level, the California Therapeutic Abortion Act has been challenged in three cases. Two cases involving Doctors Robb and Gwynne are still pending, but preliminary decisions involving these doctors have held the California statute unconstitutional. In *People v. Barksdale* (Cal. 1972), a municipal court in Alameda County held the current California law unconstitutional as violative of the equal protection clause of the 14th Amendment, as a vague and improper delegation of legislative authority to the Joint Commission on Accreditation of Hospitals, as discriminatory between the rich and the poor, as lacking the certainty required for a criminal statute with respect to the definition of mental illness, and as violative of the fundamental right of the woman to make a free choice whether or not to bear children. In rejecting the argument that the state has a compelling interest in protecting the embryo, Judge T. L. Foley added the following poignant words:

> I might say that I belong to the religion that was just referred to, and I dislike to render this opinion. I must follow the law under my oath as a judge. I am a Catholic which makes it very, very difficult—but my oath of office calls for me to follow the law *as* stated and set out by the Appellate Courts of this State.

The judicial picture is in constant flux as new cases are filed in federal and state courts; as the defense of unconstitutionality is raised in criminal prosecutions of doctors; as issues are raised concerning jurisdiction of courts and standing of plaintiffs to sue; and as decisions come down and appeals are taken.

On at least eight occasions, the United States Supreme Court has declined to review state court decisions that involved restrictive anti-abortion laws. One of these cases was the landmark decision of the California Supreme Court in *Belous*....

Although the final outcome cannot be predicted, three eventualities' seem fairly certain. First, more and more states will change their laws in accordance with one or another of the three patterns now prevailing in the United States. Second, as in other nations of the world, moderately reformed laws will be amended to expand the grounds and to simplify the procedures; alternatively, anti-abortion laws will be repealed. Third, in every state pressure will mount for making abortion available *de facto* as well as *de jure* to women, rich and poor, faced with the despair and desperation occasioned by unwanted pregnancy.

....

THE DYNAMIC LEGISLATIVE and judicial developments in the laws governing abortion in the United States have generated a ground swell of change. The action of the U.S. Supreme Court is crucial to the rate of progress, but, regardless of the outcome of cases pending before the court, the clock can never be turned back. Safe, legal abortion is now recognized as a fundamental right of women, a protection of maternal health and family welfare, and an assurance that every child is a loved and wanted child. Abortion, however, should be only one service in an array of services that should also include effective contraception, education for responsible sexual relationships, and health protection for mothers and children.

LEGISLATION: NEW YORK

Everywoman's Abortions:
"The Oppressor Is Man" (March 27, 1969)

by Susan Brownmiller

Until 1970, New York law threatened imprisonment for women who sought abortions as well as those who assisted them. The only abortions permitted were those necessary to save the life of a pregnant woman. Women seeking legal abortions had to demonstrate that their lives were at risk—that the abortion was "therapeutic." At the turn of the 20th century, this often meant feigning a case of vomiting so severe as to be fatal. By the 1960s, it meant convincing a psychiatrist to attest to a hospital committee charged with deciding which abortions to permit that a woman would commit suicide if forced to continue her pregnancy. As the New York Times reported in 1967, "Getting a hospital abortion in New York" was often "a question of knowing the right words to use"—words like "[i]f I have this baby I'll kill myself."

Negotiating the system required money. A woman's ability to obtain a legal abortion was frequently dependent upon whether a psychiatrist and a hospital committee were willing to interpret the law liberally in her case. But psychiatric consultations were expensive: doctors received far more money performing abortions in private hospitals than in the municipal hospitals where poorer women received care; and poor women lacking psychiatric referrals often did not know the magic words that would give doctors confidence to authorize an abortion. Between 1951 and 1962, over 92 percent of women who received hospital abortions in New York City were white, while over three-quarters of those who died from illegal abortions in the city were women of color.

Doctors and practitioners were most commonly prosecuted under statutes criminalizing abortion like New York's, and doctors provided much of the initial impetus for reform. Although there were a few people, like Planned Parenthood attorney Harriet Pilpel, who argued that free choice in the area of procreation was a "fundamental civil liberty and constitutional freedom," the first debates over abortion reform in the New York legislature focused on enlarging the scope of doctors' authority to prescribe abortions, not on women's freedom to obtain them; and those given the authority to testify about abortion reform were the (male) professionals who performed abortions, not the women who sought them.

But the conversation was changing. The women's movement had begun to contest constraints on women's roles in politics, the market, and the family, and pointed to statutes criminalizing abortion as evidence of inequality in each of these spheres.

In February 1969—just as Friedan was delivering "Abortion: A Woman's Civil Right" to the Chicago conference at which NARAL was founded— a women's liberation group protested a hearing on abortion reform in the New York legislature. Objecting to the slate of witnesses the state had called to testify as experts—fourteen men and one woman, a Catholic nun—the Redstockings argued that the legislators ought to "hear from some real experts...women." Shut out of the legislative hearings, the Redstockings took their protest to the public, with a speak-out in a Washington Square church. By testifying at the speak-out, women were insisting that women's voices and experiences should shape the law, and challenging norms that consigned abortion to silence and shame.

Twelve young women faced an audience of more than 300 men and women last Friday evening and with simplicity and calm and occasional emotion and even humor, told of incidents in their personal lives which they formerly had consigned to the very private. They rapped about their abortions.

The evening was put together by the Redstockings, an action group linked to the women's liberation movement. The meeting began with a playlist that was more diatribe than dialogue, and ended with a rambling speech by America's most loquacious abortionist, Dr. Nathan H. Rappaport. The real drama and unprecedented honesty occurred in between. For three hours, in the borrowed sanctuary of Reverend Finley Schaef's Washington Square Methodist Church, the group of women "testified" from their own experience with unwanted pregnancy and illegal abortion.

Last month, the Redstockings had stormed a hearing of a New York State legislative committee studying abortion law reform, and predictably, they had been rebuffed. The committee, they were told, was interested in the testimony of "experts." The "experts" had been 14 men and one woman, a nun. The radical women had fashioned this evening as their own public hearing. As one of the younger girls said, "We are the true experts, the only experts, we who've had abortions."

There were no legislators in the audience at the Washington Square church on Friday evening. There were, surprisingly, a large number of men....

....

It was the politics of confrontation and catharsis, and as such it was successful beyond the expectations of the organizers. It was, some of the women agreed, their most successful endeavor in a year and a half of intensive self-analysis and sporadic "actions" (their term for hit-and-run demonstrations like the assault on the legislative hearing, and last spring's infiltration of the Miss America pageant in Atlantic City).

The "testifying" method was an outgrowth of the confessional style of the weekly meetings of the woman's liberation groups, leaderless introspective sessions of free-form discussion where each woman is encouraged to "speak from your own experience, sister." The panelists prepared no speeches for the Friday night open meeting. They set up an unobtrusive tape recorder, kept the lights comfortably dim to encourage conversation, and protected their anonymity by using first names only. The result, which could have been exhibitionistic or melodramatic, was neither—it was an honest rap. And it worked.

....

[O]ne small fragile girl on the panel...had been telling her story of getting therapeutic (legal) abortion in New York. She had applied to 11 hospitals before she had accomplished her mission. "The tenth," she said in a quivering little voice, "offered me a deal. The deal was, they'd give me an abortion if I'd agree to get sterilized. I was 20 years old."

Each bit of testimony from the panel was met with a knowing response from the floor. The nameless Redstocking in this church this evening was Everywoman:

"I finally found a doctor in West New York, New Jersey. The doctor was very sweet. He had pictures of crucifixes on the walls. It only cost $900. I went to a bank and got a vacation loan. I'm still paying it off."

"I found two psychiatrists who said that for $60 each they would write a report which said I was mentally unable and ought to have the abortion. I had to prove I was crazy to get a legal abortion—and the abortion was the sanest thing I had ever done in my life."

"When you tell the man you're pregnant, he says, "How do I know it was me? I'm not the only guy you ever slept with, am I?"

"The first time I got pregnant, I was a young little thing. The man didn't use any contraceptive. He told me something like, "Don't worry, when I come the second time, it washes away the sperm."

"I was just living with this middle-class guy, and my life was just like his. We were just going along, together. I didn't do anything strange or unusual. I didn't make any decisions. But one day I was pregnant. Then there was a difference."

From the audience: "I've had three abortions and let me tell you, without anesthetic it's the most scary thing in the world. You're on the table and you feel the scraping and scraping. You get hit when you're young and inexperienced. All I wanted was love, and there I was, pregnant."

"It's only when you fulfill your so-called biological role as a woman that you get a lot of attention. Women in this society are defined by their service, nurturing, and maintenance roles. When I got pregnant, relatives I hadn't seen in 10 years said, 'I'll take the baby.' I guess maybe because I was helpless. When I said I was going to have an abortion; they lost interest. They didn't care any more. Just like they never had any interest when I told them I wanted to be a painter."

At one point in the evening, a young man in the audience arose to ask a question. "You keep talking about a woman's right to have a legal abortion," he said. "What about the man's rights, in or out of wedlock? You didn't make yourselves pregnant."

"He was told off, politely and firmly. Women have the ultimate control, over their own bodies," a Redstocking told him with the patience a weary teacher uses for a dear but exceptionally slow child. Neither he nor any other male in the hall felt like challenging that simple yet not so obvious statement.

Susan Brownmiller, "Everywoman's Abortions: The Oppressor Is Man," *Village Voice*, March 27, 1969. Copyright *Village Voice*. Printed by permission of Susan Brownmiller.

Constitutional Question: Is There a Right to Abortion?
New York Times (January 25, 1970)

by Linda Greenhouse

The Redstockings protest did not move the New York legislature, at least not immediately. Although bills were introduced as early as 1965, no abortion liberalization bill even made it out of committee until 1968. Supported by diverse organizations such as the New York County Medical Society, the state's bar association, the (Protestant) State Council of Churches, and the Federation of Reform Synagogues of New York, this first bill sought not to decriminalize abortion but only modestly to increase the exceptional cases in which doctors were permitted to perform therapeutic abortion. Despite the bill's limited scope and broad-based support, the New York Catholic Conference was successful in ensuring its defeat for several years.

With abortion reform stalled in the legislature, those seeking to overturn the state's abortion law turned to the courts—and to new arguments, focusing not on abortion as a policy choice but on abortion as a constitutional right. The article below was one of the first in the popular press to lay out the emerging constitutional arguments. It offers a window on the process through which claims in public debate were translated into claims in law, such as "void for vagueness," "the right to privacy," "equal protection," "the right to practice medicine," "the fundamental right of a woman to choose whether to bear children," the right to freedom from "cruel and unusual punishment," the right to freedom from "establishment of religion"—and "the right to life."

For years, reformers have tried to persuade state legislatures to except certain women from the general ban on abortion those women made pregnant by rape or incest, for example, or those likely to bear a severely deformed child.

Except in a few states, the reformers have not gotten very far. Most notably in New York, where an 1828 abortion law is still the model for the laws of 36 other states, they have failed completely. And when the mild Blumenthal reform bill, in a last-minute defeat of stunning surprise and drama, was rejected by the New York State Legislature last spring, it appeared to many people that the reformers had nowhere else to go.

But that was not the case. Even before the bill, sponsored by Assemblyman Albert H. Blumenthal (D., Manhattan) died, small groups of reformers throughout the country had begun to look to a new forum: the courts. As 1969 drew to a close, their efforts had already been startlingly effective. By the end of 1970, they may be rewriting history.

More important than the change of tactics is the change of philosophy that underlies the new abortion-reform movement. The reformers no longer claim that the states, basically correct in regulating abortion, are simply too rigid in the way they apply this power. Now, they are seeking to establish abortion as a positive legal right, like the right to free speech or the right to be secure against unlawful search and seizure, protected by the United States Constitution against interference by the state on any but the most pressing grounds. If they succeed, it is just possible that there will not be an abortion law left standing in any state by the end of this year.

A right to abortion. Such a notion, at first hearing, sounds fantastic, illusory. The Constitution is searched in vain for any mention of it. The very phrase rings of the rhetoric of a Women's Liberation meeting. But last September, the Supreme Court of the State of California threw out a state statute essentially identical to New York's abortion law on the ground that allowing abortion only when it is "necessary to preserve the life" of the mother is unconstitutionally vague and violates the fundamental notion of due process of law. Such a statute, Justice Raymond A. Peters wrote in his opinion, is not "sufficiently certain to satisfy due process requirements without improperly infringing on fundamental constitutional rights." His opinion contained another thought: "The rights involved in the instant case are the woman's rights to life and to choose whether to bear children.... The fundamental right of the woman to choose whether to bear children follows from the Supreme Court's and this court's repeated acknowledgment of a 'right to privacy' or 'liberty' in matters related to marriage, family, and sex."

Two months later, United States District Court Judge Gerhard A. Gesell overturned the District of Columbia's more liberal statute, which permitted abortion to preserve the mother's life *or* health, on essentially the same grounds. Judge Gesell wrote: "There has been, moreover, an increasing indication in decisions of the Supreme Court of the United States that as a secular matter a woman's liberty and right of privacy extends to family, marriage and sex matters and may well include the right to remove an unwanted child at least in early stages of pregnancy. Matters have certainly reached a point where a sound, informed interest of the state must affirmatively appear before the state infringes unduly on such rights."

Those two decisions, *People v. Belous* in California and *United States v. Vuitch* in Washington, D.C., are expected to be preludes to what could be the most important decision of all In New York on April 15, a three-judge Federal court will hear four combined test cases that challenge the constitutionality of New York's abortion law on a variety of grounds—some old and some very new.

The four suits, which technically are being brought against State Attorney General Louis J. Lefkowitz and New York City's district attorneys, ask for a permanent injunction against the enforcement of New York's abortion law. Should the injunction be granted, the state will appeal the decision to the United States Supreme Court, which automatically hears an appeal from a three-judge Federal court. But, because of scheduling problems, that will, almost certainly not be until late next fall. "And by then," says Roy Lucas, "New York will be a different place."

If Roy Lucas's optimism seems premature, that is not surprising. At the age of 28, he could properly be called the father of the new abortion-reform movement, and he is getting used to success. He seems at first glance an unlikely choice for such a role. The son of a Baptist deacon from Columbia, S.C., Lucas is a rather reserved young man who speaks quietly with a mild Southern drawl.

In 1967, his last year at New York University Law School, he had to choose a topic for a senior project. He had been interested in abortion reform, and decided that trying to prove that abortion laws were unconstitutional would be a good legal challenge.

To set out to prove that abortion was a right that the state could not abridge was surprising, to say the least; it had never been done. "People thought it was a weird idea," Lucas recalls. "My professors kind of laughed at me, but I went ahead and spent six months at it. Then I figured that was the end of it."

But that was not the end of it. In June, 1968, his paper, now called "Federal Constitutional Limitations on the Enforcement and Administration of State Abortion Statutes," was published in the *North Carolina Law Review* and, from there, reprinted and widely distributed by the Association for the Study of Abortion, Inc., a research organization based in New York. More than a year later, the California Supreme Court was to cite the paper in the *Belous* decision.

The Association for the Study of Abortion gave Lucas a grant to prepare a model trial brief that could be used to test the abortion laws of any state, based on the New York model—abortion only to preserve the mother's life. The brief was a 104-page document. But the core of the new approach was still the statement Lucas had made in his senior paper: "Although interests at stake in the abortion controversy are diverse, subtle, novel, and sensitive, the case appears ultimately to fit within the classical framework of governmental interference with important interests of individual liberty and to be capable of resolution in traditional constitutional terms."

The four cases are all different. Each was developed separately by its own lawyers, although the lawyers were all aware of the others' work and agreed to file their suits at approximately the same time last October. "It was almost a case of simultaneous scientific discovery," says Nancy Stearns, one of five women lawyers who are representing several hundred plaintiffs—married pregnant women, unmarried pregnant women, nonpregnant women, social workers and psychologists, physicians and nurses—in a class action suit which is the largest of the four cases.

The single plaintiff in another of the cases is the Rev. Jesse Lyons, pastoral minister of the Riverside Church in New York and founder of the Clergymen's Consultation Service on Abortion, who claims that the abortion law interferes with his right to refer his pastoral counselees to qualified physicians.

A third suit is being brought by Community Action for Legal Services, Inc., the Federally funded legal aid office that serves New York City, on behalf of a couple afflicted with severe cerebral palsy, a pregnant woman and two women with unwanted children. All these plaintiffs claim that the burden of the abortion laws falls most heavily on the poor, in violation of the right to equal protection of the law.

The remaining case is Roy Lucas's suit, cosponsored by the Association for the Study of Abortion. The plaintiffs are four physicians, including Dr. Alan F. Guttmacher, president of Planned Parenthood, who claim that the abortion law deprives them and their patients of constitutional rights. Lucas's brief is based on his model test-case brief, already a year and a half old.

Lucas's constitutional arguments are central to the other three cases as well as to his own, although each case emphasizes different points. All the lawyers do implicitly agree on one point, although it is not spelled out in any of the cases: that the unquestioned right of abortion applies to the earliest stages of pregnancy. Lucas admits to uneasiness about the spectre of aborting, by Caesarian section, late-term, nearly complete fetuses. Several of the states with liberalized laws require that abortions which are not necessary to preserve the mother's life be performed before a certain time, usually between 16 and 26 weeks of pregnancy. Lucas, however, claims that the question is nearly moot: almost any woman, if abortion were readily available, would end an unwanted pregnancy as soon she learned of it. At 11 weeks the fetus is only two inches long and nearly every abortion would take place considerably before that.

What follows is a summary of Lucas's principal arguments:

The New York State penal code—as well as the penal codes in 36 other states—defines a "justifiable abortional act" as one "committed upon a female by a duly licensed physician acting under a reasonable belief that such is necessary to preserve the life of such female." Any other abortion is a felony, with the seriousness of the offense depending on whether the operation was performed before or, during the final trimester of pregnancy.

The phrase "necessary to preserve the life" is scarcely self-explanatory, and the law contains no procedures for determining necessity. "Does it mean that without an abortion a woman has to die immediately, or that she will have her life span shortened by two days?" Lucas asks. A basic common-law requirement for due process of law, the essential guarantee of the 14th Amendment, is specificity, so that a citizen can know precisely what is or is not within the law. The argument claims that the law is thus constitutionally vague, especially since a physician is in jeopardy of criminal prosecution if his interpretation of the statute does not agree with that of law-enforcement authorities. This "void for vagueness" doctrine has been established in several Supreme Court cases.

Second, the argument claims, the law violates the right to privacy of physicians and their patients in the doctor-patient relationship. There is, of course, nothing in the Constitution referring to doctors and patients. But the argument places this right within the broad areas of personal freedoms guaranteed by the Bill of Rights. The New York Education Law provides that a physician's license can be revoked if he "did undertake or engage in any manner or by any ways or means whatsoever to perform any criminal abortion or to procure the performance of the same by another...or did give information as to where or by whom such a criminal abortion might be performed or procured." The verbal exchange of ideas outlawed here, the argument claims, is protected both by the Constitution itself and by a series of Supreme Court precedents protecting the "freedom to associate and privacy in one's associations."

Third, the argument claims, the law violates a right of marital privacy, especially as it was established by the Supreme Court in *Griswold v. Connecticut,* the 1965 decision overthrowing Connecticut's law against the use of contraceptives....

"We deal with a right of privacy older than the Bill of Rights—older than our political parties, older than our school system," Justice Douglas wrote. "Marriage is a coming together for better or for worse, hopefully enduring, and intimate to the degree of being sacred." Thus, Lucas's argument claims, a right to abortion is only a logical extension of the right to contraception, especially since not all means of contraception are perfect. A woman should not have to forfeit her protected right to plan a family simply because contraception fails or has not been used.

Fourth, the argument holds, the laws deprive physicians of their right to practice medicine according to the highest standards of medical practice. All of the plaintiffs in Lucas's case claim that the law interferes with their personal freedom in the conduct of their professional lives.

Fifth, the Lucas brief quotes the decision in the *Belous* case that the law violates "the fundamental right of a woman to choose whether to bear children," and that the law infringes on her "right to life [which] is involved because childbirth involves risks of death," a violation of liberty without due process of law.

Sixth, the argument claims that the law violates the standard of equal protection by having widely differing effects on different women. Women with money, knowledge and an influential private physician, for example, can obtain legal abortions much more easily than can poor women whose only contact with doctors is at clinics, where they may never see the same one twice, and whose only knowledge of the law is a negative one that has taught them to avoid the law rather than to exploit it.

Seventh, the law violates the First Amendment prohibition against laws establishing a religion. This argument refers partly to the role of the Catholic Church in opposing abortion reform, and partly to the broader issue of imposing by law upon a woman a belief about the nature of life that is not necessarily her own. In his senior paper at N.Y.U. Lucas had written: "If a woman believes that life began in the 'prehistoric slime' and is not created but only passed along by conception and that a fetus in early development need not be accorded a right to continue growing within her body, she is nonetheless prohibited from acting freely on that belief."

Eighth, the argument claims that laws forcing women to bear each child they conceive violate the Eighth Amendment prohibition against cruel and unusual punishment.

Finally, the argument concludes that the laws must be voided because the state can claim no "compelling or overriding justification" for abridging these constitutionally protected rights.

THE CLASS ACTION SUIT brought by the five women lawyers stresses the women's rights argument, an aspect that Lucas does not emphasize, although he is personally sympathetic to it. "It's absurd that women should be turned into little incubators for the human race," he says in conversation. Nancy Stearns, a staff lawyer with Arthur Kinoy's Law Center for Constitutional Rights, who did most of the work on the brief, says: "Our job is to convince the judges of something that to me is as plain as day—that every woman has the right to bring this suit, that these laws affect every woman's sex life whether she is pregnant or not. It can't be more obvious that this is one law that has been incredibly oppressive of women and has seriously hurt many, many women."

Cyril C. Means, Jr., a professor at the New York Law School and the attorney for the Rev. Jesse Lyons, has studied the history of abortion laws perhaps more extensively than anyone else in the field....

Means, who was one of three lawyers appointed in 1968 to Governor Rockefeller's 11-member Commission to Review New York State's Abortion Law, has constructed an argument against the law based on one of the oldest common-law principles: *"Cessante ratione legis cessat et ipsa lex"* (Once the reason for a law has ceased to exist, the law itself ceases to exist).

Under the common law of England, which was the law of New York for 165 years, abortion in early pregnancy was not a punishable offense, and abortion in late pregnancy was only a misdemeanor. The dividing line was the time of "quickening"—when the mother first feels movement in her womb which usually occurs sometime during the second trimester of pregnancy. (This is much earlier than viability—the age at which a fetus could survive outside the womb.) Only at quickening was fetal life considered developed enough to deserve the protection of the state.

In the 1820s, New York's lawmakers decided to gather the diverse common law provisions into a modern, unified code of law. The commissioners appointed to this task changed the common law regarding abortion, and made abortion before quickening a misdemeanor and abortion before quickening a felony, except when necessary to preserve the life of the mother. Means tried to discover why the revisers had changed the common law, and he thinks he has found the reason in a section of the proposed revisions that the Legislature did not adopt: a prohibition against *all* surgery, unless necessary to save the patient's life.

Based on New York hospital records of those days, before the era of antiseptic surgery, about 30 per cent of all serious operations, including abortion, resulted in death. During the same period, the death rate from childbirth was about 2 percent. Means concludes that the revised abortion law was drawn up not out of any legislative concern for the unborn child—in whom the Legislature had never expressed an interest—but out of concern for the life of the mother, who had 15 times as great a chance of surviving childbirth as of surviving an abortion.

"Under those circumstances," Means says, "for a legislature to say to a woman, 'You bloody idiot, no matter how tragic this pregnancy is, we prohibit you from undergoing this great risk of death,' was justifiable. Any court in its right mind would say that this was a legitimate exercise of police power."

But today the situation is reversed.... In the United States, the maternal mortality rate, excluding deaths from abortion, is about 23 per 100,000, making abortion statistically almost 8 times safer than a term pregnancy instead of 15 times more dangerous.

In all its revisions of the 1828 law, the New York Legislature has never offered a new rationale for the abortion prohibition to replace the original one that Means claims is no longer relevant. In fact, the law now frustrates what Means sees as the Legislature's original purpose by compelling women to choose the more dangerous of the two alternatives. Means does not claim that the state legislators, in their wisdom, have been wrong about abortion from the beginning. He says that their once-valid reasoning no longer applies, and that for that reason the law should no longer apply either.

The lawyers for the four cases will not be alone as they argue before United States District Court Judge Edward Weinfeld, United States District Court Judge Harold R. Tyler Jr. and United States Court of Appeals Judge Henry J. Friendly. The State of New York is the defendant, with Assistant Attorney General Joel Lewittes handling the defense. Lewittes, a 35-year old Yale Law School graduate, has based the state's defense of its law on two major grounds: that the issue is one that should be decided by the Legislature rather than by the court, and that the state has an interest in the protection of the unborn child that overrides any other personal rights that the laws might otherwise be deemed to threaten.

"Our feeling about the abortion law doesn't alter its constitutionality," Lewittes says. "Our mood changes, but that mood must be reflected in the Legislature. It's a slow and frustrating process, but it is still important to segregate the law and social reform. Is every social reform matter to be presented to the courts? What are legislatures for? We've grown—happily away from strict construction, but that doesn't mean that the legislatures should be browbeaten by the courts."

Lewittes dismisses the vagueness argument. "Any surgeon knows what 'necessary to preserve life' means. A surgeon makes that decision every day, no matter what kind of operation he is performing. The abortion law presents him with no new choices." Lewittes contends that abortion cannot be covered by extending the *Griswold* doctrine of a right to marital privacy. In his memorandum opposing the convening of a three-judge court, Lewittes wrote about such an extension: "But here [when dealing with abortion] we are no longer in the sacred precincts of the marital bedroom. The act is complete, the doors are open, and the zone of privacy is no more. A potential human being's life has begun and new competing rights are at stake; competing rights which the state has seen fit to recognize."

This basic right of the fetus to state protection, similar to that given fully developed human beings, also overrides whatever right the woman may have to control the use of her body. "It is at once naive and dangerous," Lewittes wrote, "to contend that such an absolute right [abortion on demand] flows from the 'sovereign' right of females over their own bodies. We are not concerned here with an appendix or tonsils or vaccination or blood transfusions but with an entity apart from the person of the mother."

The arguments that abortion was not a crime in common law or that the legislature enacted the original statute for a reason which is no longer valid are, Lewittes claims, essentially irrelevant. "History is interesting," he says, "but harkening back to the common law can be disastrous. We know more now. There is a science of fetology. A doctor, when he is treating a pregnant woman, knows he is treating two patients."

And so, after all the constitutional arguments have been heard, the abortion issue comes back to what it has really always been—a question of how one views the fetus. If the unquickened fetus is, as Roy Lucas contends, "just a mass of protoplasm," then the legal questions raised by abortion are no more difficult than any in other problems of law. But if, as others argue, a fetus at whatever stage of development is a potential human being with the same right to life as any other human being, the other rights claimed in the abortion issue must of necessity take second place, even if their existence is conceded in the abstract.

IF THE COURT STRIKES down the New York law merely on the grounds of unconstitutional vagueness, then the state may—and Joel Lewittes is convinced that it would—enact a statute with more precise terminology. "To prevent the state from making a new law, the court has to say nothing less than that the fetus is not an entity that the state has a legitimate interest in protecting," Lewittes says.

Many observers feel that that is exactly what is likely to happen. Assemblyman Blumenthal now favors total repeal of abortion laws and hopes that a decision on the current cases will have that effect. "It may be the only answer," he said recently. "And I'd gladly accept it. Repeal is the correct route now, and if the courts could solve the problem it would be both preferable and faster."

The only certainty is that the cases will not be over at the end of the scheduled one day of oral argument. The judges will probably take several months to announce their decision—the Supreme Court of California took more than six months in the *Belous* case—and then the cases will undoubtedly go to the Supreme Court on appeal from the losing side. There, of course, any decision on the New York law will have an equal and immediate effect on the 36 other similar state laws.

Plaintiffs' Brief, *Abramowicz v. Lefkowitz* (March 9, 1970)

by Nancy Stearns, Catherine G. Roraback, Kathryn Emmett,
Marjorie Gelb, Barbara Milstein, and Marilyn Seichter,
Attorneys for the Plaintiff-Appellants

In October 1969, with reform bills still stalled in the legislature, four lawsuits were filed challenging New York's 19th-century abortion ban. Although focused on constitutional claims rather than policy arguments, three of the four cases were rooted in familiar arguments for abortion reform: the economic inequality of access to abortion and the ability—the right—of professionals to prescribe a course of action to those that seek their guidance. But the fourth case, Abramowicz v. Lefkowitz, was novel, for not only did it make claims on the Constitution, but it added to the claims of doctors and of poor women a new claim advanced for women as a class. The Abramowicz suit, brought on behalf of over 100 women—as well as male and female lawyers, clergy, counselors, and medical professionals—challenged New York's abortion ban "to ensure that women will have the right to control their own lives and bodies." It asserted this then-novel constitutional claim on several grounds.

In their brief, excerpted below, the Abramowicz plaintiffs argued that the New York abortion law forced women who would not otherwise make such choices to undergo childbirth, seek illegal abortions, or take oral contraceptives (which at that time were still of questionable safety), thereby endangering their lives as well as their physical and mental health. The law thus violated the Fourteenth Amendment's requirement that the state not deprive persons of life without due process of law. The plaintiffs also argued that the physical and mental anguish caused by forced childbirth were sufficient to constitute "cruel and unusual punishment" under the Eighth Amendment.

But the core of the brief argued that the criminalization of abortion violated women's rights to privacy and to equal protection of the laws. The privacy claim invoked and extended the Supreme Court's decision in Griswold v. Connecticut, which struck down criminal bans on the sale of contraception; the right to privacy was familiar in law although, to this point, not commonly used in conversations about abortion. The equal protection claim in Abramowicz was groundbreaking. Whereas previous equal protection arguments had focused on the disparity in access to abortion between wealthy and poor women, the Abramowicz brief represents one of the first attempts to argue that the abortion right is essential to ensure equality between men and women. At the time the brief was written, the Supreme Court had yet to strike down any law on equal protection/sex discrimination grounds. Interestingly, the equal protection argument of the *plaintiffs' brief in Abramowicz is identical to the argument made later by the plaintiffs' lawyer, Nancy Stearns, in an amicus brief she submitted to the Supreme Court in Roe v. Wade (see Appendix). The brief argues that laws criminalizing abortion deny women sexual freedom, and inflict on women the many disparate burdens that mothers face.*

Aware that they were advancing novel claims and committed to changing the law, the plaintiffs' lawyers repeatedly appealed to women's experiences and even integrated women's voices into their constitutional argument by citing a transcript containing testimony to support points or claims then not recognized by law. This strategy reiterated the larger argument the Abramowicz plaintiffs were advancing: that the law governing abortion should more fully respect and incorporate women's concerns and experiences.

SUMMARY OF TESTIMONY

This is an action brought by approximately 300 plaintiffs—women, medical workers, lawyers, social workers—all seeking to ensure that women will have the right to control their own lives and bodies.

Fourteen witnesses testified, some of whom were plaintiffs; all were women, except for a Rabbi, author of *Birth Control and Abortion in Jewish Law*. All testified concerning the harshness of the abortion laws upon women and the interference of the laws with women's constitutionally protected rights.

Women spoke of their experiences, as women, with the New York State abortion laws. Some testified concerning the experience of undergoing an illegal abortion; some about leaving the United States to have the operation; others spoke of giving up a baby for adoption and the agony of the home for unwed mothers. One testified about a forced marriage. Women involved were Catholic, Protestant, Jewish, and Atheistic. The women were white and middle class, by and large, writers, teachers, an artist, and an editor.

One witness who had an abortion, spoke of the trauma, "(the illegality)...that was the main trauma for me, to go underground and not know whether I could get it or not and go through the underground and calling doctors and being scared as to who would do it and whether I would live or die and ever be able to have babies again." (Tr. Judith Leavitt). Another spoke of the responsibility in having a child: "I personally feel that to bring a child into this world is a fantastic human responsibility that should only be carried out when man and woman together desire a child and are willing to take full responsibility for that child's upbringing." (Tr. Susan Brownmiller)

Two population experts testified (Judith Bruce and Emily Moore) and one former case worker for the Department of Welfare in New York (Judith Leavitt).

Two of the witnesses were doctors. Dr. Natalie Shainess, psychiatrist and psychoanalyst, spoke of the psychological trauma suffered by women due to the fact that abortion is a criminal act. Dr. June Finer, who works with the Judson Church Clinic at 7th St. and Ave. B, spoke of how her ability to refer a woman for an abortion was predicated upon the financial condition of the woman:

Q. Now, does there come a time when young women have occasion to come to you with a problem of unwanted pregnancies?

A. Yes.

Q. How is it that you deal with this problem?

A. I try and evaluate their financial resources, which is a bad thing by medical standards... To have to evaluate the financial resources of a person... Before you can decide what medical advice to give them. I am afraid that's a problem. Given that they have the capacity to raise $400.00 or more, I would refer them to the Clergy Consultation Service... It's a group of Clergy from all over the country who believe that abortion is the right of every woman and they are able to recommend ways and places to obtain safe abortion, many of which are out of the country and which are relatively expensive... I find that they have no financial resources, I am in a very difficult situation, because I am unable to give very effective advice.

I may feel that, abortion is indicated, but by the New York Statute, I am really tied.

I cannot give the advice that I would like to give. I cannot point them to the resources that I would like to be able to. (Tr. June Finer, H.S.)

The defendants (Louis J. Lefkowitz, Attorney General of the State of New York; Burton B. Roberts, District Attorney, City of New York—Bronx County; and Frank Hogan, District Attorney, City of New York—New York County) presented no witnesses.

The Intervenors (a group of eight doctors) presented seven doctors as witnesses—all male and all Catholic. None of them has ever applied the New York Statute in his practice, either because he did not practice in New York State or because his personal and/or religious scruples prohibited him from performing an abortion even to preserve the mother's life. Three gynecologists testified. They all stated that abortion law was clear; nevertheless, not all Intervenors witnesses agreed on practical application. One psychiatrist, staff doctor to Our Lady of

Victory Home for Unwed Mothers, in Buffalo, testified. His testimony and that of Dr. Natalie Shainess were in sharp conflict. A fetologist and embryologist also testified. In addition, Intervenors presented a Battered Child expert (Dr. Helfers). His testimony, however, did not support their original working hypothesis that an unwanted pregnancy was not a relevant factor in the likelihood of whether a child would become physically abused by its parents.

II. THE NEW YORK ABORTION LAWS EFFECT A DENIAL OF EQUAL PROTECTION OF THE LAW, GUARANTEED TO WOMEN BY THE FOURTEENTH AMENDMENT

The equal protection clause of the Fourteenth Amendment was originally drawn to protect black people. Since that time, its protection has been greatly extended. First the courts extended equal protection to protect Chinese. More recently it has been extended to protect aliens, and in 1954 it was applied to Mexican Americans.

In 1966 the United States District Court for Connecticut applied the Equal Protection Clause to women. The court held that a state law providing for greater punishment for a woman than for a man committing the same offense constitutes an "invidious discrimination against her which is repugnant to the equal protection of the laws guaranteed by the Fourteenth Amendment." Nonetheless, New York does just this to a woman for performing an act which is not a crime. Man and woman have equal responsibility for the act of sexual intercourse. Should the woman accidentally become pregnant, however, against her will she endures in many instances the entire burden or "punishment."

In getting an abortion, the threats and punishments fall on the woman. This happens even where the decision to have an abortion has been a mutual one:

> although (the relationship) was a mutual consent and the abortion was also mutual consent it was I who endured all the consequences of it when the gynecologist threatened to have me put in jail. He didn't also threaten to have the father of the child put in jail although the father of the child was half responsible for conception and responsible for the decision on the abortion. (Tr. Mainardi)

It is often said that if men could become pregnant or if women sat in the legislatures there would no longer be laws prohibiting abortion. This is not said in jest. It reaches to the heart of the unequal position of women with respect to the burdens of bearing and raising children and the fact that they are robbed of the ability to choose whether they wish to bear those burdens.

And the woman carries an unequal and greater share of the burden, not merely for nine months, but for many years all in violation of the equal protection of the laws, as we shall discuss below. The abortion laws therefore present a rather unusual constitutional situation. At first glance, it would appear that the concept of equal protection of the laws might not even apply since the laws relate only to women. However, when we look beyond the face of the laws to their effect we see that the constitutional test of equal protection must be applied to them. For the effect of the laws is to force women, against their will, into a position in which they will be subjected to a whole range of de facto types of discrimination based on the status of motherhood.

As we have discussed at length above, a woman who has a child is subject to a whole range of de jure and de facto punishments, disabilities and limitations to her freedom from the earliest stages of pregnancy. In the most obvious sense, she alone must bear the pains and hazards of pregnancy and childbirth. She is suspended or expelled from school and thus robbed of her opportunity or education and self development. She is fired from her employment and thereby denied the right to earn a living and if single and without independent income, forced into the degrading position of living on welfare. If she has pre-school age children employers may refuse to hire her despite the provisions of the Civil Rights Act of 1964 which states that it is unlawful for an employer "to fail or refuse to hire or to discharge any individual...because of such individual's sex...," for according to the Fifth Circuit, it is inconceivable that Congress intended to:

> exclude absolutely any consideration of the normal relationship of working fathers to their pre-school age children and to require that an employer treat the two exactly alike in the administration of its general hiring policies.

If she is unmarried unless she succeeds in obtaining an abortion, she has no choice but to bear the child while the man who shares responsibility for her pregnancy can and often does just walk away. One plaintiff had the following experience which has been duplicated so often:

> Up until this point (the pregnancy) we had been like engaged and planning to get married you know in the future and at this point he said "Well I changed my mind about the whole thing. I don't want anything to do with it. You do what you want with the baby." So the whole thing rested on me and he disappeared. After this I never saw him again (Tr. Leavitt)

The woman is then alone with the problem of seeking and financing the abortion and if that fails, she is alone paying the expenses of pre-natal care and child-birth and raising and supporting the child. Under New York law, the mother is liable for child support if the father is unable to support the child or cannot be found within the state [Family Court Act §414]. If the father denies paternity, the mother is forced to initiate a paternity action where she must prove his paternity by "clear and uncontradicted evidence," not merely by a preponderance of the evidence. This exposes her to accusations concerning her sexual behavior from the father if he is seeking to avoid legal responsibility for the child.

Having been forced to give birth to a child she did not want she is subject to criminal sanctions for child neglect if she does not care for the child to the satisfaction of the state. She is held responsible if the child becomes a juvenile delinquent. Even here the disabilities for the woman are greater than for the man, for the New York courts seem to have found as a matter of law that the mother has a greater responsibility for the child than the father. In the case of *People v. Edwards*, though the father and mother were jointly indicted for failure to provide shelter and medical attention for their baby, the court held that only the mother could be punished for failing to bring the baby to a doctor when a condition which began with a diaper rash resulted in the child's death. Of course, again, if the woman is unmarried and paternity was never legally established, the woman bears these legal burdens alone.

Even where the father is present, the mother rather than the father is forced to be primarily responsible for raising the children. As long as "women, as a class earn less than men," and women have less opportunity for advancement, they, rather than the father, will remain at home to raise the family.

If such a broad range of disabilities are permitted to attach to the status of pregnancy and motherhood, that status must be one of choice. And it is not sufficient to say that the women "chose" to have sexual intercourse, for she did not choose to become pregnant. As long as she is forced to bear such an extraordinarily disproportionate share of the pains and burdens of childrearing (including, of course, pregnancy and childbirth), then, to deprive her of the ultimate choice as to whether she will in fact bear those burdens violates the most basic aspects of "our American ideal of fairness" guaranteed and enshrined in the Fourteenth Amendment.

III. THE NEW YORK ABORTION LAWS VIOLATE PLAINTIFFS' FUNDAMENTAL RIGHTS OF PRIVACY PROTECTED BY THE UNITED STATES CONSTITUTION

...In holding unconstitutional the Connecticut birth control laws the Supreme Court in *Griswold v. Connecticut* (1965), reminded us that the "Right to privacy [is] no less important than any other right carefully and particularly reserved to the people."

Just as women are guaranteed the right to determine whether to utilize various forms of birth control in order to prevent and/or terminate pregnancy they have the right to determine whether to seek abortion if and when those other methods fail. For under the Constitution, abortion may and should be considered no more nor less than back-up or last resort methods of birth control.

....

Freedom and privacy in the decision of whether to limit family size by means of birth control is essential to any meaningful constitutional right of privacy. The freedom to limit family size by means of abortion is equally essential. For as will be discussed more fully below, no valid legal distinction can be made between these several methods of controlling family size. Such an arbitrary and invidious discrimination which forces women into the underworld of abortion and even defines those same women criminals themselves in order to implement personal decisions which are their right, constitutes the most basic egregious "governmental [invasion] of the sanctity of a man's home and the privacies of life." *Griswold*.

In developing the concept of privacy as a right penumbral to the First Amendment, Justice Douglas noted in *Griswold* that the First Amendment protects not only freedom to associate, but also, privacy in one's associations. For as the Supreme Court noted in *N.A.A.C.P. v. Alabama* (1958), there is a "vital relationship between freedom to associate and privacy in one's associations." When the privacy is invaded, all too often the associations are too. This happens not only in the political sphere, which *N.A.A.C.P. v. Alabama* sought to protect, but also in the personal sphere. That is just what happens when the state interferes in what should be the decision of a man and woman as to whether they will have a child. Arbitrarily told they must bear and raise a child they have unintentionally conceived, the strain is often far too great for the relationship and destroys it. As we have seen above, this leaves the woman totally on her own. Even when the relationship survives, the additional unwanted child cannot help but place strains on the family relationship.

It is impossible to separate the fact of pregnancy from the sexual relations that precede it. Just as in the inability to obtain contraceptives cannot but affect the sexual relations of a couple, the inability to terminate an accidental pregnancy has the same destructive effects....

As the Supreme Court stated in the case of *Terry v. Ohio* (1968), "no right is more sacred...than the right of every individual to the possession and control of his own person...." For a woman, the control of her own body—the decision concerning whether she will or she will not bear a child—must be her own private decision. This private decision is inextricably linked to a woman's right of liberty to control her life and with her privacy of association. It is an area which may not be invaded by the state of New York with its abortion laws.

Excerpted from plaintiffs' brief, *Abramowicz v. Lefkowitz*, No. 69 Civ. 4469, United States District Court for the Southern District of New York, March 9, 1970.

Memorandum of Assemblywoman Constance E. Cook (1970)

Feminist protest in the Washington Square speak-out and in the Strike for Equality, coupled with the Abramowicz *litigation, helped disseminate the feminist argument for repeal, which converged with public health, social justice, and population control arguments for the decriminalization of abortion.*

In 1969, Assemblywoman Constance Cook (1919–2009) introduced a bill that would (partially) repeal, rather than simply reform, New York's abortion law. Whereas previous reform bills had sought only to broaden the circumstances under which therapeutic abortion was authorized, Cook's bill would remove all restrictions on abortion within the first 24 weeks of pregnancy. The reform bill had prompted internal debate among supporters about which circumstances were bad or dangerous or difficult enough to justify an abortion. The repeal bill obviated divisive debates among reformers over particular grounds for abortion, thereby unifying those in favor of liberalization—doctors, lawyers, clergy, and feminists—in support of a single bill.

In the following memorandum, Assemblywoman Cook, a Republican from Ithaca, argues for repeal advancing many of the policy arguments that were previously advanced to justify abortion reform: doctors' ability to practice medicine, women's health, and the importance of having the same law for the wealthy and the poor. Note, however, that the memo increasingly argues in a constitutional realm as it emphasizes disparities in access to abortion along racial lines, and concludes by reframing the abortion issue as one of individual liberty. Whereas the church is free to sanction individuals' moral decisions, the state is not. Cook argues that abortion is a matter of the "civil rights of women"—"a matter of private decision, a matter of a person's own conscience and her doctor's medical judgment" that is appropriately beyond government's control. Abortion, Cook argues, is now in the zone of beliefs that religious authorities may debate, but government may not impose.

Penal Law, §125.05. The purpose of this act is to eliminate abortion performed up to the twenty-fourth week from the commencement of a female's pregnancy as a crime. If this bill is adopted, abortion would be subject only to the concerned conscience of the individual and the best medical advice of her physician.

Illegal abortions are the single largest cause of maternal death in the United States. The tragedy is compounded by the fact that virtually no deaths result when an abortion is conducted in accordance with proper medical procedures. Tietze and Lewit, in the January 1969 *Scientific American*, state that hundreds of thousands of illegal abortions are done each year. Many authorities believe, however, that the figure should be a million to a million-and-a-half.

Most abortions are done on unwed girls or women who are married and who already have at least one child. It is generally believed that one out of every five pregnancies ends in abortion; that one out of every five women will have an abortion by the time she is 45. Most of the forty-one women who died in New York City as a result of illegal abortions during the last two years were married and left children behind. In view of the above a reform bill would not make a dent in the problem of illegal abortions.

The preponderance of legal abortions are done on white middle class women in hospitals. Therapeutic abortions are generally based on "suicidal threats" and require extensive psychiatric medical evidence. The price is very high. In New York City (1960–1961), the ratio of therapeutic abortions per 1,000 deliveries was 2.6 for white women, .5 for Negro women and .1 for Puerto Rican women. A reform bill would probably preserve this ratio. Only repeal would bring equality.

Since the law prohibiting abortion except to save the life of the women was first enacted, health care has changed radically. The law was enacted at the time when abortion could prove fatal to the person upon whom it was performed because of lack of aseptic techniques. Historic reasons for the criminal abortion laws are obsolete. An excellent statement of the reasons for repealing the abortion laws was contained in *People v. Belous,* 71 A. C. 996 (1969). In that case the highest court in California held unconstitutional the old California abortion statute which was similar to the present New York law. The California decision challenged the law on the grounds of being vague, an invasion of privacy, a limitation of the civil rights of women, and obsolete. The Washington, D.C. abortion law has also been declared unconstitutional by the courts. Several suits to declare the New York law unconstitutional have been initiated. Twenty-four weeks was the dividing point under the old law for the seriousness of the penalty. Twenty-four weeks has generally been recognized as a time under which a fetus is not viable.

The medical profession is being unjustifiably inhibited by the present law. Doctors are often forced to choose between ignoring their best medical judgment, or referring the patient to someone who will perform an abortion.

There has been increasing support for a liberalized bill from various church groups around the state. The New York State Council of Churches has declared that the state should limit its involvement to requirements that abortions be carried out under normal medical and health laws. Similar shifts were voted by the American Jewish Congress, Presbytery of New York City, American Baptist Convention, Council of Churches of the City of New York, the Episcopal Diocese of New York and the National Assembly of Unitarian Churches.

Support for such a measure can also be found in Catholic circles. The Rev. Robert F. Drinan, Dean of the Boston College Law School, argues that it would be preferable to "keep the state out of the business of decreeing who is to be born" and to place abortion in the same category as adultery and other acts that are condemned by the Church as immoral but not punished by the state as criminal.

Statistics on illegal abortions in the United States indicate that the effort to make an immoral act illegal has failed. On the other hand, great personal tragedies have resulted from attempts to end unwanted pregnancies.

It is respectfully submitted that abortion should be a matter of private decision, a matter of a person's own conscience and her doctor's medical judgment. It should not be determined by the state. The legislation is permissive. It would force no one to live under its dictates or to live in a moral or religious environment foreign to his upbringing or training.

This memorandum was published by the New York Legislative Service in the *New York State Legislative Annual* (1970).

Plaintiff-Appellant's Brief, *Byrn v. New York City Health & Hospitals Corporation* (June 2, 1972)

The vote on Assemblywoman Cook's repeal bill was nothing if not dramatic. Just as it appeared to have suffered a narrow defeat in the New York Assembly, the bill was saved by one legislator's last-minute change of heart. Standing to get the attention of the Speaker, Assemblyman George M. Michaels reversed his initial vote against the bill: "I realize, Mr. Speaker," explained Michaels, "that I am terminating my political career, but I cannot in good conscience sit here and allow my vote to be the one that defeats this bill." And so, with his vote, Cook's bill was passed in April 1970.

Within the next year, 164,000 legal abortions were performed in New York City. Nearly one-quarter took place in the city's municipal hospitals, and nearly one-third of all abortions performed on New York residents were covered by Medicaid—figures that indicate that poor women who previously had very limited access to legal abortions were now able to terminate their pregnancies safely, and were choosing to do so. The proportion of abortions performed during the first trimester of pregnancy grew substantially during the first year of legalization, from 68.6 percent during the first two months (July and August 1970) to 85.8 percent by March 1971.

The 1970 law repealing New York's abortion statute rendered Abramowicz, the lawsuit contesting the ban's constitutionality, moot. But legalization of abortion prompted opponents to employ litigation as the feminist movement had: to mount a constitutional challenge to the state's abortion law. In 1971, Robert M. Byrn—a Fordham University law professor, early leader of New York's Catholic anti-abortion movement who provided legal guidance and soon would author of the National Right to Life Committee's brief in Roe—brought a class action suit against New York City's municipal hospitals on behalf of all fetuses scheduled to be aborted there under New York's new law.

Appealing to science and civil rights, Byrn argued that New York's new law was unconstitutional. He argued that the embryo/fetus, which he termed the "unborn child," is a human being—and constitutionally protected person—from conception. He then claimed for the unborn the same bundle of constitutional rights that feminist lawyers had claimed for women in the recently filed Abramowicz case, arguing that abortion at public hospitals discriminates against the fetus, in violation of the equal protection clause; denies the fetus life without due process; and subjects the fetus to cruel and unusual punishment. The lawsuit mirrored the feminist lawsuit in key respects; Nancy Stearns, the attorney who filed the Abramowicz case, observed of the Byrn complaint that "if you take our original complaint and you take their complaint, you will discover that where we said that women have constitutional rights to liberty, to life, to privacy, and to be free from cruel and unusual punishment and to the equal protection of the laws, they said a fetus has those rights. It's virtually the same argument word for word." The state of New York responded to the Byrn complaint by defending its recently enacted abortion law, arguing that the fetus is not a legal person and therefore not entitled to constitutional protection.

Just as the Abramowicz *suit expressed claims in support of enacting New York's 1970 abortion law, the* Byrn *suit supported efforts to repeal the law. As* Byrn *was progressing through the courts, the right-to-life movement was organizing its members to defeat legislators who had voted for the state's 1970 repeal statute and to secure legislative support for repealing the repeal statute—an effort that very nearly prevailed in 1972, the year the case reached the New York Court of Appeals, the state's highest court.*

Without explicitly referencing this debate, the Court of Appeals denied Byrn's claim, explaining that although the issues presented by the lawsuit were "real," they were nonetheless neither "legal [n]or justiciable." The court held that "[t]he Constitution does not confer or require legal personality for the unborn; the Legislature may, or it may do something less, as it does in limited abortion statutes, and provide some protection far short of conferring legal personality." The concurrence emphasized this point, presaging the legislative debate that would soon follow: "[T]he formidable task of resolving this issue is not for the courts. Rather, the extent to which fetal life should be protected is a value judgment not committed to the discretion of judges but reposing instead in the representative branch of government."

Below is an excerpt of Byrn's brief before the New York State Court of Appeals (New York's highest court).

THE FACTS

Plaintiff's wards are infant Roe and other unborn living human beings within 24 weeks of gestation whose mothers have been scheduled, are scheduled or will be scheduled during the course of this action for abortions in the municipal hospitals of defendant-respondent Hospitals Corporation, for reasons other than necessary to preserve their lives. For the purposes of this appeal, the facts as pleaded and as set forth in the supporting medical affidavits submitted by plaintiff have not been disputed and are before this Court. They are as follows:

....

1. Each individual member of the unborn class is an unmistakable individual human being.

2. Each member of the class has been determined to be in existence by a confirmation of pregnancy and is between the 4th and 24th week of gestation.

3. Each member of the class is genetically human and genetically distinct and distinguishable from his mother.

4. Each member of the class is an irreversibly individuated, living human being.

5. Each member of the class is dependent on his mother only for sustenance and for a place to live, develop and grow.

6. Each member of the class is in existence less than 24 weeks from the commencement of the pregnancy of the female with whom each resides *en ventre sa mere*.

7. At 4 weeks each member of the class has a pulsating, albeit primitive, human heart. The foundation of the brain, spinal cord and entire nervous system has been established and the eyes have begun to form. Each member of the class, by the 4th week of gestation, has completed the period of greatest growth and physical change of his lifetime.

8. At 8 weeks each member of the class (a) responds to tickling of the lips by bending the upper body to one side and making a quick backward motion with his arm, (b) possesses a brain which in configuration is already like the adult brain and which transmits recordable impulses that coordinate the function of various organs, (c) possesses a stomach that produces digestive juices, a liver that manufactures blood cells and kidneys that extract uric acid from the infant's blood.

9. From the 8th week until adulthood, when full growth is achieved, the changes in the bodies of the members of the class will be in development and gradual refinement of the systems and organs of the body already established.

10. Each member of the class, if his life is not terminated, will normally develop and grow in a continuous natural process in which birth, puberty and other events are merely steps along the way.

....

SUMMARY OF ARGUMENT

Respondents did not dispute the medical and biological testimony submitted by appellant at Special Term. To the contrary, they conceded that there is no disputed issue of fact. On the undisputed evidence, each member of appellants' class is a live human being—a fact which goes to the very heart of this action because it is inextricably intertwined with the constitutional rights of the members of the class. As an ultimate fact, upon which constitutional rights depend, the issue of the human beingness of the members of the class is necessarily and appropriately before this Court. Whether this Court decides the issue here and now or remands the case for trial, this issue of constitutional fact must be resolved (Point I, *infra*).

Outside of the aberration of abortion "reform," the law recognizes and protects the unborn human being as a person whenever his health or safety is threatened. This is true in equity, when a court as *parens patriae,* invades such treasured rights as religious freedom and personal, family, and residential privacy, to protect the unborn child; it is true in social services law, when Aid to Dependent Children is granted for the benefit of an unborn child; it is true in the criminal law which requires that a reprieve be granted a pregnant woman condemned to death to guard against the taking of the life of an unborn child for the crime of the mother; it is true in tort law when a child after birth brings an action for pre-natal injuries grounded on a violation of his pre-natal rights; and it was true from time immemorial (up to the "reform" movement) in the law of abortion which had striven for centuries to find, and had evolved, ways of protecting the unborn child from the moment his biological existence could be medically established, while at the same time meeting the requirements of proof in an abortion prosecution.

This whole body of "pre-natal law" was not erected to protect a legal fiction— a physiological part of the mother. Rather it was and is meant to protect a human person. History, law, and logic compel a finding that the unborn child, from the moment his biological existence can be confirmed and was and is a person at common law, under the Declaration of Independence, the Bill of Rights, the Constitution of the State of New York, and the Due Process of the Equal Protection Clauses of the Fourteenth Amendment of the United States Constitution—at least for the protection of life afforded all human persons under those guarantees.

....

ACTING UNDER COLOR of a purportedly civil statute, respondent Hospitals Corporation is inflicting death upon innocent human persons who have been legislated out of the law's protection by the Amended Abortion Act. The infliction of death is punitive not civil. Whether one characterizes abortion-at-will as a denial of due process to the innocent for disturbing by their presence the sensibilities of others, or as cruel and unusual punishment for occupying the status of being unborn and unwanted, the Amended Abortion Act, on its face, in its effect and as applied, particularly, by respondents Hospitals Corporation is an unconstitutional deprivation of the right to live of each member of appellant's class.

The protection of the unborn child's constitutional right to life is not a value judgment reposing in the representative branch of government. The protection of rights enshrined in the Constitutions of the United States and the State of New York has been entrusted to the courts precisely so that their erosion by legislatures may be prevented.

It is to this end, that appellant's wards, through their guardian, have brought this action.

....

III. THE AMENDED ABORTION ACT, ON ITS FACE, IN ITS EFFECT AND AS APPLIED (PARTICULARLY BY RESPONDENT HOSPITALS CORPORATION), VIOLATES FUNDAMENTAL FEDERAL AND STATE CONSTITUTIONAL RIGHTS OF THE MEMBERS OF APPELLANT'S UNBORN CLASS.

....

Constitutional protection of fundamental rights is not doled out to some human beings and selectively withheld from others. To say that an individual is a living human being in fact, but not a "person" entitled to constitutional protection of, for instance, so basic a right as the right to live, is to make a sham of the Constitution. History, law and logic are against it. Each member of appellant's unborn class is a human person entitled to constitutional protection.

....

UNBORN CHILDREN ARE human beings. The very rationale which requires that women be "persons" under the Fourteenth Amendment, requires also that unborn children be "persons" within the Due Process and Equal Protection Clauses.

....

...[N]otions of due process and equal protection are not tied to ancient prejudices and obsolete science: "We agree, of course, with Mr. Justice Holmes that the Due Process clause of the Fourteenth Amendment 'does not enact Mr. Herbert Spencer's Social Statistics.' Likewise, the Equal Protection Clause is not shackled to the political theory of a different era." Today, "[T]he clauses protect all persons of any class or race, whether they be Arab, Japanese, or Chinese, Jews, Christians or atheists, aliens or citizens, residents or nonresidents, men or women, individuals or corporations." There is no warrant in history, logic or pre-natal law for excluding unborn children from this list.

....

THE DUE PROCESS AND Equal Protection guarantees of the Fourteenth Amendment are too important to admit of subjective definitions of "person" which place
an entire class of human beings outside its scope. Defining "person" by reference
to criteria other then biological realities inflicts upon the Fourteenth Amendment
the very subjective prejudices which the framers sought to overcome.

...."[T]he very idea that one man may be compelled to hold his life at the mere
will of another, seems to be intolerable in any country where freedom prevails."
The Fourteenth Amendment loses its potency when it is put at the mercy of subjective definitions of personhood. It is for this reason that the Due Process and
Equal Protection Clauses know no standard for determining who is a "person"
and thus entitled to protection, other than the biological standard that reveals the
existence of life, humanness and being, as confirmed, by a practical medical test.

....

THE POLICE POWER OF the state includes the power to legislate for the health
and safety of its inhabitants. But in this case, the inhabitants include both pregnant women and their unborn children. The Amended Abortion Act promotes
the death of unborn children, not their safety or health. Further, respondents must
concede that the police power in respect of eradicating crime is not unlimited.
In *Cooper v. Aaron* (1958), a local school board asked to be relieved of the "with-
all-deliberate-speed" integration order of *Brown v. Board of Education* (1955). The
board asked for the delay on the grounds:

> that the past year at Central High School had been attended by conditions
> of "chaos, bedlam and turmoil;" that there were "repeated incidents of more
> or less serious violence directed against the Negro students and their proper-
> ty;" that there was "tension and unrest among the school administrators, the
> class-room teachers, the pupils, and the latters' parents, which inevitably had
> an adverse effect upon the educational program;" that a school official was
> threatened with violence; that a "serious financial burden" had been cast on
> the School District; that the education of students had suffered "and under
> existing conditions will continue to suffer;" that the Board would continue
> to need "military assistance or its equivalent;" that the local police depart-
> ment would not be able "to detail enough men to afford the necessary protec-
> tion;" and that the situation was "intolerable."

The Court rejected the request:

> As this Court said some 41 years ago in a unanimous opinion in a case in-
> volving another aspect of racial segregation: "It is urged that this proposed

segregation will promote the public peace by preventing race conflicts. Desirable as this is, and important as is the preservation of the public peace, this aim cannot be accomplished by laws or ordinances which deny rights created or protected by the Federal Constitution." Thus law and order are not here to be preserved by depriving the Negro children of their constitutional rights.

Similar conclusions have been reached with respect to segregation of public facilities, and public housing.

The right to live is superior to the right to be free of segregation. If the prevention of crime is not such a compelling state interest as will justify a legislative classification which invades the right to be free of segregation, neither can it justify a legislative classification which invades the right to live. In each case, the victims—the integrated Black and the intrauterine baby—are unwanted. But unwantedness is not an excuse for violence against the unwanted person. In turn the prevalence of violence against unwanted persons is no justification for invading their rights whether they be Blacks or babies. Unwantedness, whether expressed by violence; by vote; by poll; or by amicus brief before this court, cannot justify the invasion of the baby's fundamental right to live. The compelling answer to this contention is that "constitutional rights may not be denied simply because of hostility to their assertion or exercise."

....

THE FACT THAT THE child may be a source of strain upon family finances and relationships does not justify his family's killing him. And as for family finances if the state is seeking to ameliorate poverty, it must do so by less drastic means than legalizing the killing of the children of the poor.

....

THE PRIVACY OF THE family and of the home are no more compelling than personal privacy as a justification for the legalized killing of unborn children. *Griswold v. Connecticut* (1965) held only that the state had failed to show the necessary compelling interest to support an invasion of family privacy consisting of a prohibition on the use of contraceptives in the conjugal relationship. *Griswold* cannot be stretched to create a discretionary family right to kill unborn children. The right and obligation of the state and its courts of equity, as *parens patriae*, to interfere in family practices, which endanger the child both before and after birth, are too well settled and to indispensable to be questioned now. Nor can *Pierce v. Society of Sisters* (1925), vindicating the right of parents to direct the upbringing and education of children, be used as authority for a parental right to destroy children.... Similarly, although *Loving v. Virginia* (1967) and *Skinner v. Oklahoma* (1942), may have recognized fundamental rights to marry and procreate, they most certainly do not recognize any right, fundamental or otherwise, to abort the procreated children of the marriage.

....

Neither sexual freedom nor women's rights is the central issue in the abortion cases. The nature and commencement of human life, as a live human being, is.

Excerpted from brief of plaintiff-appellant, *Byrn v. New York City Health & Hospitals Corporation*, 31 N.Y.2d 194, New York Court of Appeals, June 2, 1972.

Letter from President Richard Nixon to Terence Cardinal Cooke (May 16, 1972)

Just as the feminist movement had employed protest actions and litigation to challenge the state's abortion law, so too did their rapidly mobilizing opponents. Seeking the repeal and reinstatement of the state's ban on abortion, on April 16, 1972—designated "Right to Life Sunday" by Terence Cardinal Cooke, Archbishop of New York—over 10,000 attended an anti-abortion rally sponsored by the Roman Catholic Knights of Columbus. The same week, about 600 anti-abortion protestors demonstrated at the state capitol, and, in an action ironically reminiscent of the Redstockings, a group of women stormed onto the floor of the New York Assembly demanding that legislators "Stop abortion!" The New York Right to Life Committee spent 10,000 dollars on mailings. In addition to the Roman Catholic Church, there were over 50 right-to-life groups, comprising a claimed 200,000 people, making phone calls, writing letters, and threatening primary fights if legislators did not vote to revoke the repeal.

On May 16, 1972, President Richard Nixon sent the following letter to Cardinal Cooke, expressing support for the Church's campaign to reinstate New York's abortion ban. The letter represented an early gambit in a new campaign waged by the Republican Party to woo Catholic voters away from the Democratic Party. Republican strategist Kevin Phillips had identified Catholics as a target group for party realignment, and, by 1972, with speechwriter Patrick Buchanan's assistance, the administration had identified abortion as an issue through which the president could speak to Catholic voters. The president's letter—ostensibly leaked unintentionally—drew criticism as interfering in local affairs in the media as well as from New York Governor Nelson Rockefeller, a vocal supporter of New York's liberalized abortion law, and New York chairman of Nixon's reelection campaign.

Recently, I read in the *Daily News* that the Archdiocese of New York, under your leadership, had initiated a campaign to bring about repeal of the state's liberalized abortion laws. Though this is a matter for state decision outside federal jurisdiction, I would personally like to associate myself with the convictions you deeply feel and eloquently express.

The unrestricted abortion policies now recommended by some Americans, and the liberalized abortion policies in effect in some sections of this country seem to me impossible to reconcile with either our religious traditions or our Western heritage. One of the foundation stones of our society and civilization is the profound belief that human life, all human life, is a precious commodity—not to be taken without the gravest of causes.

Yet, in this great and good country of ours, in recent years, the right to life of literally hundreds of thousands of unborn children has been destroyed—legally—but in my judgment without anything approaching adequate justification. Surely, in the on-going national debate about the particulars of the "quality of life," the preservation of life should be moved to the top of the agenda.

Your decision, and that of tens of thousands of Catholics, Protestants, Jews, and men and women of no particular faith, to act in the public forum as defenders of the right to life of the unborn, is truly a noble endeavor. In this calling, you and they have my admiration, sympathy and support.

With personal regards,
Sincerely, RN

Reprinted from correspondence archived by National Archives and Records Administration, ARC Identifier 2115465.

Governor Nelson A. Rockefeller's Veto Message (May 13, 1972)

The anti-abortion mobilization was successful, or nearly so. The legislature rejected Governor Rockefeller's attempt at a compromise—a bill that would limit permissible abortion to the first 18 weeks rather than the 24 permitted under the 1970 law—and voted to revoke entirely the law repealing the abortion ban. But Rockefeller had promised that he would veto any bill banning abortion, and he kept his promise, leaving New York's liberalized abortion law intact—barely.

In a message accompanying his veto, Governor Rockefeller did not expressly invoke the Constitution. But he emphasized matters of fundamental principle—justifying the veto as protecting the life and health of poor women, ensuring the equality of rich and poor before the law, and defending a zone of private conscience from control by the state.

The same strong reasons that led me to recommend abortion law reform in my Annual Messages to your Honorable Bodies for 1968, 1969 and 1970 and to sign into law the reform that was ultimately adopted in 1970, now compel me to disapprove the bill just passed that would repeal that reform.

The abortion law reform of 1970 grew out of the recommendations of an outstanding select citizens committee, representative of all affected parties, that I appointed in 1968.

Under the distinguished leadership of retired Court of Appeals Judge Charles W. Froessel, the select committee found that the then existing, 19th-century, near-total prohibition against abortion was fostering hundreds of thousands of illegal and dangerous abortions. It was discriminating against women of modest means who could not afford an abortion haven and the often frightened, unwed, confused young woman. It was promoting hypocrisy and, ultimately, human tragedy.

I supported the majority recommendations of the Froessel committee throughout the public debate of this issue extending over three years, until the Legislature acted to reform the state's archaic abortion law. I can see no justification now for repealing this reform and thus condemning hundreds of thousands of women to the dark age once again.

There is, further, the recent Federal court decision invalidating the Connecticut abortion law, which is substantially the same as the pre-reform New York law. The law of that case, if upheld, would clearly invalidate the old New York law, as well, were the repeal of abortion reform allowed to stand. In such a circumstance, this state would be left with no law on the subject at all.

I fully respect the moral convictions of both sides in this painfully sensitive controversy. But the extremes of personal vilification and political coercion brought to bear on members of the Legislature raise serious doubts that the vote to repeal the reform represented the will of a majority of the people of New York State.

The very intensity of this debate has generated an emotional climate in which the truth about abortions and about the present State abortion law have become distorted almost beyond recognition.

The truth is that this repeal of the 1970 reform would not end abortions. It would only end abortions under safe and supervised medical conditions.

The truth is that a safe abortion would remain the optional choice of the well-to-do woman, while the poor would again be seeking abortions at a grave risk to life in back-room abortion mills.

The truth is that, under the present law, no woman is compelled to undergo an abortion. Those whose personal and religious principles forbid abortion are in no way compelled against their convictions under the present law. Every woman has the right to make her own choice.

I do not believe it right for one group to impose its vision of morality on an entire society. Neither is it just or practical for the State to attempt to dictate the innermost personal beliefs and conduct of its citizens.

The bill is disapproved.

Reprinted from *Public Papers of Nelson A. Rockefeller, Fifty-third Governor of the State of New York, Memoranda on Legislative Bills Vetoed* (1972).

The City Politic: The Case of the Missing Abortion Lobbyists (May 29, 1972)

by Hope Spencer

How did abortion opponents convince the legislature to revoke a bill that a majority of New Yorkers still favored? The anti-abortion mobilization seems to have taken pro-choice supporters by surprise. Whereas abortion opponents had been writing, calling, threatening, and rallying around their legislators for months, those in favor of retaining the 1970 law were slow to engage—becoming active only in the weeks leading up to the vote. While the coalition that had succeeded in passing the 1970 repeal had begun to fragment and turn its attention to other issues, the anti-abortion movement was becoming increasingly unified around a single issue, capable of delivering votes to support state legislators who acted with them and punishing those who did not, and able to communicate its concerns in terms that appealed to an increasingly broad-based constituency.

We women copped out in Albany, and we're in trouble. We have three women in the Legislature. We have almost no lobbyists. We nearly lost the right to choose whether or not we shall bear children. Only the grace of a Rockefeller veto prevented the repeal of legal abortion in New York. That reprieve certainly wasn't the work of the women, who have the most to lose.

Remember all the noise about women's lib? Remember the mass turnout of 10,000 at the rally on August 26, 1970, with everyone carrying those signs, "Abortion on Demand?" Where were they these last weeks in Albany?

There stood Betty Friedan on the Capitol steps, shouting into the microphone at the May 4 rally, wrapped in a red raincoat, her gray hair awry and frizzled in the steady downpour, while a paltry 400 people gathered beneath her. The scarred veteran was there, but where were the young troops? During the whole campaign not more than 700 supporters and lobbyists appeared to back the cause and put some muscle in the intimidated legislators' backs.

It was the established planned-population groups that made the round-the-clock last-minute efforts to save the existing law. They ran tape recordings of bus schedules on their phones and sat up nights printing yellow stickers saying "Don't Doom Women to Coat Hanger Abortions."

The stalwarts included the white-haired Dr. Alan Guttmacher from Planned Parenthood, Dr. Christopher Tietze from the Population Council, and Gordon Chase from the Health Services Administration, who stood outside the Assembly doors hour after hour, jostled in the crush of Right-to-Lifers, waiting patiently to see if an Assemblyman would answer their notes and come out of the chamber. Only to be told brusquely, "Excuse me, Doctor, I only speak with my constituents," or, "If I hear one more person talk about" mongoloids..."

Where were all the other doctors, the young doctors who are specializing in abortion techniques? Where were the staffs of those proprietary hospitals that have turned over 80 per cent of their beds to abortion patients? Where were the huge counseling staffs from the outpatient clinics whom I've watched give hours of sincere attention to abortion patients each day? And where were some of the 200,000 New York State women who have *had* legal, safe abortions since July, 1970?

THE DETERMINATION AND organizational abilities of the Right-to-Lifers, in contrast, were extraordinary. "You may win this time, but we'll get you next time," I heard one member threaten an Assemblyman. They meticulously prepare their lobbyists, even their child lobbyists. "Do you know who your Assemblyman is?" I asked a cluster of 40 St. Fidelis eighth-graders pressed against the Assembly doors. "John Lopresto," they chirped in unison. "And Bronston is our Senator."

Of the 50 of us who showed up to lobby against repeal that first Monday in May, perhaps five had ever been to the Capitol building before.... Up and down the cavernous stone stairwells we tramped, along the endless halls, hopelessly, utterly lost. Later, several of us felt foot-weary; we asked a uniformed guard at the Assembly doors if we might sit in the visitors' gallery upstairs. No, he told us politely, only relatives and guests. "No lobbyists." But why, we pressed him? "Well, you see, the Assemblymen are afraid that you women may drop down into the chamber some of them...uh...them fetuses, you call them."

The self-appointed guardians of our morals in Albany seem to have become obsessed by a horror of dead fetuses. Watch Assemblyman Kelleher in action. He leaps to his feet crying, "We forgot the voiceless victim." He waves aloft a tiny jar which supposedly contains a fetus. Immediately cameramen from every point in the Chamber scramble frantically up the aisles; they approach the Fatal Fetal Jar, surrounding Kelleher until all we can see is his blond head above the press of bodies.

Such melodrama—and less dramatic daily lobbying—got the votes. Assemblywoman Connie Cook, co-sponsor of the '70 abortion bill, had spoken in the Assembly the previous day. There was an aura of loneliness around her. In an upstate accent, rather dry-voiced, she concluded her speech to keep the present law: "I speak to you as the only mother in the Assembly, as the mother of two very loved and wanted children. Life is hard. The very least a child can start out with is the love of its own mother..."

After the repeal vote passed, reporters and cameramen converged on her from all sides, bombarding her with endless questions. "What will women think? What will women do?..." I asked her if she had something to say to New York women about the future. She spoke in brisk tones: "Tell them to get smart. Women are great at going to parades, but I want to see women *run*."

Agreed. But before they can run for office—or at least *while* they run—they might try walking, too. Walking up and down Albany's corridors doing the hard, necessary work of leaning on legislators to keep the present abortion law on the books. The Right-to-Lifers are certain to be doing plenty of leaning at the next session.

Reprinted by permission of *New York* magazine.

LITIGATION: CONNECTICUT

Women vs. Connecticut, "Some Thoughts on Strategy" (Circa February 1970)

Whereas the abortion debate in New York was largely—though, as we have seen, by no means exclusively—focused on the legislature, in Connecticut the legislature resisted efforts to reform the state's abortion law, a factor that led advocates for change to focus on the courts instead.

Under Connecticut's 19th-century statute, a woman could be imprisoned for seeking or receiving an abortion, as could anyone who performed an abortion or helped a woman procure one, unless it was necessary for the life of the woman or her fetus. Neither a 1967 bill to add rape as an exception to the abortion law, nor a 1969 bill that would permit therapeutic abortion, ever made it out of committee. There was, however, a deep normative divide between the legislature and many doctors and clergy in the state. As the materials in Part I show, many in the state believed in repeal and counseled women on obtaining legal abortions, in and out of state.

When a group of women's liberation activists organized to challenge Connecticut's statute in the early 1970s, they looked for new pathways of change. The group considered organizing a referral service (with or without the assistance of clergy seeking repeal) in order to increase access to abortion, educate women, and mobilize support for change, and, eventually, to force the question of the law's constitutionality. In ultimately deciding to file a lawsuit arguing that Connecticut's abortion law was unconstitutional, their goal was not only—or perhaps even primarily—to repeal the law. On their list of objectives, "get[ting] rid of Connecticut's law" was third, behind "educat[ing] the world and bring[ing] the subject into the open more..." and "involv[ing] women (lots of them) in a winning fight about an issue that is peculiarly theirs."

I. Objectives

    A. To educate the world and bring the subject into the open more (along with questions about women's health care generally);

    B. To involve women (lots of them) in a winning fight about an issue that is peculiarly theirs;

    C. To get rid of Connecticut's law;

    D. To enable as many women as possible to get abortions when they want them.

II. Referral

    A. To meet various objectives, this service would have to

        1. be efficient and capable of dealing with perhaps hundreds of women a month;

        2. be clandestine (to avoid arrests, which would frustrate objective D at least) and therefore involve considerable security consciousness (which would limit our ability to attain objectives A and possible B and D); OR

        3. be provocatively public (which would meet objectives A and B and D until the bust and possibly A, B and C after the bust);

        4. involve sensitive and sophisticated counseling and other related support services.

    B. Arguments for a clandestine service

        1. It is needed. We already get calls. The only other organized service is run mostly by men (CCS).

        2. We could involve a more or less limited number of women in doing something that's needed for themselves and for their sisters.

        3. It would be educational (but in a limited way).

    C. Arguments against clandestine service

        1. We could only serve a limited number of women and involve a limited number of women in working.

        2. If we were seriously worried about getting busted, we would have to be very security conscious. That would be nerve-wracking and possibly destructive to the proper spirit of women's organizing.

3. Our educational and propaganda impact would be minimal.

4. We would be fitting our institutions to meet a stupid law and have less chance of dumping the law altogether.

D. Arguments for a public referral service

1. It could put as much emphasis on education and propaganda as on its basic service. Education is more effective in the context where the subject counts.

2. It could involve lots of women in a public fight for a while.

3. We would be challenging Connecticut to enforce or dump its law. If we were busted we would have a more urgent and perhaps better case (First Amendment rights, too) then in a civil suit.

4. We could see that more women got helped because they would know about us.

E. Arguments against a public referral service

1. We might not be in business long enough to accomplish anything.

2. We might not be able to control who got busted. We would be risking things for women coming to us for help and for doctors. Getting busted is a drag; someone could even end up serving time.

3. Doctors and women might not come or cooperate for fear of the stuff mentioned in number (2) above.

4. We would be prosecuted in Connecticut rather than federal courts; in other words, in courts less likely to react positively to our arguments.

5. The demand might be greater than we (or the "profession") could handle. We might find we do more servicing than educating or organizing.

III. Law suit

A. We have a couple ways of doing it:

1. We can join up with the clergy and Doug Schrader, their lawyer, in one federal suit (not a class suit) involving clergy, women, and possibly doctors all together; <u>OR</u>

2. We can try to do our "own" strictly women's suit in the style of the now-moot New York suit.

B. To meet various objectives we would have to

   1. Involve as many plaintiffs and witnesses as possible and/or get women working on publicity, demonstrations and other aspects of the suit;

   2. Make a lot of noise about it all;

   3. Be willing to press on up to the Supreme Court, which means time, among other things;

   4. Press the basic issues of women's rights rather than vagueness arguments which are more likely to win.

C. Arguments for a suit in general

   1. Without risking our necks we might succeed in getting rid of Connecticut's law.

   2. We cannot really wait for the NY suit because it is nullified by the new NY law.

   3. It is a convenient vehicle for publicity (otherwise known as education or propaganda).

   4. It could be done in various ways—with greater or smaller numbers of people involved and more or less devotion of our resources. In other words, it could be grand scale or just one of several more modest projects.

D. Arguments against a suit in general

   1. The Law is pretty remote from most people and difficult to get people meaningfully involved in.

   2. For all our energy and time, it might not work. We might not win.

E. Arguments about going in with the clergy rather than doing our own

   1. They would supply money, lawyers, respectability.

   2. There would be more kinds of plaintiffs and thus more issues to be raised.

   3. We could supply as many women plaintiffs and women's issues as we could come up with.

   4. They will probably go ahead without us and before we get going on our own suit if we do not join. They would get ACLU support. That would all be wasted resources.

5. <u>BUT</u> A lot of things would be at their initiative ("they" being mostly men).

6. We might not have time to muster maximum publicity and support for the women's part.

IV. General agitation

(We have never discussed this possibility but probably should. Some women in Washington State had demonstrations of 2000 + people in the state capital. Washington is now one state with a bill for abortion on demand before its legislature.)

V. Doing nothing

(The tide of history seems to be running in our direction. Is this the time for us to get involved or the time to become the vanguard in some less popular cause?)

Reprinted by permission of Gail Falk.

Women vs. Connecticut Organizing Pamphlet (Circa November 1970)

Women versus Connecticut, as the group came to be called, presented a new model of abortion activism. Abortion reform during the 1960s initially sought to protect women; Women versus Connecticut sought to empower them. Once the group decided to mount a challenge to Connecticut's law, only women, and as many as possible, were to be the plaintiffs, lawyers, organizers, and experts.

What follows is an organizing pamphlet used by Women versus Connecticut to recruit plaintiffs for the lawsuit. The signatories to the document included members of the New Haven women's liberation group, which drew on the students of Yale Law School and the surrounding community. The organizing pamphlet sets forth the group's arguments, explains the process of bringing a lawsuit, and then sets out the grounds of the group's constitutional arguments. Once the group had decided to sue, it was determined to make clear that Women versus Connecticut's effort to legalize abortion was part of a larger struggle for equal voice and equal citizenship. As in New York, the movement recruited hundreds of women as plaintiffs in the case. When filed, there were 858 women named in the complaint; as the suit progressed, that number reached 1,700. Lawyers for the group included Nancy Stearns of the Center for Constitutional Rights, who played a key role in the Abramowicz *case in New York, and Catherine Roraback (1920–2007), a graduate of Yale Law School who had worked with Professor Thomas Emerson in challenging Connecticut's ban on birth control, which the Supreme Court ruled unconstitutional in the* Griswold *case.*

FOREWORD

About fifteen women came together in February, 1970 because we wanted to do something about abortion. Most of us were also in Women's Liberation; about half had had abortions; most of us had been contacted by women desperate to obtain abortions. As we talked, we began to discover that "the abortion issue" is inseparable from many other dimensions of our lives as women—we just think of it as separate because society has isolated it by making it a crime. In our meetings we began to understand that it was important for us to figure out how abortion connected to the rest of our lives and couch our action in those terms.

At the end of eight months of discussion of our experiences, and research we did on abortion and health care, we decided to try to reach all the women in Connecticut who wanted to work with us to abolish Connecticut's law against abortion. We decided that bringing a lawsuit against Connecticut's anti-abortion law was an important first step toward a decent health care system and women's control over their bodies.

We wrote the statement which follows to summarize for ourselves and new people our thoughts about the relationships we came to see after long discussion and struggle. Newer members need not agree with all of what we now believe, and we expect that the newly expanded group which has decided to call itself Women versus Connecticut will probably evolve its own position. We present it as an introduction because it is the basic stance from which the suit was initiated.

As women in this society, we lack control over our own bodies.

For years women have been under constant pressure to have children. Our culture teaches us that we are not complete women unless we have children. Our husbands and boyfriends encourage us to bear children as proof of their masculinity. Contraception is almost always our responsibility. Contraceptives that are known to be safe are not always effective; contraceptives that are known to be effective are not always safe. Abortion is illegal, and women who get abortions often risk their lives.

Other pressures compel some of us not to have children. If we are unmarried, we become social outcasts by bearing children. Those of us who are poor and live on welfare know that opponents of welfare want to limit the size of our families. We are pressured to use contraceptives or be sterilized; each time we have another child the meager allowance per child gets even smaller. Population control advocates tell us that overpopulation is the reason our environment is polluted. They imply that unless women everywhere stop having babies, thousands of children in underdeveloped countries will starve, and all people will be deprived of clean air, pure water, and space in which to live.

We want control over our own bodies. We are tired of being pressured to have children or not to have children. It's our decision.

But control over our bodies is meaningless without control over our lives. Women must not be forced into personal and economic dependence on men or on degrading jobs in order to assure adequate care for the children they bear. Our decisions to bear children cannot be freely made if we know that aid in child care is not forthcoming and that we will be solely responsible for the daily care of our children.

We are a group of women associated with Women's Liberation who want to bring suit to challenge Connecticut's abortion law. For the past several months we have been meeting regularly to talk about abortion, population control, health care, and our lives as women. We have decided to act to change some of the oppressive realities of our lives.

We believe that women must unite to free themselves from a culture that defines them only as daughters, wives, and mothers. We must be free to be human whether or not we choose to marry or bear children.

We believe it is wrong for this society to put the economic needs of corporations first and human needs second. These corporations rob Third World countries of resources with which their populations could be fed. At home, they make their profits by exploiting workers and polluting the environment. We think the issue is not control of the world's population but control of the world's resources. The question is not how many children but what proportion of the world's resources each child receives.

We believe all people have a right to meaningful work, an adequate income, access to good health care, and parent-controlled child care. We believe children have a right to be born into a world where many adults will be able to love and care for them according to their needs.

We don't expect these things to be given to us; we will have to fight for them. The abortion suit is just a beginning. If we succeed in changing the law, we will still have to fight to make abortions cheap enough so all women can afford them. We will have to struggle to prevent abortion from being used as a weapon against women who want to have children. We will have to fight to create a health care system controlled by those who use and work in it. And we know there are many other struggles ahead.

We are women committed to working together for these changes. Join us!

Betsy Gilbertson Wilhelm, Gretchen Goodenow,
Michele Fletcher, Ann Freedman, Sasha Harmon,
Marione Cobb, Jill Hultin, Harriet Katz, Ann Hill,
Gail Falk, Joan Gombos, Nancy Greep

WOMEN VERSUS CONNECTICUT

We are initiating a suit to try to get Connecticut's abortion law declared unconstitutional.

Under present Connecticut law, abortions are only legal if they are necessary to preserve the life of the mother. Women who have abortions as well as anyone who either performs them or helps women arrange to get them can be imprisoned and/or fined. The abortionist can be fined $1000 and imprisoned up to five years; the woman who had the abortion can be fined $500 and imprisoned up to two years; anyone who helped her arrange the abortion can be fined $500 and imprisoned for up to one year.

The law is used. Dr. Morris Sullman, a doctor in New London, was recently convicted of performing an abortion. There have been a number of arrests of those suspected of performing and arranging illegal abortions in the New Haven area in the past few months. (The woman who had the abortion rarely gets arrested. The usual pattern is for police or medical personnel to threaten women who are desperately ill following botched abortions with prosecution unless they agree to reveal the name of their abortionist.)

Women vs. Connecticut has not chosen to try and change the law because we believe in the power of the law to bring about the liberation of women, or even because we are convinced that once the law is declared unconstitutional all women who need them will be able to get abortions in Connecticut.

We see changing the law only as a <u>necessary first step</u> toward making those things possible.

As long as the law is on the books, doctors and hospitals can always hide behind it. Hospitals which choose not to do abortions have an iron-clad defense;

hospitals like Yale-New Haven which do some abortions are protected from community pressure to do more by the argument that if their current practices are publicized they will be forced to stop doing any.

And as long as the law makes obtaining an abortion a criminal act, we will continue to be forced to behave like—and thus to feel like—criminals.

We doubt that our troubles will be over once the law is changed. We suspect that hospitals will be reluctant to reallocate their priorities to make giving abortions to thousands of women possible; that doctors will not want to spend much of their valuable time doing this brief, uninteresting (and possibly unlucrative) procedure. But we will never get to this stage without first getting rid of the law.

Connecticut's abortion law was enacted in 1821 and amended in 1860. Many states have laws similar to Connecticut's, although in the past few years nine states have enacted "reform" laws which make abortion legal under several categories of circumstances: if the mother's mental health is threatened, if there is evidence indicating the child will be born with a deformity, if the child is the product of rape or incest, etc. However, a recent study indicates that only 15% of all women who have abortions do so for reasons covered by "reform" laws—and expense prevents many eligible women from getting them.

During the past year there have been some important legal changes. A Federal court in Washington, D.C. has declared the abortion law there unconstitutional because it is too vague (it specifies that abortions are legal to preserve the life and health of the mother). The Wisconsin abortion law, which is similar to Connecticut's, has been found unconstitutional by a Federal three-judge panel which found that the police power of the state did not entitle it to deny to women the right to decide for themselves whether or not to bear a child. Hawaii (which has a 90-day residency requirement) and New York (no residency requirement) have passed new laws which make abortion legal when performed in a hospital by a doctor. The New York legislature appears to have been favorably influenced by four suits—one brought by several hundred women, the others by a minister, a group of doctors, and several women for whom childbearing presented special burdens—which were pending before a Federal three-judge panel in New York at the time of passage of the new law.

These changes in other states create a favorable climate for change in Connecticut. There are a couple of ways the Connecticut law could be changed: by getting a new law—like New York's for example—passed by the legislature, or by bringing a suit which asks the courts to find Connecticut's abortion law unconstitutional.

Getting a new law that we would approve of through Connecticut's heavily Catholic legislature seems unlikely. Previous efforts to introduce even moderate reform measures have been unsuccessful. Asking the courts to find Connecticut's abortion law unconstitutional seems more apt to succeed.

What it means to "ask the courts to find Connecticut's abortion law unconstitutional:"

1. In every state there are two sets of courts—state courts and Federal courts. State courts make decisions about cases that result from violation of state law. Federal courts make decisions about cases that arise from violations of Federal law and about conflicts between state law and the Federal Constitution.

2. There are two ways we could go about asking the courts to make a decision on the constitutionality of the Connecticut abortion law.

    A. We could get arrested under the law—one way to do this might be to set up a flagrantly public referral service—and if we were convicted we could appeal through the state courts, hoping eventually to win in the U.S. Supreme Court. The problems with this approach are these: we would be unlikely to get the law declared unconstitutional by Connecticut courts since they are subject to the same political pressures as the legislature; it takes a long time and a lot of money to go from the lowest state court to the U.S. Supreme Court; some of us would have to get arrested and might go to jail.

    B. We could go into Federal court and ask for a declaratory judgment. This means that we would ask the U.S. District Court of Connecticut to analyze the Connecticut abortion law in terms of the U.S. Constitution and find the law unconstitutional. This amounts to asking the Federal court to use its power as interpreter of the Constitution to make a ruling on a state law which is ordinarily the territory of the state courts. To do this, no one has to get arrested. Those of us who want the law declared unconstitutional become plaintiffs in a civil action. The attorney general of Connecticut, who represents the state judicial system, is the defendant.

Advantages of this approach are that it takes less time and costs less than bringing a test case by getting arrested; no one has to risk jail; the suit is a positive statement of our position, instead of a defense to criminal charges.

Any group or combination of groups that feel themselves "irreparably harmed" by the law can be plaintiffs in this type of suit. All women fit in this category. We have planned in terms of a women's suit, in which the plaintiffs would be as many women as possible single, married, professional, laywomen—all those who feel the law denies them their constitutional rights. Twelve hundred New Jersey women are bringing such a suit there. In New York, where a group of women brought a similar suit, the plaintiffs included professionals—like doctors and ministers who are frequently asked to give abortions or information about abortion. Any woman who feels she might be in the position to advise another woman about abortion is welcome to join our suit.

Since the constitutionality of abortion laws is being challenged in a number of states, many of the legal arguments we are apt to use have already been set forth in briefs written for other states. The legal arguments we plan to use are outlined in the next section of this pamphlet.

Because the legal system is so chauvinist—only 4% of lawyers are women, less than 1% of judges, and the law has been slow to recognize the rights of women— the idea of bringing a women's suit which demands that the legal system recognize women's rights is particularly appealing.

LEGAL ARGUMENTS

The legal arguments we are making to show that Connecticut's abortion law violates women's rights under the United States Constitution are summarized as follows:

1. Right to Privacy

The Connecticut abortion law violates a woman's right to privacy, because it denies her the right to control over her own body and the right to make her own decisions in intimate personal matters related to marriage, family, and sex. It is every woman's decision, not the State's decision, as to whether she wants to bear a child. It is a personal decision, made in privacy and not to be interfered with by the State.

2. Right to Life, Liberty, and Property

A woman's right to life is jeopardized by the abortion law in that childbirth carries with it a risk to the life and health of the woman. This risk is higher than the risk involved in getting an abortion in the early stages of pregnancy.

In Connecticut, the actuality of an unwanted pregnancy, or the possibility of such a pregnancy, severely limits a woman's liberty and freedom to engage in the political process, to choose her own profession, and to fulfill herself in any way which does not relate to the bearing and raising of children. Unmarried women who become pregnant and are forced to bear children against their will suffer an extreme deprivation of liberty and human dignity by the social stigma placed on them as unwed mothers.

Women also suffer loss of property in that they are denied jobs solely on the basis of possible pregnancy, or motherhood. Pregnant women are forced to leave their jobs without compensation and without any guarantee of returning to work after they give birth.

Women who are forced to bear children they cannot support suffer extreme economic hardship. Because there are few facilities for child care outside the home, these women are effectively excluded from seeking employment and are forced to rely on welfare or charities to help in raising their children, at a loss to their liberty and independence in economic matters.

3. Right to Equal Protection
(Right of Rich and Poor Alike to Get Abortions)

Rich women in Connecticut can afford to travel to London or Puerto Rico for abortions. They also have greater opportunity to learn of private New York hospitals that perform abortions for out-of-state women at fees of $500–600. Thus, Connecticut's abortion law places a much heavier burden on poor women, who cannot afford the prices charged by hospitals in New York for therapeutic abortions, nor can they afford a trip out of the country.

4. The Abortion Law Imposes a Cruel and Unusual Punishment
on Women by Forcing Them to Bear Children

Forcing a person to give up his citizenship and to leave the country has been called a cruel and unusual punishment by the U.S. Supreme Court. We are arguing that forcing a woman, who does not want a child, to carry a pregnancy to term imposes on her the highest form of mental cruelty, as well as the physical hardship of pregnancy and childbirth and the economic burden of supporting a child for 21 years. Obviously, women who want children do not see pregnancy and childbirth as punishment. But for women who are forced to have children against their will, the abortion law creates a devastating torture of body and mind and often turns a woman's life into hell.

5. Connecticut's Abortion Law Is Unconstitutionally Vague

A criminal law, like the abortion law, must be worded so that the people affected by it know what is being forbidden. The words, "necessary to preserve the life of the mother," which are used in the state abortion law do not meet the standard, because the terms "necessary," "preserve" and "life" are ambiguous. They could mean that an abortion is not permitted unless the woman will die in pregnancy or childbirth or if she attempts suicide during her pregnancy; it could also mean that a woman's health will be injured in childbirth so that her life span will be shortened; it could also mean that a woman's quality of life will be changed for the worse, if she has a child. If no one is clear about the meaning of the law, how can it be enforced?

6. Right to Freedom of Religion

The Connecticut abortion law is kept on the books by people who hold the religious belief that human life begins at the moment of conception and that abortion means killing a person. They are imposing their religious views on all the other people who do not think abortion is murder, and who have the constitutional right to hold their beliefs without interference by state laws, such as the abortion law.

7. Right to Free Speech

People who want to help women get abortions can be prosecuted under the Connecticut abortion law. This violates their right to freedom of expression, to give out information on how to do abortions, who will do abortions and where they can be obtained.

8. The State Has No Justification for Its Abortion Law

When the abortion law was passed in the nineteenth century, the State was worried about the health hazards of performing abortions. At that time, even the most minor operation was dangerous. The State also showed an interest in protecting the morals of women, and keeping them out of the hands of scurrilous men, who would force them to risk their lives getting abortions. Times have changed—medically, abortion under proper conditions is now a safe minor operation, and the law intended to protect women now forces them to depend on racketeers and profiteers for dangerous illegal abortions.

9. Women's Rights

Two other arguments we have yet to develop are:

a) The abortion law violates the Nineteenth Amendment, which women fought for to give them equal footing with men in the public sphere. As long as women are forced to have and raise children, they are denied that equal footing guaranteed by the Nineteenth Amendment.

b) The Thirteenth Amendment forbids involuntary servitude. We think forced pregnancies are definitely a form of slavery against a woman's will.

Legal information for plaintiffs—

WHO CAN BE PLAINTIFFS:

1. Any woman who is living in Connecticut and is of childbearing age and who does not wish to bear a child at this time.

2. Women medical workers, such as doctors or nurses, who have been or may be asked to perform or help perform an abortion.

3. Women, especially in a professional position of counselor, clergywoman, social worker, or doctor, who have been asked or may be asked to advise or refer persons about abortions.

Named plaintiffs will be representing all other persons in Connecticut in similar situations. The decision that the Court makes about the validity of the abortion statute will affect everyone in the state. The list of hundreds of named plaintiffs, plus their personal participation in various public activities and the hearings could have an important influence on the outcome.

RESPONSIBILITIES AND OPPORTUNITIES OF PLAINTIFFS

In this type of lawsuit you will not face any kind of fines or sentence, or be restricted from leaving the state.

Plaintiffs may have to answer written or oral questions about the subject matter or the suit. This is a formal procedure available to the defendants (who will be the state's attorneys representing Connecticut). To present such questions would be costly and time-consuming for them and it seems unlikely that they will do so. Attendance in court at the preliminary hearings and eventually at the trial will not be compelled, but is strongly urged. A packed courtroom will be important and it is your right to know what is happening.

A brief questionnaire will be given each plaintiff. Your answers will help establish particular reasons needed to claim the right to be in court at all. This material will only be for the use of your lawyers and their assistants and it will not be turned into the court.

You will need to sign a statement authorizing your attorney to represent you.

Women under 21 may be plaintiffs if one of their parents is willing to sign as guardian. If not, we are hoping to make arrangements for one of the over 21 plaintiffs to act as "guardian ad litem" (guardian for the purpose of this suit).

Reprinted by permission of Gail Falk.

Memorandum of Decision, *Abele v. Markle* I (April 18, 1972)

On March 2, 1971, Women versus Connecticut filed a complaint in federal court on behalf of 858 women. The lawsuit, captioned Abele v. Markle, *alleged that "[t]he Connecticut abortion laws compel women of childbearing age, doctors, and other medical personnel and those who counsel or assist women to procure an abortion, to forego their constitutional rights to life, liberty and property, to freedom of speech and expression, to privacy, against cruel and unusual punishments, against involuntary servitude and to due process of law and equal protection of the laws." The case challenged socioeconomic inequality in access to abortion and emphasized the need for abortion in cases where pregnancy endangers a woman's health. But the value animating many of its claims on the Constitution was women's right to equal freedom with men. The lawsuit argued that the state, through its abortion laws, "classif[ies]...women not as full and equal citizens but as limited and inferior persons—persons denied the right to choose a life style or an occupation other than one consistent with bearing all the children they conceive" and that the abortion ban unconstitutionally "discriminate[s] against women by forcing a woman to bear each child she conceives without imposing like burdens on the man for the child whom he has helped create." The lawsuit also claimed that Connecticut's abortion laws impermissibly infringed upon the rights of doctors and counselors, but these claims were secondary to those concerning the indignity and injuries the abortion ban inflicted on women.*

On April 18, 1972, a federal court held Connecticut's abortion laws unconstitutional, with two judges supporting the decision and one dissenting. Each of the three judges who heard the case wrote a separate opinion.

Judge Joseph Edward Lumbard (1901–1999), named to the federal appeals court in New York by President Dwight D. Eisenhower in 1955, based his decision clearly and unequivocally on the constitutional arguments advanced by the women's movement. In Abele, *Judge Lumbard responded to women's testimony about the injuries and indignities that laws criminalizing abortion imposed on them and recognized that laws criminalizing abortion inflicted constitutionally cognizable harms on women, and not doctors only, as earlier judgments had found. He reasoned that constitutional protection for women's decision whether to abort a pregnancy was warranted because of changing social views about women's "status" and "roles." He cited the Nineteenth Amendment's conferring on women the right to vote; Reed v. Reed, the first equal protection sex-discrimination decision; federal employment-discrimination law; and the Equal Rights Amendment, which had just been sent to the states. In striking down Connecticut's 19th-century statute, he recognized that the nation's understanding of women had changed since the law was first enacted, emphasizing that "society now considers women the equal of men." Women, therefore, "are the appropriate decisionmakers about matters affecting their fundamental concerns." The state's interest in protecting the fetus, he continued, is insufficient to abridge a woman's constitutional right "to determine within an appropriate period after conception whether or not she wishes to bear a child."*

Judge Jon O. Newman, a Yale Law School graduate named to the federal district court in Connecticut months earlier by President Richard M. Nixon, concurred but based his decision on narrower grounds, emphasizing the uncertain legislative history of the state's abortion law. Judge Newman reasoned that in the 19th century, the legislature criminalized abortion either to protect pregnant women from dangerous surgery—an interest made obsolete by improvements in medical technology—or to preserve a woman's morals; that is, to deter her from engaging in nonmarital, nonprocreative sex. Neither rationale offered sufficient reason to restrict women's decisionmaking in the 20th century. Judge Newman left open the question of whether the state could criminalize abortion in order to protect the unborn, explaining that he saw no evidence that this was the state's purpose in passing its 1860 abortion law.

Judge T. Emmet Clarie (1913–1997), a former chairman of the Connecticut State Liquor Commission named to the district court by President John F. Kennedy, was the dissenter. He would have held that Connecticut's abortion laws were not, in fact, unconstitutional. Rather, any intrusion upon a woman's privacy that they cause is justified by the state's compelling interest in protecting the unborn. His opinion gives voice to movement concerns about protecting human life and traditional family roles.

Although the Abele case has, until now, been largely forgotten, it was one of many cases to address the abortion conflict in the years preceding Roe. Abele presented several of the most prominent legal arguments being made at the time that Roe was decided—arguments emphasizing far-reaching changes in women's legal status, in sexual mores, and in medical science as reasons to reconsider the constitutionality of criminal laws adopted a century earlier.

LUMBARD, CIRCUIT JUDGE.

In Connecticut, statutes prohibit all abortions, all attempts at abortion, and all aid, advice and encouragement to bring about abortion, unless necessary to preserve the life of the mother or the fetus....We think that by these statutes Connecticut trespasses unjustifiably on the personal privacy and liberty of its female citizenry. Accordingly we hold the statutes unconstitutional in violation of the Ninth Amendment and the Due Process Clause of the Fourteenth Amendment.

The decision to carry and bear a child has extraordinary ramifications for a woman. Pregnancy entails profound physical changes. Childbirth presents some danger to life and health. Bearing and raising a child demands difficult psychological and social adjustments. The working or student mother frequently must curtail or end her employment or educational opportunities. The mother with an unwanted child may find that it overtaxes her and her family's financial or emotional resources. The unmarried mother will suffer the stigma of having an illegitimate child. Thus, determining whether or not to bear a child is of fundamental importance to a woman.

The Connecticut anti-abortion laws take from women the power to determine whether or not to have a child once conception has occurred. In 1860, when these statutes were enacted in their present form, women had few rights. Since then, however, their status in our society has changed dramatically. From being wholly excluded from political matters, they have secured full access to the political arena. From the home, they have moved into industry; now some 30 million women comprise forty percent of the work force. And as women's roles have changed, so have societal attitudes. The recently passed equal rights statute and the pending equal rights amendment demonstrate that society now considers women the equal of men.

The changed role of women in society and the changed attitudes toward them reflect the societal judgment that women can competently order their own lives and that they are the appropriate decisionmakers about matters affecting their fundamental concerns. Thus, surveying the public on the issue of abortion, the Rockefeller Commission on Population and the American Future found that fully 94% of the American public favored abortion under some circumstances and the Commission itself recommended that the "matter of abortion should be left to the conscience of the individual concerned." Similarly, the Supreme Court has said, "If the right of privacy means anything, it is the right of the individual, married or single, to be free from unwarranted governmental intrusion into matters so fundamentally affecting a person as the decision whether to bear or beget a child." Eisenstadt v. Baird (1972); Griswold v. Connecticut (1965).

The state has argued that the statutes may be justified as attempts to balance the rights of the fetus against the rights of the woman. While the Connecticut courts have not so construed the statutes,[1] we accept this characterization as one fairly drawn from the face of the statutes. Nevertheless we hold that the state's interest in striking this balance as it has is insufficient to warrant removing from the woman all decisionmaking power over whether to terminate a pregnancy.

The state interest in taking the determination not to have children from the woman is, because of changing societal conditions, far less substantial than it was at the time of the passage of the statutes. The Malthusian specter, only a dim shadow in the past, has caused grave concern in recent years as the world's population has increased beyond all previous estimates. Unimpeachable studies have indicated the importance of slowing or halting population growth. And with the decline in mortality rates, high fertility is no longer necessary to societal survival. Legislative and judicial responses to these considerations are evidenced by the fact that within the last three years 16 legislatures have passed liberalized abortion laws and 13 courts have struck down restrictive anti-abortion statutes similar to those of Connecticut. In short, population growth must be restricted, not enhanced, and thus the state interest in pronatalist statutes such as these is limited.

Moreover, these statutes restrict a woman's choice in instances in which the state interest is virtually nil. The statutes force a woman to carry to natural term a pregnancy that is the result of rape or incest. Yet these acts are prohibited by the

[1] The statutes, infrequently considered by the Connecticut courts, have been construed as advancing two distinct legislative goals: inhibition of promiscuous sexual relationships by prohibiting escape from unintentional pregnancy, and the protection of pregnant women from the dangers of nineteenth century surgery. However laudable a purpose the goal of reducing the frequency of promiscuous sexual relationships may have been considered one hundred years ago, it does not amount to a compelling interest today in the face of changed moral standards. Moreover, advances in medical science since 1860 have made abortion in the early stages of pregnancy no more dangerous than childbirth. Only a narrowly drawn statute prohibiting abortions endangering the life of the pregnant woman would be justified in light of a legislative intent to protect the woman's health.

state at least in part to avoid the offspring of such unions. Forcing a woman to carry and bear a child resulting from such criminal violations of privacy cruelly stigmatizes her in the eyes of society. Similarly, the statutes require a woman to carry to natural term a fetus likely to be born a mental or physical cripple. But the state has less interest in the birth of such a child than a woman has in terminating such a pregnancy. For the state to deny therapeutic abortion in these cases is an overreaching of the police power.

Balancing the interests, we find that the fundamental nature of the decision to have an abortion and its importance to the woman involved are unquestioned, that in a changing society women have been recognized as the appropriate decisionmakers over matters regarding their fundamental concerns, that because of the population crisis the state interest in these statutes is less than when they were passed and that, because of their great breadth, the statutes intrude into areas in which the state has little interest. We conclude that the state's interests are insufficient to take from the woman the decision after conception whether she will bear a child and that she, as the appropriate decisionmaker, must be free to choose. What was considered to be due process with respect to permissible abortion in 1860 is not due process in 1972.

The essential requirement of due process is that the woman be given the power to determine within an appropriate period after conception whether or not she wishes to bear a child. Of course, nothing prohibits the state from promulgating reasonable health and safety regulations surrounding abortion procedures.

In holding the statutes unconstitutional, we grant only declaratory relief to this effect as there is no reason to believe that the state will not obey our mandate.

NEWMAN, DISTRICT JUDGE (CONCURRING IN THE RESULT)

I fully agree with Judge Lumbard's conclusion that the plaintiffs are entitled to a judgment declaring the Connecticut abortion statutes unconstitutional, but my reasons for reaching that conclusion cover somewhat less ground. Moreover, having found the statutes unconstitutional, I would grant plaintiff Doe injunctive relief.

...[T]he question to be faced is whether the state interests being advanced in 1860 are today sufficient to justify the invasion of the mother's liberty. I agree with Judge Lumbard that protecting the mother's health, which plainly was a state interest in 1860 and may well have provided a valid state interest for these statutes when enacted, will not furnish a subordinating state interest today, when the mother's life is exposed to less risk by abortion than by childbirth.

The second justification advanced by the state, protecting the mother's morals, may well have been an objective in 1860. This justification apparently proceeds from the premise that if abortion is prohibited, the threat of having to bear a child will deter a woman from sexual intercourse. Protecting the morals of the mother thus turns out to mean deterring her from having sexual relations. But the Supreme Court has decided that such a purpose cannot validate invasion of a woman's right to privacy in matters of family and sex. Griswold v. Connecticut (1965); Eisenstadt v. Baird (1971).

That leaves the state's third justification, protecting the life of the unborn child. Judge Lumbard is willing to assume this was a purpose of the 1860 legislature and finds it constitutionally insufficient. Judge Clarie concludes it was in fact a purpose of the 1860 legislature and finds it constitutionally sufficient. With deference, I am persuaded that protecting the life of the unborn child was most likely not a purpose of the 1860 legislature. At a minimum it has not been shown with sufficient certainty that this was the legislature's purpose as to warrant a weighing of this purpose against the mother's constitutionally protected rights. Whether a fetus is to be considered the sort of "life" entitled to the legal safeguards normally available to a person after birth is undeniably a matter of deep religious and philosophical dispute. If the Connecticut legislature had made a judgment on this issue and had enacted laws to accord such protection to the unborn child, the constitutionality of such laws would pose a legal question of extreme difficulty, since the legislative judgment on this subject would be entitled to careful consideration. Compare with Byrn v. New York City Health & Hospitals Corporation (N.Y. 1972).... Since that legislative determination has not been shown to have been made, I think it is inappropriate to decide the constitutional issue that would be posed if such a legislative justification was before us.

Because I believe the only interests which the 1860 legislature was seeking to advance are not today sufficient to justify invasion of the plaintiff's constitutionally protected rights, I join with Judge Lumbard in holding these statutes unconstitutional.

....

CLARIE, DISTRICT JUDGE (DISSENTING):

I respectfully disagree and accordingly dissent from the majority opinion. This Court's bold assumption of judicial-legislative power to strike down a time-tested

Connecticut Statute constitutes an unwarranted federal judicial intrusion into the legislative sphere. The state legislature long ago made a basic choice between two conflicting human values. It chose to uphold the right of the human fetus to life over a woman's right to privacy and self-determination in sexual and family matters. The legislature has repeatedly refused to alter this decision to the present date.

The majority has reached out and grasped at the nebulous supposition that the protection of fetal life is not the purpose of the Connecticut anti-abortion laws. This assumption is unwarranted. The history of these statutes indicates that they were designed to protect fetal life.

....

PRIOR TO 1860, the Connecticut statutes concerned only abortions performed upon a woman "quick with child." This indicates a legislative determination that human "life" began at that point. The statute of 1860 amended that law to forbid abortion at any stage of fetal development. This amendment reflected a legislative judgment that fetal life at any stage merited the protection of the law. If the primary purpose of the anti-abortion laws was to protect the woman from the dangers of 19th century surgical techniques, as the majority suggests, it is impossible to understand why the original law prohibited abortions only after quickening. Certainly, the risk of infection caused by unsterilized instruments was as great before the fetus had quickened.

....

THE CASE OF *GRISWOLD*, which is relied upon by the majority, decided that the state could not, consistent with the zone of privacy emanating from the Bill of Rights, completely prohibit the use of contraceptives. The Court ruled that prohibiting contraceptives served no compelling state purpose. However, this decision is not applicable to the facts of the present case. It is one thing to prevent the impregnation of the ovum by the spermatozoa, and quite another to deliberately destroy newly formed human life. Different values are invoked. While the marital privacy referred to in *Griswold* limits itself to the personal conjugal relationship of only two people, abortion projects itself far beyond the bounds of personal intimacy. It is directed against an innocent victim, a third human being endowed with unique genetic characteristics....

The majority cite as an extreme illustration that the Connecticut law proscribes abortions, even in situations where the pregnancy is the result of incest or rape, or where there is a likelihood that the child will be born with a serious mental or physical defect. While it is conceded that such pregnancies and births are often fraught with personal hardship, the proper forum in which to present and test such concerns is the legislature....

The people, acting through their legislature, have in effect decreed that this new life is an innocent victim, not an unjust aggressor.

....

CERTAINLY, THE REPEATED failure of the successive attempts to repeal or liberalize the anti-abortion laws can be attributed realistically, only to a legislative determination to protect fetal life. As recently as December 10, 1968, the Legislative Council recommended to the legislature that no legislative action should be taken on the proposal to liberalize our present laws on abortion. At page 10 in this report, it stated:

> The Council feels that should an unborn child become a thing rather than a person in the minds of people, in any stage of its development, the dignity of human life is in jeopardy. The family, too, which is the very basis of our society, would be minimized or perhaps destroyed.

The aforesaid conclusion by the legislative leaders leaves no room to question, but that their real concern was the protection of fetal life.

....

IT SHOULD BE NOTED that the majority decision leaves the State of Connecticut with no law or control in this area of human relationships. It invites unlimited foeticide (the murder of unborn human beings), as a way of life, in a state long known as the land of steady habits. The Connecticut legislature has historically, consistently, and affirmatively expressed its determination to safeguard and respect human life. The action of the majority constitutes an unwarranted federal judicial intrusion into the legislative sphere of state government. The judiciary was never intended nor designed to perform such a function. I would uphold the constitutionality of the challenged state statutes and deny relief.

Excerpted from *Abele v. Markle*, 351 F. Supp. 224, United States District Court for the District of Connecticut (1972).

Connecticut Legislative Hearing Testimony

Soon after the court declared Connecticut's abortion laws unconstitutional—and just one day before Governor Rockefeller vetoed the New York legislature's attempt to repeal the state's 1970 liberal abortion statute—Connecticut's governor Thomas Meskill called for the legislature to enact a new law. The new abortion bill, introduced in a special ses-

sion of the assembly, closely resembled the law the court had invalidated, but authorized even more severe punishment for its violation. In response to Judge Newman's opinion, the bill featured a new preamble, which stated that the legislative intent in passing the bill "is to protect and preserve human life from the moment of conception."

Citizens from all over the state spoke out at a hearing on the bill that would recriminalize abortion in Connecticut. As the historian Amy Kesselman observes, "The atmosphere at the hearing held by the Joint Committee on Public Health and Safety on May 19, 1972, was light-years away from the hearings held three years earlier on the reform bill sponsored by the Connecticut Medical Society.... The rhetoric had...changed on both sides." Doctors spoke less of "their own professional prerogatives" and more about the needs and rights of women patients, and a number of the speakers opposing abortion—including the representative of the Family Life Bureau of the Diocese of Bridgeport—"felt it necessary to declare their respect for women's rights before speaking against abortion."

[Connecticut State Representative Dr. Morris] Cohen:

...[D]o you think it wise for us legislators to pass a law which is clearly unpopular in the State? To pass legislation which the public apparently do not want and wouldn't we be putting ourselves in the same position, if we did, that happened in the 1920s when we passed the Volstead Act which was so unpopular (that was the Prohibition Law) that was before your time—which was so unpopular that it had to be repealed, and it was impossible to enforce it and, at the same time, we are facing the same situation in the State today, I believe, that we are not enforcing the law as we had it because there are clinics in the State that are performing abortions and people can get abortions and many hospitals in the State are performing abortions on their—what they call a D&C—and since many of our people go to New York to get abortions, is it wise for us as legislators to pass legislation which might go down the drain and become unpopular...?

Representative Francis J. Collins:

If I can reply to those series of questions, Doctor, I don't agree to your analogy of the Volstead Act. I do think that we have an obligation as members of this body representing the public at large to enact things whether they be popular or unpopular. I don't agree with your conclusions that this is a very unpopular cause by any means. I think that it is a matter of opinion. Certainly, my mail, the comments that I get from my constituency does not concur with yours.... In any event, I do think this is a matter that the State must act on, particularly in view of the fact that at the present time, since the Federal court has ruled that the present law we

have is unconstitutional, we now have no law. I think that that is wrong. I think
we should have a law. I think the law when it's on the books, I concur with you in
that respect, the law should be enforced.

Attorney Catherine Roraback:

...I would like to note for the record that I am, in fact, the first female speaker on
this issue and I am also a little aware of the fact that the Committee sitting up
there on the podium and so forth, the women members seem to be relegated to
the lower row.

I was invited here to speak today as one of the attorneys [for the Women versus Connecticut case, see *Abele v. Markle* (Conn. 1972), discussed in Part II.B]....
However, today I wish to speak not as a lawyer, but as a woman and I wish speak
on behalf of my clients and I am going to read at this time, as that testimony, a
statement prepared being filed on behalf of all the lawyers in that suit....

We are here to speak as women on behalf of the 1,700 women in Connecticut
who join together to strike down the ban on abortion in this State. We want to
present to you a few facts of life—facts of life for women. These are facts we feel
are important for you to remember if you are to clearly understand the feelings
of women concerning abortions. In the first place, you should know that the risk
of death in childbirth is far greater than that arising from a medical abortion.
Indeed, abortion in the first trimester of pregnancy is almost seven times safer
than carrying the pregnancy to term, but even where this is not involved the consequences for the woman of carrying the pregnancy to term and delivering a child
may have serious medical implications for her. In any other circumstance, a doctor
would be free and indeed would be called upon by his professional obligation to
provide appropriate medical service. Here, however, the doctor is prohibited to
providing the care called for because of the criminal statutes.... Even if the woman
does not have medical indications calling for an abortion, yet the alternative of
enforced child-bearing has huge implications for her. Probably nothing but death
itself can affect a woman's life more seriously than enforce bearing of children and
enforced responsibility for them perhaps for the remainder of her and their lives.
The birth of a child is the beginning of a responsibility which affects every aspect
of this woman's life and does so for her lifetime. Even before childbirth, she will
probably lose her employment, at least temporarily, and during that lay-off she is
not entitled to receive unemployment compensation benefits. Indeed, in this State
she is ineligible for such benefits for a period of two months before childbirth and

for two months after. Afterwards, the woman that has given birth to a child will find her employment opportunities severely limited. Given the primary responsibility of home care of the child, the woman has less mobility, sometimes has to be away from the job and often is only able to give secondary attention to her job. The employer sees her as a less desirable employee. This has ramifications for the whole family. Family income and living standards may well be affected. The woman who has previously had children and returns to the job market is unable to continue so during a current pregnancy—thus the whole family suffers.

   ....

THIS HAS RAMIFICATIONS for the whole family. Furthermore, if the woman was a student at the time of the pregnancy, she will probably be forced to drop out of school or be greatly restricted in her school activities and education if she comes to term. This may be required by school regulations. It may be necessary for only physical reasons; on the other hand, she may have to do so in order to care for the child. The interruption of her education and training, for whatever reason and whatever level, places her and her family at a permanent disadvantage because her capacities will never be fully trained or utilized. Perhaps more important are the psychiatric and the emotional ramifications for the woman, the child and the family if she has to carry the unwanted pregnancy to term. The economic factor alone can create psychological and emotional stress for the woman and the family, a stress which ultimately affects the unwanted child born into such a situation. Yet, it is not only the economic factor that is relevant.... Children who are unwanted suffer from emotional starvation, often exhibit delayed physical and mental development; they cannot do as well in school, have greater need for psychiatric care, have a higher incidence of juvenile delinquency and child welfare referrals, and later in life need greater public assistance. A Connecticut woman faced with an unwanted pregnancy and desiring an abortion can, of course, go to New York. To do so, though, she makes arrangements at home for her family, pays for her travel, and pays for the operation and for accommodations away from home. If she chooses another jurisdiction where psychiatric evaluation [and] opinion...are a prerequisite to abortion, even greater expense is involved. Quite apart from the money involved you should think of the woman's emotional and physical stress having to be away from home during such a procedure.

   ....[Request from State Senator to summarize her point]

   It's the first time the women's point of view has been presented to this Hearing. It's the first time these very important factors, which are involved in her choices, are being presented in a sort of testimony that I understood that you and the Com-

mittee were looking for. The types of considerations we think you should consider.
....

...For centuries, women who have needed abortions have gotten them; they will continue to do so. The real question is who will perform them and how they will be done—by a trained doctor in a clean medical facility or by a dirty old man—in a back room. When women are forced by circumstances to seek abortions, they should be able to have them in dignity and safety. We call upon the State of Connecticut and this Committee to assure to women that right.

Mrs. Richard Albright:

Mr. Chairman, I have over 6,000 signatures from New London and Norwich area against abortion ready to be delivered to you now.
....

MEMBERS OF THE COMMITTEE and Ladies and Gentlemen, my name, as I have stated, is Mrs. Richard Albright. My religion is a Mormon and I am the wife of a Mormon bishop. I have kept myself pretty much up-to-date on the pros and cons of legalizing abortion. One major issue which is constantly brought up by those who would have legalized abortion is that women should have complete control over their bodies and the final say as to whether or not they should carry life. This I completely agree with; however, a baby's body belongs to him and it is a separate body from that of the mother. If you think you should be able to control your own bodies, why would you get pregnant in the first place. There the control of your body goes out the window. The simple fact is if you have relations with a member of the opposite sex of your own free will and become pregnant as a result, then this is the risk you took with your eyes wide open to the fact of what could happen. If you know this and realize that you want it this way, why should the result of your act be up to someone else to take away? The logic behind this whole issue if you don't want a pregnancy, don't do anything to get pregnant. What is being said is that I want my fun and my pleasure but if I get caught, I refuse the responsibilities of my action. I suppose responsibility for one's actions is becoming a thing of the past. Someday the problem of overpopulating our homes for the aged will become so acute that our liberals will again get up on the bandwagon and because they can't solve the problem, they will legalize the inhumane murder of our elderly at a certain age. Don't think it couldn't happen; a few years ago no one worth her salt could have considered killing her unborn baby. Yet, here it is.

Down through the ages women have been getting pregnant out of wedlock.

They have survived without an abortion. They accepted their responsibility and saw it through to completion. Namely, putting their babies out for adoption or keeping them if they had the means to do so.

Now, first of all, what is wrong with adoption? If you can be so cold as to justify in your mind the killing of your baby, some at even six months of pregnancy, why couldn't you go the rest of the way in your pregnancy and give your baby the chance for life, to a family who would love it and above all want it? So many couples today are going through life childless because of some medical reason and cannot adopt because babies just are not available. After being told by several adoption agencies that it would be impossible to adopt and after the strong advice of several doctors not to try to have another child because of my poor health,...we prayed about it and decided to try again. When I did become pregnant, my doctors offered me a very legal abortion at Yale-New Haven Hospital and each time now that I feel my baby moving inside of me I thank God for entrusting this little one to me, to love and for just the privilege of bringing life into this world. It is a blessing He gave to each and every woman whether they believe it or not—it's a gift. It is such a shame to know that some of His female children would take this gift and slap Him in the face with it and feel it a curse. It is a disgrace that some women have to protect themselves from other women. Surely with all the contraceptive advice made available to us, a married couple that really feels that after praying about it that they shouldn't have another pregnancy because of health or finances, should seek out these devices. Finally, the opposition would tell us that legalizing abortion would just be for the ones who wanted it and it would still be their free choice. I say in answer to this if a young girl becomes pregnant out of wedlock her first thought is sheer panic. What should she do? Should she seek out an abortion or go through her pregnancy and put her baby out for adoption. If abortion is made legal, then in all probability she will if she is weak take the easy way out, but if she has to struggle to get an abortion she may go the other way and take the responsibility of her action.... Every time I look at our little adopted child which we have, I thank God over and over for her and her biological mother that thought enough of God and her priceless womanhood to go through with her pregnancy and I thank her also for giving us a beautiful baby made in His own image to raise with our two natural children and to love so deeply. Thank you.

....

Mrs. Thomas Licciardello:

Ladies and gentlemen. My name is Trudy Licciardello, Mrs. Thomas Licciardello from Trumbull. I am a housewife, a practicing Episcopalian and since April, 1971, President of the Greater Bridgeport Planned Parenthood. I would like to speak against Governor Meskill's proposed anti-abortion bill.

I personally have been very fortunate, having had four pregnancies, each of which resulted in a normal baby after an uneventful course. I did not have heart failure of the sort which forbids carrying a baby to term, and I never caught German measles or one of the other viral infections which deforms a fetus. Luckily after each of my deliveries, I recovered without the nightmare of postpartum psychosis which strikes many women, the sort of homicidal or suicidal destructiveness which, if lived through, precludes against repeating the process of childbearing. My family life is such that I have never been forced to become pregnant, as some women literally are, against my will; and my chosen method of birth control has proven effective.

However, I know these fortunate conditions are not the result of my own virtue, and that the opposite could easily have been the case, so that instead of having four children I might have had to have three children and an abortion, or two children and an abortion. No woman wants to need an abortion. She finds herself forced to because of the conditions of her life. All women want wholesomeness, and if married, husbands who'll support them and stay with them and if children, then children who are intact and pure and well fed. I suggest that a lawmaker who votes for the Meskill proposal is not championing a defenseless fetus, so much as tormenting an already distressed woman. Do not deceive yourselves that the object of Governor Meskill's law would be some fantasied wayward hussy in need of punishment. She is more likely to be a law-abiding circumspect woman, married, but sick in body or in mind. Certainly she will be poor, for those who can afford to do so will travel to some other place to have their operations. She'll probably be someone with a husband and children at home who need her back in good health and good spirits. Do not be glib and fancy yourselves more loving than the woman who must have an abortion. The legislator who supports Governor Meskill's proposal indulges himself in a deliberate act of tight-lipped cruelty. He would be harsh and presumptuous and this is a time which calls for self-discipline on his part, and an understanding of some of the tragedies of other people's lives.

....

Frances Harwood:

I am Frances Harwood, Assistant Professor of Anthropology. I live in Middletown, Connecticut. I would like to say that a number of speakers today have stressed the control by women over their own bodies. I would be for this entirely. However, it is often out of our hands. I was assaulted and raped six years ago. I was impregnated at that time. I then had to make a decision. I did not want the child. I did not think I could care for it and so I went and obtained an abortion. I had five hundred dollars in my savings, luckily. For those who don't, things can get and be much worse. You go, you put the cash on the barrelhead and it is then done, often without any anesthesia. In my case, the abortionist insisted on further intercourse. This is not something that women should be subjected to. I ask you therefore if this legislation cannot be written in such a way as to make sure that these individuals do not practice abortion without a license. How many abortionists, illegal abortionists have been arrested under the old law which was recently declared unconstitutional? Does anyone on the committee have a notion of that in numbers?

....

...It is really important that these people be put out of business. I don't think that the bill 6002 will suppress abortion. I think abortions will go underground and the risk of danger is much greater. I urge you, therefore, to support liberalized abortion where those who require or would like an abortion can have it done in a therapeutic and supportive setting. Thank you.

Excerpted from transcript of Joint Standing Committee on Public Health and Safety, Connecticut Legislature, Hearing on Abortion, May 19, 1972.

Memorandum of Decision, *Abele v. Markle* II (September 20, 1972)

Responding to the energetic advocacy of Governor Meskill, the Connecticut Citizens Right to Life Committee, and the Connecticut Catholic Conference, state legislators re-enacted the state's criminal abortion statute, raising maximum penalties from two to five years and resisting efforts to include an exception for rape. "There's no question what I would have had to contend with if I had voted against the abortion bill," said House Majority Leader Carl R. Ajello at the time. Ajello continued, "There are five Catholic churches in my area, and they told their worshipers in no uncertain terms what my

position should be. I never received so many postcards, letters, petitions and phone calls."
Amy Kesselman quotes another legislator as reporting that "[t]he impetus for the bill
as it was drafted...came directly from the Hartford archdiocese. They didn't want any
loopholes, and there weren't any." Another, who switched his vote to support the bill,
confessed that "the governor hands out all the goodies, and when he really wants to put
the pressure on, it works."

On September 20, 1972, the same panel of judges who had declared Connecticut's
abortion laws unconstitutional just a few months earlier did so again. Judge Newman,
this time writing for the majority, held that women have a constitutional right of pri-
vacy that is infringed when the state criminalizes all abortion. However, this right,
he explained, is not unlimited. Rather, the right may be balanced against the state's
legitimate interest in protecting fetal life. Newman's opinion, excerpted here, begins to
outline a framework for balancing these interests that hinges on viability—the ability of
the fetus to survive outside of the uterus. This is the framework that Justice Blackmun
developed in Roe.

Newman, District Judge

The issue in this case is the constitutionality of Connecticut's recently enacted
law prohibiting all abortions except those necessary to save the physical life of the
mother.

....

The substantive provisions of the 1972 legislation prohibiting abortions are
quite similar to the 1860 statutes. However, the 1860 exception which had permitted an abortion when necessary to preserve the life of the woman or that of the
unborn child has been limited in the new statute to an abortion "necessary to
preserve the physical life of the mother." The maximum penalties which had been
two years for the woman, five years for performing an abortion, and one year for
encouraging an abortion have all been set at five years. More significantly, while
the former statutes made no explicit reference to the state interest they were pur-
porting to advance, the first section of the 1972 legislation reads as follows: "The
public policy of the state and the intent of the legislature is to protect and preserve
human life from the moment of conception...."

Thus the Connecticut General Assembly has expressed its judgment, in the
text of the challenged statute, that the life of a fetus should be protected. That
specification of legislative purpose raises the constitutional question of whether
the state has power to advance such a purpose by abridging almost totally the constitutionally protected right of a woman to privacy and personal choice in matters

of sex and family life.

The existence of a woman's constitutional right to such privacy has been set forth by the Supreme Court. Eisenstadt v. Baird (1972); Griswold v. Connecticut (1965). Indeed, *Baird* may have anticipated the outcome of cases such as this when the Court observed:

> If the right of privacy means anything, it is the right of the *individual,* married or single, to be free from unwarranted governmental intrusion into matters so fundamentally affecting a person as the decision whether to *bear* or beget a child.
>
> ....

But there are two distinguishing aspects of this case that require consideration before the state interest can be weighed against the woman's right. The first concerns the nature of the rights possessed by the fetus for whose benefit the state interest is asserted. The second concerns the nature of the state interest being asserted.

A. The initial inquiry is whether the fetus is a person, within the meaning of the fourteenth amendment, having a constitutionally protected right to life. If it is, then a legislature may well have some discretion to protect that right even at the expense of someone else's constitutional right. But if the fetus lacks constitutional rights, the question then becomes whether a legislature may accord a purely statutory right at the expense of another person's constitutional right.

Our conclusion, based on the text and history of the Constitution and on cases interpreting it, is that a fetus is not a person within the meaning of the fourteenth amendment. There is nothing in the history of that amendment nor in its interpretation by the Supreme Court to give any support whatever to the contention that a fetus has constitutional rights. No decision has come to our attention holding that a fetus has fourteenth amendment rights. The issue was squarely faced by at least two of the courts that have sustained the constitutionality of state laws permitting abortions: *Byrn v. New York City Health & Hospitals Corp.* (N.Y. 1972) and *McGarvey v. Magee-Woman's Hospital* (W.D.Pa. 1971). *Byrn* and *McGarvey* reject the claim that a fetus has fourteenth amendment rights. Indeed, it is difficult to imagine how a statute permitting abortion could be constitutional if the fetus had fourteenth amendment rights....

If the fetus survives the period of gestation, it will be born and then become a person entitled to the legal protections of the Constitution. But its capacity to become such a person does not mean that during gestation it is such a person.

The unfertilized ovum also has the capacity to become a living human being, but the Constitution does not endow it with rights which the state may protect by interfering with the individual's choice of whether the ovum will be fertilized. *Griswold*.

Of course, the fact that a fetus is not a person entitled to fourteenth amendment rights does not mean that government may not confer rights upon it. A wide range of rights has been accorded by statutes and court decisions....

It is one thing to permit a legislature some discretion in adjusting conflicting rights between groups of people, each of whom has a claim to constitutional protection. It is altogether different to suggest that a legislature can accord a statutory right to a fetus which lacks constitutional rights when doing so requires the abridgement of a woman's own constitutional right. No doubt a right to be born is of greater significance than the right to receive compensation for tortious injury or other pecuniary or property rights. But it is doubtful whether the constitutional right of the mother can be totally abridged by a legislative effort to confer even a significant statutory right upon a fetus which does not have any fourteenth amendment rights.

....

IF A STATUTE SOUGHT to protect the lives of all fetuses which could survive outside the uterus, such a statute would be a legislative acceptance of the concept of viability. While authorities may differ on the precise time, there is no doubt that at some point during pregnancy a fetus is capable, with proper medical attention, of surviving outside the uterus. And it is equally clear that there is a minimum point before which survival outside the uterus is not possible. A statute designed to prevent the destruction of fetuses after viability has been reached would be subject to these considerations. Like the present statute, it would be conferring statutory rights on a fetus which does not have constitutional rights. However, the state interest in protecting the life of a fetus capable of living outside the uterus could be shown to be more generally accepted and, therefore, of more weight in the constitutional sense than the interest in preventing the abortion of a fetus that is not viable. The issue might well turn on whether the time period selected could be shown to permit survival of the fetus in a generally accepted sense, rather than for the brief span of hours and under the abnormal conditions illustrated by some of the state's evidence. As to the latter situations, the nature of the state interest might well not be generally accepted. Finally, and most important, such a statute would not be a direct abridgement of the woman's constitutional right, but at most a limitation on the time when her right could be exercised. The present statute, however, does not present any of the considerations favorable to the state that might be found in either type of statute of more limited scope.

For these reasons, we hold, as have most courts that have considered similar statutes, that plaintiffs are entitled to a judgment declaring Public Act No. 1 unconstitutional.

....

Clarie, District Judge (dissenting):

My earlier dissenting opinion in *Abele v. Markle* (D. Conn. 1972) concluded that the Legislature, not the Judiciary, was designed by our founding fathers to reflect the standards of human decency which must be weighed in any choice between the competing moral values which are to guide governmental policy. By reenacting legislation which declared the paramountcy of the human fetus' right to life over a woman's right to privacy, except where it could be demonstrated that the mother's life would be jeopardized, the Connecticut Legislature *reaffirmed* that basic choice.

....

"IN A DEMOCRATIC SOCIETY legislatures, not courts, are constituted to respond to the will and consequently the moral values of the people"...."We should not allow our personal preferences as to the wisdom of legislative and congressional action...to guide our judicial decision." That the majority has taken unto itself the legislative task of measuring degrees of public acceptance is evident in its pronouncement that "the state interest in protecting the life of a fetus capable of living outside the uterus could be shown to be more generally accepted and, therefore, of more weight...."

The constitutional structure of our democracy demands judicial restraint where the choice of human values embodied by a legislative act does not unwarrantedly invade constitutionally protected rights. The Connecticut Legislature has weighed these factual considerations on society's scale of standards of decency.

The Legislature was undoubtedly aware that biologists, fetologists, and medical science commonly accept conception as the beginning of human life and the formation of an individual endowed with its own unique genetic pattern.

....

Similarly available to the Connecticut Legislature were the abortion experience statistics of New York City under that State's statute which allowed abortion upon request. During the twelve-month period from July 1, 1970, through June 30, 1971, in that one city alone, there were officially recorded 139,042 induced abortions; and for the six-month period from July 1, 1971, through December 31, 1971, there were 111,590. If these latter statistics were to be projected on a national population scale, the total number would amount to several million induced deaths of innocent victims annually. It is a legislative choice of societal values, which must decide a public policy of such magnitude, for that choice of values could either demean human life or ennoble mankind's destiny.

All of these considerations were undoubtedly pondered by the Legislature before the determination was made that human life should not be compromised in the name of personal comfort or convenience. It is nothing less than judicial usurpation of a legislative prerogative to decide that at one point in fetal development, through an obscure process of legal metamorphosis (in this case, the degree and quality of "public acceptance") the state may constitutionally protect fetal life, but that prior to such point in time, the state may not protect what it also regards, with substantial popular and medical justification, as human life.

It is for these reasons, and for those expressed in my earlier opinion in *Abele v. Markle, supra,* that I respectfully dissent.

Excerpted from *Abele v. Markle,* 342 F. Supp. 800, United States District Court for the District of Connecticut (1972).

CROSSCURRENTS IN
THE NATIONAL ARENA, 1972

The abortion conflict had spread across the nation. When Judge Lumbard struck down Connecticut's 19th-century statute in April 1972, he observed that "within the last three years 16 legislatures have passed liberalized abortion laws and 13 courts have struck down restrictive anti-abortion statutes similar to those of Connecticut." As the pace of change accelerated, conflict escalated and assumed constitutional form. Advocates for repeal and their opponents both argued from first principles and expressed these arguments about the just polity as claims on the Constitution. Those who supported change began to assert the right to be free of legal coercion in decisions concerning child bearing—and went to court when they were unable to move the legislature to respond. They inspired their opponents to respond similarly. And with the aid of the Catholic Church, those who opposed change were increasingly able to draw voters into the political arena on a single-issue basis to block abortion's liberalization.

In what follows, we trace these developments in constitutional politics as they reverberated in the national arena in 1972—a year that saw Congress send the Equal Rights Amendment to the states for ratification and Richard Nixon defeat George McGovern in the campaign for president. In the first several excerpts, we follow discussion of abortion in a sex discrimination-equal protection case that Ruth Bader Ginsburg took to the Supreme Court; in the recommendation of the Rockefeller Commission report on population control; and in polls conducted by Gallup. These selections reflect the increasing association of abortion rights with the equal citizenship claims of the women's movement, and increasing support for the liberalization of abortion laws, with majorities supporting decriminalization even among Catholics and Republicans.

We then consider President Nixon's repudiation of the Rockefeller Commission's recommendation that states liberalize their abortion laws—and situate his shifting position on abortion in the context of the 1972 presidential campaign. As we shall see, strategists for the Republican Party had identified Catholics as a group that might be persuaded to shift its party allegiance and by 1972, had begun to focus on abortion as an issue that might serve this end. As importantly, wider social conflict had begun to reshape abortion's meaning. By 1972, opponents of the Equal Rights Amendment and of McGovern's bid for the presidency began to frame abortion as a symbol of women's liberation and of a new morality that they encouraged Americans, of all faiths, to oppose.

Plaintiff's Brief, *Struck v. Secretary of Defense* (December 4, 1972)

Abortion policy in the military provides a window on shifting attitudes in the growing national conflict. In 1970, the Department of Defense had quietly adopted a policy permitting military hospitals to perform therapeutic abortions, regardless of the law of the state in which the hospital was located. But less than a year after the directive had been promulgated, President Nixon revoked the policy, using the occasion to declare for the first time his stance on abortion. "Historically," he explained, "laws regulating abortion in the United States have been the province of States, not the Federal Government.... That is where the decisions should be made." As states made these decisions, he continued, Americans had "a right to know [his] personal views." Based on his "personal and religious beliefs," he considered "abortion an unacceptable form of population control." Further, "unrestricted abortion policies, or abortion on demand" could not be "square[d] with [his] personal belief in the sanctity of human life."

But there was yet another abortion policy governing the small, but growing, number of women who served in the military. An air force regulation provided that: "A woman officer shall be discharged from the service with the least practical delay when a determination is made by a medical officer that she is pregnant" or "has given birth to a living child," unless the "pregnancy is terminated." In other words, military policy required female air force officers who became pregnant to abort the pregnancy or lose their jobs.

Captain Susan R. Struck, a career officer in the air force, became pregnant while serving in Vietnam. Captain Struck was subject to immediate discharge. Although legal abortion was available to her, as a Catholic, she decided she had no choice but to have the baby, which she gave up for adoption nine days after birth. Subject to discharge, she went to court. Represented by the American Civil Liberties Union, Struck obtained a stay of the discharge but lost on the merits in both the United States District Court in Seattle and in the United States Court of Appeals for the Ninth Circuit. The United States Supreme Court agreed to hear her appeal.

But before the case was argued, the air force amended the regulation to permit government officials to waive enforcement of the policy—perhaps out of concern about the adverse publicity that enforcing the policy might generate. In November 1972, the military decided to waive the policy in Struck's case, and the Court dismissed the appeal as moot.

Ruth Bader Ginsburg, cofounder of the ACLU's Women's Rights Project, had already filed a 70-page Supreme Court brief on Captain Struck's behalf, arguing that the regulation violated the rights of military women to equal protection, due process, privacy, and—in the case of women with religious-based opposition to abortion—the free exercise of religion. The brief in Struck v. Secretary of Defense *was one of Ginsburg's earliest equal protection briefs, filed in 1972, the same year that Congress sent the Equal Rights Amendment to the states for ratification. Ginsburg's brief linked women's right to equal protection of the laws to their right to privacy in decisions concerning family life. It sought for women the same opportunity as men to combine work and family, and argued that women's decisions whether or not to bear children should be free from government coercion. It is this principle of noncoercion that links equal protection and privacy arguments in* Struck—*and links the claim for abortion rights to the claim to freedom from coerced abortion and sterilization.*

III. The sex-based classification in the Air Force regulation applied to petitioner, directing discharge for pregnancy, a physical condition unique to the female sex, while no other temporary physical condition occasions peremptory discharge, is inconsistent with the equal protection principle inherent in the due process clause of the fifth amendment.

....

B. ...[T]he court below should have subjected the involuntary discharge for pregnancy regulation to close scrutiny, identifying sex as a "suspect" criterion for governmental distinctions.

In very recent years, a new appreciation of women's place has been generated in the United States. Activated by feminists of both sexes, legislatures and courts have begun to recognize and respond to the subordinate position of women in our society and the second-class status our institutions historically have imposed upon them. The heightened national awareness that equal opportunity for men and women is a matter of simple justice has led to significant reform, most notably on the federal level....

....

FOR A LARGE SEGMENT of the female labor force, gainful employment is dictated by economic necessity.... Discharge for pregnancy, attended by termination of income and fringe benefits, and denial of the right to return after childbirth, disables these women far more than their temporary physical condition.

For the more fortunate woman, for whom work is not dictated by economic necessity, mandatory pregnancy discharge reinforces societal pressure to relinquish career aspirations for a hearth-centered existence. Loss of her job and accumulated benefits profoundly affect the choices open to her....

....

Petitioner was presumed unfit for service under a regulation that declares, without regard to fact, that she fits "into the stereotyped vision...of the 'correct' female response to pregnancy." This Court has several times considered the "rationality" of presumptions of the kind operative here.... Based on a sexual stereotype no less invidious that one racial or religious, the regulation is patently unreasonable and constitutionally infirm.

....

The discriminatory treatment required by the challenged regulation, barring pregnant women and mothers from continued service in the Air Force, reflects the discredited notion that a woman who becomes pregnant is not fit for duty, but should be confined to the home to await childbirth and thereafter devote herself to child care. Imposition of this outmoded standard upon petitioner unconstitutionally encroaches upon her right to privacy in the conduct of her personal life.

Individual privacy with respect to procreation and intimate personal relations is a right firmly embedded in this nation's tradition and in the precedent of this Court. *Griswold v. Connecticut* (1965) emphatically reaffirmed the Court's position on the fundamental right to personal privacy....

The Air Force regulation applied to petitioner substantially infringes upon her right to sexual privacy, and her autonomy in deciding "whether to bear...a child." ...Her "choice" operates in one direction only. If she wishes to continue her Air Force career, she must not give birth to a child.

Significantly, men in the Air Force are not "encouraged," on pain of discharge, to use contraceptives and avoid fatherhood.... [T]he plain fact is that no regulation discourages men in the Air Force, whether married or single, from fathering children. If a man and a woman, both Captains in the Air Force, conceive a child, the man is free to continue his service career, but the woman is subject to involuntary discharge.

....

IF A SERVICEMAN AND a servicewoman conceive a child, the serviceman is not even disciplined; on the other hand, the servicewoman is discharged, regardless of who is responsible for the failure of contraception, if indeed either is responsible. On what rational basis does the Air Force assume that a woman alone bears responsibility for a planned or unplanned pregnancy?

Brief for the petitioner, *Struck v. Secretary of Defense*, No. 72–178 (U.S. Supreme Court, December 4, 1972).

Rockefeller Commission Report

When President Richard M. Nixon called for a major study of the role of population growth in July 1969, he declared, "One of the most serious challenges to human destiny in the last third of this century will be the growth of the population." Congress responded by chartering the Commission on Population Growth and the American Future, usually known as the Rockefeller Commission, after its chairman, philanthropist John D. Rockefeller III. The commission's 24 members, most appointed by Nixon, spent two years studying the issues.

On May 5, 1972, the commission presented its three-volume report to the president. The report was wide ranging in analysis and recommendations. The commission understood its recommendations concerning population growth as not only "increasing public knowledge of the causes and consequences of population change," and "facilitating and guiding the processes of population movement," but also "maximizing information about human reproduction and its consequences for the family, and enabling individuals to avoid unwanted fertility."

The Rockefeller report addressed the implications of unrestrained population growth for the planet and for persons, in terms inflected by concerns of ecology and equality. "[U]nfortunately, for many of our citizens, quality of life is still defined only as enough food, clothing, and shelter. All human beings need a sense of their own dignity and worth, a sense of belonging and sharing, and the opportunity to develop their individual potentialities." The report took care to distance itself from race- and class-based claims about population control and instead spoke of population control in terms that advanced understandings of human dignity, freedom, and equality advocated by

*contemporary civil rights movements, although in more temperate terms. The report
contained more than 70 policy recommendations, which advocated for social supports
ranging from sex education and contraception, to government housing aid aimed at
diminishing residential "racial polarization," to support for child care and ratification
of the Equal Rights Amendment.*

*By the time the commission presented its report to Nixon, countermobilization
against the Equal Rights Amendment had begun, and, as we have seen, opponents of
abortion repeal were organizing to recriminalize abortion in New York and Connecticut. Advisors to the president encouraged him to align himself with these efforts in the
interests of his reelection campaign. As we will see, the president shifted ground and chose
to distance himself from the report's recommendations.*

CHAPTER 7: SOCIAL ASPECTS
Racial and Ethnic Minorities

...This nation cannot hope to successfully address the question of future population without also addressing the complex network of unemployment, poor housing, poor health services, and poor education, all of which combine to act upon,
and react to, the pressures of population.

At the outset, we must recognize that our population problems cannot be
resolved simply by inducing our "have-not" groups to limit the number of children they have. Although the fertility of minority groups is higher than that of
the rest of the population, it is not they who bear the primary responsibility for
population growth.

Despite their higher fertility rates, minorities—precisely because of their
smaller numbers—contribute less to population growth than does the rest of the
population....

    ....

THE IDEA THAT OUR population growth is primarily fueled by the poor and the
minorities having lots of babies is a myth. There is nonetheless a strong relationship between high fertility and the economic and social problems that afflict the
13 percent of our people who are poor, and we must address it....

    ....

[T]HE SORDID HISTORY OF race relations in our nation has left a widely felt leg-
acy of fear and suspicion that will poison any population policy unless it is clear
that such a policy is being developed to enhance the quality of life for all Americans, and not to restrict or curtail the gains made by minorities....

    ....

WHILE EXCESS FERTILITY among blacks and other minorities is not the main source of the problem of national population growth, nonetheless it is clear that many minority families regard excess fertility as a serious *personal* problem. The evidence for this is the response of minority families to family planning services when these are made available in an acceptable manner. Like other groups, minority members seek to limit their family size as a means of achieving a better quality of life for themselves and their children....

....

...[U]nless we address our major domestic social problems in the short run—beginning with racism and poverty—we will not be able to resolve fully the question of population growth.

CHAPTER 11: HUMAN REPRODUCTION

....

...How far down the road toward population stabilization would the prevention of unwanted births take us? Since fertility has been changing so rapidly in recent years, such an estimate is difficult to make. The record of women who are approaching the end of their childbearing, those 35 to 44 years old in 1970, indicates that 27 percent had at least one unwanted birth, a total of one in every six births. The prevention of the unwanted births in this group would have carried them about three-fifths of the way to the replacement level. But women in those age groups were the main participants in the post-war baby boom and have had the highest fertility of any women in modern time. And there has been a significant change downward in the family-size expectations of young couples.

We conclude that there are many "costs" associated with unwanted fertility, not only financial, but health, social, psychological, and demographic costs as well.

The Commission believes that all Americans, regardless of age, marital status, or income, should be enabled to avoid unwanted births. Major efforts should be made to enlarge and improve the opportunity for individuals to control their own fertility, aiming toward the development of a basic ethical principle that only wanted children are brought into the world.

In order to implement this policy, the Commission has formulated the following recommendations that are developed in detail in the remainder of this chapter:

- The elimination of legal restrictions on access to contraceptive information and services, and the development by the states of affirmative legislation to permit minors to receive such information and services.

- The elimination of administrative restrictions on access to voluntary contraceptive sterilization.

- The liberalization of state abortion laws along the lines of the New York State statute.

- Greater investments in research and development of improved methods of contraception.

- Full support of all health services related to fertility, programs to improve training for and delivery of these services, an extension of government family planning project grant programs, and the development of a program of family planning education.

ABORTION

The Moral Question

The Commission recognizes that abortion is a complex issue requiring a thoughtful balancing of moral, personal, and social values. As the Commission moves toward a population policy for the United States, our principal objective is the enrichment of life, not its restriction. We share with our fellow citizens an abiding concern for the sanctity of all human life. Thus, we appreciate the moral decisions involved in abortion, as well as the possible insensitivity to all human life implied in the practice of abortion. It is from this perspective that we have approached three moral issues concerning abortion which we believe to be of foremost importance.

The first issue relates to the fetus, both as to the termination of potential life and determining when that life actually begins. The second relates to bringing into the world an unwanted child, particularly when the child's prospects for a life of dignity and self-fulfillment are limited. Third, there is the question of the woman who in desperation seeks an abortion. Our society faces a difficult decision when the woman believes her well-being is threatened and she sees no other way out but an illegal abortion with all its attendant dangers.

The Commission believes that a wise and sound decision in regard to the abortion question requires a careful balancing of the moral problems relating to the woman and the child along with those concerning the fetus.

In the development of western culture, the tendency has been toward a greater protection of life. At the same time, there is a deep commitment in our moral tradition to individual freedom and social justice. The Commission believes that the various prohibitions against abortion throughout the United States stand as obstacles to the exercise of individual freedom: the freedom of women to make difficult moral choices based on their personal values, the freedom of women to control their own fertility, and finally, freedom from the burdens of unwanted childbearing. Restrictive statutes also violate social justice, for when abortion is prohibited, women resort to illegal abortions to prevent unwanted births. Medically safe abortions have always been available to the wealthy, to those who could afford the high costs of physicians and trips abroad; but the poor woman has been forced to risk her life and health with folk remedies and disreputable practitioners.

Public Health

Abortion is not new; it has been an alternative to an unwanted birth for large numbers of American women (estimates ranged from 200,000 to 1,200,000 illegal abortions per year in the United States). The Commission regards the issue of illegal abortion with great concern and supports measures to bring this medical procedure from the backrooms to the hospitals and clinics of this country. It is becoming increasingly clear that, where abortion is available on request, one result is a reduction in the number of illegal abortions. Deaths as a consequence of illegal abortion have dropped sharply in New York since the enactment of a liberal abortion statute....

What is the effect of abortion on out-of-wedlock births? The best information comes from New York, where out-of-wedlock births have been on the rise since they were first recorded in 1954. Statistics for the first eight months of 1971 indicate that, for the first time, the rate is declining. Moreover, the New York City programs for unmarried pregnant girls have reported a sharp decline in the number of applicants this year.

In summary, we are impressed that the availability of abortion on request causes a reduction in the number of illegal abortions, maternal and infant deaths, and out-of-wedlock births, thereby greatly improving the health of women and children.

Family Planning

The Commission affirms that contraception is the method of choice for preventing an unwanted birth. We believe that abortion should not be considered a substitute for birth control, but rather as one element in a comprehensive system of maternal and infant health care. For many, the very need for abortion is evidence of a social and personal failure in the provision and use of birth control. In the year beginning July 1, 1970, an estimated 505,000 legal abortions and an unknown number of illegal abortions were performed in the United States. Far too many Americans must resort to abortion to prevent an unwanted birth. It is our belief that the responsible use of birth control can be achieved only when sex counseling and contraceptive information and services are easily accessible to all citizens.

The Commission expects that, with the increasing availability of contraceptives and improvements in contraceptive technology, the need for abortion will diminish....

Public Opinion

Public opinion on abortion is changing, tending recently to grow more liberal. Some 14 to 20 percent more women in 1970 than in 1965 approve of abortion for various reasons, according to interview data collected in the 1965 and 1970 National Fertility Studies. The public opinion survey conducted in 1971 for the Commission indicates that half of all Americans believe that abortion should be a matter decided solely between individuals and their physicians; an additional 41 percent would permit abortion under certain circumstances; and 6 percent flatly oppose abortions under any circumstances. Estimates of the current state of attitudes on abortion doubtless depend very much on the phrasing of the question and the interpretation of the respondent.

In general, support for increasing the availability of legal abortions is strongest among non-Catholics and among those who are well-educated. Among the general public, 38 percent feel that the government should help make abortion available to all women who want it.

RECOMMENDATIONS

The abortion issue raises a great number of moral, legal, public health, and demographic concerns. As a group, the Commission has carefully considered these issues, and based on their personal views, individual members of the Commission have resolved these questions differently....

The majority of the Commission believes that women should be free to determine their own fertility, that the matter of abortion should be left to the conscience of the individual concerned, in consultation with her physician, and that states should be encouraged to enact affirmative statutes creating a clear and positive framework for the practice of abortion on request.

Therefore, with the admonition that abortion not be considered a primary means of fertility control, the Commission recommends that present state laws restricting abortion be liberalized along the lines of the New York State statute, such abortions to be performed on request by duly licensed physicians under conditions of medical safety.

In carrying out this policy, the Commission recommends:

> That federal, state, and local governments make funds available to support abortion services in states with liberalized statutes. That abortion be specifically included in comprehensive health insurance benefits, both public and private.

SEPARATE STATEMENT OF MARILYN BRANT CHANDLER

Beyond my own personal feelings, I oppose open abortion on demand and support limited therapeutic abortion laws for the following reasons:

1. The Commission report does stress that abortion should not be a substitute for birth control, but has not intimated that liberal abortion takes the responsibility away from sexual activity. Impulsive, irresponsible sexual involvement can be rationalized without fear of pregnancy if abortion is open, legal, and free.

Excerpted from *Population and the American Future: The Report of the Commission on Population Growth and the American Future* (March 27, 1972).

Abortion Seen Up to Woman, Doctor
by George Gallup

In recommending that "the matter of abortion should be left to the conscience of the individual concerned, in consultation with her physician, and that states should be encouraged to enact affirmative statutes creating a clear and positive framework for the practice of abortion on request," the Rockefeller Commission was not merely reflecting the views of its members but—as Gallup polls in 1972 suggested—also those of a growing majority of Americans.

In June 1972, the Gallup Organization conducted a nationwide poll on attitudes toward abortion. George Gallup's syndicated article describing the poll results was published in the Washington Post *on August 25, 1972, and was carried in other newspapers throughout the country. The results showed substantial majorities in all demographic categories, including Catholics, in favor of leaving the abortion decision up to a woman and her doctor. The Gallup poll reported that more Republicans than Democrats were in favor of liberalized abortion laws, an outcome that likely reflected the fact that most*

Catholics in 1972 identified themselves as Democrats; a majority of Catholics supported abortion reform, but by a closer margin than Protestants.

   Presumably, those justices who were at home in Washington, or who read an American newspaper elsewhere, were aware of this poll. Clearly, Justice Blackmun was; a copy of the Washington Post *article reporting the poll results was in his* Roe v. Wade *file.*

Princeton, N.J.—Two out of three Americans think abortion should be a matter for decision solely between a woman and her physician, according to a recent survey conducted by The Gallup Organization.

   An even larger majority, 73 per cent, believes that professional birth control information, services and counseling should be made available to unmarried, sexually-active teenagers.

   The Gallup survey, conducted in June, reveals that a record high of 64 percent support full liberalization of abortion laws, agreeing with the statement that "the decision to have an abortion should be made solely by a woman and her physician." Three in ten persons (31 per cent) disagree with the statement, while five per cent do not express an opinion.

   Two in three among those who disagree, however, would make an exception in the case of a woman whose mental health is in danger.

   Majority support for legal abortion has increased sharply since January when a comparable survey by The Gallup Organization found 57 per cent of the belief that abortion should be a decision made by a woman and her physician.

   A still earlier survey, in November, 1969, found 40 per cent in favor of "a law which would permit a woman to go to a doctor and end a pregnancy at any time during the first three months."

   On the question of contraception for teenagers, almost three out of four—73 per cent—agree with the statement that "professional birth control information, services and counseling should be made available to unmarried sexually-active teenagers." Twenty-three per cent disagree with this statement, while four per cent do not express an opinion.

   The majority of Catholics agree with both statements, contrary to the traditional stand of the Roman Catholic Church. Fifty-six per cent of Catholics believe that abortion should be decided by a woman and her doctor, and 68 per cent of Catholics express approval of making birth control information and services available to teenagers. The comparable percentages for Protestants are 65 per cent in favor of legal abortion and 72 per cent in favor of birth control information and services for teenagers.

The issue of abortion is of political significance in this presidential election year. Gallup interviewers find that a greater proportion of Republicans (68 per cent) and independents (67 per cent) than Democrats (59 per cent) holding the belief that abortion should be a decision between a woman and her physician.

Approval of birth control information and services for teenagers was indicated by 70 per cent of Republicans, 71 per cent of Democrats interviewed, and 79 per cent of independents.

Agreement with both statements was found to be greatest among persons of higher income and educational levels. Geographically, approval on the issue of abortion ranged from 53 per cent in the South to 73 per cent in the West. Approval of contraceptive information and services for teenagers was above 70 per cent in all regions of the nation—rising to 81 per cent in the Far West.

Little difference in opinion is found between young and middle-aged respondents. About the same percentage of all age groups agreed with the statement on abortion, while approval of teenage birth control information and services was slightly greater among those under 30 (82 per cent) than among those aged 30–44 years (77 per cent). Persons 45 and older were 64 per cent in agreement on the teenage question.

Following are statements on a card handed to respondents, and the findings:

As you may have heard, in the last few years a number of states have liberalized their abortion laws. Do you agree or disagree with the following statement regarding abortion: "The decision to have an abortion should be made solely by a woman and her physician."

	AGREE	DISAGREE	NO OPINION
Total	64	31	5
Men	63	32	5
Women	64	31	5
Protestants	65	31	4
Catholics	56	39	5
Republicans	68	27	5
Democrats	59	36	5
Independents	67	28	5
College	74	22	4
High School	65	30	5

	AGREE	DISAGREE	NO OPINION
Grade School	47	45	8
East	69	27	4
Midwest	62	34	4
South	53	40	7
West	73	21	6
Less than $5,000 per yr.	53	38	9
$5,000–$6,999	55	40	5
$7,000–$9,999	71	26	3
$10,000–$14,999	68	27	5
$15,000 and over	74	24	2
Under 30 years old	64	31	5
30–44 years old	63	33	4
45 and over	63	31	6

[The second question was the teenage contraception question described in the article.]

Printed with permission of the Gallup Organization. Original article published Aug. 25, 1972.

Statement about the *Report of the Commission on Population Growth and the American Future*
by Richard M. Nixon (May 5, 1972)

By 1972, there was steadily increasing support for the repeal of abortion laws; the Gallup poll registered a clear majority of Americans, even Catholic Americans, supporting liberalization. In response, opponents of liberalization, with the aid of the Catholic Church, redoubled their efforts to organize. They entered politics, mobilizing constituencies of single-issue voters who would support and oppose legislators in response to their votes on abortion. Politicians responded.

By the time the Rockefeller Commission presented its three-volume report to the president on May 5, 1972, Nixon's reelection campaign was under way, and the domestic political climate had changed significantly from when the report was commissioned in 1969. The commission's work had attracted criticism from cultural conservatives and, most notably, from the Catholic Church. As we have seen, Nixon himself had publicly advocated against abortion liberalization, first by repudiating the military's liberal abortion policy in 1971, and, subsequently, by writing—with the guidance of his speechwriter and advisor Patrick Buchanan—a letter to Cardinal Cooke of New York, supporting Cooke's efforts to repeal New York's 1970 abortion statute. The ostensibly private letter was immediately leaked, furthering Nixon's public image as anti-abortion. In a more public, and nonsectarian, gesture, the president distanced himself from the population-control study he himself had commissioned just a few years earlier.

Nixon explicitly rejected two of the Rockefeller Commission's recommendations: for legalized abortion and for teenagers' access to birth control; he made no comment on the remainder of the recommendations and never proposed adopting any of them as federal policy. Abortion was "an unacceptable means of population control," the president said in an official statement that ignored the fact that the commission's report disclaimed any such objective, instead depicting liberalized access to abortion as contributing to "the exercise of individual freedom."

The Commission on Population Growth and the American Future has formally presented its report to me today, thus completing its 2 years of work.

The men and women on this panel have performed a valuable public service in identifying and examining a wide range of problems related to population, and have contributed to an emerging debate of great significance to the future of our Nation.

I wish to thank the able and energetic Chairman of the Commission, Mr. John D. Rockefeller 3d, for his tireless efforts, not only on this Commission but in other capacities, to focus the Nation's attention on these important issues.

The extensive public discussion already generated by this report clearly indicates the need to continue research in areas touching on population growth and distribution.

While I do not plan to comment extensively on the contents and recommendations of the report, I do feel that it is important that the public know my views on some of the issues raised.

In particular, I want to reaffirm and reemphasize that I do not support unrestricted abortion policies. As I stated on April 3, 1971, when I revised abortion policies in military hospitals, I consider abortion an unacceptable form of population control. In my judgment, unrestricted abortion policies would demean human life. I also want to make it clear that I do not support the unrestricted distribution of family planning services and devices to minors. Such measures would do nothing to preserve and strengthen close family relationships.

I have a basic faith that the American people themselves will make sound judgments regarding family size and frequency of births, judgments that are conducive both to the public interest and to personal family goals—and I believe in the right of married couples to make these judgments for themselves.

....

MANY OF THE QUESTIONS raised by the report cannot be answered purely on the basis of fact, but rather involve moral judgments about which reasonable men will disagree. I hope that the discussions ahead will be informed ones, so that we all will be better able to face these questions relating to population in full knowledge of the consequences of our decisions.

Richard M. Nixon, statement about the *Report of the Commission on Population Growth and the American Future,* May 5, 1972.

Swing to Right Seen Among Catholics, Jews (August 5, 1972)

by Louis Cassels

The report of the Rockefeller Commission reflected growing public support for the liberalization of abortion law, but it did not fully register the debate that was escalating sharply during the period that the commission officially delivered its report. The commission's report endorsing repeal in New York State was delivered in May 1972, just as New York legislators were voting to repeal the state's liberalized abortion statute, and as a special session of the Connecticut legislature was reenacting the statute that Abele v. Markle had invalidated. By 1972, thirteen states had enacted laws permitting therapeutic abortion, and four—Alaska, Hawaii, New York, and Washington—had legalized abortion entirely, at least if performed sufficiently early in pregnancy. But abortion reform in fact had stalled. Despite increasing support for liberalization in this period, no state legislature voted to repeal its abortion law after 1970.

A similar paralysis affected Congress. Only two bills proposing national abortion legislation were introduced, one in each house. Both attempted to enact at the national level the decriminalization of abortion already in force in four states. Neither passed. In the Senate, Oregon Republican Robert Packwood, who urged the importance of population control, introduced the National Abortion Act in 1970; Bella Abzug, a New York Democrat and a leader of the women's movement, introduced a bill in the House in 1972. Despite repeatedly sponsoring the National Abortion Act in the Senate, Senator

Packwood never believed it would actually pass. He understood the abortion issue as politically risky. Explaining the inability of Congress to enact national abortion legislation, Packwood stated in 1970: "Most of the legislators in the nation I have met and certainly many members of Congress would prefer the Supreme Court to legalize abortion, thereby taking them off the hook and relieving them of the responsibility for decision-making."

Several factors seem to account for the legislative deadlock. To begin with, passage of the four repeal statutes in 1970 signaled the possibility of significant change in the law, and helped mobilize opposition to the liberalization of abortion law. Second, the nascent opposition movement organized around abortion as a single issue. In New York and Connecticut, those opposed to abortion targeted legislators district by district on the basis of their vote on abortion. Under pressure of this kind, support for repeal became more costly, even when a majority of voters supported liberalization.

Third, the Catholic Church worked directly and indirectly—through the National Right to Life Committee and other organizations—to draw Catholic, and, increasingly, even non-Catholic voters into voting on the basis of abortion. Church leadership addressed abortion as an issue of Catholic faith and identity, and, by 1972, the press was covering abortion as a Catholic voting issue, even though, as we have seen, Catholics were in fact divided in attitude toward the liberalization of abortion law.

The article excerpted here captures a moment when the political tectonic plates were beginning to shift. The writer, Louis Cassels (1922–1974), was United Press International's religion editor and a widely read columnist.

The vast majority of America's Catholics and Jews have traditionally been Democrats. This year, a large number is likely to vote Republican.

That is the consensus of Catholic and Jewish leaders who are intimately familiar with trends and attitudes in these two large religious communities.

There are several reasons for this historic shift in political allegiance. The first is economic. Rising affluence has caused many Catholic and Jews to identify with the haves rather than the have-nots. "There is no question about it," says Rabbi Louis Bernstein, president of the Rabbinical Council of America, "a lot of Jews are swinging to the right in politics."

Racial issues have played a part in the swing to the right, particularly among so-called "ethnic" Catholics and among Jews who live near black neighborhoods in big cities. Many Jews who once considered themselves liberal allies of black men in the struggle for civil rights now feel that they are targets of virulent anti-Semitism among blacks and have become defensive about it.

MOST IMPORTANT ISSUES

Most important issues in switching Catholic and Jewish votes, however, are (1) abortion and (2) Israel.

Sen. George McGovern, the Democratic presidential nominee, is trying to sidestep the abortion issue by saying it's one for states to decide. But Catholics know—and Republicans won't let them forget it—that McGovern was saying only a few months ago that "abortion is a private matter which should be decided by a pregnant woman and her own doctor." In other words, he favored abortion-on-demand with no legal restrictions.

This position is deeply repugnant to many Americans—not only Catholics—who feel that the state has a responsibility to provide protection to the most helpless form of human life—a quickened but unborn fetus.

President Nixon has squarely aligned himself with this latter sentiment—and again you can rest assured this point will be made perfectly clear in the election campaign. On April 3, 1971, Nixon said:

> From personal and religious beliefs I consider abortion an unacceptable form
> of population control. Further, unrestricted policies of abortion on demand
> I cannot square with my personal belief in the sanctity of human life—
> including the life of the yet unborn.

MCGOVERN'S RECORD QUESTIONED

Jews aren't much concerned with the abortion issues but are quite concerned about American support of Israel. The general feeling of the American Jewish community, according to qualified informants within it, is that Nixon has proved himself a stalwart supporter of Israel, both in diplomatic maneuvers and in shipments of U.S. arms, including Phantom jet planes.

McGovern, on the other hand, is widely remembered among Jews as a man who once advocated making Jerusalem an open city. No amount of present and future waffling on that issue will erase the memory or the distrust of McGovern it inspired among the Jews.

McGovern indicated at the Democratic Convention in Miami Beach that he is aware of the possibility of large-scale Catholic and Jewish defections from the Democratic fold. He sought to placate Catholics by choosing one as his running mate and by having his forces defeat a proposed platform plank advocating abortion on demand. He tried to make character with Jews by having his name placed in nomination by a Jew and by having his delegates write into the platform a plank pledging firm U.S. support of Israel.

It is possible, however, that some Catholics and Jews may consider these gestures too little and too late.

Taking all in all, it appears probable at this moment that the two major religious components of Franklin D. Roosevelt's famous Democratic coalition will take a walk this year.

Printed by permission of United Press International.

Assault Book

by Patrick Buchanan

Catholic voters' increasing willingness to vote on the basis of the abortion question was of great interest to the national political parties. In the late 1960s, strategists had identified Southern Democrats and Catholics in the Northeast as target groups whom Republicans might persuade to shift party affiliation. As the concluding document in Part I shows, by 1970, the Republican Party in California was experimenting with using the abortion issue to persuade Catholics to affiliate with the GOP.

By 1972, a national presidential campaign was under way. Richard Nixon, seeking reelection, had decided that the abortion issue was an effective way to encourage Catholic voters to shift party alignment. His public rejection of the Rockefeller Commission's recommendations was part of that strategy. Kevin Phillips, then a Republican Party strategist, described a key prong of Nixon's 1972 reelection plan as "wooing conservative Catholics, senior citizens, and other traditionalists."

Catholic voters thus emerged as an important swing vote in the national campaign, and abortion was emerging as an issue with the power to capture their vote. But as the campaign unfolded, abortion acquired new politically charged meanings of concern to an audience that reached far beyond Catholic constituencies. The shift most noticeably began during the primary campaign for the Democratic presidential nomination, when Senator George McGovern emerged as a candidate associated with the left and, as importantly, as candidate associated with the women's movement. On April 27, 1972, the widely read political columnists Rowland Evans and Robert Novak, writing in the Washington Post, *quoted "one liberal senator" as saying, "The people don't know McGovern is for amnesty, abortion, and legalization of pot.... Once middle America—Catholic middle America, in particular—finds this out, he's dead." The column famously associated McGovern with demands for amnesty for the antiwar protesters who evaded the Vietnam draft, with the abortion rights claims of the women's movement, and with the counter-cultural tastes of the youth movement. Abortion, in this usage, broadly signified a refusal to conform to traditional social norms—to practice restraint (in sex and drugs) and to fulfill role obligations requiring women to raise children and men to defend family and nation. (Interestingly, the twin targets of this social critique were women who refused the role of nurturer in the nursery and men who refused to kill on the battlefield.)*

Soon Senate Republican leader Hugh Scott of Pennsylvania was to turn this idea into a catchy alliterative phrase, tarring McGovern as the "triple-A candidate" who was for abortion, amnesty and "acid" (the legalization of LSD, and of narcotics in general). The claim spread, carried by other Democrats campaigning for the party's nomination, by advertisements placed in Catholic newspapers, and by anti-abortion groups. McGovern had associated himself with repeal of abortion laws in only a few public statements, but his feminist supporters sought more visible and unequivocal support for repeal in the Democratic Party platform; increasingly sensitive to the political cost, McGovern forces defeated the abortion plank, expressing the view—not unlike President Nixon's—that the abortion question was for the states to decide.

Despite these similarities in the candidates' position, Republican Party strategists sought to make the most of the abortion issue—not only to use it to persuade Catholics to shift party alignment but to reframe it to speak to a wider audience. An important tactic of the Nixon campaign was, as Kevin Phillips described it, to "link McGovern to a culture and morality that is anathema to Middle America"; to portray him as "a radical whose election could jeopardize the fabric and stability of American society." The strategy succeeded: Nixon won the majority vote in 49 states.

During the campaign, Patrick Buchanan, a key Nixon advisor, compiled an "assault book," as he labeled it, outlining strategies for the general election. It began with an account of "social issues" understood to be "Catholic/Ethnic concerns" in which abortion figured first.

DOMESTIC POLICY

    I. SOCIAL ISSUES—Catholic/Ethnic Concerns

        1. Abortion/ZPG [Zero Population Growth] /Contraceptives

        2. Amnesty [for Vietnam War draft evaders]

        3. Marijuana

        4. Aid to Nonpublic Schools

ABORTION

Though McGovern says "we should leave the matter to the States"; "I simply don't think the Federal Government should be involved at all," he clearly has come down hard on the side of unrestricted abortion policies—in favor of abortion on demand. No other conclusion can be drawn from the following statement in *Newsweek* (direct quote)

> "abortion is a private matter which should be decided by a pregnant woman and her own doctor. Once the decision is made, I do not feel the law should stand in the way of its implementation."
>
> (RNC [Republican National Committee] has this quote from
> Zero Population Group [sic], *National Reporter,* January, 1972)

Before Catholic groups and ethnic groups, McGovern can rightly be charged with favoring "abortion on demand, unrestricted abortion," and repeal of all state abortion laws. Though McGovern is attempting to back off his hard-line pro-abortion position saying, we should leave the matter to the states, his statement above clearly suggests that he opposes any law which interferes with the decision of a pregnant woman and her doctor.

Recommendation

That a flyer, contrasting RN [Richard Nixon] and McGovern positions on abortion be prepared and distributed at the Right to Life Convention in Philly in June—and that we attempt to have the flyer included in at least one mailing by every right-to-life group in the United States. Further, our position vis a vis McGovern on abortion should be included in a Position Flyer in October, on major issues of concern to Catholics—i.e. parochial schools, abortion, pornography, etc.

Reprinted from document archived at Richard Nixon Presidential Library and Museum, (Nixon-WHSF-Buchanan, box 10, folder 1.)

Women's Libbers Do NOT Speak for Us

from The Phyllis Schlafly Report, *February 1972*

By the early 1970s, youthful advocates for an end to the war in Vietnam, social justice, sexual freedom, and women's liberation had triggered countermobilization among those who opposed the new "permissive" morality. It was in this context that the strategies outlined in the Buchanan "assault book" and the "triple-A" label that the Republicans pinned on Senator McGovern acquired such resonance. In 1970, the Women's Strike for Equality had firmly linked the claim for a right to abortion to the call for a radical change in women's place in society, in the process changing the claim's meaning and associations. The abortion conflict was now part of a more wide-ranging conflict about sex and family roles. In 1972, the "triple-A" label harnessed backlash against the women's movement as a powerful political weapon, deriving its energies in some good part from one of feminism's most prominent critics, Phyllis Schlafly, a longtime conservative activist. In 1972, Congress sent the Equal Rights Amendment to the states for ratification, and the ratification process became a lightning rod for hostility to the women's movement. Schlafly spearheaded organizing against ERA ratification, building grassroots networks state by state in which opposition to abortion would figure prominently. A Catholic, Schlafly added to arguments about when life begins a new ground of objection focused on women's roles.

In this early newsletter mobilizing opposition to the ERA, Schlafly associated abortion with the ERA and attacked both as the twin aims of women's liberation. In organizing against the ERA and associating it with abortion, she led the way in building a "pro-family" constituency and in reframing the abortion issue itself. Here Schlafly attacks abortion by associating it, as the Strike for Equality did, with child care—that is, care provided by someone other than a child's mother. The ERA frame associates abortion with women's abdication of motherhood, rather than murder. The frames and networks of Schlafly's campaign against the ERA laid the foundation for the family values movement that would help carry Ronald Reagan to the White House in 1980. Abortion remained at the heart of the conservative defense of traditional family values long after the ERA was defeated.

The "women's lib" movement is *not* an honest effort to secure better jobs for women who want or need to work outside the home. This is just the superficial sweet-talk to win broad support for a radical "movement."

Women's lib is a total assault on the role of the American woman as wife and mother and on the family as the basic unit of society. Women's libbers are trying to make wives and mothers unhappy with their career, make them feel that they are "second-class citizens" and "abject slaves." Women's libbers are promoting free sex instead of the "slavery" of marriage. They are promoting Federal "day-care centers" for babies instead of homes. They are promoting abortions instead of families.

Why should we trade in our special privileges and honored status for the alleged advantage of working in an office or assembly line? Most women would rather cuddle a baby than a typewriter or factory machine. Most women find that it is easier to get along with a husband than a foreman or office manager. Offices and factories require many more menial and repetitious chores than washing dishing and ironing shirts.

Women's libbers do *not* speak for the majority of American women. American women do *not* want to be liberated from husbands and children. We do *not* want to trade our birthright of the special privileges of American women—for the mess of pottage called the Equal Rights Amendment.

Modern technology and opportunity have not discovered any nobler or more satisfying or more creative career for a woman than marriage and motherhood. The wonderful advantage that American women have is that we can have all the rewards of that number-one career, and still moonlight with a second one to suit our intellectual, cultural or financial tastes or needs.

And why should the men acquiesce in a system which gives preferential rights and lighter duties to women? In return, the men get the pearl of great price: a happy home, a faithful wife, and children they adore.

If the women's libbers want to reject marriage and motherhood, it's a free country and that is their choice. But let's not permit these women's libbers to get away with pretending to speak for the rest of us. Let's not permit this tiny minority to degrade the role that most women prefer. Let's not let these women's libbers deprive wives and mothers of the rights we now possess.

Tell your Senators NOW that you want them to vote NO on the Equal Rights Amendment. Tell your television and radio stations that you want equal time to present the case FOR marriage and motherhood.

Published by permission of Phyllis Schlafly.

PART III

Speaking
to the Court

SPEAKING
TO THE COURT

The Supreme Court that decided Roe v. Wade. This formal group photograph of the 1972 Burger Court was taken in August 1972. Seated, left to right: Justice Potter Stewart, Justice William O. Douglas, Chief Justice Warren E. Burger, Justice William J. Brennan Jr., Justice Byron R. White. Standing, left to right: Justice Lewis F. Powell Jr., Justice Thurgood Marshall, Justice Harry A. Blackmun, and Justice William H. Rehnquist.

Photograph by Robert Oakes, National Geographic Society, courtesy of the Supreme Court of the United States, photo #2005.7.11. The formal group photograph of the 1972 Burger court. Taken in August 1972.

Roe v. Wade in Context

As we have seen, the reframing of the abortion issue from a question of public health to a weapon in an escalating culture war happened swiftly and, to a degree that is surprising in retrospect, took place beneath the radar of those observers who were not themselves direct combatants. One reason may be that those who aimed to associate abortion with the "new morality" and with threats to traditional family values spoke in select venues that allowed them to target particular segments of the electorate. The Gallup Poll on abortion, taken at the height of the 1972 presidential campaign, did not catch the change; a substantial majority of the public, and more Republicans than Democrats, supported leaving the abortion decision up to a woman and her doctor.

As illustrated in Part II, as the evolution in abortion's meaning was taking place, the litigation campaign to constitutionalize a right to abortion was in full swing in courts around the country. The Connecticut legislature's response to the successful litigation in that state demonstrates that neither litigation nor legislation proceeded in a vacuum. The same mix of forces, illustrated in the preceding parts of this book, were at work, propelling abortion to its visible position on the country's political, social, and legal agenda.

The Texas law at issue in *Roe v. Wade* dated to 1857 and prohibited all abortions not necessary to save a pregnant woman's life. Two recent graduates of the University of Texas Law School, Sarah Weddington and Linda Coffee, had filed the case. They had recruited three plaintiffs: a married couple, Marsha and David King (Mrs. King was not pregnant, but had medical reasons for avoiding pregnancy and feared the consequence of a failure of birth control) and an unmarried and pregnant 21-year-old, Norma McCorvey. McCorvey had already borne two children and had relinquished custody of both. This time, she wanted an abortion. In the lawsuit, the Kings became Mary and John Doe, and Norma McCorvey became Jane Roe. The defendant, Henry Wade, was the Dallas district attorney.

The lawyers filed the case in federal district court in Dallas on March 3, 1970. On June 17, a three-judge panel agreed unanimously that the Texas law violated a woman's "fundamental right to choose whether to have children." The court said the law was unconstitutionally broad in its "monolithic interdiction," sweeping "far beyond any areas of compelling state interest" in regulating abortion. In addition, the court held, the law was unconstitutionally vague in failing to define the sole exception specifically enough to let doctors know whether they would face or avoid criminal liability in terminating a patient's dangerous pregnancy.

But while ruling in favor of Jane Roe, the judges dismissed the Does from the case on the ground that they lacked a sufficiently concrete stake in the outcome. And the court, adhering to "the federal policy of non-interference with state criminal prosecutions," declined to issue an injunction (an order that would bar the state from future enforcement of the law). The decision was a nominal victory that lacked practical utility. On October 6, 1970, the plaintiffs' lawyers appealed to the Supreme Court.

Since another abortion case was already before the Court, the justices set the Texas appeal aside. The other case, *United States v. Vuitch*, was an appeal by the government from a federal district court decision that had struck down the District of Columbia's abortion statute as unconstitutionally vague. The statute contained a health exception that the lower court had found imprecise and constitutionally problematic because it failed sufficiently to inform doctors of how they could distinguish a permitted abortion from a prohibited one. In April of 1971, the Supreme Court handed down a decision in the *Vuitch* case that dealt with the vagueness problem by interpreting the health exception to apply broadly to mental as well as physical health. It was a significant ruling that signaled the Court's receptivity to constitutional criticism of laws criminalizing abortion, but it had no bearing on *Roe*'s challenge to the Texas law, which lacked a health exception.

Only a day after issuing the *Vuitch* decision, the Court announced that it would hear *Roe v. Wade* during the following term. But developments affecting the case continued to unfold. In September, just before the new term was to begin, two elderly justices, Hugo L. Black and John M. Harlan, announced their retirements, leaving the Court with only seven members. The Court nonetheless proceeded with oral argument in the case on December 13, 1971.

A second abortion case was argued the same day: *Doe v. Bolton,* a challenge to Georgia's recently enacted reform law based on the American Law Institute's 1962 proposal. [See page 24.] This 1968 law, which replaced an 1876 statute like the Texas statute at issue in *Roe* was more liberal in allowing abortions under certain circumstances. The Georgia law authorized doctors to terminate pregnancies that threatened a woman's life; "that would seriously and permanently injure her health"; that resulted from rape; or that would lead to the birth of a baby with a "grave, permanent, and irremediable mental or physical defect." Three doctors, each conducting an independent examination, had to certify that a woman met at least one of these criteria; even then, the abortion could not take place until approved by a special hospital committee.

The 24 plaintiffs in *Doe v. Bolton* included doctors, nurses, social workers, and members of the clergy. The lead plaintiff, "Mary Doe," whose real name was Sandra Bensing, was a 22-year-old married woman with three children and a history of mental illness. Pregnant again, she had sought permission for an abortion, but was turned down because she was found not to meet any of the criteria. A three-judge panel of the Federal District Court in Atlanta declared the restrictions on eligibility to be unconstitutional but upheld the procedural requirements and declined, like the court in Texas, to issue an injunction.

Complications affecting the Court's decision to hear the cases continued. Two new justices, Lewis F. Powell Jr. and William H. Rehnquist, had been confirmed to the Court on the eve of the December arguments, but they had not yet taken their seats. Concluding that the two cases should be re-heard by a full Court, the justices scheduled a new argument for October 11, 1972—almost exactly two years after the appeal in *Roe v. Wade* had been filed. More than 27 months would elapse between the time the case was filed and the day it was decided, along with *Doe v. Bolton,* on January 22, 1973.

A Changing Landscape

Two years is an unusually long time for a case to remain on the Supreme Court's docket. As we have already discussed, these were a crucial two years for the meaning of abortion, and it is clear that *Roe* arrived at the Court's doorstep in one world and emerged, 27 months later, into another. In October 1970, when the case reached the Supreme Court, New York's repeal of its abortion law appeared to many people to suggest an inexorable march toward reform. Two years later— during which time 402,100 women, two-thirds of them from out of state, had obtained legal abortions in New York—the Legislature's attempted repeal of the repeal failed only because of Governor Rockefeller's veto. In the November 1972 elections, voters in Michigan and North Dakota had defeated proposals to liberalize those states' abortion laws—and, as we have seen, abortion was one of a constellation of factors playing a role in McGovern's landslide defeat. In early January 1973, the New York Legislature reconvened in the full expectation of a new effort to recriminalize abortion.

As we now turn to the arguments that were formally presented to the Supreme Court in legal briefs, an intriguing question arises: What did the justices perceive of the turmoil over abortion outside their own quiet precincts? Clearly, they knew that they had on their hands "a most sensitive, emotional, and controversial" issue, as Justice Harry A. Blackmun described it when he announced *Roe* and *Doe* from the bench (see page 245). Further, as Justice Blackmun observed, the Court knew that "the controversy will continue." The justices had not been hermetically sealed off in their chambers during the long months in which the cases were pending. They lived in the world as husbands and fathers. They had set the cases for a second argument, a sign that they regarded the cases as something other than routine.

It does appear, however, that the justices in the 7-to-2 majority were responding to a consensus among the elites, particularly of the legal and medical professions, that change was appropriate and necessary. They appreciated that the decision would provoke controversy, but decided the case on grounds that they had reason to suppose would find broad public acceptance. Non-legal material in Justice Blackmun's file included the Gallup Poll from the summer of 1972, reflecting substantial majorities supporting decriminalization, even among Catholics [see page 207.] The file also contained a series of articles from the *Atlanta Journal-Constitution*, passed on to Justice Blackmun by Justice Potter Stewart. In these articles, prominently displayed in the newspaper during April 1972, an Atlanta physician, Robert A. Hatcher, M.D. asserted that Georgia's ALI-type reform law had not gone far enough and was not making enough of a difference.

Justice Blackmun's files also contained articles from the American Journal of Public Health (several of which are excerpted in parts I and II), depicting abortion reform as inevitable and highly desirable. This was not the only voice of the medical community the Court heard; among the Roe v. Wade briefs was a strongly worded one from dissenting obstetricians and gynecologists arguing for upholding the Texas law (see page 295).

Further, the justices may well have viewed organized opposition to the legalization of abortion as based almost exclusively on Catholic religious conviction, as it primarily was when *Roe v. Wade* first arrived on the Court's docket. The only Catholic justice then sitting on the Supreme Court was William J. Brennan, Jr., a liberal whose full support for an expansive right to abortion may have served to emphasize significant differences of opinion about the criminalization of abortion within the American Catholic community, and so undercut the weight of the Catholic opposition.

One significant change inside the Court while the case was pending was the arrival of Lewis Powell, a courtly Virginian appointed by President Nixon. A former president of the American Bar Association, the very embodiment of the legal establishment, Powell proved not only a surprisingly strong supporter of the right to abortion but also a strategic ally who pushed Blackmun to extend until later in pregnancy the time period during which women's abortion decisions received constitutional protection. Any fears the justices may have had that they were embarking on a radical course would have been allayed by Powell's presence and performance.

Argument and Decision

Excerpted here are the main briefs filed by the parties in Roe v. Wade. *The brief for Jane Roe incorporates many arguments about public health, medical practice, and personal liberty that will sound familiar from the advocacy and litigation documents in Parts I and II. In its constitutional argument, the brief draws on the Supreme Court's 1965 decision in* Griswold v. Connecticut, *which declared that a Connecticut law prohibiting the use of contraception violated a constitutional right to marital privacy. The brief contains some vivid language about the consequences for a woman of being compelled "to serve as an incubator for months and then as an ostensibly willing mother for up to twenty or more years." But the right of doctors to practice medicine as they see fit receives at least as much attention. (As Part II shows, this was one of the earliest justifications for challenges to the constitutionality of laws criminalizing abortion, and was presumably less controversial than the women's-rights frame.)*

The state's brief defending the statute focuses on fetal development and the rights of the unborn. It seeks to demonstrate that when prenatal development is properly understood, the "artificial distinction between born and unborn" vanishes and should not receive legal recognition. The detailed, month-by-month description of fetal development contained in the state's brief is repeated nearly word for word in several of the amicus curiae *(friend of the court) briefs filed in support of the state's position.*

The Supreme Court's decision reflected the arguments of both parties, as well as many of those contained in the friend-of-the-court briefs filed on both sides. The Court rejected the state's argument that the fetus was a "person" meriting the same protection under the Constitution as born persons. Nevertheless, the Court found that the state did have an interest in protecting "the potentiality of human life." Similarly, the Court endeavored to strike a balance in defining the scope of the right to abortion it recognized. The majority reasoned that the right to privacy protected not only the use of contraception, but also a woman's decision whether to bear a child. Yet, the decision emphasized, this right was not absolute. The Court held that in the first trimester of pregnancy, the state may not inhibit a woman's ability to obtain an abortion; abortion, during that time, "must be left to the medical judgment of the pregnant woman's attending physician." In the middle trimester, the state may regulate abortion to protect "maternal health"; and in the final trimester, "the State in promoting its interest in the potentiality of human life may, if it chooses, regulate, and even proscribe, abortion except where it is necessary, in appropriate medical judgment, for the preservation of the life or health of the mother."

Although seven justices joined the decision, there were two dissenters, each expressing an objection that opponents of abortion would later invoke in mobilizing against the abortion right and against Roe *itself. Justice Rehnquist's dissent was focused not on the moral question of whether abortion ought to be legal, but rather on the institutional question of the Supreme Court's role. Rehnquist argued that in announcing a constitutional right to abortion, the Court had overstepped its authority; the right to privacy on which it based the decision was not part of the "liberty" that the Fourteenth Amendment protects. Justice White, in a separate dissent, echoed Rehnquist's arguments about the proper role of the Court. However, he focused also on the moral questions of when abortion ought to be permissible, and who ought to be entrusted with such a decision. Without expressing a fundamentally different view of the fetus from the majority, White, like the majority, asserted the state had an interest in protecting potential life. But where the majority saw the concerns motivating women to end pregnancies as significant, and the impact of a criminal law depriving them of control over the decision as inflicting harms of constitutional magnitude, White was skeptical and suggested that the majority had extended constitutional protection to women who seek abortions for reasons of "whim" and "caprice."*

This Part begins with the briefs in which the parties presented their arguments to the Supreme Court. It then presents the statement Justice Blackmun read from the bench when he first announced the Court's decision in Roe v. Wade *and* Doe v. Bolton. *The Court's lengthy published opinion in* Roe *is widely available on the Internet. But Blackmun's brief statement exists only as typescript in the justice's files at the Library of Congress. A personal judicial pronouncement of this kind shows how the author of an opinion wants the world to understand what the Court has done.*

An afterword discusses the decision and briefly surveys the trajectory of the abortion debate in the decades after Roe.

Finally, an appendix presents excerpts of selected friend-of-the-court briefs in order to document the full range of arguments presented to the Court.

Brief for Appellants Jane Roe, et al.

The lawyers who signed this brief were Roy Lucas, Sarah Weddington, James R. Weddington, Linda N. Coffee, Fred Bruner, Roy L. Merrill, Jr., and Norman Dorsen.

STATEMENT OF THE CASE

Jane Roe [Descriptions are omitted of the other plaintiffs, "Mary Doe" and "John Doe," along with a Dallas physician, James H. Hallford, M.D., who was then under indictment for performing an illegal abortion and who joined the others in challenging the statute.]

Appellant Jane Roe sued as an unmarried pregnant adult woman on behalf of herself "and all other women who have sought, are seeking, or in the future will seek to obtain a legal, medically safe abortion but whose lives are not critically threatened by the pregnancy." At the time the action was filed, Jane Roe had been "unable to secure a legal abortion in Dallas County because of the existence of the Texas Abortion Laws." She had sought this medical procedure "because of the economic hardship which pregnancy entailed and because of the social stigma attached to the bearing of illegitimate children in our society." Miss Roe admitted that insofar as her own interpretation of Texas law was concerned, her "life [did] not appear to be threatened by the continuation of her pregnancy," other than in a qualitative sense, and in the "extreme difficulty in securing employment of any kind" because of her pregnant condition.

Jane Roe suffered emotional trauma when unable to obtain a legal abortion in Texas. She regarded herself as a law-abiding citizen and did not want to participate in a felony offense by obtaining an illegal abortion. Also, she had only a tenth grade education and no well-paying job which might provide sufficient funds to travel to another jurisdiction for a legal abortion in a safe, clinical setting.

....

RELEVANT BACKGROUND AND MEDICAL FACTS

....

The law on abortion cannot be understood without reviewing the pertinent aspects of medical and legal history which gave rise to the law. When this is done, it becomes abundantly clear that public health considerations motivated this type of legislation, and that these factors no longer justify maintaining such stringent restrictions in the criminal code.

In the 1820s when the first American abortion statutes were enacted, there was no medical profession as we know it. Physicians and quacks alike advertised their treatments and potions in the same marketplace. Both had little to offer the public. Medical science, an infant branch of learning in the 1800s, did not uncover the need for clean hands in gynecological examinations until the 1840s.

....

Still, surgical dangers warned against any medical procedure. Induced abortion, in particular, involved internal use of surgical instruments, and the inevitable introduction of infection into the womb. Far better, the legislature obviously deemed, that a woman risk childbirth, than death on the operating table. Only when the risks cancelled themselves out did she have an option.

Today the comparative risks weigh heavily in favor of permitting induced abortion, not as an emergency matter as in 1851, but as an elective medical procedure. Surgery in those times was almost always fatal. As the next section shows, medicine is a different science today.

Induced abortion, in medical practice today, is a relatively minor surgical procedure, insofar as risks to the patient's physical or mental well-being are concerned....

....

On another level as well, abortion is a safe procedure: it is without clinically significant psychiatric sequelae. A number of recent studies confirm that abortion does not produce serious psychological side-effects damaging to the mental well-being of the patient.

....

Legal and Medical Standards of Practice Regarding Induced Abortion in Texas and the United States.

...Today, only abortions performed in non-medical environments present significant risks of morbidity and mortality; with proper medical supervision, abortions are safe and simple procedures. In keeping with modern medical practice, this Court would reinforce the purpose of early abortion legislation if it invalidated the statute. This would permit abortions to be done by licensed physicians in adequate medical facilities and discourage abortions by unskilled practitioners. Moreover, it would preserve the 117-year-old purpose of the law, and the common law.

....

EVIDENCE OF AMERICAN STANDARDS of medical practice respecting induced abortion is found in the policy statements of professional organizations. Both the

American Medical Association and the American College of Obstetricians and Gynecologists have set standards of professional practice in recent years.

ACOG policy sanctions therapeutic and elective abortion "to safeguard the patient's health or improve her family life situation." ACOG recognizes that "abortion may be performed at the patient's request...." A very similar position was taken by the American Medical Association. The AMA at one time had followed the A.L.I. model, listing four or five vaguely defined situations for sanctioned abortion. This proved unworkable, and the policy was changed in order not to limit the physicians' traditional responsibility for evaluating "the merits of each individual case...."

....

The Provisions in the Texas Penal Code, Articles 1191–1194 and 1196, Which Prohibit the Medical Procedure of Induced Abortion Unless "procured or attempted by medical advice for the purpose of saving the life of the mother," Abridge Fundamental Personal Rights of Appellants Secured by the First, Fourth, Ninth, and Fourteenth Amendments, and Do Not Advance a Narrowly Drawn, Compelling State Interest.

....

The Constitution does not specifically enumerate a "right to seek abortion," or a "right of privacy." That such a right is not enumerated in the Constitution is no impediment to the existence of the right. Other rights not specifically enumerated have been recognized as fundamental rights entitled to constitutional protection including the right to marry, the right to have offspring, the right to use contraceptives to avoid having offspring, the right to direct the upbringing and education of one's children, as well as the right to travel.

....

APPELLANTS CONTEND THAT fundamental rights entitled to constitutional protection are involved in the instant case, namely the right of individuals to seek and receive health care unhindered by arbitrary state restraint; the right of married couples and of women to privacy and autonomy in the control of reproduction; and the right of physicians to practice medicine according to the highest professional standards. These asserted rights meet constitutional standards arising from several sources and expressed in decisions of this Court. The Texas abortion law infringes these rights, and since the law is not supported by a compelling justification, it is therefore unconstitutional.

The Right to Seek and Receive Medical Care for the Protection of Health and Well-Being Is a Fundamental Personal Liberty Recognized by Decisions of This Court and by International and National Understanding.

....

Although this Court has not expressly delineated a right to seek health care, the importance of such care has been recognized and the existence of such a right suggested. In *United States v. Vuitch* (1971), this Court reaffirmed society's expectation that patients receive "such treatment as is necessary to preserve their health." In this Court's invalidation of Connecticut's proscription against contraception, Justice White noted that statute's intrusion upon "access to medical assistance...in respect to proper methods of birth control." *Griswold v. Connecticut* (1965) (White, J., concurring).

....

Abortion is an accepted medical procedure for terminating pregnancy. Amici medical organizations recognize the acceptability of abortion, as their policy statements indicate; they draw no distinction between abortion and other medical procedures.

The Texas abortion law effectively denies Appellants Roe and Doe access to health care. Jane Roe was forced to bear a pregnancy to term though an abortion would have involved considerably less risk to her health. Physicians who would otherwise be willing to perform an abortion in clinical surroundings are deterred by the fear of prosecution. Since Appellant Roe could not afford to travel elsewhere to secure a safe abortion, to avoid continuation of pregnancy she would have been forced to resort to an unskilled layman and accept all the health hazards attendant to such a procedure. Even had she been able to travel out of state, the time required to make financial and travel arrangements would have entailed greater health risks inherent in later abortions.

The Fundamental Rights to Marital and Personal Privacy Are Acknowledged in Decisions of This Court as Protected by the First, Fourth, Ninth, and Fourteenth Amendments.

....

This Court has previously upheld the right to use contraceptives to avoid unwanted pregnancy [*Griswold v. Connecticut* (1965)].

As did the law considered in *Griswold*, "[t]his law...operates directly on an intimate relation of husband and wife and their physician's role in one aspect of that relation." The Texas abortion law in forbidding resort to the procedure of medical abortion, has a maximum destructive impact upon the marriage relationship.

In addition to rights associated with marital privacy, an overlapping body of precedent extends significant constitutional protection to the citizen's sovereignty over his or her own physical person.

....

PREGNANCY OBVIOUSLY DOES have an overwhelming impact on the woman. The most readily observable impact of pregnancy, of course, is that of carrying the pregnancy for nine months. Additionally there are numerous more subtle but no less drastic impacts.

Without the right to respond to unwanted pregnancy, a woman is at the mercy of possible contraceptive failure, particularly if she is unable or unwilling to utilize the most effective measures. Failure to use contraceptives effectively, if pregnancy ensues, exacts an exceedingly high price.

....

WHEN PREGNANCY BEGINS, a woman is faced with a governmental mandate compelling her to serve as an incubator for months and then as an ostensibly willing mother for up to twenty or more years. She must often forego further education or a career and often must endure economic and social hardships. Under the present law of Texas she is given no other choice. Continued pregnancy is compulsory, unless she can persuade the authorities that she is potentially suicidal or that her life is otherwise endangered. The law impinges severely upon her dignity, her life plan and often her marital relationship. The Texas abortion law constitutes an invasion of her privacy with irreparable consequences. Absent the right to remedy contraceptive failure, other rights of personal and marital privacy are largely diluted.

....

The decisions of this Court which implicitly recognize rights of marital and personal privacy have been followed by state and federal court decisions expressly holding the decision of abortion to be within the sphere of constitutionally protected privacy.

That there is a fundamental constitutional right to abortion was the conclusion of the court below in the instant case....

That view has been shared by a number of other courts which have considered the question and have affirmed that this is a fundamental right....

Without the ability to control their reproductive capacity, women and couples are largely unable to control determinative aspects of their lives and marriages. If the concept of "fundamental rights" means anything, it must surely include the right to determine when and under what circumstances to have children.

Physicians Have a Fundamental Right to Administer Health Care Without Arbitrary State Interference.

The First, Ninth, and Fourteenth Amendments protect the right of every citizen to follow any lawful calling, business, or profession he may choose, subject only to rational regulation by the state as necessary for the protection of legitimate public interests. In reviewing legislation affecting the medical profession, courts have particularly respected the knowledge and skill necessary for medical practice, the broad professional discretion necessary to apply it, and the concomitant state interest in guaranteeing the quality of medical practitioners....

Similarly, courts have been alert to protect medical practice from rash or arbitrary legislative interference....

Most recently, this Court, in *United States v. Vuitch* (1971), recognized that "doctors are encouraged by society's expectations...and by their own professional standards to give their patients such treatment as is necessary to preserve their health." The *Vuitch* decision went on to construe the term health to encompass "psychological as well as physical health," and "'the state of being sound in body or mind.'"

Here, the practice of medicine clearly includes the treatment of pregnancy and conditions associated with it. However, the Texas statute prohibits physicians from administering the appropriate remedy to preserve the patient's health or well-being. Physicians are not required to forego the right to make medically sound judgments and to act upon them with respect to any other human disease or condition. With appropriate consents they may administer electric shock therapy, excise vital organs, perform prefrontal lobotomies and take any other drastic action they believe indicated. They are not indictable for these actions. However, obstetricians and gynecologists who are asked to abort their patients for sound medical reasons risk a prison sentence if they do so. The statute severely infringes their practice and seriously compromises their professional judgments.

The state must demonstrate a legitimate interest to impair doctors' rights to practice their profession. Historically, the interest asserted by the state is a health interest, and courts have upheld laws designed to ensure the quality of medical practice. Similarly, statutes have been upheld which require doctors' intervention in sales of medically-related products in order to protect public health.

None of the above interests are applicable here, however. The statute in question here does not protect the public from unqualified practitioners. Rather the statute applies to laymen and physicians alike. Indeed, it endangers patients'

health by unduly confining doctors' exercise of medical judgment.... Further, the
statute addresses no other legitimate state interest.

    ....

The Texas Statute Does Not Advance Any State Interest of Compelling Importance in a Manner Which is Narrowly Drawn.

As shown earlier, medical abortion is a safe and simple procedure when performed
during the early stages of pregnancy; indeed, it is safer than childbirth. This fact
alone vitiates any contention that the statute here serves a public health interest.
Numerous state and federal courts have taken notice of this fact and concurred
that no health rationale supports a statute like the one here. *See e.g.* People v.
Belous (Cal. 1969).

    Moreover, no concern for mental health justifies the statute, for it does not
permit abortion even if a woman's mental health is threatened. Such a view is
untenable for the additional reason that abortion is a procedure without clinically
significant psychiatric sequelae.

    Additional data reveal that statutes like the one here actually create "a public
health problem of pandemic proportions" by denying women the opportunity to
seek safe medical treatment. Severe infection, permanent sterility, pelvic disease,
and other serious complications accompany the illegal abortions to which women
are driven by laws like this one.

    Any notion that less restrictive abortion laws would produce excessive demands
on medical resources and thereby endanger public health also is unfounded. The
experience in New York City after one year under an elective abortion law dispels
any such fears....

    The absence of a public health problem accompanying less restrictive abortion
is indicated by comparative mortality rates: for the first eleven months of operation, the mortality for abortion in New York City is approximately equal to that
of tonsillectomy in the United States.

    Against this background of medical fact, there is no support whatever for the
suggestion that public health is an interest protected by this statute.

    ....

The Statute Does Not Advance Any Public Interest in Protecting Human Life.

As counsel for appellee admitted during oral argument, "the State only has one
interest and that is the protection of the life of the unborn child." The question
then becomes whether this interest is sufficiently compelling to overcome the couple's or woman's fundamental right to privacy and autonomy. In this regard it is

revealing to examine other aspects of the State's attitude toward the fetus. Such an inquiry reveals that only in the area of abortion does the State exhibit an interest in the fetus or treat it as having legal personality.

First, the pregnant woman who searches out a person willing to perform an abortion and who consents to, if not pleads for, the procedure is guilty of no crime. Texas courts have repeatedly held that the woman is neither a principal nor an accomplice. Similarly, the women who travel from Texas to states with less restrictive abortion laws in order to secure medical abortions and avoid the alleged state interest in protecting the fetus are guilty of no crime. Moreover, self-abortion has never been treated as a criminal act. The State has failed to seek to deter through criminal sanctions the person whose interests are most likely to be adverse to those of the fetus. This suggests a statutory purpose other than protecting embryonic life.

An unborn fetus is not a "human being" and killing a fetus is not murder or any other form of homicide. "Homicide" in Texas is defined as "the destruction of the life of one human being by the act, agency, procurement, or culpable omission of another." Since the common law definition of "human being" is applicable, a fetus neither born nor in the process of birth is not a "human being" within the meaning of those words as they appear in the homicide statute. In *Keeler v. Superior Court* (Cal. 1970), a pregnant woman was assaulted by her former husband; a Caesarean section and examination in utero revealed that the fetus, of approximately thirty-five weeks gestation, had died of a severely fractured skull and resultant hemorrhaging. The California Supreme Court held the man could not be guilty of murder; the same result would apply in Texas. A fetus is not considered equal to a "human being," and its destruction involves a significantly lesser penalty.

The State does not require that a pregnant woman with a history of spontaneous abortion go into seclusion in an attempt to save the pregnancy. No pregnant woman having knowingly engaged in conduct which she reasonably could have foreseen would result in injury to the fetus (such as skiing in late pregnancy) has ever been charged with negligent homicide.

No formalities of death are observed regarding a fetus of less than five months gestation. Property rights are contingent upon being born alive. There has never been a tort recovery in Texas as the result of injury to a fetus not born alive. No benefits are given prior to birth in situations, such as workman's compensation, where benefits are normally allowed for "children."

....

It is sometimes argued that scientific discoveries show that human life exists in the fetus. Scientific studies in embryology have greatly expanded our understanding of the process of fertilization and development of the fetus and studies relating to the basic elements of life have shown that life is not only present in the fertilized egg, sperm and ova but that each cell contains elements which could conceivably constitute the beginning of a new human organism. Such studies are significant to science but only confuse the problem of defining human life.

....

Thus science only leads to a worse quandary for obviously if one goes far enough back along the continuum of human development one encounters the existence of sub-microscopic double-helix molecules which have human life potential. When does something become human?...

Once the fact that science can offer no guidance on the question of when human life begins is conceded, arguments concerning preservation of the fetus almost always fall back to the proposition of potential life....

It is obvious that the legislative decision forbidding abortions also destroys potential life—that of the pregnant woman—just as a legislative decision to permit abortions destroys potential life. The question then becomes not one of destroying or preserving potential, but one of who shall make the decision. Obviously some decisions are better left to a representative process since individual decisions on medical facilities, wars, or the release of a convict would tend toward the chaotic. It is our contention that the decision on abortion is exactly the opposite. A representative or majority decision making process has led to chaos. Indeed, in the face of two difficult, unresolvable choices—to destroy life potential in either a fetus or its host—the choice can only be left to one of the entities whose potential is threatened.

The above argument is perhaps only another way of stating that when fundamental rights are infringed upon, the State bears the burden of demonstrating a compelling interest for doing so. The question of the life of the fetus versus the woman's right to choose whether she will be the host for that life is incapable of answer through the legislative fact-finding process. Whether one considers the fetus a human being is a problem of definition rather than fact. Given a decision which cannot be reached on the basis of fact, the State must give way to the individual for it can never bear its burden of demonstrating that facts exist which set up a compelling state interest for denying individual rights.

Brief for Appellee Henry Wade, District Attorney of Dallas County, Texas

The lawyers who signed this brief were Crawford C. Martin, attorney general of Texas; Nola White, Alfred Walker, Robert C. Flowers, and Jay Floyd, lawyers in the Attorney General's Office; Henry Wade, criminal district attorney, Dallas County; and John B. Tolle, assistant district attorney.

VI. The Constitution of the United States Does Not Guarantee a Woman the Right to Abort an Unborn Fetus.

One must recognize the interest of a husband and wife in preserving their conjugal relations from state interference, an interest which, in *Griswold v. Connecticut* (1965), was found to be violated by Connecticut's statute forbidding the use of contraceptives. This law interfered with the most private aspect of the marital relation, sexual intercourse, making it criminal for a couple to engage in sexual intercourse when using contraceptives. In contrast, the usual statute restricting abortions does not affect the sexual relations of a couple except under some circumstances and only for a limited time. Prevention of abortion does not entail, therefore, state interference with the right of marital intercourse, nor does enforcement of the statute requiring invasions of the conjugal bedroom.

Assuming arguendo that there are other marital rights the state must respect, may it then be urged that the right of marital privacy includes the freedom of a married couple to raise and educate a child they do not want, or commit infanticide, incest, engage in pandering and the like. Family privacy, like personal privacy, is highly valued, but not absolute. The news media may publicize the events that occur when a family is victimized by criminals though they seek seclusion. The family may not practice polygamy, may not prohibit schooling for a child, or prohibit the child's labor, or expose the community or a child to communicable disease....

Proponents of abortion-on-demand assert that anti-abortion laws unlawfully intrude into the privacy of the physician-patient relationship. They assume necessarily that the doctor treating a pregnancy owes an obligation of good medical care to only one patient, the pregnant woman.... As a patient of the obstetrician, the child may recover damages for a prenatal injury suffered as the result of the negligence of his doctor. It is elemental that a doctor cannot be freed from legal restraints in making socio-moral judgments. The state may regulate the medical profession to protect the health and welfare of all its citizens. Appellants' contentions of intrusion upon physician-patient relationship are not self-sustaining and must be associated with and connected to a violation of some basic right.

Personal privacy is an exalted right but, as in marital privacy, it has never been regarded as absolute. A person may be subjected to a "stop and frisk" though it constitutes an intrusion upon his person, or a person may be required to submit to a vaccination, and a blood sample may forcibly be extracted from the body of an individual arrested for suspicion of driving while intoxicated. A woman has been required to submit to a blood transfusion necessary to preserve her life in order that her small child shall not be left without a mother. The "right of privacy" is a highly cherished right—however one which is nowhere expressly mentioned in the Constitution of the United States or its amendments....

....

The crux of the moral and legal debate over abortion is, in essence, the right of the woman to determine whether or not she should bear a particular child versus the right of the child to life. The proponents of liberalization of abortion laws speak of the fetus as "a blob of protoplasm" and feel it has no right to life until it has reached a certain stage of development. On the other hand, the opponents of liberalization maintain the fetus is human from the time of conception, and so interruption of pregnancy cannot be justified from the time of fertilization. It most certainly seems logical that from the stage of differentiation, after which neither twinning nor re-combination will occur, the fetus implanted in the uterine wall deserves respect as a human life. If we take the definition of life as being said to be present when an organism shows evidence of individual animate existence, then from the blastocyst stage the fetus qualifies for respect. It is alive because it has the ability to reproduce dying cells. It is human because it can be distinguished from other non-human species, and once implanted in the uterine wall it requires only nutrition and time to develop into one of us.

The recent recognition of autonomy of the unborn child has led to the development of new medical specialties concerning the unborn child from the earliest stages of the pregnancy. Modern obstetrics has discarded as unscientific the concept that the child in the womb is but tissue of the mother.... Yet the attack on the Texas statute assumes this discredited scientific concept and argues that abortions should be considered no differently than any medical measure taken to protect maternal health (see appellant's brief), thus completely ignoring the developing human being in the mother's womb.

....

It is our task in the next subsections to show how clearly and conclusively modern science—embryology, fetology, genetics, perinatology, all of biology—establishes the humanity of the unborn child. We submit that the data not only show the constitutionality of the Texas legislature's effort to save the unborn from indiscriminate extermination, but in fact suggests a duty to do so. We submit also that no physician who understands this will argue that the law is vague, uncertain or overbroad for he will understand that the law calls upon him to exercise his art for the benefit of his *two patients*: mother *and* child.

From conception the child is a complex, dynamic, rapidly growing organism. By a natural and continuous process the single fertilized ovum will, over approximately nine months, develop into the trillions of cells of the newborn. The natural end of the sperm and ovum is death unless fertilization occurs. At fertilization a new and unique being is created which, although receiving one-half of its chromosomes from each patient, it really unlike either.

(Editor's note: The brief contained ten photographs depicting fetal development, which are omitted here. These were well-known images at the time, taken by the Swedish photographer Lennart Nilsson and published in A Child Is Born: The Drama of Life before Birth, *by Axel Ingelman-Sundberg and Claes Wirsen [Dell Publishing Company, 1965].)*

....

THE DEVELOPMENT OF the child, while very rapid, is also very specific. The genetic pattern set down in the first day of life instructs the development of a specific anatomy. The ears are formed by seven weeks and are specific, and may resemble a family pattern. The lines in the hands start to be engraved by eight weeks and remain a distinctive feature of the individual.

The primitive skeletal system has completely developed by the end of six weeks. This marks the end of the child's embryonic (from Greek, to swell or teem within) period. From this point, the child will be called a fetus (Latin, young one or offspring).

In the third month, the child becomes very active. By the end of the month he can kick his legs, turn his feet, curl and fan his toes, make a fist, move his thumb, bend his wrist, turn his head, squint, frown, open his mouth, press his lips tightly together. He can swallow and drinks the amniotic fluid that surrounds him. Thumb sucking is first noted at this age. The first respiratory motions move fluid in and out of his lungs with inhaling and exhaling respiratory movements.

....

EVERY CHILD SHOWS a distinct individuality in his behavior by the end of the third month. This is because the actual structure of the muscles varies from baby to baby. The alignment of the muscles of the face, for example, follow an inherited pattern. The facial expressions of the baby in his third month are already similar to the facial expressions of his parents.

Further refinements are noted in the third month. The fingernails appear. The child's face becomes much prettier. His eyes, previously far apart, now move closer together. The eyelids close over the eyes. Sexual differentiation is apparent in both internal and external sex organs, and primitive eggs and sperm are formed. The vocal cords are completed. In the absence of air they cannot produce sound; the child cannot cry aloud until birth, although he is capable of crying long before.

....

IN THE FIFTH MONTH, the baby gains two inches in height and ten ounces in weight. By the end of the month he will be about one foot tall and will weigh one pound. Fine baby hair begins to grow on his eyebrows and on his head and a fringe of eyelashes appear. Most of the skeleton hardens. The baby's muscles become much stronger, and as the child becomes larger his mother finally perceives his many activities. The child's mother comes to recognize the movement and can feel the baby's head, arms and legs. She may even perceive a rhythmic jolting move-ment—fifteen to thirty per minute. This is due to the child. The doctor can now hear the heartbeat with his stethoscope.

The baby sleeps and wakes just as it will after birth. When he sleeps he invari-ably settles into his favorite position called his "lie." Each baby has a characteristic lie. When he awakens he moves about freely in the buoyant fluid turning from side to side, and frequently head over heel.... The child hears and recognizes his mother's voice before birth. Movements of the mother, whether locomotive, car-diac or respiratory, are communicated to the child.

....

IN THE SIXTH MONTH, the child develops a strong muscular grip with his hands. He also starts to breathe regularly and can maintain respiratory response for twenty-four hours if born prematurely. He may even have a slim chance of surviv-ing in an incubator. The youngest children known to survive were between twenty to twenty-five weeks old. The concept of *viability* is not a static one....

This review has covered the first six months of life. By this time the individual-ity of this human being should be clear to all unbiased observers. When one views the present state of medical science, we find that the artificial distinction between born and unborn has vanished. The whole thrust of medicine is in support of the motion that the child in its mother is a distinct individual in need of the most diligent study and care, and that he is also a patient whom science and medicine treat just as it does any other person.

This review of the current medical status of the unborn serves us several purposes. Firstly, it shows conclusively the humanity of the fetus by showing that human life is a continuum which commences in the womb. There is no magic in birth. The child is as much a child in those several days before birth as he is those several days after. The maturation process, commenced in the womb, continues through the post-natal period, infancy, adolescence, maturity and old age. Dr. Arnold Gesell points out in his work that no king ever had any other beginning than have had all of us in our mother's womb. [Arnold Gesell, *The Embryology of Behavior* (Harper & Bros., 1945.)] Quickening is only a relative concept which depends upon the sensitivity of the mother, the position of the placenta, and the size of the child.

The State of Texas Has a Legitimate Interest in Prohibiting Abortion Except by Medical Advice for the Purpose of "Saving the Life of the Mother"

There seems little argument necessary if one can conclude the unborn child is a human being with birth but a convenient landmark in a continuing process—a bridge between two stages of life. The basic postulates from which the Appellees' arguments proceed are: (1) the pregnant woman has a right of control over her own body as a matter of privacy guaranteed to her by the Constitution of the United States; and (2) this right cannot be interfered with by the state since the state cannot demonstrate any compelling interest to justify its intrusion. The contrary position is the state's interest in preventing the arbitrary and unjustified destruction of an unborn child—a living human being in the very earliest stages of its development. Whatever personal right of privacy a pregnant woman may have with respect to the disposition and use of her body must be balanced against the personal right of the unborn child to life.

Whatever the metaphysical view of it is, or may have been, it is beyond argument that legal concepts as to the nature and rights of the unborn child have drastically changed, based on expanded medical knowledge, over the last 2,500 years.

....

It is most seriously argued that the "life" protected by the Due Process of Law Clause of the Fifth Amendment includes the life of the unborn child. Further, it would be a denial of equal protection of law not to accord protection of the life of a person who had not yet been born but still in the womb of its mother. If it is a denial of equal protection for a statute to distinguish between a thief and an embezzler under a statute providing for the sterilization of the one and not the other, then it is surely a denial of equal protection for either the state or federal government to distinguish between a person who has been born and one living in the womb of its mother. [Note: in 1942 in *Skinner v. Oklahoma,* the Court had ruled that it violated equal protection for the state to punish by sterilization a person convicted of three or more "felonies involving moral turpitude" while not similarly punishing a felon convicted of embezzlement.]

    ....

If it be true that the compelling state interest in prohibiting or regulating abortion did not exist at one time in the stage of history, under the result of the findings and research of modern medicine, a different legal conclusion can now be reached. The fact that a statute or law may originally have been enacted to serve one purpose does not serve to condemn it when the same statute, with the passage of time, serves a different but equally valid public purpose.

ANNOUNCING THE DECISION

No. 70-18—*Roe v. Wade*
No. 70-40—*Doe v. Bolton*

On January 22, 1973, the Supreme Court issued its decisions in Roe v. Wade *and* Doe v. Bolton. *Following the Court's custom, Justice Harry A. Blackmun, as the author of the opinions, read a summary from the bench. Known in Supreme Court parlance as "hand-downs," these summaries are not casual documents. While they are not formally part of the Court's published opinion, they reflect the author's view of what matters most about the decision.*

The marked-up draft in Blackmun's file shows that he labored over the hand-down. In presenting Roe, *Blackmun strives to locate the Court's decision in history as well as in contemporary public opinion and to demonstrate how the constitutional framework that the Court announced respected and coordinated competing values.*

Although it is not clear whether anyone on the Court anticipated the passionate and prolonged conflict the abortion right has generated, the document indicates that Blackmun was aware that the decision would generate controversy; the previous week, he had sent a draft of the announcement to Chief Justice Warren E. Burger with the notation, "I anticipate the headlines that will be produced over the country when the abortion decisions are announced."

In his announcement from the bench, Justice Blackmun stressed the states' continuing ability to regulate abortion, and presented the Roe *framework as responsive to medical science and to doctors' professional judgment. In contrast to his written opinion, the hand-down was silent about women's reasons for seeking to end a pregnancy. The text of Justice Blackmun's hand-down is reprinted below. It incorporates the handwritten additions and changes that Blackmun made on his final typed draft. The document was dated, in his handwriting, January 22, 1973.*

There follows as a separate document, a concluding paragraph that Justice Black-mun crossed out on the final draft of the hand-down.

These are the two abortion cases that were argued first in December 1971 and again last October. They are appeals from three-judge federal courts in the Northern Districts of Texas and of Georgia respectively.

The lawsuits attack the constitutionality of the Texas and Georgia abortion statutes. The actions were instituted by pregnant women, both married and unmarried, by a married couple in the Texas case, and by physicians and others alleging an interest in the subject matter.

The Texas statue is representative of those presently in effect in a majority of our states and that, for the most past, were enacted during the last half of the nineteenth century. The Texas statue prohibits *any* abortion, or any attempt at an abortion, *except* where is it procured by medical advice for the purpose of saving the *life* of the woman. It makes no reference to health, as does the District of Columbia statute considered in *United States v. Vuitch* decided here in the 1970 Term.

The Georgia statute, on the other hand, was enacted only in 1968. It is a modern statute patterned after the American Law Institute's Model Penal Code. It is representative of recent legislation enacted in approximately one-quarter of our states. It makes an abortion a criminal act with certain *exceptions*. These exceptions are where the abortion is performed by a licensed physician and, "based upon his best clinical judgment," the abortion is necessary *because* the pregnancy if continued would endanger the life or health of the woman, *or* the fetus would very likely be born with a grave and permanent mental or physical defect, *or* the pregnancy resulted from forcible or statutory rape. The Georgia statute also imposes certain *procedural* conditions for the obtaining of the abortion. These are several in number, but among them are (1) Georgia residence, (2) concurrence in the abortion decision by two licensed physicians in addition to the attending [physician], (3) performance of the procedure in a hospital both licensed by the state *and* accredited by the Joint Commission on Accreditation of Hospitals, and (4) approval by a hospital abortion committee of 3 physicians.

So much for the statutes.

The *Texas* federal court held that a woman had a right, protected by the Ninth and Fourteen[th] Amendments, to choose whether to have children and that the Texas statute was therefore void on its face.

The Georgia federal court invalidated certain parts of the Georgia statute including the portion specifying the particular circumstances in which an abortion may be sought, but upheld most of the remainder of that state's statute.

The plaintiffs in both cases took appeals here, and we set the cases for argument successively.

The abortion issue, of course, is a most sensitive, emotional and controversial one, perhaps one of the most emotional that has reached the Court for some time. The issue is one of great public interest not confined to lawyers and their lawsuits. Convictions are firmly rooted and firmly held. At the same time, attitudes by no means are uniform. We are aware of this, and we are fully aware that, however the Court decides these cases, the controversy will continue. Our task, however, is to decide the cases on constitutional principles as we perceive those principles to be.

In the Texas case we have filed a lengthy opinion that attempts to review the history of attitudes toward abortion, popular, legal, civic, and moral, from ancient times down to the present. We cannot escape noting, too, the change in attitudes—in recent years—of professional bodies such as the American Medical Association, the American Public Health Association, and the American Bar Association, and, indeed, the changing attitudes among the courts of this country, both state and federal. This historical approach has revealed a number of interesting things. One is the fact, already alluded to, that nearly all the strict state abortion statutes were enacted about a hundred years ago. Another is the conclusion that it is very doubtful that abortion was ever firmly established as a common law crime, even with respect to the destruction of a *quick* fetus. A third is that there is little consensus, even among religious or medical groups, as to when life begins. Some would fix it at the moment of conception. Others would focus on quickening. Still others would regard live birth as the significant point.

We have concluded again, as the Court has done before, that there is a right of personal privacy under, and implicit in, the Constitution. It is not spelled out in so many words, but the Court has recognized this right before in varying contexts. We feel that it is founded in the Fourteenth Amendment's concept of personal liberty and restrictions upon state action. We further conclude that this right of personal privacy includes the abortion decision, but, as we say that, we emphasize that the right is *not* unqualified and that it must be considered against important state interests in regulation abortion.

There are, we feel, two important interests that a state possesses and that if it so desires, it may seek to protect by legislation. The first is the state's interest in preserving and protecting the health of the pregnant woman. The second is the state's interest in protecting the *potentiality* of human life, irrespective of the moment when life actually begins. These interests are separate and distinct. Each grows in substantiality as the woman approaches term, and at some point during pregnancy each becomes "compelling."

We thus have, in tension, the pregnant woman's right of privacy, on one hand, and these two distinct state interests, on the other.

We conclude:

1. For that portion of the pregnancy stage prior to approximately the end of the first trimester, the woman's privacy right dominates the interests of the state. It follows that, during this period, the abortion decision must be left to the medical judgment of the woman's attending physician.

2. From that point on, however, the state, in promoting its interest in health, may, if it chooses, regulate the abortion procedure in ways that are appropriately related to maternal health. Examples of permissible state regulation in this area are requirements as to the qualifications of the person who is to perform the abortion; as to the licensure of that person; as to the facility where the procedure is to be performed; and as to the licensing of the facility.

3. From and after viability, which, we judicially notice, is usually the end of approximately the 26th or 27th week, and which is the point at which the fetus has a reasonable chance of independent life if it were then born or removed from the mother, the state's interest in protecting the *potentiality* of human life dominates the woman's right to *privacy*. It follows that the state may, if it chooses, regulate and even prohibit abortion, except where it is necessary in appropriate medical judgment for the preservation of the life or health of the mother.

4. The state may define the term physician to mean only a licensed physician, and it may proscribe any abortion by a person who is not a physician.

We feel that this holding is consistent with the relative weights of the respective interests involved, with the lessons and examples of medical and legal history, with the attitude of the common law toward abortion, and with the demands of the profound problems of the present day. The states are thus left free to place increasing restrictions on abortion as the period of pregnancy lengthens so long as those restrictions are tailored to the recognized state interests. The decision, we also feel, vindicates the right of the physician and is consistent with the fact that abortion is essentially a medical decision until, of course, those points in pregnancy are reached when the state interests become dominant.

Viewed under this analysis, the Texas statute must fall, and we, therefore, affirm, with one procedural exception, the judgment of the federal court of the Northern District of Texas.

In the Georgia case we hold that the procedural requirements for J.C.A.H. accreditation for the hospital, for the hospital abortion committee, and for the additional two-doctor concurrence are unduly restrictive of the patient's rights and of the attending physician's rights. Similarly, we do not uphold the provision that the patient be a resident of Georgia. The remainder of the Georgia statute does not conflict with federal constitutional standards.

We thus strike a balance between the interests of the pregnant woman and the interests of the state in health and in potential life. Fortunately, these decisions come at a time when a majority of the legislatures of the states are in session. Presumably where these decisions cast doubt as to the constitutional validity of a state's abortion statute, the legislature of that state may immediately review its statute and amend it to bring it into line with the constitutional requirements we have endeavored to spell out today. If this is done, there is no need whatsoever for any prolonged period of unregulated abortion practice.

The Chief Justice, Mr. Justice Douglas and Mr. Justice Stewart, while joining the opinion, have each filed separate concurring opinions. Mr. Justice White has filed a dissenting opinion, and Mr. Justice Rehnquist has joined him in that dissent. Mr. Justice Rehnquist has also filed a separate dissenting opinion in each of the two cases.

H.A.B., January 22, 1973

In presenting the Court's decision throughout his oral announcement as moderate, balanced, and bounded, Justice Blackmun was, no doubt, anticipating and responding to criticism of the Court's decision. In the paragraph that Justice Blackmun eventually struck from the draft, he was even more emphatic about the decision's limits. "The Court," he wrote, "does not today hold that the Constitution compels abortion on demand."

Justice Blackmun's reasons for deleting this paragraph are unknown but can perhaps be inferred. The phrase "abortion on demand" does not appear in the majority opinion, but it is the closing line of a concurring opinion by Chief Justice Burger, who wrote: "Plainly, the Court today rejects any claim that the Constitution requires abortions on demand." While drafting the hand-down, Justice Blackmun had consulted the chief justice but had not yet seen the concurring opinion. Perhaps he inserted the reference to "abortion on demand" at Chief Justice Burger's request, and then changed his mind when he finally received the Burger concurrence on January 18. Seeing that the chief justice himself had explicitly rejected "abortion on demand," Justice Blackmun might well have concluded that he himself had no need to invoke a phrase that was increasingly acquiring negative connotations.

The meanings associated with the phrase "abortion on demand" were in flux at the time Roe *was handed down. As we saw in Part I, the feminist movement used the phrase in seeking abortion rights during the movement's Strike for Equality in 1970 [see page 44, the illustration of the flyer]. The feminist claim for abortion "on demand" sought repeal of abortion restrictions; the claim challenged as paternalistic new abortion-reform laws based on the "therapeutic" model. Those laws gave doctors the power to decide whether a woman had a sufficient reason to have an abortion, and so reduced women to supplicants of men and the state. In claiming abortion on demand, feminists asserted that women were fully competent to decide for themselves whether to continue a pregnancy, and should not have such a question decided by a stranger, even a medical professional.*

But women's assertion of decisional authority was disturbing to many. What feminists understood as a question of dignity and self-governance their critics saw as an invitation to self-indulgence. Critics of the abortion-repeal movement argued that decriminalization would allow women access to abortion for insufficient reasons, and some suggested that liberalizing access to abortion would encourage moral laxity— sexual license, abdication of maternal responsibility, and a general breakdown of self- and social control. Thus, where feminists asserted that abortion's criminalization was wrongful because it was insufficiently respectful of women, their critics expressed doubt that women's judgment in matters of abortion was respect-worthy. Backlash came to torque and flip the very meaning of "abortion on demand."

In the early 1970s, the meaning of the phrase remained unsettled as feminist and antifeminist usages circulated. In April 1971, President Nixon invoked the phrase in his official statement repudiating the Pentagon's liberal policy that permitted servicewomen to obtain abortions in any military hospital. [see annotation on p. 198, brief in the Struck case.] "Unrestricted abortion policies, or abortion on demand, I cannot square with my personal belief in the sanctity of human life," the president said.

Whether or not Justice Blackmun was aware of the original meaning of the phrase, it is highly likely that he was aware of the negative meaning that "abortion on demand" was then acquiring. In striking this original concluding paragraph of the hand-down, Justice Blackmun appears to have decided that he would address the concerns of Chief Justice Burger and others less contentiously, and emphasize Roe's *moderation in language that distanced the Court from the claims of both abortion rights advocates and their critics.*

In closing, I emphasize what the Court does not do by these decisions. The Court does not today hold that the Constitution compels abortion on demand. It does not today pronounce that a pregnant woman has an absolute right to an abortion. It does, for the first trimester of pregnancy, cast the abortion decision and the responsibility for it upon the attending physician, whose judgment is to be exercised, as always, upon long established medical standards. For the period following the first trimester, the decisions permit the state, if it chooses, to impose reasonable regulations for the protection of maternal health. And, after viability, they give the state full right to proscribe all abortions except those that may be necessary, in appropriate medical judgment, for the preservation of the life or health of the mother.

AFTERWORD

In January 1973, the Supreme Court declared unconstitutional Texas's 19th-century abortion statute and Georgia's more recent "ALI"-style legislation. The Court rested its decision on the the right to privacy, found in *Griswold v. Connecticut* (1965) to protect the use of contraceptives. *Roe v. Wade* ruled that the right to privacy protected a woman's decision in consultation with her physician whether to carry a pregnancy to term. The Court held that the unborn were not "persons" under the Fourteenth Amendment but that government had a constitutionally weighty interest in regulating the abortion decision to protect potential life. The Court explained that the strength of this interest corresponded with the stage of pregnancy. While the state was prohibited from restricting a woman's right to abortion during the first trimester of pregnancy, it was permitted to regulate abortion "in ways that are reasonably related to maternal health" in the second trimester, and could constitutionally proscribe abortion after the point of "viability" (that is, when a fetus was capable of surviving outside the womb) except if doing so would endanger the life or health of the pregnant woman.

Both the right and regulatory interest that *Roe* recognized emerged from more than a decade of searching public conversation about abortion. Reasoning about the meaning of constitutional precedent in the midst of that conversation, the justices concluded that the right to privacy recognized in *Griswold* covered not only contraception but abortion as well. The Court conducted a lengthy analysis of historical precedent before declaring that the Constitution protected the abortion decision from state interference until the point of fetal viability. But, in explaining its decision, the Court also invoked or adverted to the judgments of growing numbers of lower courts, the decisions of public authorities such as the Rockefeller Commission that endorsed the legalization of abortion, and measures of popular support for liberalizing access. (In addition to the many briefs in

Roe, Justice Blackmun had in his files the papers in *Abele v. Markle,* Connecticut's abortion case, and other lower court decisions; documents reflecting the views of organizations such as the American Medical Association and the American Bar Association; and the 1972 Gallup poll reports showing steadily rising support for decriminalization.)

Roe's holding fused old and new legal frameworks. By protecting a woman's decision whether to bear a child until the period of fetal viability, the Court recognized as constitutional a framework at least partly resembling abortion "repeal." Under *Roe,* government could no longer ban abortion or make access to the procedure conditional on ALI-type indications (for example, rape, maternal health) in the period of pregnancy before viability. But *Roe* did not altogether bar government from regulating abortion. To the contrary, *Roe* gave constitutional sanction to government interests in regulating abortion that grow with a pregnancy; it vindicated these interests alongside women's right to have an abortion through the trimester framework, which allowed government to restrict abortion in the interest of protecting potential life at the point of fetal viability. In the years since *Roe,* the Court has allowed government more leeway to regulate abortion to express its interest in protecting potential life throughout pregnancy.

Roe's reasoning fused old and new justifications for decriminalizing abortion. *Roe* indirectly reflected the abortion-rights claims of the women's movement, recognizing that laws that criminalized abortion inflict constitutionally significant harms on women, and not doctors only. But *Roe* expressed those harms in public health-inflected language. The decision barred government from coercing women to bear children, but its reasoning did not audibly express the feminist claim (1) that a woman has dignitary interests in making her own decision about whether to bear a child, or (2) that a woman needs the ability to control the timing of motherhood in order to negotiate institutional arrangements that exclude caregivers from participation in the workplace and other arenas of civic life. Instead, *Roe* observed:

> The detriment that the State would impose upon the pregnant woman by denying this choice altogether is apparent. Specific and direct harm medically diagnosable even in early pregnancy may be involved. Maternity, or additional offspring, may force upon the woman a distressful life and future. Psychological harm may be imminent. Mental and physical health may be taxed by child care. There is also the distress, for all concerned, associated with the unwanted child, and there is the problem of bringing a child into a family already unable, psychologically and otherwise, to care for it. In other

cases, as in this one, the additional difficulties and continuing stigma of unwed motherhood may be involved. All these are factors the woman and her
responsible physician necessarily will consider in consultation.

Roe justified the abortion right by appealing to Griswold and earlier decisions
that protected the right to make decisions about family life free from state interference. In extending this right to privacy to encompass the abortion decision,
Roe reasoned about abortion in terms drawn from the reform debates of the early
1960s, emphasizing the importance of protecting a doctor's autonomy as much as
that of his patients. Women's advocacy helped establish women as constitutional
rights holders who are entitled to make decisions about sex and parenting without
control by the state—but Roe barely acknowledged that such claims were circulat-
ing in public debate. Instead, the Court explained and justified its holding in language that depicted doctors as the responsible and authoritative decisionmakers,
with women as patients subject to their guidance. In Roe, the Court states:

> In view of all this, we do not agree that, by adopting one theory of life, Texas
> may override the rights of the pregnant woman that are at stake.
>
> ....This means, on the other hand, that, for the period of pregnancy prior
> to this "compelling" point, *the attending physician, in consultation with his
> patient, is free to determine, without regulation by the State, that, in his medi-
> cal judgment, the patient's pregnancy should be terminated.* If that decision is
> reached, the judgment may be effectuated by an abortion free of interference
> by the State.
>
> ....*The decision vindicates the right of the physician to administer medical
> treatment according to his professional judgment up to the points where im-
> portant state interests provide compelling justifications for intervention. Up to
> those points, the abortion decision in all its aspects is inherently, and primarily,
> a medical decision, and basic responsibility for it must rest with the physician.*
> If an individual practitioner abuses the privilege of exercising proper medical
> judgment, the usual remedies, judicial and intra-professional, are available.

In representing the abortion decision as one that a woman made under the
guidance of her doctor, the Court figured the doctor as the agent responsible for
abortion decisions and the criteria guiding those decisions as medical.

This form of talk in Roe reflected modes of reasoning current at the time of
the opinion. The recommendations of the Rockefeller Commission in 1972 presented women as having a "conscience" guiding their decisions about abortion, but
nonetheless emphasized that women make decisions with their doctors:

> The majority of the Commission believes that women should be free to de-
> termine their own fertility, that the matter of abortion should be left to the
> conscience of the individual concerned, in consultation with her physician,
> and that states should be encouraged to enact affirmative statutes creating a
> clear and positive framework for the practice of abortion on request.

Gallup polls in the summer of 1972 also expressed support for decriminalization
in terms that presented women as making decisions with their doctors' guidance.
Gallup reported that "Two out of three Americans think abortion should be a
matter for decision solely between a woman and her physician."

Roe's holding and its reasoning reflected dominant understandings about
abortion of the time. In striking down laws that banned abortion or allowed it in
only a very few circumstances, *Roe* decriminalized abortion along the lines that
the feminists and others advocated. But the Court gave only blurry and indis-
tinct expression to the values feminists argued were at stake in protecting women's
choices. Something similar might be said of the justification the Court offered
for abortion restrictions. The Court gave constitutional approval to a government
interest in regulating abortion to protect potential life, but only barely explained
or justified this interest, leaving unstated how this regulatory interest related to
the old statutes criminalizing abortion or the claims of the contemporary anti-
abortion movement.

IF *ROE* CONFORMED TO then-dominant modes of reasoning about abortion, at
a time when the Gallup poll reported the belief of two-thirds of Americans that
the abortion decision should be left to a woman and her doctor, how are we to
understand the outcry against the decision that steadily mounted over the 1970s?
Our review of the debate before *Roe* reveals several factors contributing to the
conflict over abortion that were in play well before the Court issued its decision in
January 1973, and identifies still other developments that intensified the conflict
much later in the decade.

As we have seen, in the period between 1970 and 1972, even as public support for decriminalization was continuing to grow, bitter conflict over abortion
had already begun. The story of decriminalization in New York and Connecticut
shows that, even where opponents of abortion's liberalization were numerically
outnumbered, they were single-issue focused and passionate in moral conviction.

In the period before *Roe*, the Catholic Church led opposition to decriminalization, organizing to support and punish legislators who voted for abortion's
liberalization. The fact that the Church and the burgeoning right-to-life organiza-

tions were encouraging single-issue voting around abortion caught the attention of politicians—and not only state legislators. Even as Catholics were working to build institutions and arguments opposing abortion in secular and nonsectarian terms, abortion's very identification as a "Catholic" voting issue (however Catholics were divided about abortion, in fact) made the issue of interest to strategists building coalitions for the national political parties during the 1972 presidential campaign.

And so, by 1972, abortion was beginning to find a life in national party politics. Republican Party strategists seeking to persuade Catholic voters and other so-called social conservatives to abandon their traditional alignment with the Democrats and join the Republican cause began to incorporate arguments against abortion rights into their case against the 1972 Democratic presidential nominee, George McGovern. Abortion rights, in this view, symbolized the new morality—a problematic "permissiveness" that afflicted the nation. Those who tarred McGovern as the "triple-A" candidate who favored amnesty, abortion, and acid may have suggested more of a difference between McGovern's position on abortion and that of Republican nominee Richard Nixon than existed in fact; but the anti-McGovern arguments nonetheless helped reframe abortion's meaning.

Triple-A claims about abortion had little to do with the concerns motivating public health reformers (who spoke of back alleys and coat hangers) or the claim advanced by religious opponents of abortion that abortion was murder. But the triple-A claim had much to do with feminist arguments for abortion repeal. Triple-A attacks on McGovern condemned abortion rights as part of a permissive youth culture that was corrosive of traditional forms of authority. The objection to abortion rights was not that abortion was murder, but that abortion rights (like the demand for amnesty) validated a breakdown of traditional roles that required men to be prepared to kill and die in war and women to save themselves for marriage and devote themselves to motherhood. Phyllis Schlafly's attack on abortion never mentioned murder; she condemned abortion by associating it with the Equal Rights Amendment (ERA) and child care.

These shifts in the abortion right's meaning were accelerating in 1972, as the ERA was sent to the states for ratification, and as the question of who should govern the nation was reverberating during the primaries and through the general election. But it is not clear whom these claims actually reached in the period before *Roe*. The claims reframing abortion that we have examined were designed to mobilize Catholic and conservative voters. Patrick Buchanan's "assault book" advised the president's campaign to send anti-abortion messages to Catholics and the National Right to Life Committee convention; and Phyllis Schlafly—who had worked for Barry Goldwater in the 1964 election—sent her *Phyllis Schlafly Report* to a network of conservative readers. The reframing of abortion that would take hold over the course of the 1970s had only incrementally begun at the time the Court handed down *Roe*. (The first justice to join the Court after *Roe* was John Paul Stevens, nominated in December 1975. His views on abortion were unknown, yet at his Senate confirmation hearing, he was not asked a single question about abortion.)

In the immediate aftermath of *Roe*, organized opposition to the decision was still carried by the National Right to Life Committee and the Catholic Church. The National Right to Life Committee began mobilizing in support of a constitutional amendment that would overturn *Roe* and constitutionalize an embryo's/fetus's right to life, thereby requiring all states to *re*criminalize abortion. By 1975, the National Conference of Catholic Bishops had promulgated a Pastoral Plan for Pro-Life Activities that declared that "the decisions of the United States Supreme Court (January 22, 1973) violate the moral order, and have disrupted the legal process which previously attempted to safeguard the rights of children." The plan urged "[p]assage of a constitutional amendment providing protection for the unborn child to the maximum degree possible," and "[p]assage of federal and state laws and adoption of administrative policies that will restrict the practice of abortion as much as possible."

During the years after *Roe*, opponents were unable to muster broad-based support for overturning the decision and requiring abortion's recriminalization. Many Americans supported the right recognized in *Roe*, some quite passionately. Others believed that abortion should be decriminalized but criticized the Court for deciding a question that might have been left to the political process. Those who believed the question should have been left to the legislature did not support a human life amendment constitutionalizing prohibitions on abortion of the kind the right-to-life movement was then advocating. Advocates of a human life amendment could not find the support they needed, even among religious leaders.

In the early 1970s, most Protestant denominations did not share the Catholic Church's view of abortion. As we have seen, mainline Protestant groups approved of liberalizing access to abortion; some approved repeal, while others endorsed variants of the "reform" position, advocating regulation on the "therapeutic model." In this period, conservative evangelical groups did not view abortion as a categorical wrong. Even after *Roe*, in June 1973, Southern Baptist Convention President Owen Cooper criticized the Supreme Court for decisions liberalizing abortion—and banning capital punishment—and then proceeded to observe that the Southern Baptists would support abortions "where it clearly serves the best interests of society." His view of abortion was far from absolute, and expressed in secular, not religious, terms.

When *Roe* was handed down, the family-values movement that would mobilize against the decision and ultimately carry Ronald Reagan to national office in 1980 had already begun to take shape, but it had not yet crystallized. That coalition did not form in spontaneous response to *Roe* but was instead built with the help of strategists for the Republican Party, including many brilliant Catholic conservatives. In the process, opposition to abortion as murder was married to a variety of socially conservative causes, accelerating the process of party realignment that had begun before *Roe* during the Nixon administration. When conservatives of the New Right began to assemble a pan-Christian coalition against *Roe* in the late 1970s, the crusade against *Roe* would proceed under the banner of "pro-life" and "pro-family."

Phyllis Schlafly's Stop ERA organization associated the Equal Rights Amendment with abortion and gay marriage, using this frame to mobilize opposition to the amendment's ratification in state houses across the country. During the mid-1970s, funding battles in Congress provided a lower-stakes arena in which to forge new alliances and erode support for the abortion right. By the late 1970s, Richard Viguerie and Paul Weyrich—architects of a more conservative Republican Party—were approaching such Protestant evangelicals as the Reverend Jerry Falwell and helping them to see in the abortion issue a question that could create a pan-Christian movement united against "secular humanism" and for "family values." By 1980, the *Christian Harvest Times* was denouncing abortion in its "Special Report on Secular Humanism vs. Christianity": "To understand humanism is to understand women's liberation, the ERA, gay rights, children's rights, abortion, sex education, the 'new' morality, evolution, values clarification, situational ethics, the loss of patriotism, and many of the other problems that are tearing America apart today." In this way, a new relationship was emerging among Protestant evangelicals, the Catholic right-to-life movement, and the ascendant conservatives of the New Right. Increasingly lost in this transformation was an earlier Catholic association of a pro-life position with liberal ideals of social justice; forged was an increasingly tight association of pro-life with pro-family politics.

THE DECADES OF STRUGGLE that followed *Roe*—between the pro-life and pro-choice movements and between the Republican and Democratic parties—came deeply to affect the Court and to infuse the Court's reasoning about abortion with a much clearer expression of the convictions of the Americans arrayed in passionate support and opposition to the decision.

The Court's decision in *Roe* was written by Justice Blackmun, whom President Nixon appointed to the Supreme Court in 1970, and supported by other of Nixon's conservative appointees, including Lewis Powell, who during the Court's deliberations actually advocated lengthening the time period in which women's abortion decision was protected—from the end of the first trimester to the end of the second. But over the course of the 1970s, prominent Republicans shifted positions on abortion, acting on alignments and framings that were already in evidence by the 1972 election. By the decade's end, conservatives of the New Right—led by Ronald Reagan, who, in the late 1960s, had signed California's legislation liberalizing abortion—urged fundamentalist Christians to make common cause with Catholics in opposition to abortion and in support of family values. They attacked *Roe* as a threat to life and family and as a symbol of judicial overreaching. Republican Party platforms began regularly to support "the appointment of judges who respect traditional family values and the sanctity of innocent human life."

With Republican presidents appointing justices who might be counted on to oppose *Roe*, judicial support for the decision narrowed, and by the late 1980s, *Roe* looked vulnerable to outright reversal. But the women's movement continued energetically to mobilize in support of the decision, and in 1987 it helped defeat the nomination of Robert Bork, a prominent critic of the Court's privacy decisions. Ensuing Supreme Court appointments by Presidents Reagan and Bush seemed to provide sufficient votes to overturn *Roe*. And yet, in 1992—during a presidential campaign in which the abortion right was a burning issue—the Supreme Court decided *Planned Parenthood v. Casey*, a case that both reaffirmed and narrowed *Roe*.

Casey justified both the abortion right *and* its regulation in terms that reflected the views of mobilized proponents and opponents of abortion rights more clearly than *Roe* itself had in 1973. Like *Roe*, *Casey* held that women had a constitutionally protected right to decide whether to bring a pregnancy to term, but, unlike *Roe*, *Casey* allowed government to regulate the exercise of that right from the beginning of pregnancy in the interests of protecting potential life— so long as the regulation did not impose an "undue burden" on a woman's decision. Even as *Casey* narrowed the right recognized in *Roe*, it justified that right more expansively than *Roe* did. *Casey* tied constitutional protection for women's abortion decisions to the fundamental liberty to choose one's family life, as well as to the understanding—forged in the Court's sex-discrimination cases—that government cannot use law to enforce traditional sex roles: "Her suffering is too intimate and personal for the State to insist, without more, upon its own vision of the woman's role, however dominant that vision has been in the course of our history and our culture. The destiny of the woman must be shaped to a large extent on her own conception of her spiritual imperatives and her place in society."

Casey's account of the constitutional values that the abortion right vindicates makes clear that government respects not only women's freedom but also their equal citizenship. Yet, *Casey* also listens carefully to *Roe*'s critics. It allows government to regulate women's abortion decisions to express respect for the value of human life, so long as government does so in ways that express respect for the decisional autonomy of women: "[T]he State may enact rules and regulations designed to encourage her to know that there are philosophic and social arguments of great weight that can be brought to bear in favor of continuing the pregnancy to full term and that there are procedures and institutions to allow adoption of unwanted children as well as a certain degree of state assistance if the mother chooses to raise the child herself." In ways that *Roe* did not, *Casey* situates the abortion right in a community deeply divided over the basic values implicated by the debate. That conflict continues—on and off the Court.

In *Gonzales v. Carhart* in 2007, the Court voted 5 to 4 to uphold the federal Partial-Birth Abortion Ban Act of 2003. The law had been devised by the right-to-life movement to focus attention on abortions that doctors perform late in pregnancy for medical reasons; the law was designed to provoke public unease with abortion, and it succeeded. Doctors developed the regulated procedure as safer for the woman under some circumstances; abortion opponents succeeded in portraying the procedure as a step from infanticide.

The five justices in the majority insisted that Congress could regulate the method doctors employed in later-term abortions in order to differentiate abortion and infanticide, and so express respect for human life. At the same time, the opinion reaffirmed a woman's right to terminate her pregnancy before viability, as spelled out in *Casey*. But while in *Casey* the Court had, at last, placed women at the center of the abortion decision, in *Carhart* the Court spoke less clearly. To the majority, led by Justice Anthony M. Kennedy, a woman seeking to terminate a pregnancy needed the state's protection against making an unwise choice that she would come to regret. The four dissenters, led by Justice Ruth Bader Ginsburg, recalled *Casey*'s understanding that the abortion right vindicates women's equality and liberty as citizens, objected that the majority had reverted to a view of women as not fully capable of acting in their own best interests.

The future of abortion rights under the United States Constitution remains uncertain. The Supreme Court will again speak to the question, but the record suggests that it is not likely to have the last word. The future lies in the Court's ongoing dialogue with the American people. And the documents that tell *that* story remain to be written.

APPENDIX

Briefs Filed by "Friends of the Court"

Fifteen individual or collective "friends of the court"—*amici curiae*—filed briefs in *Roe v. Wade,* eight for the challengers to the Texas law and seven in the state's defense. (Several on both sides also filed supplemental briefs for the second argument.) This was a substantial number for the time, although it looks small by the standards of today, when even in cases of only moderate importance, the Court often receives two dozen briefs or more.

Here, we present excerpts from ten briefs, six for Jane Roe and four for the state. The ten were selected either because of the significance of the organizational voices, or because a brief differs from others in a distinctive way. (There was, not surprisingly, a fair amount of repetition among the briefs.)

As indicated by its signers, this first brief speaks for the medical establishment. Its perspective is that of medical professionals who believe that criminalizing abortion was "fundamentally unsound in the light of present day medical and surgical knowledge, and a serious obstacle to good medical practice." Although the brief discusses the rights of women, its emphasis is on the rights of doctors to act in their patients' interest, free from fear of criminal prosecution.

Amicus Curiae Brief in Support of Jane Roe

American College of Obstetricians and Gynecologists, American Psychiatric Association, American Medical Women's Association, New York Academy of Medicine, and a Group of 178 Physicians

This brief was filed by Carol Ryan, Esq. Each of the 178 physicians signed individually. All were medical school deans, department chairmen, or professors. One signer was

Charles E. Gibbs, M.D., at the time president of the Texas Association of Obstetricians and Gynecologists.

INTEREST OF AMICI CURIAE

The individuals whose names are appended hereto as amici curiae are deans and vice presidents of medical schools, heads of departments of obstetrics, gynecology and pediatrics in medical schools, practicing physicians and surgeons who are specialists in those fields, and other physicians and psychiatrists having a particular interest in the subject matter of this brief. The organizations whose names are appended hereto are among the largest, oldest and most respected national organizations in the medical profession. These organizations are devoted to the promotion of the highest possible quality health care and it is toward that end that they join in this brief as amici. They include many leaders in the medical profession and renowned teachers in medical schools. As teachers, they are impelled to seek to protect the right of their students—the future generations of doctors—to give their patients the benefit of knowledge acquired in the medical schools. As practicing physicians, amici are bound by oath to give their patients the benefit of the best medical knowledge. These physicians are concerned that the Texas anti-abortion law prevents them from fulfilling their sworn duties and responsibilities in the highest traditions of their profession. They believe that the Texas anti-abortion statute is wrong in principle, fundamentally unsound in the light of present day medical and surgical knowledge, and a serious obstacle to good medical practice. Amici believe that the restrictions imposed by the Texas statute on the performance of medically indicated therapeutic abortions interfere with the physician-patient relationship and with the ability of physicians to practice medicine in accordance with the highest professional standards. Amici are also concerned with the burden the law places on physicians to interpret, at their peril, a statute whose meaning and scope are not clear. Accordingly, amici deem it appropriate to offer arguments with respect to this area of law which is of vital concern to them.

The American Psychiatric Association is a non-profit, tax exempt, scientific and educational medical organization, comprised of those 18,783 qualified Doctors of Medicine who specialize as psychiatrists in the diagnosis, care and treatment of mental diseases and defects of the mind. Abortions are of prime interest to psychiatrists because pregnancy, child bearing, birth and abortions can have material effects upon the mental processes of patients requiring psychiatric diagnosis, evaluation and care.

The Board of Trustees of the APA on December 12–13, 1969, upon recommendation of the Committee on Psychiatry and Law, approved the following:

Position Statement on Abortion

A decision to perform an abortion should be regarded as strictly a medical decision and a medical responsibility. It should be removed entirely from the jurisdiction of criminal law. Criminal penalties should be reserved for persons who perform abortions without medical license or qualification to do so. A medical decision to perform an abortion is based on the careful and informed judgments of the physician and the patient. Among other factors to be considered in arriving at the decision is the motivation of the patient. Often psychiatric consultation can help clarify motivational problems and thereby contribute to the patient's welfare.

ARGUMENT

The Statute Is Unconstitutionally Vague.

Under Texas law, abortion is permitted only "for the purpose of saving the life of the mother." If, following the performance of an abortion, under this law, a physician is brought to trial and the jury disagrees with the physician's interpretation of the meaning of these quoted words, the physician is liable to imprisonment for from two to five years in the penitentiary.

This Court has declared that "a statute which either forbids or requires the doing of an act in terms so vague that men of common intelligence must necessarily guess at its meaning and differ as to its application, violates the first essential of due process of law." Under this standard the statute must fall, because amici respectfully submit that neither they, nor Dr. Hallford nor any other similarly situated physician receive proper notice from the statute of what acts and consultations in their daily practice of medicine will subject them to criminal liability.

Amici contend that the phrase "for the purpose of saving the life" is so indefinite and vague that physicians must guess at its meaning and do in fact differ as to the meaning of the phrase. The word "save" has a broad range of possible meanings. The Random House Dictionary lists, inter alia, "to rescue from danger or possible harm...to avoid...the waste of...to treat carefully in order to reduce wear, fatigue, etc...."

...Life may mean the vitality, the joy, the spirit of existence, as well as merely not dying. The possible interpretations of the statute range therefore from a test requiring imminence of death to one which would permit abortion if desirable to preserve an enjoyable life, i.e., a test under which the physician could consider the effect of pregnancy upon the quality of the patient's life and not merely upon the fact of life as not death. The statute forces the physician to decide at his peril whether a strict or liberal interpretation, or one in between, is the one intended by the statute. It forces him at his peril to make a decision which may be gainsaid by a jury of non-peer laymen whose guess will be as good as his as to the meaning of this statute. In sum the statute fails to provide the certainty required of penal laws.

Physicians have a professional obligation to preserve and advance the health of their patients. Assuming arguendo that the statute should be read as requiring a judgment by the physician that without an abortion the patient will die, the statute conflicts with the physician's obligation because it commands him to ignore all the health interests of his patient with respect to termination of pregnancy unless he can predict that she will die without an abortion. Moreover, the statute does not tell the doctor what factors he may properly consider in making this prediction; nor how certain his prediction must be before he may decide to terminate his patient's pregnancy; nor how soon she must die if she does not have an abortion.

HE MUST GUESS WHETHER the statute allows abortion only if his patient would otherwise die before delivery or if it is sufficient that her life would be significantly shortened thereafter.

If a patient threatens suicide, physicians do not know if they may rely upon the threat as a basis for abortion to save life. Psychiatric consultation may not be available because the woman may refuse such treatment. The non-psychiatrist may then be forced to evaluate the probability of suicide. The physician does not know how he may determine safely whether the patient is sincere in her threat. Furthermore, a woman who does not overtly threaten may be as inclined toward suicide as one who makes clear her threat. The non-psychiatrist doctor is not told whether he may consider suicidal tendencies whether they are stated by his patient, or not.

If a doctor may properly consider the fact that his patient may take her own life unless she receives an abortion, the question is opened whether he may consider the fact that she may seriously imperil her life by obtaining an illegal abortion. For a doctor to consider his patient's threat to obtain an illegal abortion by an unlicensed person is a logical step from his considering her threat of suicide, because such illegal abortions are extremely hazardous and are in fact a common cause of maternal deaths.

Physicians are unable to agree on the meaning of the statute because its words have no medical meaning. Medical standards have been established for treating patients and for terminating pregnancy as part of that treatment. The statute cuts across those standards and requires physicians to apply an unclear legal test which supersedes and may negate their medical judgment.

II. THE TEXAS ANTI-ABORTION STATUTE INFRINGES UPON CONSTITUTIONALLY PROTECTED FUNDAMENTAL RIGHTS OF PHYSICIANS AND OF PATIENTS.

Unquestionably there is a constitutionally protected right to practice one's chosen profession.

The practice of medicine clearly includes the treatment of pregnancy and its attendant conditions. The statute interferes with a physician's practice of medicine by substituting the mandate of a vague legalism for the doctor's best professional judgment as to the medically indicated treatment for his pregnant patients.

Physicians and surgeons in many special branches of medicine routinely make extremely serious decisions regarding their patients' best medical welfare, often with life or death in the balance. But those physicians treating pregnant women run the risk of criminal charges as the result of their professional decisions.

The statute unfairly discriminates against those physicians treating pregnant women and thus denies these physicians equal protection of the laws....

The statute forbids all abortions except those necessary to save the life of the mother. Construing the statute to intend its narrowest possible meaning, i.e., that abortions are lawful only when they will prevent certain and imminent death, it is clear that the operation of the statute may deny women abortions when the abortion would prevent injury or safeguard or preserve the patient's mental or physical health. Thus a woman suffering from heart disease, diabetes or cancer whose pregnancy worsens the underlying pathology may be denied a medically indicated therapeutic abortion under the statute because death is not certain. Such a patient is effectively denied a fundamental constitutional right reserved to her under the Ninth Amendment—the right to medical treatment...

A state may not require that a citizen impair his or her health, even if the individual's right to good health and medical care infringes upon some legitimate state interest. The State of Texas may not in pursuit of its policy infringe upon the constitutionally protected right of its pregnant citizens to the medical treatment they require to maintain their good health.

The anti-abortion statute denies women their right to secure the best medical treatment available and, further, positively and seriously impairs their health by forcing them to turn to illegal abortionists, most of whom are not licensed physicians and do not have the most advanced and safest medical techniques available for their use. Statistics are necessarily uncertain, but a frequent estimate is that over one million criminal abortions occur in the United States each year, resulting in an estimated 5,000 maternal deaths annually. That 5,000 American women a year should be denied medically safe procedures and thus be driven to their untimely deaths to avoid bearing unwanted children is unconscionable.

Death due to complications following illegal abortion procedures are only part of the problem. Many thousands of other women needlessly suffer serious infections following these procedures in addition to pain, suffering and emotional trauma....

A doctor has a direct, personal, substantial interest for his decision may send him to jail. Not only does the State prevent the physician from making an impartial decision about terminating his patient's pregnancy, it unfairly influences this decision in a shocking way. The State says that only if the physician wrongly decides that the operation is needed to preserve her life is he criminally liable. If he wrongly decides the operation is not needed to preserve her life, he is subject to no criminal penalties. The State of Texas thus requires that all errors in a doctor's evaluation of his patient's need for termination of pregnancy be on the side of her death...

A physician practising medicine under the Texas statute cannot keep as his sole concern his patient's life. A doctor would have to be superhuman if he were able to ignore the fact that his decision can be second-guessed by a jury which may totally disregard medical evidence. Therefore, his patient cannot receive the impartial decision required by due process of law....

The freedom to be the master of her own body, and thus of her own fate, is as fundamental a right as a woman can possess.

The Texas statute, by forcing a woman to carry to full term an embryo—regardless of her wishes, her health, her circumstances, her finances, her family or her future—is the most severe and extreme invasion of her right to privacy.

She is forced to function as a baby factory for an unwanted child. In addition to the gross invasion by the state into a pregnant woman's physical autonomy, the law imposes enormous additional obligations on this woman toward her child once it is born. Furthermore, these obligations, involuntarily assumed, continue for many years throughout the child's minority.

It is unthinkable for a state to compel reproduction against a woman's wishes. The right of a woman to avoid pregnancy following conception has been recently recognized in State and Federal Courts.

This Court should not fail to protect the fundamental constitutional right of women to decide whether they want to have children.

Amicus Curiae Brief in Support of Jane Roe

National Legal Program on Health Problems of the Poor, National Welfare Rights Organization, and American Public Health Association

The American Public Health Association had taken an early role in advocating for abortion reform. It is joined here by two organizations representing the interest of the poor. This brief stresses the practical consequences for the poor of laws prohibiting abortion. It also frames the issue as one of discrimination, in violation of the constitutional guarantee of equal protection; middle-class white women could more easily obtain safe abortions than the poor and the non-white. (In the late 1960s and early 1970s, lawyers were advancing the claim that discrimination on the basis of wealth violated equal protection, an argument that the Supreme Court rejected in 1973 in a case concerning the financing of public education.)

The lawyers who signed this brief were Alan F. Charles and Susan Grossman Alexander of the UCLA School of Law.

These organizations share the view that restrictive state abortion laws, such as the Texas statute here under review, have a negative effect on the health and well-being of American women, and have a particularly severe impact on the nation's poor and non-white populations. It is the poor and non-white who suffer most from limited access to legal abortion, and it is they who incur greatly disproportionate numbers of deaths and crippling injuries as a result of being forced to seek criminal abortion....

The State Has No Interest in Increasing Its Population; on the Contrary, Its Interest, if Any, Is in Limiting Population Growth.

In view of the increasing public concern over our rapidly multiplying population, any supposed state interest in increasing the number of lives in being can hardly be raised as a justification for the prohibition of abortion. Indeed, the growing emphasis of both federal and state agencies upon preplanning of families and limitation of their size makes manifestly inconsistent treating the termination of pregnancy as a crime, while birth control devices are not merely permitted but are openly promoted and encouraged by the government....

The Application and Effect of Restrictive Abortion Laws, Such as the Texas Abortion Law, Results in Discrimination Against Poor and Non-White Women in Exercising Their Fundamental Interest in Marital and Individual Privacy, Denying to Them the Equal Protection of the Laws.

While amici contend that to receive proper medical care in the form of an abortion approved and performed by a physician is, by itself, a fundamental interest protected by the Constitution, it is not necessary for abortion to be declared a constitutional right to hold that its discriminatory denial violates guarantees of equal protection.

The State of Texas has prohibited all abortions except for "the purpose of saving the mother's life." On its face, this permits treatment in the case of all women whose lives are similarly endangered, and excludes from treatment all others.

Presumably, therefore those women who qualify for a legal abortion according to the terms of the statute should be able to obtain one, regardless of their race or socio-economic status. There is nothing demonstrable in the differences of skin color or economic condition which suggests that a substantially smaller proportion of the poor or the non-white fall into this category than that of the white and the non-poor, or that the poor and non-white have a substantially different moral attitude on abortion.

On the contrary, a recent study of births occurring between 1960 and 1965 led investigators to conclude that one-third of Negro (as contrasted with one-fifth of white) births were unwanted. Unwanted births were in general more than twice as high for families with incomes of less than $3,000 as for those with incomes of over $10,000; this differential was "particularly marked among Negroes." The results indicated, in the view of the investigators, that there is a "coincidence of poverty and unwanted births rather than a propensity of the 'poor' to have unwanted children."

One explanation for this high level of unwanted births among the poor and the non-white is surely the fact that they do not have equal access to abortions. Data demonstrate that the poor and the non-white do not receive this medical treatment on the same terms as do others. They thus suffer a particularly harsh and adverse effect from the operation of this statute, as they do from that of the other restrictive abortion laws which have existed and currently exist in the United States....

Because the poor rely primarily upon public hospitals for their medical services, denials or delays at those institutions are tantamount to a denial of prompt medical care solely because these women are without funds.

A partial explanation for the marked disparity in these figures appears to lie in the far lower incidence of abortions performed for psychiatric reasons among poor and non-white women. While socioeconomic conditions never per se legally warrant therapeutic abortion, socioeconomic status nevertheless frequently determines whether or not an abortion will be performed, and if performed, whether that self-same abortion will be therapeutic or criminal.

Criminal abortion has been described as the greatest single cause of maternal mortality in the United States; it is one of the greatest cause of disease, infection, and resulting sterilization as well. The poor and the non-white suffer disproportionately from the "back-alley" abortionists, whose services they seek out in lieu of the medically safe hospital abortions generally denied them.

California, the only state known to officially compile such figures, notes that approximately 7 percent of that state's non-white female population subjected themselves to criminal abortion in 1968, as opposed to only 1.5 percent of the state's white female population.

The often tragic results of these abortions are also documented. In their New York study, Drs. Gold, et al. noted that the ratio of criminal abortion deaths per 1,000 live births was 4.0 for white women and 16.2 for non-whites. Likewise, Dr. Hall's 1960–62 study led him to conclude that approximately half of the puerperal deaths among New York's Negroes were due to criminal abortions as opposed to only a quarter of the puerperal deaths among white women.

In sharp contrast to the above data has been the experience in New York State since July 1, 1970, when categorical restrictions on abortion were eliminated. On April 5, 1971, New York City health officials reported that the city's public hospitals, which restricted abortions to city residents, were performing an average of 511 a week, and that the "vast majority" of those women would be unable to afford abortions in private hospitals.

It is clear from this evidence that where the law has eliminated restrictions on the obtaining of abortions, the poor and non-white women who were previously unable to exercise the financial and other kinds of leverage required to have a "therapeutic" abortion, are able to obtain medically safe abortions on an equal basis with all other women, and they do obtain them to at least the same extent as their more privileged sisters. One result has been a drop in the maternal mortality rate: New York City hospitals now report treating far fewer victims of "botched" illegal abortions than they did in years past.

It has been amply demonstrated above that poor and non-white women are not treated equally with other women in obtaining lawful abortions. However neutral its facial appearance, and however unexceptionable its underlying intent, the practical effect of a statute in denying equal treatment to classes of persons, such as the poor or the non-white, must be measured by the Court....

The Texas Abortion Law, While Permitting Abortion to Save a Woman's Life, Irrationally Excludes From Its Protection Women Whose Health May Be Seriously Threatened, Who Bear a Deformed Fetus, Who Have Been Victims of Sexual Assault, Who Are Financially, Socially or Emotionally Incapable of Raising a Child and Whose Family Tranquility and Security Would Be Seriously Disrupted by the Birth of Another Child, Exclusions Which Bear Most Heavily on the Poor and Non-White, and Which Do Not Serve Any Compelling or Reasonable State Interest, Denying to These Women the Equal Protection of the Law.

The Equal Protection Clause of the Fourteenth Amendment requires the states to "exercise their powers so as not to discriminate between their inhabitants except upon some reasonable differentiation fairly related to the object of regulations." The challenged statute operates to deny equal protection to women with compelling reasons for receiving therapeutic abortion, concurred in by their physicians, but whose physicians cannot advance as "medical advice" that the abortion is necessary to "save" their lives. Women so excluded are those who would suffer a serious impairment of physical or mental health from carrying a pregnancy to term, those whose pregnancies are the result of rape or incest, those whose fetuses will, with high medical certainty, be born with gravely disabling physical or mental defects, and those who are financially unable or emotionally incapable of supporting a child, or of adding another child to a family whose limited resources are already strained by their devotion to raising children in being.

[T]he fundamental interest involved in the case of each of the excluded classes of women is as deserving of constitutional protection as the "saving" (whatever it may mean) of the mother's life. Compelling a woman to give birth to a child which is the product of rape or incest, or which will be born deformed, or whose birth will damage the woman's own health or capacity to be a mother to the child or to her existing family, may be as unbearable to the woman as a vague threat to her life itself. That compulsion also puts her physician in the ethically questionable position of having to decide just how much injury he must allow her to bear, despite his obvious ability to prevent that injury, before he can confidently say to the prosecutor that he ultimately acted to save her life.

Certain assumptions must be made and constitutionally accepted to find that there is a basis of rationality to the exclusion of the above-mentioned classes of women from the statute's protection. One is that human-life begins with fertilization of egg by sperm. Another is that this "life" is equivalent to the life of the woman, and the life-saving exception to the abortion law is a rational balancing of interests by the state, analogous to the laws of self-defense.

It is remarkable that the existence of a one-day-old fetus is to be equaled with the life of a grown woman. The woman is—beyond doubt—a human being, one upon whom other human beings (husband, children, etc.) depend in a variety of ways essential to the sanctity of the family, and whose impaired health may be critically disruptive to that family; or one who may not have consented to sexual intercourse made felonious by the state, yet who is forced to bear the consequences of that same felonious act. This equivalency of interest between a microscopic embryo and the woman who bears it must be assumed in the Texas law, however, since that statute draws no lines, such as viability, as the time to invoke the state's protection.

Because the Texas abortion law has the clear effect of denying disadvantaged citizens access to safe hospital abortions, without any justification, it violates the Equal Protection Clause of the Fourteenth Amendment.

Amicus Curiae Brief in Support of Jane Roe

New Women Lawyers; Women's Health and Abortion Project, Inc.; and National Abortion Action Coalition

The lawyer who filed this brief, Nancy Stearns, of the Center for Constitutional Rights, also wrote the brief in the Abramowicz case challenging New York's abortion law. She also played a role in the Connecticut litigation, and in feminist movement challenges to abortion bans in several other states, always incorporating women's voices and concerns into her constitutional argument. As in the earlier cases, her brief in Roe invokes numerous clauses of the Constitution to express the harms abortion laws inflict on women, focusing in particular on the constitutional guarantees of due process and equal protection. Any justice who read this brief would have been exposed to the full range of contemporary feminist argument, vigorously expressed.

STATEMENT OF INTEREST

During the past two years the question of the constitutionality of abortion laws—of the right of a woman to control her own body and life—has become one of the most burning issues for women throughout the country. As women have become aware of the myriad levels of unconstitutional discrimination they face daily, they have become most acutely aware of the primary role which restrictions on abortions plays in that discrimination. As a result, women throughout the country have become determined to free themselves of the crippling and unconstitutional restrictions on their lives. As a major part of their efforts, thousands of women have sought and continue to seek the aid of federal and state courts in their challenges to abortion statutes....

The Georgia and Texas Statutes Restricting the Availability of Abortion Violate the Most Basic Rights of Women to Life, Liberty and Property Guaranteed by the Fourteenth Amendment to the Constitution.

Under the Fourteenth Amendment to the Constitution, no state shall "...deprive any person of life, liberty, or property without due process of law." The courts have not yet, however, begun to come to grips with the fact that approximately one half of our citizenry is systematically being denied those guarantees of the Fourteenth Amendment. That is exactly the effect of the abortion laws of Texas and Georgia, and nearly every other state in the United States. Amici urge this Court not to shrink from redressing the constitutional wrongs perpetrated on women.

For the first time, this Court has the opportunity to give serious and full consideration to the degree to which laws such as those challenged herein, in denying women the control of their reproductive life, violate their most basic constitutional rights....

The decision by a woman of whether and when she will bear children may be the most fundamental decision of her life because of its far-reaching significance, affecting almost every aspect of her life from the earliest days of her pregnancy.

THE RIGHT TO LIFE

Persons seeking to uphold restrictive abortion laws argue that the State has a compelling interest in protecting human life. Amici could not agree more. But, we argue that the responsibility of the State runs to persons who are living and that the State may not maintain laws which effect the most serious invasions of the constitutional rights of its citizens.

e any real meaning
ysical survival. The
and liberty. For the
one which must be
at fact, the Consti-
cy may be denied a

es pregnant her sta-
ions of the govern-
imarily among the
her] faculties...free
; to earn [her] live-
tion...." Pregnancy,
y. In many cases of
porarily or perma-
e employer has no
any stage of preg-
); nor is there any
ardless of whether
s of whether she is
d to stop working
en who are public
me arbitrary date
nuing work.
with pregnancy.
or work" (which
n), if she restricts
t she may care for

anti-abortion law,
inst her wishes, is
unusual punish-
n of the pregnant
rk because of an

v ch
the F
that "the
a hospital on a
the risk ordinarily
he death rate from child

deaths per 100,000 pregna
orted that the death rate due
stern Europe is 3 per 100,000
giving birth is nearly 7 times

uld not continue an unwanted
child, she will not be deterred
ould be illegal. She will do this
al health—and the great finan-
she knows that under local law

le for most women forces them
Aware of the failure rate of most
ancy which they will be unable
mselves to the known and as yet
ould prefer not to.
nat even women who have medi-
ake oral contraceptives feel com-

helming concern for human life,
ple dilemma of choosing between
onsible act of bearing and casting
rdizing their life and health, both
rtion or attempting to self-abort.
fact results in hazards to women's
skilled and unscrupulous persons
rteenth Amendment.

...t and its guarantees are to hav...
...be read to protect only women's ph...
...ent speaks not merely of life, but of life
...stitution recognized well that it is not life a...
...also personal liberty and freedom. Because of th...
...established requirements that neither life nor liber...
...without the guarantees of due process....

It should be obvious that from the moment a woman becom...
...tus in society changes as a result of both direct and indirect ac...
...ment and because of social mores. Except in very rare cases (p...
...wealthy) she is certainly no longer "free in the enjoyment of all [...
...to use them in all lawful ways; to live and work where [she] wil...
...lihood by any lawful calling; to pursue any livelihood or avoca...
...from the moment of conception, severely limits a woman's libert...
...both public and private employment women are forced to tem...
...nently leave their employment when they become pregnant. Th...
...duty to transfer a pregnant woman to a less arduous job during...
...nancy (should the woman or her doctor consider this advisable...
...statutory duty to rehire the woman after she gives birth.... [R]eg...
...the woman wishes and/or needs to continue working, regardles...
...physically capable of working, she may nonetheless be require...
...solely because of her pregnancy. In many if not most states wom...
...employees are compelled to terminate their employment at so...
...during pregnancy regardless of whether they are capable of cont...

But restrictions on a woman's liberty and property only begi...
A woman worker with children is considered "unavailable f...
means that she cannot qualify for unemployment compensatio...
her hours of availability to late afternoon and night shifts so tha...
her children during the day....

Under these circumstances, a case can well be made that the ...
in compelling a pregnant woman to continue this condition aga...
not merely a denial of liberty, but also an imposition of cruel and...
ment on the woman. "Confinement" well describes the situatio...
woman, or mother, who is denied work, or restricted in her wo...
employer's decision on her ability to work.

Here we see how inextricably the rights to life and liberty are mixed and even more how laws restricting abortion deny women both....

A further denial of liberty results from the fact that women are generally forced to arbitrarily end their education because of pregnancy. Until recently, girls who became pregnant were forced to drop out of public school in New York. In New York City, Central Harlem, more than forty percent of the girls who leave school before graduation do so because of pregnancy. This still happens in countless other cities throughout the country as well. Many women are also deprived of higher education because of college rules requiring that pregnant women leave school....

The incursions on the liberty of an unmarried woman who becomes pregnant are even more severe. She too may be fired from her job and is even more likely to be compelled to discontinue her education. Unable to terminate her pregnancy, she is often forced into marriage against her will and better judgment in an attempt to cope with the new economic and social realities of her life. Such marriages are forced on women despite the fact that the right to marry or not to marry may not be invaded by the state.

Of course, frequently, the man who is responsible for the pregnancy refuses to marry her. Then unable to support herself she may be forced to become a welfare recipient, become part of that cycle of poverty, and expose herself to the personal humiliation, loss of personal liberty and inadequate income that entails.

To further add to her difficulties, the mere fact of her out-of-wedlock pregnancy or child resulting from that pregnancy may be used as "some evidential or presumptive effect" to a decision to exclude or remove her from public housing. Thus, having been forced to bear a child she did not want, she may be deprived of her right and ability to provide for herself and her child either because of employer policies or because of her inability to leave the child. Surviving on at least marginal income, she who is most obviously in need of public housing is then deprived of decent shelter because of the existence of that very same child.

For a woman perhaps the most critical aspect of liberty is the right to decide when and whether she will have a child—with all the burdens and limitations on her freedom which that entails. But that has been robbed from her by men who make the laws which govern her....

Restrictive laws governing abortion such as those of Texas and Georgia are a manifestation of the fact that men are unable to see women in any role other than that of mother and wife....

The statutes of Georgia, Texas and nearly every other state in the nation similarly deny to women throughout the country their most precious right to control their lives and bodies.

The Georgia and Texas Statutes Restricting the Availability of Abortions Deny Women the Equal Protection of the Laws Guaranteed to Them by the Fourteenth Amendment

The express guarantee of equal protection was originally designed to protect black people. Since that time, its protection has been greatly extended....

Most recently federal estate courts have begun to apply the guarantees of the equal protection of the laws to prohibit discrimination against women....

Despite the fact that women are entitled to the equal protection of the laws, one major area in which they are daily denied that protection is in the area of abortion.

Man and woman have equal responsibility for the act of sexual intercourse. Should the woman accidentally become pregnant, against her will, however, she endures in many instances the entire burden or "punishment."

In obtaining an abortion, the threats and punishments fall on the woman. This happens even where the decision to have an abortion has been a mutual one. Only the woman is subjected to the variety of threats which often accompany the painful search for abortion—the threats of frightened or hostile doctors of giving her name to the police—the threat of subpoena and/or prosecution if the doctor who would help her is arrested.

It is often said that if men could become pregnant or if women sat in the legislatures there would no longer be laws prohibiting abortion. This is not said in jest. It reaches to the heart of the unequal position of women with respect to the burdens of bearing and raising children and the fact that they are robbed of the ability to choose whether they wish to bear those burdens.

And the woman carries an unequal and greater share of the burden, not merely for nine months, but for many years, all in violation of the equal protection of the laws, as we shall discuss below. The abortion laws therefore present a rather unusual constitutional situation. At first glance, it would appear that the concept of equal protection of the laws might not even apply to abortion since the laws relate only to women. However, when we look beyond the face of the laws to their effect, we see that the constitutional test of equal protection must be applied. For the effect of the laws is to force women, against their will, into a position in which they will be subjected to a whole range of de facto forms of discrimination based on the status of pregnancy and motherhood.

THE RIGHT TO LIBERTY

If the Fourteenth Amendment and its guarantees are to have any real meaning for women, they must not be read to protect only women's physical survival. The Fourteenth Amendment speaks not merely of life, but of life and liberty. For the framers of our constitution recognized well that it is not life alone which must be protected, but also personal liberty and freedom. Because of that fact, the Constitution has established requirements that neither life nor liberty may be denied a person without the guarantees of due process....

It should be obvious that from the moment a woman becomes pregnant her status in society changes as a result of both direct and indirect actions of the government and because of social mores. Except in very rare cases (primarily among the wealthy) she is certainly no longer "free in the enjoyment of all [her] faculties;...free to use them in all lawful ways; to live and work where [she] will; to earn [her] livelihood by any lawful calling; to pursue any livelihood or avocation...." Pregnancy, from the moment of conception, severely limits a woman's liberty. In many cases of both public and private employment women are forced to temporarily or permanently leave their employment when they become pregnant. The employer has no duty to transfer a pregnant woman to a less arduous job during any stage of pregnancy (should the woman or her doctor consider this advisable); nor is there any statutory duty to rehire the woman after she gives birth.... [R]egardless of whether the woman wishes and/or needs to continue working, regardless of whether she is physically capable of working, she may nonetheless be required to stop working solely because of her pregnancy. In many if not most states women who are public employees are compelled to terminate their employment at some arbitrary date during pregnancy regardless of whether they are capable of continuing work.

But restrictions on a woman's liberty and property only begin with pregnancy. A woman worker with children is considered "unavailable for work" (which means that she cannot qualify for unemployment compensation), if she restricts her hours of availability to late afternoon and night shifts so that she may care for her children during the day....

Under these circumstances, a case can well be made that the anti-abortion law, in compelling a pregnant woman to continue this condition against her wishes, is not merely a denial of liberty, but also an imposition of cruel and unusual punishment on the woman. "Confinement" well describes the situation of the pregnant woman, or mother, who is denied work, or restricted in her work because of an employer's decision on her ability to work.

From the very fact, as noted by the California Supreme Court in *People v. Belous* (Cal. 1969), that "childbirth involves the risk of death," it should be most obvious that laws which force women to bear every child she happens to conceive raise the most severe constitutional questions under the Fourteenth Amendment.

Nearly ten years ago a medical expert reported that "the risk to life from an abortion, performed by an experienced physician in a hospital on a healthy woman in the first trimester of pregnancy is far smaller than the risk ordinarily associated with pregnancy and childbirth." A recent study of the death rate from child-birth in the United States revealed that there are still 20 deaths per 100,000 pregnancies among American women. The same study reported that the death rate due to legalized abortions performed in hospitals in Eastern Europe is 3 per 100,000 pregnancies. And so, in the United States today, giving birth is nearly 7 times more dangerous than a therapeutic abortion.

Furthermore, if a woman truly believes she should not continue an unwanted pregnancy and give birth to and raise an unwanted child, she will not be deterred by the fact that an abortion in her circumstances would be illegal. She will do this despite the great hazards to her physical and mental health—and the great financial expense involved. She will do this even though she knows that under local law she is performing a criminal act.

The very fact that legal abortion is unavailable for most women forces them into an additional hazard to their health and life. Aware of the failure rate of most contraceptives and afraid of an accidental pregnancy which they will be unable to terminate, millions of women daily expose themselves to the known and as yet unknown dangers of the pill even though they would prefer not to.

The fear of accidental pregnancy is so great that even women who have medical histories that indicate that they should not take oral contraceptives feel compelled to do so.

Thus while governments profess their overwhelming concern for human life, they force their female citizens into the intolerable dilemma of choosing between what in many instances would be a totally irresponsible act of bearing and casting off, or even "raising" an unwanted child or jeopardizing their life and health, both physical and mental, by obtaining an illegal abortion or attempting to self-abort. What is more, this professed concern for life in fact results in hazards to women's lives, often forcing them into the hands of unskilled and unscrupulous persons directly in the face of the guarantees of the Fourteenth Amendment.

Here we see how inextricably the rights to life and liberty are mixed and even more how laws restricting abortion deny women both....

A further denial of liberty results from the fact that women are generally forced to arbitrarily end their education because of pregnancy. Until recently, girls who became pregnant were forced to drop out of public school in New York. In New York City, Central Harlem, more than forty percent of the girls who leave school before graduation do so because of pregnancy. This still happens in countless other cities throughout the country as well. Many women are also deprived of higher education because of college rules requiring that pregnant women leave school....

The incursions on the liberty of an unmarried woman who becomes pregnant are even more severe. She too may be fired from her job and is even more likely to be compelled to discontinue her education. Unable to terminate her pregnancy, she is often forced into marriage against her will and better judgment in an attempt to cope with the new economic and social realities of her life. Such marriages are forced on women despite the fact that the right to marry or not to marry may not be invaded by the state.

Of course, frequently, the man who is responsible for the pregnancy refuses to marry her. Then unable to support herself she may be forced to become a welfare recipient, become part of that cycle of poverty, and expose herself to the personal humiliation, loss of personal liberty and inadequate income that entails.

To further add to her difficulties, the mere fact of her out-of-wedlock pregnancy or child resulting from that pregnancy may be used as "some evidential or presumptive effect" to a decision to exclude or remove her from public housing. Thus, having been forced to bear a child she did not want, she may be deprived of her right and ability to provide for herself and her child either because of employer policies or because of her inability to leave the child. Surviving on at least marginal income, she who is most obviously in need of public housing is then deprived of decent shelter because of the existence of that very same child.

For a woman perhaps the most critical aspect of liberty is the right to decide when and whether she will have a child—with all the burdens and limitations on her freedom which that entails. But that has been robbed from her by men who make the laws which govern her....

Restrictive laws governing abortion such as those of Texas and Georgia are a manifestation of the fact that men are unable to see women in any role other than that of mother and wife....

The statutes of Georgia, Texas and nearly every other state in the nation similarly deny to women throughout the country their most precious right to control their lives and bodies.

The Georgia and Texas Statutes Restricting the Availability of Abortions Deny Women the Equal Protection of the Laws Guaranteed to Them by the Fourteenth Amendment

The express guarantee of equal protection was originally designed to protect black people. Since that time, its protection has been greatly extended....

Most recently federal estate courts have begun to apply the guarantees of the equal protection of the laws to prohibit discrimination against women....

Despite the fact that women are entitled to the equal protection of the laws, one major area in which they are daily denied that protection is in the area of abortion.

Man and woman have equal responsibility for the act of sexual intercourse. Should the woman accidentally become pregnant, against her will, however, she endures in many instances the entire burden or "punishment."

In obtaining an abortion, the threats and punishments fall on the woman. This happens even where the decision to have an abortion has been a mutual one. Only the woman is subjected to the variety of threats which often accompany the painful search for abortion—the threats of frightened or hostile doctors of giving her name to the police—the threat of subpoena and/or prosecution if the doctor who would help her is arrested.

It is often said that if men could become pregnant or if women sat in the legislatures there would no longer be laws prohibiting abortion. This is not said in jest. It reaches to the heart of the unequal position of women with respect to the burdens of bearing and raising children and the fact that they are robbed of the ability to choose whether they wish to bear those burdens.

And the woman carries an unequal and greater share of the burden, not merely for nine months, but for many years, all in violation of the equal protection of the laws, as we shall discuss below. The abortion laws therefore present a rather unusual constitutional situation. At first glance, it would appear that the concept of equal protection of the laws might not even apply to abortion since the laws relate only to women. However, when we look beyond the face of the laws to their effect, we see that the constitutional test of equal protection must be applied. For the effect of the laws is to force women, against their will, into a position in which they will be subjected to a whole range of de facto forms of discrimination based on the status of pregnancy and motherhood.

As we have discussed at length above, a woman who has a child is subject to a whole range of de jure and de facto punishments, disabilities and limitations to her freedom from the earliest stages of pregnancy. In the most obvious sense she alone must bear the pains and hazards of pregnancy and childbirth. She may be suspended or expelled from school and thus robbed of her opportunity for education and self-development. She may be fired or suspended from her employment and thereby denied the right to earn a living and, if single and without independent income, forced into the degrading position of living on welfare....

If a woman is unmarried, unless she succeeds in obtaining an abortion, she has no choice but to bear the child, while the man who shares responsibility for her pregnancy can, and often does, just walk away....

Having been forced to give birth to a child she did not want, a woman may be subject to criminal sanctions for child neglect if she does not care for the child to the satisfaction of the state....

If such a broad range of disabilities are permitted to attach to the status of pregnancy and motherhood, that status must be one of choice. And it is not sufficient to say that the women "chose" to have sexual intercourse, for she did not choose to become pregnant. As long as she is forced to bear such an extraordinarily disproportionate share of the pains and burdens of childrearing (including, of course, pregnancy and childbirth), then, to deprive her of the ultimate choice as to whether she will in fact bear those burdens violates the most basic aspects of "our American ideal of fairness" guaranteed and enshrined in the Fourteenth Amendment.

There is yet another way in which women are denied the equal protection of the laws. This Court has shown great concern with the "conception of political equality" and particularly with "questions of alleged 'invidious discriminations against groups or types of individuals in violation of the constitutional guaranty of just and equal laws.'" Because of this concern, in a line of cases the court has sought to guarantee that each citizen is fairly and equally represented in the legislature which make laws governing his or her life. Nevertheless, in the instance of abortion laws one finds the grossest form of lack of representation.

This court can surely take judicial notice of the fact that the state legislatures in Texas and Georgia, like state legislatures throughout the country are composed almost exclusively of men....

Therefore we have a situation in which persons are making laws which could never possibly affect them....

Abortion Laws Violate the Constitutional Guarantee Against the Imposition of Cruel and Unusual Punishment.

To understand what having an unwanted pregnancy and child means to a woman, it may be best to consider the following analogy: a group of people are walking along the street. Half the group crosses; the remainder are stopped by a red light. Those stopped by the light are told the following:

> From now on, for about nine months, you are going to have to carry a twenty-five pound pack on your back. Now, you will have to endure it, whether you develop ulcers under the load whether your spine becomes deformed, no matter how exhausted you get, you and this are inseparable.
>
> Then, after nine months you may drop this load, but from then on you are going to have it tied to your wrist. So that, where ever you go this is going to be with you the rest of your life and if, by some accident, the rope is cut or the chain is cut, that piece of rope is always going to be tied to you to remind you of it.

Of course, this analogy is not complete. It does not include the extreme, sometimes excruciating pain and risk of death involved with the process of transferring the pack from your back to your wrist, nor does it fully describe the limitations placed on your liberty by having that load chained to your wrist for a substantial portion, if not all, of your life. It does, however, begin to give some picture of the pain and burden of pregnancy and motherhood when both are involuntary. Forcing a woman to bear a child against her will is indeed a form of punishment, a result of society's ambivalent attitude towards female sexuality. The existence of the sexual "double standard" has created the social response that when a woman becomes pregnant accidentally, she must be "punished" for her transgression, particularly if she is single. This punishment falls solely on the woman: she must face the physical burdens and emotional strains of an unwanted pregnancy, the degrading experience of having an illegal abortion "often in filthy motel rooms at the mercy of quacks who are charging exorbitant fees," and if unable to get such an abortion, the responsibilities and trauma involved in raising an unwanted child. The man equally responsible for the pregnancy faces no such punishment....

The Eighth Amendment to the United States Constitution protects all persons against the infliction of "cruel and unusual punishment." Amici contend that the expanding constitutional concern, as expressed by this Court, with practices which "offend the dignity of man," are contrary to "the evolving standards of decency that mark the progress of a maturing society" and punishment "disproportionate to the offense committed" as violative of the Eighth Amendment necessitates a finding that laws restricting abortion are unconstitutional....

Laws which force women to endure unwanted pregnancy and motherhood against their will or to become criminals and take the risks to physical and mental health resulting from an illegal abortion are disproportionate to the act for which they are being punished—an act which, in many instances, is not even illegal. Further, amici contend that abortions, in fact if not in theory, punish women for private, sexual activity for which only women bear the repercussions of pregnancy therefore punishing them for their status as women and potential child-bearers.

The pain and suffering associated with an unwanted pregnancy or child, is not solely physical pain. The emotional pain and scarring which accompanies an unwanted pregnancy is an equally important and far more lasting form of pain which must be considered in the context of guarantees of the Eighth Amendment, and the emphasis given to mental anguish as a crucial component of "cruel and unusual punishment." According to Dr. Natalie Shainess, who has devoted the majority of her 25-year practice as a psychoanalyst and psychiatrist to the area of feminine psychology and particularly with experience of being a mother, a woman who does not want her pregnancy suffers depression through nearly the entire pregnancy and often that depression is extremely severe. Furthermore, according to Dr. Shainess that depression continues even after birth may even go into psychotic states, and may result in permanent emotional damage to the woman.

Such potential permanent emotional damage, the risks to physical health and safety which may also result in permanent physical harm, and the burdens of taking care of an unwanted child, constitute a form of long-term imprisonment. Such long term imprisonment "could be so disproportionate to the offense as to fall within the inhibition" of the Eighth Amendment....

Millions of women are now becoming truly conscious of the manifold forms of oppression and discrimination of their sex in our society. They are beginning to publicly express their outrage at what they have always known—that bearing and raising a child that they do not want is indeed cruel and unusual punishment. Such punishment involves not only an indeterminate sentence and a loss of citizenship rights as an independent person...great physical hardship and emotional damage disproportionate to the crime of participating equally in sexual activity with a man...but is punishment for her status as a woman and a potential child-bearer.... Abortion laws reinforce the legally legitimized indignities that women have already suffered under for too long and bear witness to the inferior position to which women are relegated. The total destruction of a woman's status in society results from compelling her to take sole responsibility for having the illegal abortion or bear the unwanted child, and suffer the physical hardship and mental anguish whichever she chooses. Only the woman is punished by society for an act in which she has participated equally, only she is punished for her "status" as child-bearer. In light of "evolving standards of decency that mark the progress of a maturing society," the basis of the Eighth Amendment...the struggle of women for full and meaningful equality in society over the last hundred years indicates that it would indeed be a sign of the immaturity of our social development if these laws were upheld. White persons have had to readjust their thinking and actions to question whether laws which discriminated against blacks were unconstitutional.

Men (of whom the legislatures and courts are almost exclusively composed) must now learn that they may not constitutionally impose the cruel penalties of unwanted pregnancy and motherhood on women, where the penalties fall solely on them....

Amicus Curiae Brief in Support of Jane Roe

Planned Parenthood Federation of American, Inc. and American Association of Planned Parenthood Physicians

This brief presents medical information designed to refute the assumption that new methods of birth control, including oral contraceptives, were so reliable that the prohibition of abortion was no longer a serious public health concern.

The lawyers who filed this brief were Harriet F. Pilpel, Nancy F. Wechsler, Ruth Jane Zuckerman, and Michael Kenneth Brown. Harriet Pilpel (1911–1991) was a well-known civil liberties lawyer who served as Planned Parenthood's general counsel. She lectured and wrote widely on free speech issues as well as on abortion.

Planned Parenthood's concern with family planning and family health necessarily includes concern with the availability of abortion and with the compelling problems which result from restrictive abortion laws which make medically safe, legal abortions unavailable to many women. Planned Parenthood has adopted a policy on abortion which states in part:

> The optimum method of birth control is the consistent employment of effective contraception but in practice this goal is sometimes not achieved. It is,

therefore, desirable that provisions respecting abortion not be contained in State Criminal Codes. Planned Parenthood believes that since abortion is a medical procedure, it should be governed by the same rules as apply to other medical procedures in general when performed by properly qualified physicians with reasonable medical safeguards."

This commitment to the principle that safe abortions should be available to all who seek them is a necessary corollary of Planned Parenthood's activities in the area of birth control. While Planned Parenthood does not view abortion as an alternative to contraception, it recognizes that abortion services are essential to protect women where contraception is unavailable, where it has not been used or where it has failed. Planned Parenthood believes that abortions must also be available to women who have been raped and in cases where the fetus may be deformed as a result of the mother's exposure to rubella, her use of drugs which affect fetal development or as a result of other factors.

Amici present the following material to bring to the Court's attention the serious health problems facing women and society where abortion is not available to terminate pregnancies which for a variety of reasons should not result in compelling the birth of a child. Such pregnancies include those resulting from contraceptive failure and from rape, as well as those which will probably result in the birth of a deformed or defective child. They also include pregnancies which if carried to full term will create severe hardship or utterly disrupt the life of the mother, particularly where she is an unmarried teenager.

THE FACTS ABOUT CONTRACEPTION

Although contraceptive services are legally available in all states to married persons and in almost all states without regard to marital status, in fact contraceptives are not readily available to a substantial portion of the population. This is particularly true of urban and rural poor in many areas of the country. In some of these areas even non-prescription and relatively ineffective contraceptives cannot be obtained. Even if some form of contraception is available there is likelihood of unwanted pregnancy since the most effective and practical contraceptives, such as the birth control pill, the intrauterine device, and the diaphragm can be obtained only on the prescription of a doctor whose services are denied to hundreds of thousands of poor....

Because of the unavailability of contraceptives to so many women, and the unavailability in most states of legal abortions, many medically indigent women, who should not be forced to bear a child for medical or other reasons, have no alternative unless willing and able to obtain illegal abortions.

....

ORAL CONTRACEPTIVES (OCS) OF the combined type are "almost 100 percent effective" when "taken according to the prescribed regimen." But the oral contraceptives have disadvantages such as side effects during their early use. Moreover, their use is medically contraindicated for certain patients, particularly those with a history of thromboembolic disease....

[E]ven the theoretically most effective or highly effective methods of contraception are not always actually effective for a number of reasons. Except for voluntary sterilization which many people will not use, even the most effective or highly effective methods have shortcomings either in terms of method failures or in terms of side effects or medical contraindications. In addition some of the methods are so difficult to practice regularly and correctly that they have little practical utility.

Amicus Curiae Brief in Support of Jane Roe

American Ethical Union, American Friends Service Committee, American Humanist Association, American Jewish Congress, Episcopal Diocese of New York, New York State Council of Churches, Union of American Hebrew Congregations, Unitarian Universalist Association, United Church of Christ, and Board of Christian Social Concerns of the United Methodist Church.

This brief presents voices from the liberal religious community. It maintains that for the government to enforce policies based on the Catholic faith—that "the product of every conception is sacred"—would amount to an unconstitutional "establishment" of religion.

The lawyers who filed this brief were Helen L. Buttenwieser and Bonnie P. Winawer. Helen Buttenwieser (1905–1989) was a civic leader and one of the most prominent female attorneys in New York City. In addition to the nine religious organizations listed on the cover, the brief was also signed by the Planned Parenthood Association of Atlanta, Inc.; Georgia Citizens for Hospital Abortion, Inc.; and 23 Georgia residents.

INTEREST OF AMICI

....The Amici do not advocate abortion. They do advocate the right of an individual to be free from State interference in the conduct of his or her private life.

That freedom includes the determination whether or not to have a child. If an individual does not want a child, the Amici believe he or she should be free to use means to that end consistent with the woman's health and safety....

The brief of the Amici stresses that the States may not unreasonably interfere with the constitutional right of an individual to determine the course of his or her own life and that the Georgia and Texas abortion laws constitute such an interference. The Amici present related issues that Appellants have not discussed in their Jurisdictional Statements—namely that there is no constitutional right of birth and that the States may not justify the abortion laws' interference with the personal liberty of all persons on the ground of moral precepts not shared by all.

The Georgia and Texas abortion laws unjustifiably restrict the reserved constitutional liberty of all persons to conduct their private lives without unwarranted governmental interference.

The religious view that the product of every conception is sacred may not validly be urged by the States as a justification for limiting the exercise of constitutional liberties, for that would be an establishment of religion.

The real basis of the claim of state interest in the foetus is a doctrinaire "moral" concern for the "potential of independent human existence." The theoretical moral concern is effected only by permitting a greater moral outrage: the deep human suffering of adults and children alike, that results from compelling one to continue an unwanted pregnancy, to give birth to an unwanted child, and to assume the burdens of unwanted parenthood.

To many minds the "moral" concern for the foetus is misplaced. Reflective judges, scholars and commentators have perceived and deplored the fact that religious beliefs underlie the retention of abortion laws....

No argument is needed to show that the police power cannot be employed in the service of sectarian moral views without violating the Establishment Clause of the First Amendment....

In *Griswold v. Connecticut,* the Court held that the right of privacy, whether drawn from the penumbras of the First, Third, Fourth, Fifth, Ninth and Fourteenth Amendments, or protected by the Due Process Clause of the Fourteenth Amendment, protects the free exercise of one's views (whether of religious or secular origin) on birth control. State laws such as the abortion laws at issue cannot be justified on the ground that they comport with one group's "moral" condemnation of the exercise of the guaranteed freedom by others.

CONCLUSION

The abortion laws invade the fundamental individual liberty reserved by the Constitution to conduct one's personal life without unwarranted governmental interference, and the laws' infringement of that liberty is not warranted by any overriding valid state interest.

Amicus Curiae Brief in Support of Jane Roe

California Committee to Legalize Abortion; South Bay Chapter of the National Organization for Women; Zero Population Growth, Inc.; Cheriel Moench Jensen; and Lynette Perkes

Presenting the most radical argument against the Texas statute, this brief, submitted on behalf of Zero Population Growth and feminist advocates for abortion rights from California, asserts that laws prohibiting abortion impose on women a condition of involuntary servitude in violation of the Thirteenth Amendment, which outlawed slavery. The brief includes a graphic description of the physical burdens of pregnancy, an interesting counterpoint to the detailed portrait of prenatal development contained in the main Texas brief. This brief also cites the Rockefeller Commission report for the proposition that the government's legitimate interest lies in limiting rather than promoting population growth.

The lawyer who filed this brief was Joan K. Bradford, Esq.

Each of the organizations and individuals urges upon the Court the position that laws restricting or regulating abortion as a special procedure violate the Thirteenth Amendment by imposing involuntary servitude without due conviction for a crime and without the justification of serving any current national or public need....

LAWS WHICH RESTRICT OR REGULATE ABORTION AS A SPECIAL PROCEDURE VIOLATE THE THIRTEENTH AMENDMENT BY IMPOSING INVOLUNTARY SERVITUDE WITHOUT DUE CONVICTION FOR A CRIME.

The Thirteenth Amendment to the Constitution provides:

> Neither slavery nor involuntary servitude, except as a punishment for crime whereof the party shall have been duly convicted, shall exist within the United States, or any place subject to their jurisdiction.

The Amendment, by its very language, prohibits both slavery and involuntary servitude, and requires due conviction of a crime as a condition precedent to all forms of involuntary servitude regardless of racial contexts.

From the outset, the Amendment has been interpreted by this Court to apply to all persons without regard to race or class, and to guarantee universal freedom in the United States....

It is the purpose of this brief to show that anti-abortion laws, which force an unwillingly pregnant woman to continue pregnancy to term, are a form of involuntary servitude without the justification of serving any current national or public need.

Involuntary Pregnancy and Childbearing as Involuntary Servitude.

Pregnancy is not a mere inconvenience. "The physical and functional alterations of pregnancy involve all the body systems," displacing body parts, depleting the body of its necessary elements and changing its chemical balance.

The pregnant woman's body is in a state of constant service, providing warmth, nutrients, oxygen and waste disposal for the support of the conceptus. These activities are always to the detriment of the woman's body. They are performed for the benefit of the conceptus alone unless an interest of the pregnant woman is also served thereby, that is, unless the pregnant woman defines the pregnancy as wanted.

During pregnancy, enlargement of the uterus within the abdominal cavity displaces and compresses the other abdominal contents including the heart, lungs and gastrointestinal tract. The resulting pressure has a direct effect on circulation of the blood and increase in venous pressure, sometimes leading to irreversible varicose veins and hemorrhoids and, with predictable frequency, to disabling thrombophlebitis. The gastrointestinal tract experiences functional interference causing constipation and displacement of the urinary tract, thus urinary tract infections occur in six to seven per cent of all pregnant women and such infections, in turn, lead to kidney infections. During the second and third months, bladder irritability is quite constant. Tearing and overstretching of the muscles of the pelvic floor occurs frequently during delivery, causing extensive and irreparable damage to the pelvic organs and their supporting connections. Surgery is often required to return these organs to position. Bladder control may be permanently lost. The weight of the contents of the uterus causes sacroiliac strain accompanied by pain and backache, with the effects of the pressure being felt as far as the outermost extremities of the woman's body. The weight causes such pressure on the cervical spine as to result in numbness, tingling and proprioceptive acuity reduction in the hands.

During pregnancy estrogen levels exhibit severe increase, this phenomenon accounting for the symptoms of nausea and vomiting occurring in one-half or more of all pregnant women. If this condition is prolonged, hospitalization is required. Evacuation of the contents of the uterus results in immediate and dramatic relief of symptoms. In severe cases blood protein may be destroyed. Bodies of women who have died from this condition exhibit the symptoms of starvation, acidosis, dehydration and multiple vitamin deficiencies.

The excess progesterone produced by the placenta causes fluid retention, increase in blood pressure, weight gain, irritability, lassitude, severe emotional tension, nervousness, inability to concentrate, and inability to sleep. At least 40 per cent of pregnant women have symptomatic edema, distorting the hands, face, ankles and feet. A woman's lungs respire 45 per cent more air than normal in an attempt to obtain the needed oxygen, but oxygen absorbed is less than normal despite the extra effort of the crowded lungs.

Because the conceptus utilizes almost twice as much calcium as the pregnant woman can assimilate from administered and dietary calcium, extra calcium must be drawn from a woman's calcium stores, mostly from her long bones. Thus, the pregnant woman is likely to suffer leg cramps. In young women, permanent bone deformation results.

Total loss of a woman's iron stores during pregnancy and delivery is measured at 680 mg. Thus anemia of pregnancy is high and almost all pregnant women, especially those having repeated pregnancies, require supplementary iron. Efforts to correct this condition may fail because many pregnant women cannot tolerate iron supplements.

With such extensive effects, can pregnancy be considered as merely a "natural" state of being?

Amici ask this Court to consider the lack of options open to the pregnant woman at the time of onset of her pregnancy.

A. Contraceptive failure.

Contraceptives are never foolproof. Any act of intercourse between a fertile man and woman constitutes some risk of conception, no matter what contraceptives are used....

If 100,000 women who do not wish to become pregnant take the pill, three will probably die within the year and 1,000 will become pregnant.

Under the present state of contraceptive failure, a woman does not have the option of remaining free of pregnancy by making careful use of contraceptives. She is at some risk in using the most effective methods of contraception available.

B. Limitations on the right to refuse.

The average married woman expects to bear two to three children, yet coitus takes place between a couple married during the period of the woman's reproductive years (age 18 to 43) an average of 2,535 times. The frequency of coitus stated in the Kinsey Report is average behavior between married couples. If the woman wishes to remain free of pregnancy once her desired family size is reached, her only sure method of remaining so free of pregnancy is complete abstinence from sexual intercourse. If she embarks on such a course, will the law uphold her decision?

A wife has no legal power to refuse to participate in the intimacies of married life. If she refuses her husband's forced attentions, there is no law to intervene in her behalf. She cannot charge her husband with rape. Indeed, if a married woman attempts to practice abstinence, the laws of most states treat her behavior as a denial of the marital right of the husband....

Under present law, a married woman has two choices: she can attempt to refuse to fulfill the sexual obligations of the marriage and thus risk termination of her marriage; or she can participate in normal marital relations and risk unwanted pregnancy and childbirth. With a choice of either alternative, she risks the consequence of a legally imposed penalty. The woman is left with no non-punishable course of action.

THE THIRTEENTH AMENDMENT INCLUDES PROTECTION AGAINST INVOLUNTARY PREGNANCY AND CHILDBEARING.

The women who bear children and the medical experts who assist them testify that pregnancy and childbearing are indeed labor. The fact that many women enter into such labor voluntarily and joyfully does not alter the fact that other women, under other circumstances, find childbearing too arduous, become pregnant through no choice of their own, and are then forced to complete the pregnancy to term by compulsion of state laws prohibiting voluntary abortion.

It is the purpose of the Thirteenth Amendment to prohibit a relationship in which one person or entity limits the freedom of another person. In the absence of a compelling state interest or due conviction for a crime, the state's forcing the pregnant woman through unwanted pregnancy to full term is a denial of her

Thirteenth Amendment right to be free from "a condition of enforced compulsory service of one to another." This is the very essence of involuntary servitude in which the personal service of one person is "disposed of or coerced for another's benefit."....

THE STATE'S INTEREST IN RIGHTS OF THE FETUS

....[E]ven if the position were accepted, arguendo, that the fetus is a "person" or "potential person," such recognition of the fetus would not provide the state with a compelling interest to justify encroachment upon the pregnant woman's possession and free control of her own person.

Let us assume, for the time being, that the pregnant woman and the fetus she carries within her body have come before the law as equal "persons." The woman desires an abortion. May the state legitimately intervene to prevent the abortion? At the present stage of medical knowledge and ability to control human incubation, the fetus cannot survive and develop into a separate self-sustaining person without contribution of the bodily force of the single female individual who carries that particular fetus within her body. Yet the laws prohibiting and regulating abortion, unlike all other laws in respect of persons, compel this pregnant woman to breathe, process food and donate blood for the sustenance of another human entity, either fully or partially developed. In no other instance does the law compel one individual to donate his/her bodily force to another individual. In no other instance does the law give another human—even a fully developed human—a right to life beyond that which the person himself can sustain.

The law does not give a person in need of blood the right to receive blood from an unwilling donor; the conclusiveness of the law on this subject being so clearly recognized that it is difficult even to imagine testing such a principle in the courts.

The law does not give a person whose kidneys or other body parts are not functioning the right to demand another person's kidneys or body parts....

Abortion laws alone compel the contribution of one individual's organs, blood, breath and life support system for another individual, either fully or partially formed....

If the pregnant woman, as potential donor, and the fetus, as potential donee, come before the law as equal "persons," one may not command involuntary servitude of the other; and so the potential donor retains her sovereignty over her body and her right to refuse. Therefore, it follows that the fetus, a potential person, can have no greater right over a potential donor. Unless the state has some other compelling interest in forcing the donation of the pregnant woman's body to the service of the fetus, the state must stand aside in the abortion conflict; it cannot legitimately intervene in preventing the pregnant woman from withholding her life force from the fetus....

THE STATE'S INTEREST IN PROMOTING POPULATION GROWTH.

....A state cannot seriously contend today that restrictions on abortion are justified by an overriding state interest in increasing population. See Ehrlich, *The Population Bomb,* 1968. On the contrary, it is accepted government policy to limit family size and to encourage family planning. Such state interest is expressed in *Population and the American Future, The Report of the President's Commission on Population Growth and the Future* (March, 1972) p. 192:

> Recognizing that our population cannot grow indefinitely, and appreciating the advantage of moving now toward the stabilization of population, the Commission recommends that the nation welcome and plan for a stabilized population.

The President's Commission recognizes the acceptability of voluntary abortion as a method of achieving population stability....

Today, this country's population has moved far beyond its needed growth, and current government policy is to encourage population control. Anti-abortion laws have outlived their purpose if regarded in historical perspective. Rights of the individual pregnant woman can no longer be ignored.

The Thirteenth Amendment's promise of freedom has long provided to male citizens the sovereign control of their own bodies.

In 1942, this Court protected the civil right of a male person, even one duly convicted of crime, to control his own reproductive system. Skinner v. Oklahoma (1942). Is it any the less important that this Court protect the right of a female person to control her body and her reproductive system?

We respectfully request this Court to recognize that the anti-abortion laws which force an unwillingly pregnant woman to continue pregnancy to term are a form of involuntary servitude without due conviction for a crime and without the justification of serving any national or public need.

Amicus Curiae Brief in Support of Henry Wade

Americans United for Life

We now turn to the briefs that were filed on behalf of Texas. For a description of Americans United for Life (AUL), see page 88. Just as the public health brief for Jane Roe made an equal protection argument for decriminalizing abortion, this brief also draws on the Supreme Court's equal protection jurisprudence to argue the other side: that permitting abortion amounts to unconstitutional discrimination against the unborn. Pursuing AUL's objective of expressing the wrong of abortion in secular terms persuasive to non-Catholic audiences, the brief locates the right to life of "the innocent child in the womb" in a civil rights framework.

The lawyer who filed this brief was Charles E. Rice, Esq.

THE CHILD IN THE WOMB IS A PERSON WITHIN THE MEANING OF THE EQUAL PROTECTION CLAUSE OF THE FOURTEENTH AMENDMENT.

In *Levy v. Louisiana* (1968), the Court said: "We start from the premise that illegitimate children are not 'nonpersons.' They are humans, live, and have their being. They are clearly 'persons' within the meaning of the Equal Protection Clause of the Fourteenth Amendment."

The child in the womb meets these criteria of personhood under the Equal Protection Clause. He is human, he lives and he has his being. That is, he is a living human being. As the highest court of New Jersey summarized the state of scientific knowledge, "Medical authorities have long recognized that a child is in existence from the moment of conception." Smith v. Brennan (N.J. 1960).

The character of the child in the womb as a person is clearly recognized in the law of torts....

It is significant that a majority of courts, keeping pace with advancing scientific knowledge, now hold that even a stillborn child may maintain a wrongful death action where his death was caused by a prenatal injury.

A similar trend can be seen in the law of property.... The law of property has long recognized the rights of the child in the womb for purposes which affect the property rights of that child....

For purposes of equity, too, the law has recognized the existence of the child in the womb. An unborn child, for example, can compel his father to provide him support. He can compel his mother to undergo a blood transfusion for his benefit, even where such transfusion is forbidden by the mother's religious beliefs....

Suffice it to say that the child in the womb satisfies the three criteria for personhood—he is human, he lives and he has his being—enunciated in *Levy v. Louisiana*. He is clearly alive and in being. As the living offspring of human parents, he can be nothing else but human. As a living human being he is therefore a person within the meaning of the Equal Protection Clause.

Even if one somehow does not concede that the child in the womb is a living human being, one ought at least to give him the benefit of the doubt. Our law does not permit the execution, or imprisonment under sentence, of a criminal unless his guilt of the crime charged is proven beyond a reasonable doubt. The innocent child in the womb is entitled to have us resolve in his favor any doubts we may feel as to his living humanity and his personhood.

IF THE LAW WERE TO ALLOW THE CHILD IN THE WOMB TO BE KILLED WHERE IT IS NOT NECESSARY TO SAVE THE LIFE OF HIS MOTHER, IT WOULD MAKE HIM THE VICTIM OF AN UNREASONABLE CLASSIFICATION AND AN INVIDIOUS DISCRIMINATION IN VIOLATION OF THE EQUAL PROTECTION CLAUSE OF THE FOURTEENTH AMENDMENT.

The right to live is more basic even than the right to procreate. And there is "no redemption" for the aborted child in the womb. The abortion is to his "irreparable injury" and by it he "is forever deprived of a basic liberty." Any law which interferes with the right to live must therefore be carefully scrutinized. It is appropriate to apply here the principles which govern the application of the Equal Protection Clause to another basic right—the right to be free from racial discrimination....

There is no sufficient necessity which justifies a law which permits the killing of the child in the womb where it is not necessary to save the life of his mother. We are not concerned in this appeal with the question of whether a state law can constitutionally allow abortion where it is necessary to save the life of the mother. Rather the issue is whether the constitution permits the child in the womb to be killed where it is not necessary to save the life of his mother. To permit the child in the womb to be killed in such a case improperly discriminates against him on account of his age and situation. For the law does not allow a born child or an adult to be killed at the discretion of another or in any other situation where his killing is not necessary to save the life of another.

Discrimination in employment on account of age is now forbidden by federal law which enunciates a strong public policy. And while age may be a reasonable criterion for determining the right to vote or to drive a car, it can hardly be contended that it is a reasonable basis for determining whether one has a right to continue living. The child in the womb should have the same right as his older brother or sister not to be killed where it is unnecessary to save the life of his mother. Nor should the fact that he temporarily reposes in his mother's womb rather than in an incubator or a crib operate to deprive the child of the right to continue living....

Amicus Curiae Brief in Support of Henry Wade

Certain Physicians, Professors and Fellows of the American College of Obstetricians and Gynecologists

This brief argues for the personhood of an obstetrician's unborn patient, and also asserts that abortion is medically dangerous for women.

The lawyers who filed this brief were Dennis J. Horan; Jerome A. Frazel, Jr; Thomas M. Crisham; Dolores B. Horan; and John D. Gorby. The brief was signed by 222 individual doctors, including medical school professors and those in private practice. Among the signers were 113 fellows of the American College of Obstetricians and Gynecologists, dissenting from the organization's official position as expressed in the brief it filed on behalf of Jane Roe. One of the signers was Dr. John C. Willke, whose Handbook on Abortion, had recently been published (see pp. 99–112). The lead counsel, Dennis J. Horan (1932–1988), was one of the country's most prominent anti-abortion lawyers and spokesmen. A legal advisor to the United States Catholic Conference, he founded Americans United for Life's legal defense fund and later served as AUL's chairman.

Ed.'s note: Omitted from this excerpt is a description of fetal development that duplicated the description contained in the main brief for Henry Wade. Another brief filed in support of the Texas law, by the Texas Diocesan Attorneys, contained a similar description.

INTEREST OF THE AMICI

[A]mici are physicians, professors and certain Fellows of the American College of Obstetrics and Gynecology who seek to place before this Court the scientific evidence of the humanity of the unborn so that the Court may know and understand that the unborn are developing human persons who need the protection of law just as do adults.

These amici also desire to bring to the Court's attention the medical complications of induced abortion, both in terms of maternal morbidity and mortality (as well as the mortality to the child), and to show that these are questions of considerable debate in medicine....

In reviewing the Briefs filed in both cases it appears that no attempt was made to advise the Court of the scientific facts of life from conception to birth, or of the medical complications of induced abortion....

An expansion of the right to privacy to include the right of a woman to have an abortion without considering the interests of the unborn person decides this question against the unborn. The necessary consequence of that expansion would be a direct and unavoidable conflict between the unborn person's right to life and the woman's extended right of privacy. Assuming such a conflict, it is the position of the amici that the more fundamental and established of the conflicting rights must prevail where they clash. The right to life is most certainly the most fundamental and established of the rights involved in the cases facing the Court today.

THE UNBORN OFFSPRING OF HUMAN PARENTS IS AN AUTONOMOUS HUMAN BEING.

MEDICAL HAZARDS OF LEGALLY INDUCED ABORTION.

The medical hazards of legally induced abortion are all too often compared to the safety of a tonsillectomy or the "proverbial tooth extraction." (See Texas Appellant's brief.) Data presented from Eastern European mortality statistics have often been used to produce such claims as "it is X-times safer to have an abortion than to carry the child to term." These claims have been widely published in newspapers and lay periodicals; when made by the non-professional, they are forgivable; when made by "medical experts," one can only assume that these "experts" have allowed a desire for "social change" to fog their ability to distinguish first-rate from second-rate medical care.

The world's medical literature does not support such claims. The medical hazards of legal abortion should be presented to the Court in their total perspective through an analysis of this literature. It is imperative to note that when one focuses only on the legal abortion mortality rates from selected countries around the world, one can only see the risks of legal abortion through tunnel vision. The total medical picture cannot be understood without a look at the early and late physical and psychological complications. Indeed, these are the complications which affect the greater number of people and result in what a World Health Organization scientific group said was "a great amount of human suffering."

....The obstetrician has two patients: mother and child. It is deplorable to think that discussions of mortality can so easily exclude the child. The court should recognize that the mortality to the child is nearly 100%. Only an occasional child has the strength to survive. Let us not forget that abortion kills children of varying ages and stages in development. The unheard voices of these little ones are our concern, and we deplore this violent trend which is turning the healing art of medicine into a source of efficient swift and sure destruction of human life. A trend which will yield a "body count" unlike any we have seen in our nation's history. We deplore the condition of a society which calls physicians to exercise their art as a tool of death for those yet unborn....

Most abortion proponents not involved in public efforts to promote their cause, admit that elective removal of the fetus is without psychiatric or medical justification. The fetus has not been shown to be a direct cause of any emotional disorder, and present medical capabilities make pregnancies safe. Almost always, other means than abortion are available to handle any medical or psychiatric complications of pregnancy. Indeed, if a woman wants her child, there are no medical or psychiatric indications that ever make an abortion necessary....

The medical hazards of legally induced abortion are significant and must be recognized. When one focuses only on selected abortion mortality rates from Eastern Europe to make claims regarding the safety of legally induced abortion, one is looking for a motive to sell abortion. While the mortality rates alone do not present a total perspective analysis, they should not, on the other hand, be isolated from the 100% mortality, numbering already in the hundreds of thousands, of innocent unborn children. Indeed, one must recognize that the performance of legally induced abortion upon healthy women is not the practice of medicine at all, but rather another example of the violence of our times; the use of one more technological skill to destroy human life....

CONCLUSION

It is respectfully submitted that the unborn is a "person" within the meaning of the 5th and 14th Amendments. Consequently, the unborn's life can be taken only with due process of law, and its life is entitled, like all other persons' lives, to equal protection under the law.

The voidance of state abortion statutes by court or legislature is governmental action which deprives the innocent unborn of the right to life, and therefore deprives them of equal protection and due process. This Court should therefore protect the unborn's constitutional rights in any decision it renders.

Amicus Curiae Brief in Support of Henry Wade
National Right to Life Committee

Presenting itself as "non-sectarian" despite its origins in, and continuing ties to, the Catholic Church, the National Right to Life Committee offers a point-by-point refutation of constitutional arguments for abortion rights. The right to privacy recognized by the Supreme Court in the 1965 birth control case, Griswold v. Connecticut, *cannot be applied to abortion, the brief argues, because "there is another important interest at stake, the life of the unborn child."*

The lawyers who filed this brief were Alfred L. Scanlan; Robert M. Byrn; Juan J. Ryan; Joseph V. Gartlan, Jr., and Martin J. Flynn. Robert Byrn had published the early and influential law review article excerpted in Part I, page 86, and also brought a lawsuit that challenged the constitutionality of New York's legalization of abortion [see page 150, Byrn v. NYC Health and Hospital*].*

INTEREST OF THE AMICUS CURIAE

The National Right to Life Committee is a non-sectarian, interdisciplinary organization that is committed to informing and educating the general public on questions related to the sanctity of human life. Protecting the right to life of the unborn child is of central concern for NRLC. The Committee believes that proposals for total repeal or relaxation of present abortion laws represent a regressive approach to serious human problems. NRLC is in favor of a legal system that protects the life of the unborn child, while recognizing the dignity of the child's mother, the rights of its father, and the responsibility of society to provide support and assistance to both the mother and child....

NEITHER THE NINTH NOR THE FOURTEENTH AMENDMENT PROHIBITS A STATE FROM PROTECTING AGAINST THE DESTRUCTION OR ABORTION OF HUMAN LIFE

....NRLC sees no point in belaboring the scientifically obvious. Life begins at conception and for practical medical purposes can be scientifically verified within 14 days. Within three weeks, at a point much before "quickening" can be felt by the mother, the fetus manifests a working heart, a nerve system, and a brain different from and independent of the mother in whose womb he resides; the unborn fetus is now a living human being. It is universally agreed that life has begun by the time the mother realizes she is pregnant and asks her doctor to perform an abortion.

The appellants, and those allied with them as amici curiae in this case, are hard put to deny that a state has a grave and important interest in preventing the destruction of human life through unjustifiable abortion. However, they argue that even assuming such an interest, the abortion laws do not reflect that interest since, they claim, such laws were passed for another purpose, i.e., to protect the life and health of pregnant women who submit to illegal, and what once were highly dangerous, operations. Their position here crumbles before the thrust of the history of Anglo-Saxon law both in England and in this Country. That history shows conclusively that the protection of the life of the unborn child was always a major purpose, if not the paramount purpose, surrounding the enactment of the abortion laws in both England and the United States....

Let us then address ourselves specifically to the question of balancing the two rights which may appear to be in conflict in these cases. That question must be: To what extent can the State protect the right of an unborn infant to continue its existence as a living being in the face of a claim of right of privacy on the part of a woman to decide whether or not she wishes to remain with child?

This Court has decided that the Constitution protects certain rights of privacy on the part of a woman arising from the marital relationship which cannot be unjustifiably interfered with by the State. NRLC believes that the genesis of such rights, to the extent such rights may exist, must be found among the "penumbral" personal liberties protected by the Due Process Clause of the Fifth Amendment. Yet equally unchallengeable is the proposition that an unborn child's right not to "be deprived of life," to quote the words of the Due Process Clause itself, is also a fundamental personal right or liberty protected by that same amendment and entitled to the traditional searching judicial scrutiny and review afforded when basic personal liberties are threatened by state action, whether legislative or judicial in character. Therefore, it is very clear that this case is not one, as the appellants would portray it, which involves merely the balancing of a right of personal liberty (i.e., a married woman's privacy) against some competing, generalized state interest of lower priority or concern in an enlightened scheme of constitutional values, such as the state's police power. Here, the Court must choose between a nebulous and undefined legal "right" of privacy on the part of a woman with respect to the use of her body and the State's right to prevent the destruction of a human life. That election involves the determination as to whether the State's judgment that human life is to be preferred is a prohibited exercise of legislative power.

There would be no question of the answer, of course, if the choice were between a woman's "right to privacy" and the destruction of an unwanted after-born child. Yet abortion is distinguishable from infanticide only by the event of birth. The recent findings of medical science now suggest that any distinction, at least from a medical if not a legal point of view, disappears very early in a woman's pregnancy and in the life of the unborn child within the womb. Contrary to the appellants' assumption in these cases, a state's interest in regulating abortion is not bottomed exclusively on concern for the health of the mother, a concern which admittedly would be of less than persuasive effect, since it cannot be successfully established that abortions during the early period of pregnancy performed by competent physicians in hospital surroundings represent a substantially high medical risk to the life and health of the mother. The state interest which justifies what Texas and Georgia have done rests on a concern for human life, even though that life be within the womb of the mother. Such an interest on the part of the State has existed since the common law of England. Now the separate, early and independent existence of fetal life has been conclusively proven by medical science. While it may be impossible for the State to insist on maintaining such a life under all circumstances, can it seriously be maintained that the Government is powerless to insist on protecting it from intentional destruction, absent danger to the mother's life?

Under the analysis set out above, the appellant's argument in support of a woman's "sovereignty...over the use of her body" cannot stand. Either (1) the argument means that she has a "private right" or personal freedom which permits her to decide, for any reason whatsoever, whether to sustain and support, or whether to eliminate, a life which she alone may decide is unwanted; or (2) it means that she has some kind of right to bodily integrity which permits her and her alone to decide under all circumstances whether to retain, or permit to be destroyed, a human life contained within her own body.

In all fairness we doubt that the first is the correct understanding of the basis of the "private right of personal freedom" for which the appellants contend. For, were that principle ever to be accepted as the law, there would have crept into the Constitution a potentially terrifying principle that, with very little more logic than the appellants have relied upon to sustain their position in these cases, would equally justify infanticide and euthanasia, at least if the victims were those in a relationship of dependence with the person or persons who wished to destroy them. Nor would the laws which forbid abandonment, failure of support and child neglect be immune from attack.

If the appellants and their supporting amici are maintaining that a woman has a right to the integrity of her body sufficient to permit her alone to decide, for whatever reason, whether to terminate a pregnancy, the proposition cannot prevail. If a woman has sovereignty over her body of the degree suggested by the appellants, how could the States ban prostitution, outlaw suicide or prohibit the use of harmful drugs?

However, in the amicus brief filed by the American Association of University Women and other women's organizations, the "sovereignty of the body" argument is made in a disguised and superficially more plausible form. These amici assert a woman's right of "reproductive autonomy." This they define as the "personal, constitutional right of a woman to determine the number and spacing of her children, and thus to determine whether to bear a particular child.... "Such a right, those amici argue, evolves inevitably from the recognition which this Court has afforded to those human interests "which relate to marriage, sex, the family and the raising of children." ...Parents may have a constitutional right to plan for the number and spacing of children. Still, that right cannot be extended to permit the destruction of a living human being absent a threat to the life of the mother carrying the unborn baby. Family planning, including the contraceptive relationship, is a matter between a man and a woman alone. The abortion relationship, on the other hand, is between the parents and the unborn child....

....NRLC disputes the assertion that a woman enjoys any right of privacy, as yet undefined in American law, which vests in her alone the absolute authority to terminate a pregnancy for any reason whatsoever. No precedents of this Court have gone so far....

In relying on the *Griswold* case, the appellants have not considered that in this case, as opposed to that decision, there is another important interest at stake, the life of an unborn child. If, despite all the medical evidence and legal history on the point, the unborn child is not to be considered a person within contemplation of the law with legally protectable interests, then *Griswold* possibly might be stretched to serve as a precedent for the result that the appellants urge this Court to reach. On the other hand, if terminating pregnancy is something different from preventing it, if abortion is different from cosmetic surgery, if the fetus is not in the same class as the wart, and if we are dealing with something other than an inhuman organism, then *Griswold* is totally inapposite. As medical knowledge of prenatal life has expanded, the rights of the unborn child have been enlarged. And even if it could still be argued that the fetus is not fully the equal of the adult, the law, through centuries of judicial decision and legislation, and following the lead supplied by medical science, has raised the equivalency of that life to such a status that the unborn child may not be deprived of it, absent the demonstrated necessity of protecting a reasonably equivalent interest on the part of the mother. *Griswold,* of course, presented no such conflict and therefore is not controlling in this case....

THE REMAINING CONSTITUTIONAL ARGUMENTS ADVANCED BY THE APPELLANTS AND THE AMICI CURIAE SUPPORTING THEM ARE WITHOUT MERIT

In both cases, the doctor-appellants alleged that the particular statute in question "chills and defers plaintiffs from practicing their profession as medical practitioners" and thus offends rights guaranteed by the First and Fourteenth Amendments. The dispositive answer to these contentions is that neither statute proscribes speech or medical advice but prohibits the commission of the criminal acts specified in the statute. If, as this amicus maintains, the acts outlawed by the statutes are within the constitutional competency of Texas and Georgia to proscribe as criminal conduct, then the argument is closed. Criminal acts do not fall within the "freedom of speech" which the First Amendment protects. On the other hand, if we are wrong and these statutes do represent unconstitutional invasions of a woman's right to privacy, then the free speech argument advanced by the doctor-appellants becomes superfluous. Apart from that, however, we do not believe that the appellants can seriously argue that these abortion statutes are vulnerable on their face as abridging a doctor's or anyone else's right of free expression.

The identical rationale also answers appellants' claims that any freedom to pursue the profession of medicine guaranteed by the Due Process Clause of the Fourteenth Amendment is offended by the statutes involved in these cases. And it legitimately could be asked whether the deliberate destruction of the unborn child, absent a threat to a mother's life or a serious menace to her health, is really the practice of the "healing art" of medicine.

As so often happens in such cases, the parties attacking abortion statutes argue that they discriminate against the economically deprived. Specifically, appellants contend that there is an advantage to the class which is able to obtain abortions and that this advantage is enjoyed only by the more affluent people of Texas, Georgia and the rest of the United States. We doubt that this contention rises to the level of a constitutional argument which must be dealt with in these cases. If it were necessary, NRLC would point out that the statutes on their face apply to all persons committing the acts condemned and that there is no suggestion that they seek to discriminate on any invidious basis, including that of income.

Of course, departing from the facts of the two cases, it might be argued abstractly that (1) a poor woman finds it more difficult than a rich woman to leave Texas or Georgia in order to get an abortion in a jurisdiction where that might be legal, and (2) she cannot afford treatment by a private physician who, some might say, would be more inclined to find a legal reason for the abortion. Hence, the two statutes bear unequally upon the poor. However, the same theoretical argument could be made of many types of conduct proscribed by the criminal laws of Texas and Georgia. There are jurisdictions to which wealthy persons may travel in order to indulge in the doubtful pleasures of gambling at will, using narcotics without restraint, and enjoying a plurality of wives. Could these doubtful "advantages" on the part of the rich be relied on as any basis to set aside the criminal statutes of Texas or Georgia proscribing such activities within those jurisdictions?

And even if it were assumed to be true that the rich are more likely than the poor to secure the services of a sympathetic physician for purposes of terminating an unwanted pregnancy, such a result, unintended by the statute, would not rise to the level of a constitutional infirmity.... If the statute is to fail, it must be shown that on its face it takes away a right guaranteed to the poor by the Constitution. No such showing is possible in these cases.

Many criminal laws in actual practice do bear with unequal severity upon the poor. It is they who are more likely than the rich to be caught, to be unable to post bail bond, to be prosecuted, to be unskillfully defended, to be convicted and to be punished. However, the remedy for these injustices of society lies in the elimination or mitigation of the conditions and causes of poverty and in the reform of the administration of criminal justice, not by the selective invalidation of otherwise lawfully enacted criminal statutes.

APPELLANTS' PUBLIC POLICY ARGUMENTS ARE MISPLACED

In addition to their arguments of unconstitutionality, the appellants, and their supporting amici, dwell at some length on what they believe is the poor public policy inherent in the Texas and Georgia abortion statutes in particular and in abortion laws generally. Attention is called to the fact that the presence of strict abortion statutes requires women often to go to non-medical practitioners for the performance of illegal abortions conducted under poor hygienic conditions. The problem of world overpopulation is also touched upon in the appellants' marshalling of their reasons why they think abortion laws are a bad thing. Finally, in the brief of at least one of the amici, there is the suggestion that abortion laws stand in the way of women's liberation and represent a stamp of servility imposed by men upon the women of America.

In our opinion, the validity of all of these arguments is very questionable. In any case, their assertion, directly or indirectly, in this litigation is misplaced. They should be directed to the legislatures of Texas and Georgia, not to this Court. Moreover, we point out that in recent years it has not been impossible to convince state legislatures that their abortion statutes should be revised. Even if the appellants' public policy arguments were addressed to a legislative body, NRLC would dispute their validity. For example, Sweden, a country not unlike ours, and the nation which has had the longest experience with state-regulated abortions in Western Europe, has produced no evidence that criminal abortions, estimated at 20,000 a year when the law was passed in 1938, have been substantially reduced since that time. Other studies confirm the belief that liberalization of abortion laws effect no reduction in the rate of criminal abortions and all that is done is to increase the total number of abortions.

So far as any alleged problem of overpopulation is concerned, abortion, whether on the free demand of a woman or on the intimidating command of the State, appears as a completely ineffective and extremely dangerous way to deal with such a problem, if it exists. For instance, one side effect of the repeal of abortion statutes and the fostering of abortion through state auspices is that no group will be more likely to feel the sting more bitingly than the mothers of illegitimate children. Already, laws making the birth of illegitimate children a crime suggest the squeeze to which the poor mother might be subjected in an age of unrestricted, and state-sponsored, abortion.

Finally, the suggestion that laws against abortion were enacted by men to constrain the behavior of women has nothing to support it except the historical accident that most of the criminal statutes, including abortion laws, were enacted by male legislators in the 19th Century when women were unable to vote. It is not evident how this general condition of political freedom influenced abortion laws more than it influenced other developments in the criminal law. Moreover, more women than men currently disapprove of elective, or unrestricted, abortion. The suggestion that abortion laws are peculiarly the product of a male-dominated government is especially inapposite in the case of Georgia, which enacted the abortion statute involved in this litigation in 1968. This amicus applauds the continuing process by which illegal discriminations against women have been removed. However, the claim that a woman should be free to destroy a human being whom she has conceived by voluntarily having sexual intercourse can only make sense if that human being be regarded as part of herself, a part which she may discard for her own good. However, at this point, the evolution of social doctrine favoring freedom for women collides squarely with modern scientific knowledge and with the medical and judicial recognition that the fetus in the womb is a living person. A woman should be left free to practice contraception; she should not be left free to commit feticide.

Amicus Curiae Brief in Support of Henry Wade
Women for the Unborn

This brief's stated goal was to present the voices of women speaking for the unborn, as opposed to those briefs filed by "groups of women who are advancing the rights of women alone." The brief argues that abortion is an "easy" but not a "true solution" to a woman's problems. We see here a use of the phrase "abortion-on-demand" with a negative connotation that suggests recklessness; should the court "extend abortion-on-demand to the entire country?" the brief asks.

The lawyer who filed the brief was Eugene J. McMahon, Esq. The brief was signed by Diane Arrigan, president, Women for the Unborn, "representing 2,000 women;" Lucille Buffalino, chairman of the Long Island Celebrate Life Committee, "representing 1,500 women;" and Mrs. Norbet Winter, president, Women Concerned for the Unborn Child, "representing 1,500 women."

INTEREST OF THE AMICI CURIAE

The interest of the organizations and the persons listed below as amici curiae in this case arises from the fact that there are appearing before this Court amici curiae and other groups of women who are advancing the rights of women alone. We are stressing the rights of the unborn without overlooking the rights of the mothers. This brief will treat the psychological, medical and other factors involved as well as legal points. However, it will not duplicate material presented in other briefs.

It is to plead on behalf of life that we have prepared this brief. As women and mothers, we ask the Justices of the Supreme Court to consider our views, which can be summed up in the following four statements:

(1) The unborn child is a distinct individual. Modern genetics has confirmed scientifically what women have long felt intuitively—the presence of another human life, a life to be reverenced and protected.

(2) Many women who seek abortions are acting from an overpowering but temporary fear. Most of these women really desire to have their baby, and they will later be glad that their effort to secure an abortion was unsuccessful. In order to react constructively to the stresses and tensions of pregnancy, women need the support of society—not the address of the nearest abortion clinic.

(3) While abortion is an easy solution for many social problems, it is not a true solution for any. Its availability may prevent more constructive solutions from emerging.

(4) The social consequences of unlimited abortion are as yet unknown.

Furthermore, both the moral and the legal arguments for abortion-on-demand have attained popularity only within the last few years. Since the test of time has not been applied, should a final decision be made which would extend abortion-on-demand to the entire country?

AS WOMEN, WE BELIEVE the state laws restricting abortions protect both thousands of unborn babies and thousands of mothers. Therefore, we respectfully ask the Justices of this Court not to strike them down.

The easy solution of abortion discourages more constructive solutions.

Even if one overlooks the biological evidence concerning the unborn child, or the psychological testimony that most women seeking to take the life of their unborn baby, like most persons seeking to take their own life, desire to be stopped by someone, is abortion really a satisfactory solution to any social problem? Will the availability of the easier abortion "solution" discourage our society from seeking deeper and more permanent solutions?

Such a fear appears to lie behind the opposition to abortion-on-demand within the black community. Despite assurances by abortion advocates, many members of the black community seem to suspect that numerous abortion clinics in ghetto areas could end up as the "white man's" solution to the problems of poverty and race.

When the poor cry out for bread, what response will they receive? The more difficult response—an equitable distribution of society's resources? Or the easier response—a list of centers where abortions can be performed on those who would not seek them except for their desperate poverty? While these two responses are not mutually exclusive, to what extent will the availability of the second lessen society's incentive to seek the first?

Sponsors of non-abortional family planning have also expressed concern that reliance on abortion could lessen the effectiveness of their efforts. Could abortion-on-demand adversely affect other programs which require a commitment of society's resources—e.g., programs to assist the unwed mother or efforts to provide easily accessible counseling services for all women who need such support in order to respond constructively to the anxieties they experience during pregnancy?

Perhaps these fears about the adverse social effects of easy abortion will turn out to be unfounded. At the moment, however, that is far from certain. Until some kind of definite evidence is available concerning the social pattern that is emerging in those states which have removed all restrictions on abortion, should a final decision be made which would extend abortion-on-demand to the entire country? For if easy abortion does indeed produce such undesirable social effects, would this not be a ground in itself for state regulation of the practice?

If a verdict of unconstitutionality is reached concerning state laws which protect the unborn child and the mother herself from an immediate decision to terminate life, then the legislative discussion is over. If these laws are held to be constitutional, their wisdom will continue to be debated in our state and national legislatures.

If any doubt exists, would it not be better to allow the discussion to continue?

On behalf of the unborn child...the mother...and society itself...we ask the Court to preserve the right of the state to protect unborn human life.

ACKNOWLEDGMENTS

Just as this book contains many voices, it is the product of many hands.

Jennifer Bennett worked on the project from its conception through its production, and played a role both creative and practical throughout; Jennifer Keighley also provided invaluable assistance. "Research assistant" does not begin to convey the contribution made by "the Jenns," two wonderfully gifted young women, both 2010 graduates of Yale Law School.

We are indebted to two remarkable Yale Law School librarians, Camilla Tubbs and Jason Eiseman, whose enthusiasm for this project carried them above and beyond the call of duty. Their help in identifying, retrieving and organizing in digital space a substantial archive of original and secondary sources was indispensable.

We thank Naomi Rogers, Barry Friedman, Hunter Smith, and Sarah Hammond for the time they devoted to reading the manuscript at various stages of its assembly and for the helpful feedback they provided. Linda Kerber, one of the country's preeminent historians, was most helpful in providing national context for our New York and Connecticut documents. We thank Barbara Consiglio for her invaluable assistance in preparing the documents for editing.

Amy Kesselman was extraordinarily generous in helping us to recover documents from *Women vs. Connecticut*, a case on which she has done significant historical research. Members of the original legal team, including Gail Falk, Ann Freedman, Kathryn Emmett, and Dina Lassow, were extremely helpful. We particularly thank Nancy Stearns and Rhonda Copelon. Judge Jon O. Newman joined the hunt for lost documents and found some in his files.

And we are especially indebted to those whose words became our primary source material. Any of the authors whose work is here reproduced could have said no, but all said yes, and so enabled us to reconstruct for our readers some sense of the national conversation about abortion that unfolded in the decade before *Roe*.

Last but not least, in consideration of the many conversations shared and evenings foregone through the production of this book, we thank, for their extraordinary partnership and their patience, Eugene Fidell and Robert Post.

SOURCES AND
SUGGESTED READING

Sources for the documents are noted with each excerpt. Here, we offer sources for additional background, as well as for the quotations and other information presented in the annotations.

Additionally, in copying the excerpts, we have corrected spelling errors in the original documents, and made spelling, punctuation and formatting consistent. The paragraph structure of the documents may differ from the originals, and headings within the original documents were not always reproduced in the excerpts. We have endeavored to mark any passages omitted from the excerpts by ellipses.

PART I: Reform

LETTER FOUND IN FILES OF SOCIETY FOR HUMANE ABORTION

On the social history of abortion and contraception, see:

Brodie, Janet Farrell. *Contraception and Abortion in 19th-Century America* (Ithaca, NY: Cornell University Press, 1994).

Gordon, Linda. *The Moral Property of Women: A History of Birth Control Politics in America* (Champaign, IL: University of Illiinois Press, 1974).

Luker, Kristin. *Abortion and the Politics of Motherhood* (Berkeley, CA: University of California Press, 1984).

Messer, Ellen & Kathryn E. May. *Back Rooms: Voices from the Illegal Abortion Era* (New York: St. Martin's, 1988).

Mohr, James C. *Abortion in America: The Origins and Evolution of National Policy, 1800-1900* (New York: Oxford University Press, 1978) 147-170.

Reagan, Leslie J. *When Abortion Was a Crime: Women, Medicine, and Law in the United States, 1867-1973* (Berkeley, CA: University of California Press, 1997).

Tone, Andrea. *Controlling Reproduction: An American History* (Wilmington, DE: SR Books, 1997).

On Jane Roe, see:

Kaplan, Laura. *The Story of Jane: The Legendary Underground Feminist Abortion Service* (Chicago: University of Chicago Press, 1995).

Kaplan, Laura. "Beyond Safe and Legal: The Lessons of Jane," *Abortion Wars: A Half Century of Struggle, 1950-2000* (Rickie Solinger ed., Berkeley, CA: University of California Press, 1998) 33.

On illegal abortions before *Roe*, see:

Solinger, Rickie. "Extreme Danger: Women Abortionists and Their Clients before Roe v. Wade," *Not June Cleaver: Women and Gender in Postwar America, 1945-1960* (Philadelphia: Temple University Press, 1994) 335.

THE LESSER OF TWO EVILS

"The Abortion Puzzle," *Tulsa Tribune*, July 27, 1962.

"The Drug that Left a Trail of Heartbreak: The Full Story of Thalidomide," *Life* (Aug. 10, 1962) 24.

ABORTION: THE LAW AND THE REALITY IN 1970

"Minnesota's Abortion Law on Trial," *Minneapolis Tribune*, November 25, 1970.

ILLEGAL ABORTION AS A PUBLIC HEALTH PROBLEM

For the proceedings of a 1955 conference on abortion organized by Calderone and Planned Parenthood, see:

Calderone, Mary Steichen. *Abortion in the United States* (New York: P. B. Hoeber, 1958).

AMERICAN MEDICAL ASSOCIATION, POLICY STATEMENTS ON ABORTION

On the role of the medical profession in enacting laws criminalizing abortion in the nineteenth century, see:

Burns, Gene. *The Moral Veto: Framing Contraception, Abortion, and Cultural Pluralism in the United States* (London: Cambridge University Press, 2005).

Mohr, James C. *Abortion in America: The Origins and Evolution of National Policy, 1800-1900* (New York: Oxford University Press, 1978) 147-170.

CLERGY STATEMENT ON ABORTION LAW REFORM AND CONSULTATION SERVICE ON ABORTION

On the Clergy Consultation Service, see:

Moody, Howard. *A Voice in the Village: A Journey of a Pastor and a People* (Bloomington, IN: Xlibris, 2009) 311-328.

Wolff, Joshua D. *Ministers of a Higher Law: The Story of the Clergy Consultation Service on Abortion* (1998).

ABORTION LAW REFORM IN THE UNITED STATES

The proceedings of the 1969 California Conference on Abortion are compiled in:

Abortion and the Unwanted Child (Carl Reiterman ed., New York: Springer, 1971).

PART I: Repeal

INTRODUCTION

For an account tracing the development of constitutional claims for abortion rights and women's equal citizenship, see:

Siegel, Reva B. "Sex Equality Arguments for Reproductive Rights: Their Critical Basis and Evolving Constitutional Expression," *Emory Law Journal* 56 (2007) 815.

NATIONAL ORGANIZATION FOR WOMEN BILL OF RIGHTS

For an overview of NOW's early history, see:

The Founding of NOW: Setting the Stage, National Organization for Women, http://www.now.org/history/the_founding.html (last visited Jan. 1, 2010).

For more on the founding of NOW, and the women's movement in the 1960s and 70s more generally, see:

Carabillo, Toni, Judith Meuli, and June Bundy Csida. *Feminist Chronicles, 1953-1993* (Women's Graphics, 1993).

Freeman, Jo. *The Politics of Women's Liberation: A Case Study of an Emerging Movement and Its Relation to the Policy Process* (Boston: Longman, 1975) 84-85.

Rosen, Ruth. *The World Split Open: How the Modern Women's Movement Changed America* (New York: Penguin, 2000) 92-93.

For information on the founding of the Women's Equity Action League, see:

> Berkeley, Kathleen C. *The Women's Liberation Movement in America* (Westport, CT: Greenwood Press, 1999) 34.

ABORTION: A WOMAN'S CIVIL RIGHT

Lawrence Lader, one of the co-founders of NARAL, documented the organization's founding in

> *Abortion II: Making the Revolution* (1973) 88-97.

For more of *Lader's* earlier writings, see:

> Lader, Lawrence. *Abortion* (Boston: Beacon Press, 1966).

Additional information on the founding of NARAL can be found in:

> Davis, Flora. *Moving the Mountain: The Women's Movement in America Since 1960* (Champaign, IL: University of Illinois Press, 1999).

> Staggenborg, Suzanne. *The Pro-Choice Movement, Organization and Activism in the Abortion Conflict* (New York: Oxford University Press, 1991).

For more on Betty Friedan, see:

> Friedan, Betty. *Life So Far: A Memoir* (New York: Simon & Schuster, 2006).

> Horowitz, Daniel. *Betty Friedan and the Making of the Feminine Mystique* (Boston: University of Massachusetts Press, 1998).

CALL TO WOMEN'S STRIKE FOR EQUALITY, AUGUST 26, 1970

The *Women's Strike for Equality* has yet to be chronicled in sufficient depth. The following sources discuss the strike in varying levels of detail:

> Freeman, Jo. *The Politics of Women's Liberation: A Case Study of an Emerging Movement and Its Relation to the Policy Process* (Boston: Longman, 1975).

> Rosen, Ruth. *The World Split Open: How the Modern Women's Movement Changed America* (New York: Penguin, 2000).

> Dow, Bonnie J. "Spectacle, Spectatorship, and Gender Anxiety in Television News Coverage of the 1970 Women's Strike for Equality," *Communication Studies* 50 (1999) 143.

> Klemesrud, Judy. "A Herstory-Making Event," *New York Times Magazine*, Aug. 23, 1970. 6, 14.

Post, Robert C. and Reva B. Siegel. "Legislative Constitutionalism and Section Five Power: Policentric Interpretation of the Family and Medical Leave Act," *Yale Law Journal* 112 (2003) 1943-2060.

The following unpublished dissertation collects primary source documents from the strike:

Bernard, Shirley. *The Women's Strike: August 26, 1970* (1975) (unpublished Ph.D. dissertation, Antioch College) (available through ProQuest Direct's Dissertation database).

WOMEN'S STRIKE FOR EQUALITY FLYER

On feminist support for abortion rights see:

Gordon, Linda. *The Moral Property of Women: A History of Birth Control Politics in America* (Champaign, IL: University of Illinois Press, 2002).

On feminist support for child care see:

Berry, Mary Frances. *The Politics of Parenthood: Child Care, Women's Rights, and the Myth of the Good Mother* (New York: Penguin, 1993).

Morgan, Kimberly J. "A Child of the Sixties: The Great Society, the New Right, and the Politics of Federal Child Care," *Journal of Policy History* 13 (2001) 215.

Umansky, Lauri. *Motherhood Reconceived: Feminism and the Legacies of the Sixties* (New York: New York University Press, 1996) 46-50.

A SPEAK-OUT-RAGE: A WOMAN'S RIGHT TO CHOOSE

Vidal, Mirta. "Chicanas Speak Out," *Women: New Voice of La Raza* 9 (1971) 14.

For an overview of the role of women of color in movements for reproductive rights, see:

Nelson, Jennifer. *Women of Color and the Reproductive Rights Movement* (New York: New York University Press, 2003).

Roberts, Dorothy E. *Killing the Black Body: Race, Reproduction, and the Meaning of Liberty* (New York: Vintage, 1997).

FEMINIST AS ANTIABORTIONIST

For background on Sidney Callahan, see:

Callahan, Sidney and Daniel Callahan. "Abortion: Understanding Differences," *Perspectives in Family Planning* 16 (1984) 219.

For more of Sidney Callahan's writings, see:

Callahan, Sidney. "Abortion and the Sexual Agenda: A Case for Prolife Feminism," *Commonweal* 25 (1986) 232.

On pro-life feminism, see:

> Grenier Sweet, Gail, ed. *Pro-Life Feminism: Different Voices* (New York: Life Cycle Books, 1985).
>
> Krane Derr, Mary, Rachel MacNair & Linda Naranjo-Huebl eds. *ProLife Feminism; Yesterday & Today* (Bloomington, IN: Xlibris, 1995).
>
> Matthewes-Green, Frederica. *Real Choices: Listening to Women, Looking for Alternatives to Abortion* (Ben Lomand, CA: Conciliar Press, 1997).

BLACK WOMEN'S MANIFESTO; DOUBLE JEOPARDY: TO BE BLACK AND FEMALE

> Center for Research on Population and Security, *Population and the American Future: The Report of the Commission on Population Growth and the American Future* (also known as the Rockefeller Commission Report) (1972), http://www.population-security.org/rockefeller/001_population_ growth_ and_the_american_future.htm.
>
> Chisholm, Shirley. *Unbought and Unbossed* (New York: Houghton Mifflin, 1970) 122.
>
> Gregory, Dick. "My Answer to Genocide: Bitter Comic Prescribes Big Families as Effective Black Protest," *Ebony* (October 1971) 66.

For more on Jesse Jackson's early abortion views, see:

> Burke, Vincent J. "Zero Growth Held 'Choice' of Nation," *Los Angeles Times* (March 12, 1972) 1.

For Jackson's views during his presidential campaign, see:

> McCarthy, Colman. "Jackson's Reversal on Abortion," *Washington Post* (May 21, 1988) A22.

For the *Chicago Daily Defender* poll results see:

> "Blacks Split on Sex," *Chicago Daily Defender* (February 15, 1971) 1.

For critical analysis of race and reproduction, see:

> Cade, Toni. "The Pill: Genocide or Liberation," *The Black Woman: An Anthology* (New York: Signet, 1970) 162.
>
> Nelson, Jennifer. *Women of Color and the Reproductive Rights Movement* (2003).
>
> Roberts, Dorothy E. *Killing the Black Body: Race, Reproduction, and the Meaning of Liberty* (New York: Vintage, 1997).
>
> Ruffin, Frances E. "Birth Control: Survival or Genocide," *Essence* (September 1972) 42.
>
> Solinger, Rickie. *Wake Up, Little Susie: Single Pregnancy and Race before* Roe v. Wade (New York: Routledge, 1992).

Beal's excerpt is reprinted in:

Morgan, Robin, ed. *Sisterhood Is Powerful: An Anthology of Writings from the Women's Liberation Movement* (New York: Vintage, 1970).

INTRODUCTION TO POPULATION CONTROL

For an overview of population control advocacy that ranges well beyond its intersection with abortion reform in the late 1960s, see:

Connelly, Matthew. *Fatal Misconception: The Struggle To Control World Population* (Boston: Harvard University Press, 2008).

ZERO POPULATION GROWTH: PROGRESS?

Ehrlich, Paul R. *The Population Bomb* (New York: Ballantine, 1968).

A SEX COUNSELING SERVICE FOR COLLEGE STUDENTS

Student Committee on Human Sexuality. *The Student Guide to Sex on Campus* (1971).

For more on the "sexual revolution," see:

Allyn, David. *Make Love Not War: The Sexual Revolution: An Unfettered History* (New York: Routledge, 2000).

Gerhard, Jane. *Desiring Revolution: Second-Wave Feminism and the Rewriting of American Sexual Thought, 1920 to 1982* (New York: Columbia University Press, 2001).

PART I: Religion

INTRODUCTION TO RELIGION SECTION

For a compilation of official statements on abortion from a wide variety of religious denominations over time, see:

Melton, J. Gordon, ed. *The Churches Speak on Abortion: Official Statements from Religious Bodies and Ecumenical Organizations* (Gale Group, 1989).

UNION FOR REFORM JUDAISM, 49TH GENERAL ASSEMBLY, MONTREAL, QUEBEC

Rabbinical Council of America. *Statement on Abortion* (1972).

UNITED METHODIST CHURCH, STATEMENT OF SOCIAL PRINCIPLES

United Methodist Church, Methodist Board of Social Concerns. *Statement on Responsible Parenthood* (1969).

SOUTHERN BAPTIST CONVENTION, RESOLUTION ON ABORTION

American Baptist Convention. *Resolution on Abortion* (1968).

Southern Baptist Convention. *Resolution on Abortion* (1979).

On the Conservative Resurgence, and the history of American Baptists generally, see:

Leonard, Bill J. *Baptists in America* (New York: Columbia University Press, 2007).

NATIONAL ASSOCIATION OF EVANGELICALS, STATEMENT ON ABORTION

National Association of Evangelicals. *Resolution on Abortion* (1973).

National Association of Evangelicals. *Resolution on Man and Woman* (1979). Resolutions of the National Association of Evangelicals are available at *www.nae.net/resolutions/* (accessed Jan. 31, 2010).

HUMANAE VITAE

Lambeth Conference of Anglican Bishops. *The Life and Witness of the Christian Community—Marriage and Sex, Resolution* (1930) 15.

Pope Pius XI. *Casti Connubii: Encyclical on Christian Marriage* (1930).

"Pope Paul's Remarks on Birth Control," *New York Times* (June 24, 1964) 3.

Hoyt, Robert G. *The Birth Control Debate* (Kansas City, MO: National Catholic Reporter, 1968) (reprinting majority and minority reports of Papal Birth Control Commission).

For the American Catholic Church's reaction to *Griswold*, see:

"Birth Control Information To Be Available in State," *Hartford Courant* (June 8, 1965) 11.

For a history of *Humanae Vitae* and the Catholic Church's position on birth control, see:

Shannon, William H. *The Lively Debate: Response to Humanae Vitae* (Riverside, NJ: Andrews McMeel, 1970).

On Catholic involvement in American politics, see:

Byrnes, Timothy A. *Catholic Bishops in American Politics* (Princeton, NJ: Princeton University Press, 1991).

HUMAN LIFE IN OUR DAY: PASTORAL LETTER BY THE NATIONAL CONFERENCE OF CATHOLIC BISHOPS

"Text of the Statement by Theologians," *New York Times* (July 31, 1968) 16.

On opposition to *Humanae Vitae*, see:

Callahan, Daniel. "Contraception and Abortion: American Catholic Responses," *Annals of the American Academy of Political and Social Science* 109 (1970) 112-13.

Keely, Charles B. "Limits to Papal Power: Vatican Inaction After Humanae Vitae," *Population and Development Review* 220 (1994) 225.

Fleming, Thomas J. "Confrontation in Washington: The Cardinal vs. The Dissenters," *New York Times* (November 24, 1968) SM54.

"Religion: Catholic Freedom v. Authority," *Time* (November 22, 1968).

Shannon, William H. *The Lively Debate: Response to Humanae Vitae* (Riverside, NJ: Andrews McMeel, 1970).

PART I: Reaction

NEW JERSEY CATHOLIC CONFERENCE PAMPHLET

The history of the National Right to Life Committee before *Roe v. Wade* is not well-documented. Although there is widespread agreement that the NRLC was initially funded by the Catholic Church, accounts differ about the specific details of its founding, and particularly the date upon which it was founded. Our account is based on unpublished NRLC documents from the time period retrieved from the archive at the Gerald R. Ford Library. Published sources on the origins of the NRLC include:

Blanchard, Dallas A. *The Anti-Abortion Movement and the Rise of the Religious Right: From Polite to Fiery Protest* (New York: Twayne, 1994) 28, 82.

Fiske, Edward B. "Bishops To Press Abortion Battle," *New York Times* (April 14, 1967) 35.

Gorney, Cynthia. *Articles of Faith: A Frontline History of the Abortion Wars* (New York: Simon & Schuster, 1998).

Munson, Ziad W. *The Making of Pro-Life Activists* (Chicago: University of Chicago Press, 2008) 82-83.

Risen, James and Judy L. Thomas. *Wrath of Angels: The American Abortion War* (1999).

ABORTION AND SOCIAL JUSTICE

Forsythe, Clark D. *A Strategic History of Americans United for Life (1971-2008)*, http://www.aul.org/AUL_History (last visited Jan. 31, 2010).

Miriam Ottenberg, "Some Fund-Raisers Dream Up Causes To Win Your Dollar for Charity," *Iowa City Press-Citizen*, June 21, 1972.

On the founding of Americans United for Life, see:

Allitt, Patrick. *Catholic Intellectuals and Conservative Politics in America 1950-1985* (Ithaca, NY: Cornell University Press, 1993) 186-89.

Mason, Carol. *Killing for Life: The Apocalyptic Narrative of Pro-Life Politics* (Ithaca, NY: Cornell University Press, 2002) 140-41.

HANDBOOK ON ABORTION

For more on the *Willkes,* see:

Gorney, Cynthia. "The Dispassion of John C. Willke," *Washington Post Magazine* (April 22, 1990) 20.

ABORTION MAKES STRANGE BEDFELLOWS: GOP AND GOD

Phillips, Kevin P. *The Emerging Republican Majority* (New York: Arlington House, (1969).

PART II

ABORTION LAW REFORM AND REPEAL: LEGISLATIVE AND JUDICIAL DEVELOPMENTS

For an overview of state legislative reform efforts before *Roe,* see:

Burns, Gene. *The Moral Veto: Framing Contraception, Abortion, and Cultural Pluralism in the United States* (London: Cambridge University Press, 2005).

LEGISLATION: NEW YORK

Everywoman's Abortion: "The Oppressor is Man"

Barden, Jim. "Getting Hospital Abortion in New York City Depends on Words Used in Request," *United Press International* (Mar. 6, 1967).

Garrow, David J. *Liberty and Sexuality: The Right to Privacy and the Making of* Roe v. Wade (New York: Scribner, 1994) 311.

On access to hospital abortions, see:

Reagan, Leslie J. *When Abortion Was a Crime: Women, Medicine, and Law in the United States, 1867-1973* (Berkeley, CA: University of California Press, 1997) 201-02.

For more on the *Redstockings,* see:

Brownmiller, Susan. *In Our Time: Memoirs of a Revolution* (New York: Dial Press, 1999).

Nelson, Jennifer. *Women of Color and the Reproductive Rights Movement* (2003) 30-38.

For an overview of the availability of abortions before *Roe* in New York, see:

Tolchin, Martin. "Doctors Divided on Issue," *New York Times* (Feb. 27, 1967) 1.

Plaintiffs' Brief, *Abramowicz v. Lefkowitz*

For more on *Abramowicz,* see:

Schulder, Diane and Florence Kennedy. *Abortion Rap* (New York: McGraw-Hill, 1971).

Stearns, Nancy. "Commentary: Roe v. Wade: Our Struggle Continues," *Berkeley Women's Law Journal* 4 (1990) 1, 2-5.

For the preliminary opinion in the case (which was consolidated with other abortion litigation in New York), see:

Hall v. Lefkowitz, 305 F. Supp. 1030 (S.D.N.Y. 1969).

For a discussion of the draft opinion that might have been issued if the case had not become moot, see:

Randolph, Raymond. "Address: Before Roe v. Wade: Judge Friendly's Draft Abortion Opinion," *Harvard Journal of Law and Public Policy* 29 (2006) 1035.

Memorandum of Assemblywoman Constance E. Cook

For Constance Cook's account of mobilization in support of the repeal bill, see:

Nossiff, Rosemary. *Before Roe, Abortion Policy in the States* (Philadelphia: Temple University Press, 2001) 66.

Brief of Plaintiff-Appellant, *Byrn v. New York City Health & Hospitals Corporation*

Kovach, Bill. "A Last-Minute Switch Rescues Bill After Bitter Debate," *New York Times* (Apr. 10, 1970) 1.

Goodman, Janice, Rhonda Copelon Schoenbrod, and Nancy Stearns. "Doe and Roe: Where Do We Go From Here?" *Women's Rights Law Reporter* 20 (1973) 28.

Byrn v. New York City Health & Hospitals Corp., 31 N.Y. 2d 194 (1972).

For an account of the legislative reform effort in New York, see:

Nossiff, Rosemary. *Before Roe, Abortion Policy in the States* (Philadelphia: Temple University Press, 2001) 77-105.

Letter from President Richard Nixon to Cardinal Terence Cooke

For information on the antiabortion rally sponsored by the Knights of Columbus, see:

"Thousands Here Urge Repeal of Abortion Statute," *New York Times* (Apr. 17, 1972) 27.

For an account of antiabortion demonstrations in Albany, see:

Narvaez, Alfonso A. "Abortion Repeal Urged in Albany," *New York Times* (Apr. 18, 1972) 43.

Farrell, William E. "Women Protesting Easier Abortions Storm Assembly and Halt Proceedings," *New York Times* (Apr. 19, 1972) 94.

On the efforts of antiabortion advocacy groups, see:

> McFadden, Robert D. "Lobbying on Abortion Increases at Capitol," *New York Times* (May 8, 1972) 43.

For Rockefeller's criticism, see:

> McFadden, Robert D. "President Supports Repeal of State Law on Abortion," *New York Times* (May 7, 1972) 1.

Governor Rockefeller's Veto Message

For the legislative response to the antiabortion mobilization, see:

> Garrow, David J. *Liberty and Sexuality: The Right to Privacy and the Making of* Roe v. Wade (New York: Scribner, 1994) 546-47.

The City Politic: The Case of the Missing Abortion Lobbyists

On popular support for the 1970 law, see:

> Garrow, David J. *Liberty and Sexuality: The Right to Privacy and the Making of* Roe v. Wade (New York: Scribner, 1994) 546-47.

On political mobilization in support of the 1970 law, see:

> McFadden, Robert D. "Lobbying on Abortion Increases at Capitol," *New York Times* (May 8, 1972) 43.

On continuing efforts to recriminalize abortion in New York in the period before *Roe,* see:

> Garrow, David J. "Abortion Before and After *Roe v. Wade*: An Historical Perspective," *Albany Law Review* 62. (1999) 833, 840-41.
>
> Buckley, Tom. "Both Sides Gird for Renewal of Fight on Legalized Abortion, Explosive Legislative Issue," *New York Times* (Jan. 2, 1973) 78.

LITIGATION: CONNECTICUT

For the only historical account of the Connecticut case and its social movement origins, see:

> Kesselman, Amy. "Women Versus Connecticut: Conducting a Statewide Hearing on Abortion," *Abortion Wars: A Half Century of Struggle* (Rickie Solinger ed., Berkeley, CA: University of California Press, 1998) 42.

For more of *Kesselman's* research on the women's liberation movement in Connecticut, see:

> Kesselman, Amy. "Women's Liberation and the Left in New Haven, Connecticut, 1968-72," *Radical History Review* 81 (2001) 15.

Class action style lawsuits modeled on the New York and Connecticut litigation were also filed in other states, including Illinois, Massachusetts, New Jersey, Pennsylvania, and Rhode Island. Nancy Stearns, one of the key participants in the Connecticut and New York litigation, played an integral role in many of these suits. Stearns was personally involved with the New Jersey and Rhode Island cases, and she shared her papers with the litigants in the Massachusetts and Pennsylvania suits. For more on these cases (some of which did not result in any published opinions), see:

Doe v. Scott, 321 F. Supp. 1385 (N.D. Ill. 1971).

Complaint, Women of Mass. v. Quinn, Civ. No. 71-2420-W (D. Mass. November 1, 1971).

YWCA v. Kugler, 342 F. Supp. 1048 (D.N.J. 1972).

Ryan v. Specter, 321 F. Supp. 1109 (D. Pa. 1971).

First Amended Complaint, Women of Rhode Island v. Israel, No. 4605 (D.R.I. May 14, 1971).

Women v. Connecticut Organizing Pamphlet

For more on Nancy Stearns's involvement in pre-*Roe* abortion litigation, see:

Goodman, Janice, Rhonda Copelon Schoenbrod, and Nancy Stearns. "Doe and Roe: Where Do We Go From Here?" *Women's Rights Law Reporter* 20 (1973) 28.

Stearns, Nancy. "Commentary: Roe v. Wade: Our Struggle Continues," *Berkeley Women's Law Journal 4* (1990) 1,2.

For more on *Catherine Roraback,* see:

Connecticut Women's Hall of Fame. "Catherine G. Roraback," *www.cwhf.org/browse_hall/hall/people/roraback.php* (accessed Jan. 21, 2010).

Weisberg, Jonathon T. "In Control of Her Own Destiny: Catherine G. Roraback and the Privacy Principle," *Yale Law Reporter* (Winter 2004) 39.

Memorandum of Decision, *Abele v. Markle* I

Complaint, *Abele v. Markle*, 342 F. Supp. 800 (D. Conn. 1972) (Civ. No. 14291).

For Judge Lumbard's full opinion, see *Abele v. Markle*, 342 F. Supp. 800 (D. Conn. 1972). Judge Lumbard cites to the Nineteenth Amendment, which gave constitutional protection to women's right to vote, as recognizing women's equal citizenship. Lumbard also references the then-pending Equal Rights Amendment, and cites to Title VII, which prohibits employment discrimination on the basis of sex. See 42 U.S.C. §§ 2000e to 2000e-15. He also cites *Reed v. Reed*, the first Supreme Court case striking down a law under the Fourteenth Amendment's Equal Protection Clause because the law discriminated on the basis of sex. See *Reed v. Reed*, 404 U.S. 71 (1971).

Memorandum of Decision, *Abele v. Markle* **II**

For Judge Newman's full opinion, see *Abele v. Markle*, 351 F. Supp. 224 (D. Conn. 1972).

For more on Judge Newman's opinion, see:

Hurwitz, Andrew D. "Jon O. Newman and the Abortion Decisions: A Remarkable First Year," *New York Law School Law Review* 46 (2002) 231.

Legislative Hearing

Fellows, Lawrence. "Connecticut Assembly Weighs Strict Abortion Bill," *New York Times* (May 17, 1972) 53

Kesselman, Amy. "Women Versus Connecticut: Conducting a Statewide Hearing on Abortion," *Abortion Wars: A Half Century of Struggle* (Rickie Solinger ed., 1998) 42, 57.

Memorandum of Decision, *Abele v. Markle* **II**

Kandell, Jonathan. "Tough Abortion Law in Connecticut is Attributed to Meskill and Catholics," *New York Times* (May 25, 1972) 38.

CROSS-CURRENTS IN THE NATIONAL ARENA

Plaintiff's Brief, *Struck v. Secretary of Defense*

Nixon, Richard. *Statement About Policy on Abortions at Military Base Hospitals in the United States* (Apr. 3, 1971).

Struck v. Secretary of Defense, 460 F.2d 1372, 1374 (9th Cir. 1971) (quoting Air Force Regulation 36-12).

On *Struck*, see:

Siegel, Neil and Reva B. Siegel. "Struck By Stereotype: Ruth Bader Ginsburg on Pregnancy Discrimination as Sex Discrimination," *Duke Law Journal* 59 (2010) 771.

Ginsburg, Ruth Bader. "A Postscript to *Struck* by Stereotype," *Duke Law Journal* 59 (2010) 799.

The Commission on Population Growth and the American Future

Nixon, Richard. Special *Message to the Congress on Problems of Population Growth* (July 18, 1969).

Rockefeller, John D. and the Commission on Population Growth and the American Future. *Transmittal Letter to the President and Congress of the United States* (Mar. 27, 1972).

Swing to Right Seen Among Catholics, Jews

Packwood, Bob. "The Role of the Federal Government," *Clinical Obstetrics & Gynecology* 14 (1971) 1212.

For Senator Packwood's bill, see:

U.S. Senate. *National Abortion Act*, S. 3746, 91st Congress.

For Representative Abzug's bill, see:

U.S. House of Representatives. *Abortion Rights Act of 1972*, H.R. 14715, 92d Congress.

On public opinion on abortion in the late sixties, see:

Rossi, Alice. "Public Views on Abortion," *The Case for Legalized Abortion Now* (Alan Guttmacher, ed., 1967).

Assault Book

Associated Press. "Acid Comment." (May 25, 1972).

Evans, Rowland and Robert Novak. "Behind Humphrey's Surge," *Washington Post* (Apr. 27, 1972) A23.

Phillips, Kevin. "How Nixon Will Win," *New York Times* (Aug. 6, 1972) SM8.

On *Nixon* and the party realignment in the early 1970s, see:

Mason, Robert. *Richard Nixon and the Quest for a New Majority* (2004).

Naughton, James M. "McGovern Defeat: A Look at Some Factors," *New York Times* (Nov. 9, 1972) 24.

Perlstein, Rick. *Nixonland* (New York: Scribner, 2008).

Women's Libbers Do NOT Speak for Us

For more on Phyllis Schlafly and the Equal Rights Amendment, see:

Critchlow, Donald T. *Phyllis Schlafly and Grassroots Conservatism: A Woman's Crusade* (Princeton, NJ: Princeton University Press, 2005).

Post, Robert and Reva Siegel. "*Roe* Rage: Democratic Constitutionalism and Backlash," *Harvard Civil Rights-Civil Liberties Law Review* 42 (2007) 373, 419-23.

Siegel, Reva B. "Constitutional Culture, Social Movement Conflict and Constitutional Change: The Case of the De Facto ERA," *California Law Review* 94 (2006) 1323, 1389-96.

PART III

SPEAKING TO THE COURT

Roe v. Wade, 314 F.Supp. 1217, 1222-24 (1970).

Doe v. Bolton, 410 U.S. 179, 183 (1973).

AFTERWORD

Griswold v. Connecticut, 381 U.S. 479 (1965).

Roe v. Wade, 410 U.S. 113 (1973).

Planned Parenthood v. Casey, 505 U.S. 833 (1992).

Gonzales v. Carhart, 550 U.S. 124 (2007).

The account of *Roe*'s reception draws on:

Post, Robert and Reva Siegel. "*Roe* Rage: Democratic Constitutionalism and Backlash," *Harvard Civil Rights-Civil Liberties Law Review* 42 (2007) 409-24.

INDEX

ABOUT THE AUTHORS

LINDA GREENHOUSE, a Pulitzer-Prize-winning journalist, covered the Supreme Court for *The New York Times* for many years and now teaches at Yale Law School. She is the author of a biography, *Becoming Justice Blackmun: Harry Blackmun's Supreme Court Journey* (2005). A graduate of Radcliffe College (Harvard), she holds a Master of Studies in Law degree from Yale.

REVA B. SIEGEL is the Nicholas deB. Katzenbach Professor of Law at Yale University. She teaches constitutional law, civil rights, and legal history, and writes on the ways courts interact with representative government and popular movements in interpreting the Constitution. She is co-editor of *The Constitution in 2020* and *Processes in Constitutional Decisionmaking*. She received undergraduate, graduate, and law degrees from Yale.